McGraw-Hill Reading
Wonders

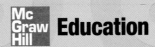

McGraw Hill Education

Bothell, WA • Chicago, IL • Columbus, OH • New York, NY

 TextEvaluator.

ETS and the ETS logo are registered trademarks of Educational Testing Service (ETS).
TextEvaluator is a trademark of Educational Testing Service.

Cover and Title Pages: **Nathan Love**

www.mheonline.com/readingwonders

C

The *McGraw·Hill* Companies

Mc Graw Hill Education

Send all inquiries to:
McGraw-Hill Education
Two Penn Plaza
New York, New York 10121

Printed in the United States of America.

8 9 RMN 17 16 15 14

McGraw-Hill Reading Wonders

CCSS Reading/Language Arts Program

Program Authors

Dr. Diane August
Managing Director,
American Institutes
for Research
Washington, D.C.

Dr. Donald Bear
Iowa State University
Ames, Iowa

Dr. Janice A. Dole
University of Utah
Salt Lake City, Utah

Dr. Jana Echevarria
California State University, Long Beach
Long Beach, California

Dr. Douglas Fisher
San Diego State University
San Diego, California

Dr. David J. Francis
University of Houston
Houston, Texas

Dr. Vicki Gibson
Educational Consultant
Gibson Hasbrouck and Associates
Wellesley, Massachusetts

Dr. Jan Hasbrouck
Educational Consultant
and Researcher
J.H. Consulting
Vancouver, Washington
Gibson Hasbrouck and Associates
Wellesley, Massachusetts

Margaret Kilgo
Educational Consultant
Kilgo Consulting, Inc.
Austin, Texas

Dr. Jay McTighe
Educational Consultant
Jay McTighe and Associates
Columbia, Maryland

Dr. Scott G. Paris
Vice President, Research
Educational Testing Service
Princeton, New Jersey

Dr. Timothy Shanahan
University of Illinois at Chicago
Chicago, Illinois

Dr. Josefina V. Tinajero
University of Texas at El Paso
El Paso, Texas

 **McGraw Hill Education**

Bothell, WA • Chicago, IL • Columbus, OH • New York, NY

PROGRAM AUTHORS

Dr. Diane August

American Institutes for Research, Washington, D.C.

Managing Director focused on literacy and science for ELLs for the Education, Human Development and the Workforce Division

Dr. Donald R. Bear

Iowa State University

Professor, Iowa State University

Author of *Words Their Way, Words Their Way with English Learners, Vocabulary Their Way,* and *Words Their Way with Struggling Readers, 4–12*

Dr. Janice A. Dole

University of Utah

Professor, University of Utah

Director, Utah Center for Reading and Literacy

Content Facilitator, National Assessment of Educational Progress (NAEP)

CCSS Consultant to Literacy Coaches, Salt Lake City School District, Utah

Dr. Jana Echevarria

California State University, Long Beach

Professor Emerita of Education, California State University

Author of *Making Content Comprehensible for English Learners: The SIOP Model*

Dr. Douglas Fisher

San Diego State University

Co-Director, Center for the Advancement of Reading, California State University

Author of *Language Arts Workshop: Purposeful Reading and Writing Instruction* and *Reading for Information in Elementary School*

Dr. David J. Francis

University of Houston

Director of the Center for Research on Educational Achievement and Teaching of English Language Learners (CREATE)

Dr. Vicki Gibson

Educational Consultant
Gibson Hasbrouck and Associates

Author of *Differentiated Instruction: Grouping for Success, Differentiated Instruction: Guidelines for Implementation,* and *Managing Behaviors to Support Differentiated Instruction*

Dr. Jan Hasbrouck

J.H. Consulting
Gibson Hasbrouck and Associates

Developed Oral Reading Fluency Norms for Grades 1–8

Author of *The Reading Coach: A How-to Manual for Success* and *Educators as Physicians: Using RTI Assessments for Effective Decision-Making*

Margaret Kilgo

Educational Consultant
Kilgo Consulting, Inc., Austin, TX

Developed Data-Driven Decisions process for evaluating student performance by standard

Member of Common Core State Standards Anchor Standards Committee for Reading and Writing

Dr. Scott G. Paris

Educational Testing Service,
Vice President, Research

Professor, Nanyang Technological
University, Singapore, 2008–2011

Professor of Education and Psychology,
University of Michigan, 1978–2008

Dr. Timothy Shanahan

University of Illinois at Chicago

Distinguished Professor, Urban Education

Director, UIC Center for Literacy

Chair, Department of Curriculum &
Instruction

Member, English Language Arts Work
Team and Writer of the Common Core
State Standards

President, International Reading
Association, 2006

Dr. Josefina V. Tinajero

University of Texas at El Paso

Dean of College of Education

President of TABE

Board of Directors for the American
Association of Colleges for Teacher
Education (AACTE)

Governing Board of the National Network
for Educational Renewal (NNER)

Consulting Authors

Kathy R. Bumgardner

National Literacy Consultant

Strategies Unlimited, Inc.
Gastonia, NC

Jay McTighe

Jay McTighe and Associates

Author of *The Understanding by Design
Guide to Creating High Quality Units* with
G. Wiggins; *Schooling by Design: Mission,
Action, Achievement* with G. Wiggins;
and *Differentiated Instruction and
Understanding By Design* with C. Tomlinson

Dr. Doris Walker-Dalhouse

Marquette University

Associate Professor, Department
of Educational Policy & Leadership

Author of articles on multicultural
literature, struggling readers, and
reading instruction in urban schools

Dinah Zike

Educational Consultant

Dinah-Might Activities, Inc.
San Antonio, TX

Program Reviewers

Kelly Aeppli-Campbell
Escambia County School District
Pensacola, FL

Marjorie J. Archer
Broward County Public Schools
Davie, FL

Whitney Augustine
Brevard Public Schools
Melbourne, FL

Antonio C. Campbell
Washington County School District
Saint George, UT

Helen Dunne
Gilbert Public School District
Gilbert, AZ

David P. Frydman
Clark County School District
Las Vegas, NV

Fran Gregory
Metropolitan Nashville Public Schools
Nashville, TN

Veronica Allen Hunt
Clark County School District
Las Vegas, NV

Michele Jacobs
Dee-Mack CUSD #701
Mackinaw, IL

LaVita Johnson Spears
Broward County Public Schools
Pembroke Pines, FL

Randall B. Kincaid
Sevier County Schools
Sevierville, TN

Matt Melamed
Community Consolidated School
District 46
Grayslake, IL

Angela L. Reese,
Bay District Schools
Panama City, FL

Eddie Thompson
Fairfield City School District
Fairfield Township, OH

Patricia Vasseur Sosa
Miami-Dade County Public Schools
Miami, FL

Dr. Elizabeth Watson
Hazelwood School District
Hazelwood, MO

TEACHING WITH

McGraw-Hill Reading
Wonders

INTRODUCE

Weekly Concept
Grade Appropriate
Topics, including Science
and Social Studies

- **Videos**
- **Photographs**

Reading/Writing Workshop Big Book

TEACH AND APPLY

**Listening
Comprehension**
Complex Text

**Shared Reading
Minilessons**

Comprehension
Skills and Strategies,
Genre, Phonics,
High-Frequency
Words, Writing,
Grammar

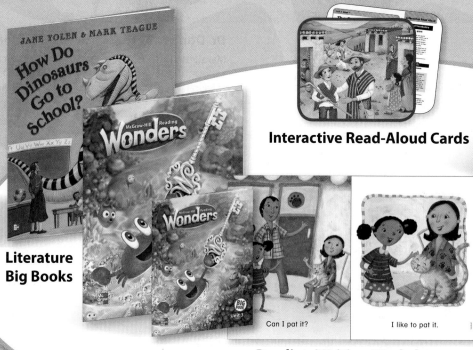

Interactive Read-Aloud Cards

- **Visual Glossary**
- **eBooks**
- **Interactive Texts**
- **Listening Library**
- **English/Spanish
  Summaries**

**Literature
Big Books**

**Reading/Writing Workshop
Big Book and Little Book**

UNIT 3 CONTENTS

Unit Planning

Weekly Lessons

Program Information

Week 1
RULES TO GO BY

Week 2
SOUNDS AROUND US

READING

Oral Language
ESSENTIAL QUESTION
What rules do we follow in different places?

Build Background

CCSS **Oral Vocabulary Words**
L.K.5c *cooperate, rules, guard, prank, responsible*

CCSS Category Words: Action Words
L.K.1b

Comprehension
Genre: Fantasy

Strategy: Visualize

CCSS **Skill**
RL.K.7 Key Details

Word Work
CCSS **Phonemic Awareness**
RF.K.2d Phoneme Isolation
Phoneme Blending
Phoneme Categorization

CCSS **Phonics** /i/i ♪
RF.K.3b **Handwriting:** Ii

CCSS **High-Frequency Words:** *to*
RF.K.3c

Fluency
Letter and Word Automaticity
Model Fluency

Oral Language
ESSENTIAL QUESTION
What are the different sounds we hear?

Build Background

CCSS **Oral Vocabulary Words**
L.K.5c *listen, volume, chat, exclaimed, familiar*

CCSS Category Words: Sound Words
L.K.1b

Comprehension
Genre: Fiction

Strategy: Visualize

CCSS **Skill**
RL.K.7 Key Details

Word Work
CCSS **Phonemic Awareness**
RF.K.2d Phoneme Isolation
Phoneme Blending
Phoneme Categorization

CCSS **Phonics** /n/n ♪
RF.K.3a **Handwriting:** Nn

CCSS **High-Frequency Words:** *and*
RF.K.3c

Fluency
Letter and Word Automaticity
Model Fluency

LANGUAGE ARTS

Writing
Trait: Sentence Fluency
Use Complete Sentences

CCSS Shared Writing
W.K.2 Complete Sentence

Interactive Writing
Complete Sentence

Independent Writing
Complete Sentence

CCSS **Grammar**
L.K.1f Sentences

Writing
Trait: Ideas
Use Interesting Details

CCSS Shared Writing
W.K.3 Personal Narrative Sentence

Interactive Writing
Personal Narrative Sentence

Independent Writing
Personal Narrative Sentence

CCSS **Grammar**
L.K.2a Sentences

UNIT 3

Week 3
THE PLACES WE GO

Oral Language
ESSENTIAL QUESTION
What places do you go to during the week?

Build Background

CCSS **Oral Vocabulary Words**
L.K.4a *local, neighborhood, routine, intelligent, volunteer*

CCSS Category Words: Sequence Words
L.K.1b

Comprehension
Genre: Fantasy

Strategy: Visualize

CCSS **Skill**
RL.K.3 Character, Setting, Events

Word Work
CCSS **Phonemic Awareness**
RF.K.2d Phoneme Isolation
Phoneme Blending
Phoneme Identity
Phoneme Segmentation

CCSS **Phonics** /k/c♪
RF.K.3a **Handwriting:** Cc

CCSS **High-Frequency Words:** *go*
RF.K.3c

Fluency
Letter and Word Automaticity
Model Fluency

> **Unit 3 Assessment**
> **Unit Assessment Book**
> pages 29–42

Writing
Trait: Sentence Fluency
Use Complete Sentences

CCSS Shared Writing
W.K.1 Opinion Sentence

Interactive Writing
Opinion Sentence

Independent Writing
Opinion Sentence

CCSS **Grammar**
L.K.2b Sentences

Half Day Kindergarten

Use the chart below to help you plan your kindergarten schedule to focus on key instructional objectives for the week. Choose Small Group and Workstation Activities as your time allows during the day.

Oral Language

• **Essential Questions**
• **Build Background**
• **Oral Vocabulary**
• **Category Words**

Word Work

• **Phonemic Awareness**
• **Phonics** /i/i, /n/n, /k/c♪
• **High-Frequency Words** *to, and, go*
• **Letter and Word Automaticity**

Reading/Comprehension

• **Reading/Writing Workshop**
Can I Pat It?; Tim Can Tip It; Nat and Tip; Tim and Nan; We Go to See Nan; Can We Go?
• **Big Books:**
How Do Dinosaurs Go to School?; Clang! Clang! Beep! Beep! Listen to the City; Please Take Me for a Walk
• **Interactive Read-Aloud Cards**
"The Boy Who Cried Wolf;" "The Turtle and the Flute;" "Field Trips"

Language Arts

• **Shared Writing**
• **Interactive Writing**
• **Independent Writing**

Independent Practice

• **Practice Book pages**
• **Workstation Activity Cards**

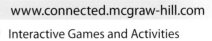
www.connected.mcgraw-hill.com
Interactive Games and Activities

Reading/Writing Workshop Big Book

Unit 3

Going Places

Train Station

The Big Idea
What can you learn by going to different places?

Going to the Train Station

Going to the station,
early in the morning,
See the engineer,
as he pulls on the lever.
Choo, choo, puff, puff,
going away.

4

5

READING/WRITING WORKSHOP, pp. 4–5

The Big Idea *What can you learn by going to different places?*

Talk About It

Ask children to discuss the different places they go to during the week and on weekends with family and friends. As the children suggest places, invite the class to discuss how they get to those places, whom they see there, and whom they go with. Encourage children to discuss what they learn while they are there. As children participate in the discussion, help keep them on topic. If they do stray from the topic, acknowledge their responses and ask them questions to get them back on track in the discussion.

Sing the Song

Introduce the unit song: *Going to the Train Station*. Read the lyrics of the song. Ask children:

→ *How are trains, airplanes, and buses similar?*

→ *What are some other types of transportation that carry many people at once?*

→ *How are those types of transportation different from cars, motorcycles, and bicycles?*

Play the song "Going to the Train Station." After listening to the song a few times, ask children to join in. Audio files of the song can be found in the Teacher Resources on www.connected.mcgraw-hill.com.

Research and Inquiry

Weekly Projects Each week children will be asked to find out more about the topic they are reading about. Children will be asked to work in pairs or small groups to complete their work. Children use what they learn from their reading and discussions as well as other sources to find additional information.

Shared Research Board You may wish to set up a Shared Research Board in the classroom. You can post illustrations and other information that children gather as they do their research.

WEEKLY PROJECTS
Students work in pairs or small groups.

Week 1 Rule Book

Week 2 School Sound Chart

Week 3 Page for a Class Book

Writing

Write about Reading Throughout the unit children will write in a variety of ways. Each week, writing is focused on a specific writing trait. Scaffolded instruction is provided through Shared Writing and Interactive Writing. Children review a student writing sample together and then write independently, practicing the trait.

WEEKLY WRITING
Week 1 Use Complete Sentences

Week 2 Use Interesting Details

Week 3 Use Complete Sentences

Music Links

www.connected.mcgraw-hill.com Integrate music into your classroom using the downloadable audio files in the Teacher's Resources online. Songs for this unit include:

WEEKLY SONGS
→ The Bus

→ Kim Hears an Insect

→ Nellie's Nest

→ Can Your Camel Do the Can-Can?

HOLIDAY SONGS
→ Buenos Dias, Amigo (Good Day, Friend)

→ Boo!

→ I Caught a Rabbit

→ Five Fat Turkeys (speech piece)

→ A Mince Pie and Pudding

Celebration Posters

Celebrate Display the Fall Celebrations poster. Use it to remind students of important holidays during the season. Commemorate the holidays by selecting from the activity suggestions provided in the Teacher Resources found at www.connected.mcgraw-hill.com.
Teaching Posters are available for Fall, Winter, Spring, and Summer.

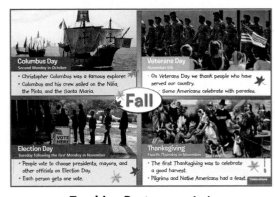

Teaching Posters, pp. 1–4

WEEKLY OVERVIEW

Literature Big Book

Listening Comprehension

How Do Dinosaurs Go to School?, 3–32
Genre Fantasy

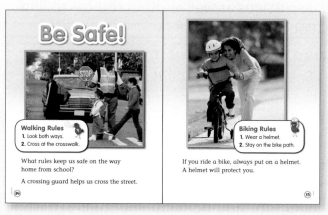

"Be Safe!" 34–36
Genre Informational Text

Interactive Read-Aloud Cards

"The Boy Who Cried Wolf"
Genre Fable

Oral Vocabulary

cooperate   responsible
guard   rules
prank

Minilessons   ✔ TESTED SKILLS (CCSS)

✔ **Comprehension Strategy** .... Visualize, T13

✔ **Comprehension Skill** .... Key Details, T22

☞ **Go** Digital

www.connected.mcgraw-hill.com

Nathan Love

Essential Question
What rules do we follow in different places?

WEEK 1 →

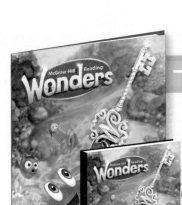

**Big Book and Little Book
Reading/Writing Workshop**

Shared Reading

"Can I Pat It?" 8–13
Genre Fiction

"Tim Can Tip It," 14–19
Genre Fiction

High-Frequency Word to, T17

Minilessons   ✓ TESTED SKILLS CCSS

✓ **Phonics** . . . . Short *i*, T15

Writing Trait . . . . Sentence Fluency, T18

Grammar . . . . Sentences, T19

Differentiated Text

Approaching   On Level   Beyond   **ELL**

TEACH AND MANAGE

What You Do

INTRODUCE

Weekly Concept
Rules to Go By

**Reading/Writing Workshop
Big Book, 6–7**

TEACH AND APPLY

Listening Comprehension

Big Book
How Do Dinosaurs Go to School?
Genre Fantasy
Paired Read "Be Safe!"
Genre Informational Text

Minilessons
Strategy: Visualize
Skill: Key Details

Shared Reading

Reading/Writing Workshop
"Can I Pat It?"
"Tim Can Tip It"

Minilessons
Short *i*, High-Frequency Word: to
Writing, Grammar

 Go Digital

 Interactive Whiteboard

Interactive Whiteboard

Mobile

What Your Students Do

WEEKLY CONTRACT

PDF Online

PRACTICE AND ONLINE ACTIVITIES

Your Turn Practice Book, pp. 77–84

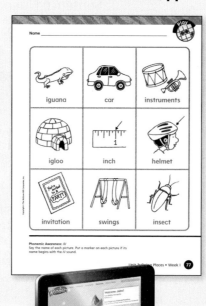

Leveled Readers

Go Digital

Online To-Do List

Online Activities

Mobile

DIFFERENTIATE

Small Group Instruction
Leveled Readers

We Run
by Edward Fender
Illustrated by Javier Gonzalez Burgos

Go, Nat!
by Herbert Thomas

The Birdhouse

Go, Nat!
by Herbert Thomas
Illustrated by Dan Andreasen

Mobile

INTEGRATE

Research and Inquiry
Rule Book, pp. T52–T53

Text Connections
Compare Rules, p. T54

Talk About Reading
Becoming Readers, p. T55

**Online
Research**

WORKSTATION CARDS

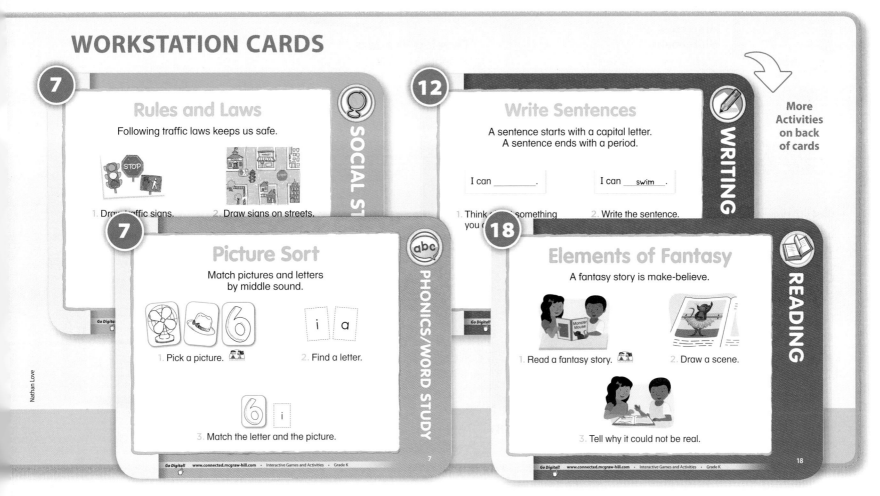

7

Rules and Laws
Following traffic laws keeps us safe.

SOCIAL S...

1. Draw traffic signs.
2. Draw signs on streets.

12

Write Sentences
A sentence starts with a capital letter.
A sentence ends with a period.

I can _____ .
I can ___swim___ .

WRITING

1. Think ... something you ...
2. Write the sentence.

**More
Activities
on back
of cards**

7

Picture Sort
Match pictures and letters
by middle sound.

i   a

1. Pick a picture.
2. Find a letter.

6   i

3. Match the letter and the picture.

PHONICS/WORD STUDY

Go Digital!   www.connected.mcgraw-hill.com   •   Interactive Games and Activities   •   Grade K   7

18

Elements of Fantasy
A fantasy story is make-believe.

Monster Mouse

1. Read a fantasy story.
2. Draw a scene.

3. Tell why it could not be real.

READING

Go Digital!   www.connected.mcgraw-hill.com   •   Interactive Games and Activities   •   Grade K   18

Nathan Love

DEVELOPING READERS AND WRITERS

Write to Sources and Research

Respond to Reading, T13, T61, T69, T75, T79

Connect to Essential Question, T13, T45

Key Details, 22

Research and Inquiry, T52

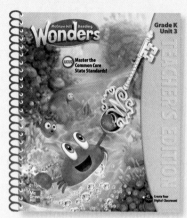

Teacher's Edition

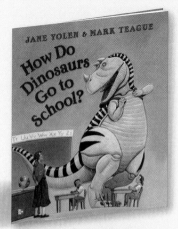

Literature Big Book
How Do Dinosaurs Go to School?
Paired Read: *Be Safe!*

Interactive Whiteboard

Leveled Readers
Responding to Texts

Narrative Text

Sentences About a Rule, T40–T41, T50, T58

Conferencing Routines

Peer Conferences, T50

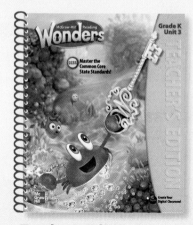

Interactive Whiteboard

Teacher's Edition

Leveled Workstation Card
Write Sentences, Card 12

Writing Traits • Shared and Interactive Writing

Writing Trait:
Sentence Fluency
Sentences About a Rule, T18, T32

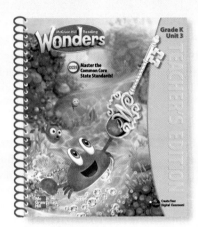

Teacher's Edition

Sentences, pp. 22–23

Reading/Writing Workshop

Leveled Workstation Card
Write Sentences, Card 12

Go Digital

Interactive Whiteboard

Grammar and Spelling/Dictation

Grammar
Sentences, T19

Spelling/Dictation
Words with Short *i*, *a*, and *s*, *p*, *t*, T47, T57

Go Digital

Interactive Whiteboard

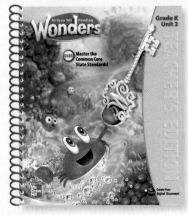

Teacher's Edition

Go Digital

Online Grammar Games

Handwriting

SUGGESTED LESSON PLAN

✔ TESTED SKILLS CCSS		DAY 1	DAY 2

Whole Group

READING

Teach and Model

Literature Big Book   Reading/ Writing Workshop

DAY 1

Build Background Rules to Go By, T10
Oral Vocabulary Words rule, cooperate, T10
✔ **Listening Comprehension**
• Genre: Fantasy
• Strategy: Visualize, T13
Big Book *How Do Dinosaurs Go to School?*
✔ **Word Work**
Phonemic Awareness
• Phoneme Isolation, T14
Phonics
• Introduce /i/i, T15
Handwriting Ii, T16
High-Frequency Word to, T17

Practice *Your Turn* 77–78

DAY 2

Oral Language Rules to Go By, T20
✔ **Category Words** Action Words, T21
✔ **Listening Comprehension**
• Genre: Fantasy
• Strategy: Visualize, T22
• Skill: Key Details
• Guided Retelling
• Model Fluency, T27
Big Book *How Do Dinosaurs Go to School?*
✔ **Word Work**
Phonemic Awareness
• Phoneme Blending, T28
Phonics
• Blend Words with Short *i*, T29
High-Frequency Word to, T29
Shared Reading "Can I Pat It?" T30–T31

Practice *Your Turn* 79

Small Group

DIFFERENTIATED INSTRUCTION
Choose across the week to meet your student's needs.

Approaching Level

DAY 1
Leveled Reader *We Run*, T60–T61
Phonological Awareness Recognize Rhyme, T62 TIER 2
Phonics Sound-Spelling Review, T64 TIER 2
High-Frequency Words Reteach Words, T66 TIER 2

DAY 2
Leveled Reader *We Run*, T60–T61
Phonemic Awareness Phoneme Blending, T62 TIER 2
Phonics Connect *i* to /i/, T64 TIER 2
High-Frequency Words Reread for Fluency, T66 TIER 2

On Level

DAY 1
Leveled Reader *Go, Nat!* T68–T69
Phonemic Awareness Phoneme Isolation, T70

DAY 2
Leveled Reader *Go, Nat!*, T68–T69
Phonemic Awareness Phoneme Blending, T70
Phonics Review Phonics, T71
High-Frequency Words Review Words, T72

Beyond Level

DAY 1
Leveled Reader *The Birdhouse*, T74–T75
Phonics Review, T76

DAY 2
Leveled Reader *The Birdhouse*, T74–T75
High-Frequency Words Review, T76

English Language Learners

DAY 1
Leveled Reader *Go, Nat!* T78–T79
Phonological Awareness Recognize Rhyme, T62 TIER 2
Phonics Sound-Spelling Review, T64 TIER 2
Vocabulary Preteach Oral Vocabulary, T80
Writing Shared Writing, T82

DAY 2
Leveled Reader *Go, Nat!* T78–T79
Phonemic Awareness Phoneme Blending, T62 TIER 2
Phonics Connect *I* to /i/, T64 TIER 2
High-Frequency Words Reread for Fluency, T66 TIER 2
Vocabulary Preteach ELL Vocabulary, T80

Whole Group

LANGUAGE ARTS

Writing and Grammar

DAY 1
Shared Writing
Writing Trait: Sentence Fluency, T18
Write a Sentence, T18
Grammar Sentences, T19

DAY 2
Interactive Writing
Writing Trait: Sentence Fluency, T32
Write a Sentence, T32
Grammar Sentences, T33

Nathan Love

DAY 3	DAY 4	DAY 5 Review and Assess

READING

Oral Language Rules to Go By, T34	**Oral Language** Rules to Go By, T42	**Integrate Ideas**
Oral Vocabulary guard, prank, responsible, T34	✓ **Category Words** Action Words, T43	• Text Connections, T54
✓ **Listening Comprehension**	✓ **Listening Comprehension**	• Talk About Reading, T55
• Genre: Fable	• Genre: Informational Text	• Research and Inquiry, T55
• Strategy: Visualize, T35	• Strategy: Visualize, T44	✓ **Word Work**
• Make Connections, T35	• Text Features: Lists	**Phonemic Awareness**
Interactive Read Aloud "The Boy Who Cried Wolf," T35	• Make Connections, T45	• Phoneme Categorization, T56
✓ **Word Work**	**Big Book** Paired Read: "Be Safe," T44	**Phonics**
Phonemic Awareness	✓ **Word Work**	• Blend Words with Short *i, a,* and, *s, p, t,* T56
• Phoneme Isolation, T36	**Phonemic Awareness**	**High-Frequency Word** to, T57
Phonics	• Phoneme Blending, T46	
• Blend Words with Short *i,* and *m, s, t, p,* T37	**Phonics**	
• Picture Sort, T38	• Blend Words with Short *i, a,* and *s, p, t,* T46	
High-Frequency Word to, T39	**High-Frequency Word** to, T47	
	Shared Reading "Tim Can Tip It," T48–T49	
	Integrate Ideas Research and Inquiry, T52–T53	
Practice *Your Turn* 80–82	**Practice** *Your Turn* 83	**Practice** *Your Turn* 84

DIFFERENTIATED INSTRUCTION

Leveled Reader *We Run,* T60–T61	**Leveled Reader** *We Run,* T60–T61	**Leveled Reader** Literacy Activities, T61
Phonemic Awareness Phoneme Isolation, T63	**Phonemic Awareness** Phoneme Categorization, T63	**Phonemic Awareness** Phoneme Categorization, T63
Phonics Reteach, T64	**Phonics** Blend Words with Short *i,* T65	**Phonics** Build Words with Short *i,* T65
High-Frequency Words Reteach Words, T66	**Oral Vocabulary** Review Words, T67	Build Fluency with Phonics, T65
		Comprehension Self-Selected Reading, T67

Leveled Reader *Go, Nat!* T68–T69	**Leveled Reader** *Go, Nat!,* T68–T69	**Leveled Reader** Literacy Activities, T69
Phonemic Awareness Phoneme Categorization, T70	**Phonics** Blend Words with Short *i,* T72	**Comprehension** Self-Selected Reading, T73
Phonics Picture Sort, T71	**High-Frequency Words** Reread for Fluency, T73	

Leveled Reader *The Birdhouse,* T74–T75	**Leveled Reader** *The Birdhouse,* T74–T75	**Leveled Reader** Literacy Activities, T75
Vocabulary Oral Vocabulary: Synonyms, T77	**High-Frequency Words** Innovate, T76	**Comprehension** Self-Selected Reading, T77

Leveled Reader *Go, Nat!* T78–T79	**Leveled Reader** *Go, Nat!,* T78–T79	**Leveled Reader** Literacy Activities, T79
Phonemic Awareness Phoneme Isolation, T63	**Phonemic Awareness** Phoneme Categorization, T63	**Phonemic Awareness** Phoneme Categorization, T63
Phonics Reteach, T64	**Phonics** Blend Words with Short *i,* T65	**Phonics** Build Words with Short *i,* T65
High-Frequency Words Review Words, T81	**Vocabulary** Review Category Words, T81	Build Fluency with Phonics, T65
Writing Writing Trait: Sentence Fluency, T82	**Grammar** Sentences, T83	

LANGUAGE ARTS

Independent Writing	**Independent Writing**	**Independent Writing**
Writing Trait: Sentence Fluency, T40	Writing Trait: Sentence Fluency, T50	Write a Sentence
Write a Sentence	Write a Sentence	Prepare/Present/Evaluate/Publish, T58
Prewrite/Draft, T40–T41	Revise/Final Draft, T50	**Grammar** Write a Sentence, T59
Grammar Sentences, T41	**Grammar** Sentences, T51	

DIFFERENTIATE TO ACCELERATE

  A C T Scaffold to **A**ccess **C**omplex **T**ext

IF ▶ the text complexity of a particular section is too difficult for children

THEN ▶ see the references noted in the chart below for scaffolded instruction to help children Access Complex Text.

Qualitative / Quantitative
Reader and Task
TEXT COMPLEXITY

	Literature Big Book	**Reading/Writing Workshop**	**Leveled Readers**
	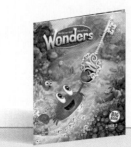		
Quantitative	*How Do Dinosaurs Go to School?* **Lexile** 500	"Can I Pat It?" **Lexile** BR	**Approaching Level** **Lexile** BR / **On Level** **Lexile** BR
	Paired Selection: "Be Safe!" **Lexile** 260	"Tim Can Tip It" **Lexile** 300	**Beyond Level** **Lexile** BR / **ELL** **Lexile** BR
Qualitative	**What Makes the Text Complex?** • **Organization** Questions and Statements, T22 • **Connection of Ideas** Synthesize Information, T22 **A C T** *See Scaffolded Instruction in Teacher's Edition, T22.*	**What Makes the Text Complex?** **Foundational Skills** • Decoding with short *i*, T28–T29 • Identifying high-frequency words, T29	**What Makes the Text Complex?** **Foundational Skills** • Decoding with short *i* • Identifying high-frequency words *to* *See Level Up lessons online for Leveled Readers.*
Reader and Task	The Introduce the Concept lesson on pages T10–T11 will help determine the reader's knowledge and engagement in the weekly concept. See pages T12–T13, T23–T27, T44–T45 and T52–T55 for questions and tasks for this text.	The Introduce the Concept lesson on pages T10–T11 will help determine the reader's knowledge and engagement in the weekly concept. See pages T30–T31, T48–T49 and T52–T55 for questions and tasks for this text.	The Introduce the Concept lesson on pages T10–T11 will help determine the reader's knowledge and engagement in the weekly concept. See pages T60–T61, T68–T69, T74–T75, T78–T79 and T52–T55 for questions and tasks for this text.

BR = Epitome of a beginning reader   ***Go Digital!*** www.connected.mcgraw-hill.com

Nathan Love

Monitor and *Differentiate*

IF	you need to differentiate instruction
THEN	use the Quick Checks to assess children's needs and select the appropriate small group instruction focus.

✓ Quick Check

Comprehension Strategy Visualize, T35

Phonemic Awareness/Phonics Short *i*, T17, T29, T39, T47, T57

High-Frequency Words *to*, T17, T29, T39, T47, T57

If No → | Approaching | **Reteach,** pp. T60–T67 |
| ELL | **Develop,** pp. T78–T83 |

If Yes → | On Level | **Review,** pp. T68–T73 |
| Beyond Level | **Extend,** pp. T74–T77 |

Level Up with Leveled Readers

IF	children can read their leveled text fluently and answer comprehension questions
THEN	work with the next level up to accelerate children's reading with more complex text.

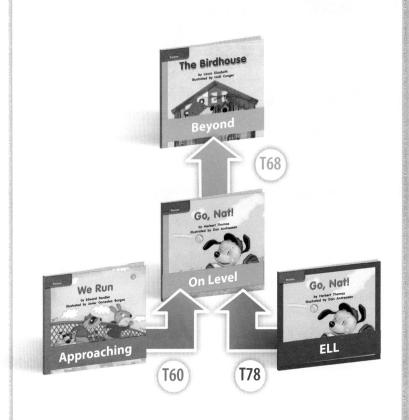

ENGLISH LANGUAGE LEARNERS
ELL SCAFFOLD

| IF | ELL students need additional support | THEN scaffold instruction using the small group suggestions. |

Reading-Writing Workshop T11 "Let's Play Ball" Integrate Ideas T52	Leveled Reader T78–T79 *Go, Nat!*	Phonological Awareness Recognize Rhyme, T62 Phoneme Blending, T62 Phoneme Isolation, T63 Phoneme Categorization, T63	Phonics, /i/i, T64–T65	Oral Vocabulary, T80 cooperate, rules, guard, prank, responsible High-Frequency Word, T81 to	Writing Shared Writing, T82 Writing Trait: Sentence Fluency, T82	Grammar T83 Sentences

Note: Include ELL Students in all small groups based on their needs.

Materials

Reading/Writing Workshop Big Book
UNIT 3

Literature Big Book
How Do Dinosaurs Go to School?

Visual Vocabulary Cards
rule
cooperate

Response Board

Photo Cards
inch
inchworm
invitation
jump
sing
write

Sound-Spelling Cards
insect

High-Frequency Word Cards
I
like
to
we

Think Aloud Clouds

"Kim Hears an Insect"

→ Introduce the Concept

 MINILESSON **10 Mins**

Build Background

Reading/Writing Workshop Big Book

OBJECTIVES

CCSS Confirm understanding of a text read aloud or information presented orally or through other media by asking and answering questions about key details and requesting clarification if something is not understood. **SL.K.2**

CCSS Identify real-life connections between words and their use. **L.K.5c**

ESSENTIAL QUESTION

What rules do we follow in different places?

Read aloud the Essential Question. Tell children that you are going to recite a rhyme about a girl who didn't follow the rules at school.

Mary Had a Little Lamb

Mary had a little lamb
Its fleece was white as snow,
And everywhere that Mary went
The lamb was sure to go.

It followed her to school one day,
That was against the rule.
It made the children laugh and play
To see the lamb at school.

Say the weekly rhyme, "Mary Had a Little Lamb," with children.

Ask children what rule Mary and the little lamb did not follow. Tell children that this week they will be reading to find out about rules we follow in different places.

Oral Vocabulary Words

Use the **Define/Example/Ask** routine to introduce the oral vocabulary words **rule** and **cooperate**.

Discuss the theme of "Rules to Go By" and explain that we all follow rules. Have children name some rules they follow at home.

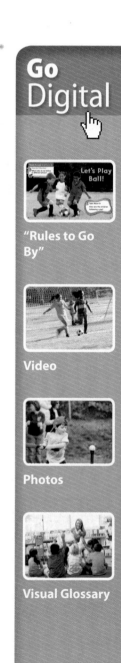

Go Digital

"Rules to Go By"

Video

Photos

Visual Glossary

Oral Vocabulary Routine

<u>Define:</u> A **rule** is something that tells you what you can or can't do, such as the rules of a game.

<u>Example:</u> In school, everyone follows the classroom rules.

<u>Ask:</u> What is a rule you follow at school?

Visual Vocabulary Cards

<u>Define:</u> To **cooperate** is to work with others toward a goal.

<u>Example:</u> The three boys cooperated to make a clubhouse.

<u>Ask:</u> When have you had to cooperate to get a task completed?

Talk About It: Rules to Go By

Discuss what rules we follow when we play a sport or game. List children's responses. Why do we need to cooperate when we play sports? Display pages 6–7 of the **Reading/Writing Workshop Big Book** and have children do the **Talk About It** activity with a partner.

Weekly Concept Rules to Go By

Essential Question
What rules do we follow in different places?

? Go Digital!

Let's Play Ball!

Talk About It
How are the children following rules?

READING/WRITING WORKSHOP BIG BOOK, pp. 6–7

Collaborative Conversations

Take Turns Talking As children engage in partner, small group, and whole group discussions, encourage them to:

→ take turns talking.

→ listen carefully to the speaker.

→ ask others to share their ideas and opinions.

ENGLISH LANGUAGE LEARNERS SCAFFOLD

Beginning

Use Visuals Explain that the children in the picture are playing a game and following rules. Tell children that they are playing outside. Point out children with the same color uniforms and explain that they are on the same team. Point out two children on the opposite team. *Are these children on the same team? Are they playing outside?* Allow children ample time to respond.

Intermediate

Describe Ask children to describe what is happening in the picture. Ask them to tell which children are on the same teams. *Who is cooperating?* Correct grammar and pronunciation as needed.

Advanced/Advanced High

Discuss Have children elaborate on how the teams in the picture cooperate. Elicit more details to support children's answers.

→ # Listening Comprehension

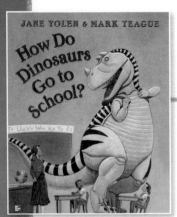

Literature Big Book

JANE YOLEN & MARK TEAGUE
How Do Dinosaurs Go to School?

OBJECTIVES

CCSS With prompting and support, name the author and illustrator of a story and define the role of each in telling the story. **RL.K.6**

CCSS Actively engage in group reading activities with purpose and understanding. **RL.K.10**

• Recognize characteristics of fantasy

• Connect Big Book to Weekly Concept

• Strategy: Visualize

ACADEMIC LANGUAGE

• *fantasy, author, illustrator, visualize*

• Cognates: *fantasía, autora, ilustrador, visualizar*

MINILESSON **10** Mins

Read the Literature Big Book

Connect to Concept: Rules to Go By

Tell children that you will now read about some dinosaurs and the rules at their school. *What are some rules that you follow at school?*

Concepts of Print

Book Handling Display the **Big Book** cover and point out that we hold a book so the words are right side up. Model directionality as you explain that we read from left to right, from top to bottom, and from page to page.

Genre: Fantasy

Model *How Do Dinosaurs Go to School?* is a fantasy story. Share these characteristics of fantasy with children.

→ Fantasy is a kind of fiction: the events are made up.

→ Some events, such as animals talking, could never happen in real life.

Story Words Preview these words before reading:

roughhouse: play hard
fidgets: moves around a lot
tidies: cleans up

Set a Purpose for Reading

→ Read aloud the title and the names of the author and the illustrator.

→ Remind children that the author wrote the words in the story and the illustrator drew the pictures.

→ Ask children to listen as you read aloud the Big Book to find out if a dinosaur can follow the rules when it goes to school.

Go Digital

How Do Dinosaurs Go to School?

I was able to picture in my mind...

Think Aloud Cloud

Strategy: Visualize

Explain Tell children that sometimes they can use the words and pictures on a page to make pictures in their minds of what is happening in a story.

Think Aloud When I look at the cover I see a very big dinosaur standing in a classroom. I wonder what it would be like with a dinosaur in the classroom. In my mind, I picture the dinosaur standing in front of me. I picture his big feet and long tail. He is too big to fit in the chairs.

Model As you read, use the **Think Aloud Cloud** to model the strategy.

Think Aloud On pages 28–29, I read "At recess he plays with a number of friends, and growls at the bullies till bullying ends." I see in the illustration that this dinosaur is flying and has big wings. I picture in my mind that he can fly very fast to help the boy who is being bullied. I think that the boy would be glad to have this dinosaur as a friend!

Respond to Reading

After reading, prompt children to share what they learned about how the dinosaurs behaved in school. Discuss what pictures they made in their minds as they listened to the story. Then have children draw a picture of a dinosaur at their school. Ask: *What rule is the dinosaur in your picture following?*

Make Connections

Use *How Do Dinosaurs Go to School?* to discuss school rules. Revisit the concept behind the Essential Question *What rules do we follow in different places?* by paging through the Big Book.

Write About It Have children write about one of the rules that both they and the dinosaur follow at school.

ENGLISH LANGUAGE LEARNERS SCAFFOLD

Beginning

Describe Display and describe the picture on the cover pointing out the details. Ask children to visualize, or make pictures in their minds, about what would happen if a dinosaur was in their classroom right now. *Would you like to have a dinosaur in our school?*

Intermediate

Discuss Ask children to visualize, or make pictures in their minds, of their favorite part of the story. Have them describe it and tell you why they like that part of the story. Model correct pronunciation as needed.

Advanced/Advanced High

Express Ask children to visualize, or make pictures in their minds, of a dinosaur in the story that did not follow rules. *Why should the dinosaur follow the rules? What might happen if we do not follow rules in school?* Correct the meaning of children's responses as needed.

→ # Word Work

MINILESSON 5 Mins

Phonemic Awareness

Photo Card

Go Digital

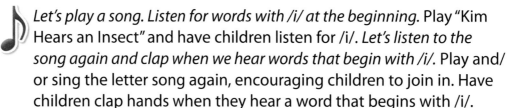

Phonemic Awareness

Phonics

OBJECTIVES

CCSS Isolate and pronounce the initial, medial vowel, and final sounds in three–phoneme words. **RF.K.2d**

CCSS Associate the long and short sounds with the common spellings for the five major vowels. **RF.K.3b**

ACADEMIC LANGUAGE

• *isolate, phoneme*
• Cognates: *fonema*

Phoneme Isolation

❶ **Model** Display the **Photo Card** for *insect*. *Listen for the sound at the beginning of this word:* insect. *Say the sound with me: /iii/.* Insect *has /i/ at the beginning.* Say *it, is, in* and have children repeat. Emphasize phoneme /i/.

♪ *Let's play a song. Listen for words with /i/ at the beginning.* Play "Kim Hears an Insect" and have children listen for /i/. *Let's listen to the song again and clap when we hear words that begin with /i/.* Play and/ or sing the letter song again, encouraging children to join in. Have children clap hands when they hear a word that begins with /i/.

❷ **Guided Practice/Practice** Display and name each Photo Card: *inch, inchworm, invitation. Say each picture name with me. Tell me the sound at the beginning of the word.* Guide practice with the first word.

Photo Cards

ARTICULATION SUPPORT

Demonstrate how to say /i/. Relax your face and let the front part of your tongue rise in your mouth. Do not let your lips round. Have children practice the sound /i/ with you. Say these words: *itch, igloo, if, inside.* Stretch the initial sound when you say the word, then have children repeat.

Phonics

MINILESSON 10 Mins

Ii

insect

Sound-Spelling Card

Introduce /i/*i*

1 Model Display the *Insect* **Sound-Spelling Card**. *This is the* Insect *card. The sound is /i/. The /i/ sound is spelled with the letter* i. *Say the sound with me: /iii/. This is the sound at the beginning of the word* insect. *Listen: /i/ /i/ /i/,* insect. *What is the name of this letter?* (i) *What sound does this letter stand for?* (/i/)

Display the song "Kim Hears an Insect" (see **Teacher's Resource Book** online). Read or sing the song with children. Reread the title and point out that the word *insect* begins with the letter *i*. Model placing a self-stick note below the *i* in *insect*.

2 Guided Practice/Practice Read each line of the song. Stop after each line and ask children to place self-stick notes below words that begin with *I* or *i* and say the letter name.

Kim Hears an Insect

Kim hears an insect buzzing
'round and 'round her head.
It's buzzing in the kitchen.
It's buzzing 'round her bed.
Kim hears an insect buzzing.
Why can't it sing instead?

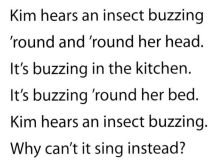

Corrective Feedback

Sound Error Model the sound /i/ in the initial position, then have children repeat the sound. Say: *in, /i/ /i/ /i/. Now it's your turn.* Have children say *is* and *it* and isolate the initial /i/.

ENGLISH LANGUAGE LEARNERS

Minimal Contrasts Focus on articulation. Make the /i/ sound and point out your mouth position. Have children repeat. Use the articulation photos. Repeat for the /a/ sound. Have children say both sounds, noticing the differences.

YOUR TURN PRACTICE BOOK pp. 77–78

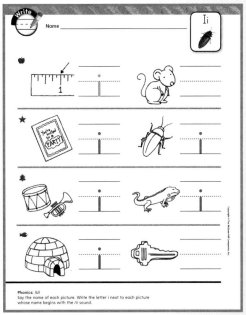

→ # Word Work

MINILESSON 5 Mins

Handwriting: Write *Ii*

OBJECTIVES

CCSS Write a letter or letters for most consonant and short-vowel sounds. **L.K.2c**

CCSS Read common high-frequency words by sight. **RF.K.3c**

ACADEMIC LANGUAGE
uppercase, lowercase

❶ **Model** Say the handwriting cues below as you write and identify the upper and lowercase forms of *Ii*. Then trace the letters on the board and in the air as you say /i/.

Straight down. Go back to the top. Straight across. Go to the bottom line. Straight across.

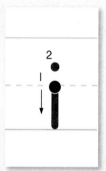

Straight down, dot above.

Handwriting

| the | is |
| you | do |

High-Frequency Word Routine

❷ **Guided Practice/Practice**

→ Say the cues together as children trace both forms of the letter with their index finger. Have them identify the uppercase and lowercase forms of the letter.

→ Have children write *I* and *i* in the air as they say /i/ multiple times.

→ Distribute **Response Boards**. Observe children's pencil grip and paper position, and correct as necessary. Have children say /i/ every time they write the letter *Ii*.

Daily Handwriting

Throughout the week teach uppercase and lowercase letters *Ii* using the Handwriting models. At the end of the week, have children use the **Your Turn Practice Book**, page 84 to practice handwriting.

MINILESSON 5 Mins

High-Frequency Words

to

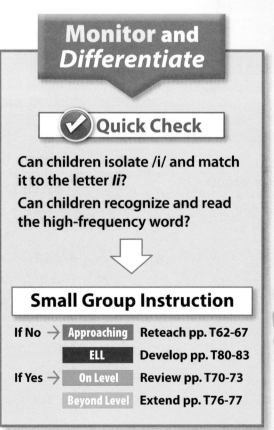

to

High-Frequency Word Card

❶ Model Display **Big Book** *How Do Dinosaurs Go to School?* Read the title. Point out the word *to.* Then display the **High-Frequency Word Card** *to* and use the **Read/Spell/Write** routine to teach the word.

→ **Read** Point to the word *to* and say the word. *This is the word to. Say it with me: to. I like to swim.*

→ **Spell** *The word* to *is spelled t-o. Spell it with me.*

→ **Write** *Let's write the word in the air as we say each letter: t-o.*

→ Point out that the /t/ sound in the word *to* is the same as the /t/ sound in the word *tap.*

→ Have partners create sentences using the word.

❷ Guided Practice/Practice Build sentences using High-Frequency Word Cards, **Photo Cards**, and teacher-made punctuation cards. Have children point to the high-frequency word *to.* Use these sentences.

Also online

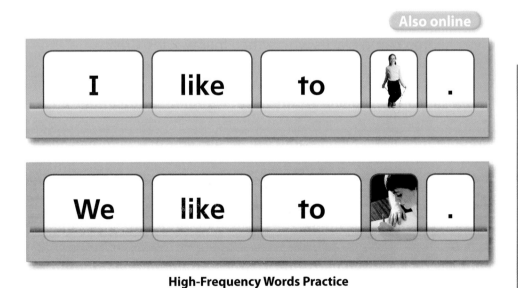

| I | like | to | | . |

| We | like | to | | . |

High-Frequency Words Practice

Monitor and *Differentiate*

✔ Quick Check

Can children isolate /i/ and match it to the letter *Ii*?

Can children recognize and read the high-frequency word?

⬇

Small Group Instruction

If No →	Approaching	Reteach pp. T62-67
	ELL	Develop pp. T80-83
If Yes →	On Level	Review pp. T70-73
	Beyond Level	Extend pp. T76-77

→ # Language Arts

Shared Writing
10 Mins MINILESSON

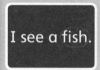
Writing Trait: Sentence Fluency

1 Model Tell children that a sentence is a group of words that tells a complete thought. A sentence has two parts: it tells about someone or something doing an action and what the action is.

→ Write and read aloud this sentence: "The dinosaur raises his hand." *The sentence tells about the dinosaur. It tells what the dinosaur is doing. He is raising his hand.*

2 Guided Practice/Practice Write this sentence to show a different action: "The dinosaur helps the teacher." Read aloud the sentence and help children identify the action.

Write a Sentence

Focus and Plan Tell children that this week they will write their own sentence about a rule.

 Brainstorm Have children name places where they follow rules. Create lists for some of the places. *What rules do we follow in these places?*

In a Library
talk in quiet voices
return books on time
listen to the librarian

Crossing the Street
walk with an adult
follow the street signs
look both ways

Write Model writing a sentence using an idea from the list. *I can take one of these rules and make it into a sentence:* I return books on time. *This is a sentence that tells about a rule in a library. It tells about someone doing an action.* (I; return books).

Model writing sentences using other rules on the lists. Read aloud the sentences with children.

OBJECTIVES

 CCSS Use a combination of drawing, dictating, and writing to compose informative/ explanatory texts in which they name what they are writing about and supply some information about the topic. **W.K.2**

CCSS Capitalize the first word in a sentence and the pronoun *I*. **L.K.2a**

• Write lists
• Learn to recognize sentences

ACADEMIC LANGUAGE

• *sentence, punctuation, capital, period*
• Cognates: *puntuación*

Grammar

MINILESSON
5 Mins

Sentences

1 Model Explain that a sentence always begins with a capital (uppercase) letter and ends with a mark. Write the following group of words:

> *our teacher*
> *Our teacher reads a story.*

→ Read aloud: *our teacher*. Explain that it is not a sentence because it does not tell about someone doing an action.

→ Read aloud: *Our teacher reads a story*. Explain that it is a sentence. It tells about someone, *our teacher*, who does an action, *reads*. Point to the capital letter: *This is a capital letter. A sentence must begin with a capital letter.*

→ Point to the period: *A sentence must end with a mark. This end mark is called a period.*

2 Guided Practice/Practice Write and read aloud the groups of words: *the teacher; I go to the store; We play in the park*. Work together to identify which groups are sentences and which are not. Have children identify the capital letters and the punctuation at the end of the sentences. Remind children that the word "I" is always capitalized.

Model how to make more sentences from groups of words. Add "writes on the board" to "the teacher." Write the new sentence. Read the sentence aloud. Encourage children to think of other words to make the phrase into a sentence. Have them identify capital letters and end marks.

Talk About It

COLLABORATE

Have partners work together to orally generate sentences about rules they follow in class. Challenge them to create sentences for more than one rule.

ENGLISH LANGUAGE LEARNERS SCAFFOLD

Beginning

Explain Tell children that a sentence has two parts: a naming part and a telling part. Say: *The cat jumps*. Explain that this is a complete sentence. Tell children that the cat names who or what and *jumps* tells what the cat does. *Tell me if this is a complete sentence*: went to school. *How can I make it complete?* Allow children ample time to respond.

Intermediate

Practice Ask children to tell you if these are complete sentences: *the little bear; Ana went to the playground; tastes sweet; I like rice; goes to the store*. Have children correct the incomplete sentences. Correct the meaning of children's responses as needed.

Advanced/Advanced High

Practice Have partners make up complete sentences. *Who is doing the action in your sentence? What is the action?* Clarify children's responses as needed by providing vocabulary.

Daily Wrap Up

• Review the Essential Question and encourage children to discuss it, using the new oral vocabulary words. *What did we learn about rules in different places today?*

• Prompt children to share the skills they learned. How might they use those skills?

Materials

Literature Big Book
How Do Dinosaurs Go to School?

Visual Vocabulary Cards

rule
cooperate

Response Board

Word-Building Cards

Photo Cards
bird
jet
man
dog

Puppet

insect

Sound-Spelling Cards

High-Frequency Word Cards

a   like
see
the
we
to

Retelling Cards

→ Build the Concept

MINILESSON
10 Mins

Oral Language

OBJECTIVES

CCSS Use words and phrases acquired through conversations, reading and being read to, and responding to texts. **L.K.6**

CCSS Recognize and produce rhyming words. **RF.K.2a**

Develop oral vocabulary

ACADEMIC LANGUAGE

• *rhyme, action*
• Cognates: *rima, acción*

ESSENTIAL QUESTION

What rules do we follow in different places?

Remind children that this week they are learning about following rules in different places. Point out that there are rules at home, in the community, and at school. Ask them to share some school rules.

Recite the rhyme "Mary Had a Little Lamb" with children.

> **Phonological Awareness**
> **Recognize Rhyme**
> Tell children that the words *rule* and *school* rhyme. Remind them that words that rhyme have the same ending sounds. Say the following word pairs and have children raise their hands if the words rhyme: *pin, fin; mat, mud; Tim, dim; lid, hid; pet, pig*.

Review Oral Vocabulary

Use the **Define/Example/Ask** routine to review the oral vocabulary words **rule** and **cooperate**. Prompt children to use the words in sentences.

Vocab...
Define...
Examp...
Ask:

Visual Vocabulary Cards

Go Digital

Visual Glossary

Category Words

Category Words: Action Words

1 Model Use the **Big Book** *How Do Dinosaurs Go to School?* to point out action words: *walk, ride,* p. 5; *stomp,* p. 7. Explain that these are action words. They tell what someone or something does. Point out the illustrations that represent each action word. *What actions do the dinosaurs do?* (walk, ride, stomp)

Sing the following song to the tune of "Here We Go 'Round the Mulberry Bush." Ask children to listen for action words.

This is the way we walk *to school,* walk *to school,* walk *to school, This is the way we* walk *to school,* walk *to school today.*

Repeat the verse using the action words *ride* and *drive.*

→ Sing the first two lines of the song again and ask children how we get to school. (walk) Repeat with the remaining verses of the song. Tell children that the words *walk, ride,* and *drive* are action words. The words name something we do. Act out each of the action words with children.

2 Guided Practice/Practice Have children stand. Tell them that you will say some words. If the word is an action word, they will act out the action.

| jump | potato | clap | sing | clock |
| wiggle | pencil | march | chair | stomp |

Ask children why *jump, clap, sing, wiggle, march* and *stomp* are action words. (Possible answers: The words tell what someone or something does; I can act out the word.)

ENGLISH LANGUAGE LEARNERS

Reinforce Meaning Help children understand action words that are often used in the classroom, such as *listen, point, watch, find, write.* Demonstrate these words and have children mirror your actions as they repeat the words with you.

LET'S MOVE!

Have children dramatize the category words used in sentences. As you say "We bike to school," the children act out riding their bikes to school.

WHOLE GROUP

DAY 2

→ # Listening Comprehension

CLOSE READING

Literature Big Book

Reread Literature Big Book

Genre: Fantasy

Display *How Do Dinosaurs Go to School?* Remind children that fantasy stories are fiction. They are made-up stories. Some things in fantasy stories could never happen in real life. Ask: *How do you know that* How Do Dinosaurs Go to School? *is a fantasy story?* Have children point to evidence in the text and the pictures to show that this is a fantasy.

Strategy: Visualize

Remind children that good readers use the words and pictures to make a picture in their minds of what is happening in a story. Ask: *As we reread, you can make pictures in your mind about the dinosaur in the classroom.*

Skill: Key Details

Tell children that they can learn about what is happening in stories by looking for information in the text and illustrations. Point out that illustrations sometimes give information that is not in the author's words. Say: *Details from the illustrations can help you make pictures in your mind of what is happening.* As you read, have children listen for evidence in the text to find details.

OBJECTIVES

CCSS With prompting and support, ask and answer questions about key details in a text. **RL.K.1**

CCSS With prompting and support, retell familiar stories, including key details. **RL.K.2**

• Strategy: Visualize
• Skill: Key Details

ACADEMIC LANGUAGE

• *details, illustrations, retell*
• Cognates: *detalles, ilustraciones*

Go Digital

How Do Dinosaurs Go to School?

Retelling Cards

A C T
Access Complex Text

Organization The book is divided into two parts: questions and statements.

→ Point out that on pages 5–24 all the sentences are questions. The questions are asking if the dinosaurs are behaving badly at school. The "No" on page 24 is the answer to all of these questions. The rest of the book tells about how the dinosaurs really act at school.

Connection of Ideas The connection of ideas between pages is not clearly stated. Children may need help in making connections.

→ Guide children to understand that all the pages give details about certain school rules.

LITERATURE BIG BOOK   PAGES 4–5

HIGH-FREQUENCY WORDS

Have children identify and read the high-frequency word *to*.

pp. 4–5

car pool: When I ride in a car pool, my friends and I are in the same car. Our family members and friends take turns driving us places. Ask children if any of them ride to school in a car pool.

LITERATURE BIG BOOK   PAGES 6–7

VISUALIZE

Think Aloud I read that the dinosaur might make a big fuss. What would that be like? I see his big feet and tail in the picture. I can picture in my mind the dinosaur running and yelling to try and catch the bus. I imagine that he is so heavy that the ground shakes!

pp. 6–7

make a big fuss: Point to the picture of the dinosaur. Act out how the dinosaur is making a fuss by stomping.

Say: *I am making a fuss.* Have children join you in the action and say the phrase.

LITERATURE BIG BOOK   PAGES 8–9

KEY DETAILS

What is the dinosaur doing? How do you know? (He is grabbing a girl's lunch. I read it in the text and see it in the picture.)

pp. 8–9

roughhouse: When you roughhouse, you play hard. If you are not careful, someone could get hurt. Ask children why they shouldn't roughhouse in school.

LITERATURE BIG BOOK   PAGES 10–11

CONCEPTS OF PRINT

Point out the question mark at the end of the sentence. Explain that question marks are used at the ends of questions.

pp. 10–11

right ahead of the bell: Have you ever rushed to school because you did not want to be late? If you got to school just before the bell rang, you were "right ahead of the bell."

Listening Comprehension

CLOSE READING
ELL

LITERATURE BIG BOOK　　**PAGES 12–13**

VISUALIZE

Think Aloud I can picture in my mind giving a show and tell. I can also picture the big dinosaur interrupting. He is so big and loud that all of the other kids look at him instead. I think this would make me feel sad.

pp. 12–13

interrupt: You interrupt *people if you stop them from talking or finishing what they were doing.* Ask children how they might feel if someone interrupted them.

LITERATURE BIG BOOK　　**PAGES 14–15**

KEY DETAILS

I read that the dinosaur yells. Why do you think he might yell? What do you see in the illustration that makes you think that? (If he loses a tooth he would be excited and yell. I see the dinosaur holding a tooth, and he has a space in his mouth.)

LITERATURE BIG BOOK　　**PAGES 16–17**

PHONICS

Reread page 17 and have children identify the word that begins with the /i/ sound. (in) Hint: *I see this word three times.*

pp. 16–17

fidget: Move around in your seat a lot to demonstrate *fidget.* Tell children that when they can't sit still someone might tell them not to fidget. Have children act out fidgeting and say the word.

LITERATURE BIG BOOK　　**PAGES 18–19**

KEY DETAILS

How does the teacher feel? How do you know? (The teacher is angry that the dinosaur is roaring out of turn. She has an angry face in the illustration.)

pp. 18–19

out of turn: Tell children that if you do something "out of turn" that means it is not your turn. Say: *It is important to wait for your turn in Show and Tell.*

LITERATURE BIG BOOK   **PAGES 20–21**

PHONICS

Reread the sentence on page 21 and have children identify the word with the /i/ sound. (it)

LITERATURE BIG BOOK   **PAGES 22–23**

KEY DETAILS

How does the dinosaur feel about making a noise? What do you see in the illustration that makes you think that? (The dinosaur thinks he is being funny. The dinosaur is smiling; the children are laughing.)

pp. 22–23

stir up the classroom: If something happens in the classroom that usually doesn't happen, it might make everyone laugh. That's what we mean by "stir up the classroom." If someone makes a loud noise, it might stir up the classroom.

LITERATURE BIG BOOK   **PAGES 24–25**

ASK AND ANSWER QUESTIONS

I read the word "no" on this page. The author is telling us that the dinosaur doesn't do these things. What does a dinosaur really do at school? We can keep reading to find out the answer.

pp. 24–25

pick on the boys: Point to the picture of the dinosaur holding the boy. *The dinosaur has picked up the boy, but he also picks on the boy. When the dinosaur picks on the boy, he is bothering him or being mean to him.* Have children say the phrase.

LITERATURE BIG BOOK   **PAGES 26–27**

VISUALIZE

Think Aloud Picture in your mind the dinosaur sitting quietly at a desk with its hand raised. Why do you think he is raising his hand?

Listening Comprehension

ELL

LITERATURE BIG BOOK   PAGES 28–29

VISUALIZE

Think Aloud I see that the dinosaur is looking at a boy who is being mean to another boy. I imagine the dinosaur growling at the boy because he is being a bully. I think this will scare the boy and make him stop bullying the other children.

pp. 28–29

Point to bully in the illustration. Say: *This boy is being mean. He is a bully.*

LITERATURE BIG BOOK   PAGES 30–31

KEY DETAILS

What is the dinosaur doing? How do you know? (The dinosaur is going home. He has his backpack on. The words on the page say he is leaping out the door.)

pp. 30–31

tidies his desk: Demonstrate tidying your desk and say: *I tidy my desk when it is messy. When I tidy my desk, I clean it up.* Say the phrase *tidies his desk* and have children repeat.

LITERATURE BIG BOOK   PAGE 32

AUTHOR'S PURPOSE

Why do you think the author wrote this story? (Possible answer: She wanted to remind us how we should behave when we are in school.)

Text Evidence

Explain Remind children that when they answer a question they will need to show where in the story (both words and pictures) they found the answer.

Discuss *How do you know that the yellow and blue dinosaur behaves in school?* (He keeps his desk clean. The author writes, "Good work, little dinosaur.")

Guided Retelling

Tell children that now they will use the **Retelling Cards** to retell the story.

→ Display Retelling Card 1. Based on children's needs, use either the Guided, Modeled or ELL retelling prompts. The ELL prompts contain support for English language learners based on levels of language acquisition. Repeat with the rest of the cards, using the prompts as a guide.

→ Discuss the story. Choose a scene from the book and talk about the dinosaur's behavior. Talk about whether the behavior shown by the dinosaur follows the rules or not. Have children defend their answers.

→ Have children choose their favorite part of the story and act it out.

Model Fluency

Reread the questions on page 5 of *How Do Dinosaurs Go to School?* and emphasize the intonation. Point out to children that when they read a sentence that ends in a question mark, they should raise their voice at the end. Then reread the sentence *How does a dinosaur go to school?* and have children repeat. Continue with other questions in the book.

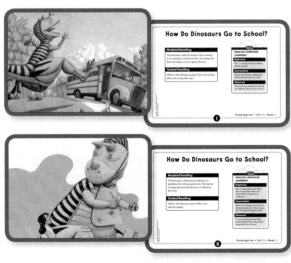

Retelling Cards

YOUR TURN PRACTICE BOOK p. 79

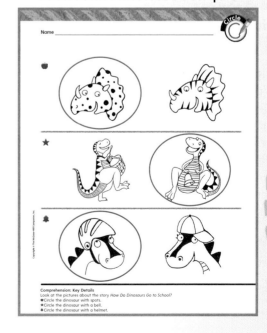

→ # Word Work

MINILESSON **5 Mins**

Phonemic Awareness

Puppet

Phoneme Blending

OBJECTIVES

CCSS Associate the long and short sounds with the common spellings for the five major vowels. **RF.K.3b**

CCSS Read common high-frequency words by sight. **RF.K.3c**

Blend phonemes to make words

1 Model Use the puppet to demonstrate how to blend phonemes to make words. *The puppet is going to say sounds in a word, /i/ /t/. The puppet can blend those sounds to make a word: /iiit/ it. When the puppet blends the sounds together, it makes the word* it. *Listen as the puppet blends more sounds to make words.* Model blending with the following.

/i/ /z/ is   /i/ /n/ in   /i/ /n/ /ch/ inch

2 Guided Practice/Practice Tell children that the puppet is going to say the sounds in a word. *Listen to the puppet as it says each sound. Repeat the sounds, then blend them to say the word.* Guide practice with the first word.

/i/ /ch/ itch   /i/ /n/ /ch/ inch   /i/ /f/ if   /i/ /z/ is

MINILESSON **5 Mins**

Phonics

Ii
insect
Sound-Spelling Card

Review Short /i/*i*

ELL

ENGLISH LANGUAGE LEARNERS

High-Frequency Words: Build Meaning Reinforce the meaning of the word *to* by saying aloud the following sentences and demonstrating them.

• Talk *to* a child.
• Point *to* the window.
• Walk *to* the door.
• Go *to* a bookcase.

1 Model Display the *Insect* **Sound-Spelling Card**. *This is the letter* i. *The letter* i *can stand for the sound /i/ as in the word* insect. *What is the letter?* (i) *What sound does the letter* i *stand for?* (/i/)

2 Guided Practice/Practice Have children listen as you say some words. Ask them to write the letter *i* on their **Response Boards** if the word begins with /i/. Do the first two words with children.

it   dinosaur   in   pan   is   if   itch   iguana

Go Digital

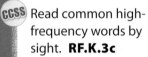
Phonemic Awareness

Phonics

High-Frequency Word Routine

Handwriting

Blend Words with Short /i/ *i*

❶ Model Place **Word-Building Cards** *i, t* in a pocket chart. Point to the letter *i*. *This is the letter* i. *The letter* i *stands for /i/. Say /i/. This is the letter* t. *The letter* t *stands for /t/. Say /t/. Listen as I blend the two sounds together: /iiit/. Blend the sounds with me to read the word.*

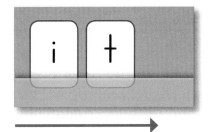

❷ Guided Practice/Practice Use Word-Building Cards or write *it*. Point to the letter *i* and have children say the sound. Point to the letter *t* and have children say the sound. Then move your hand from left to right under the word, have children blend and read the word *it*.

MINILESSON
5 Mins

High-Frequency Words

to

to

High-Frequency Word Card

❶ Guided Practice Display the **High-Frequency Word Card** *to*. Use the **Read/Spell/Write** routine to teach the word. Ask children to close their eyes, picture the spelling of the word, and then write it the way they see it. Have children self-correct by checking the High-Frequency Word Card.

❷ Practice Add the word *to* to the cumulative word bank.

COLLABORATE

→ Have partners create sentences using the word.

→ Have children count the number of letters in the word and then write the word again.

Cumulative Review Review words: *a, like, see, the, we*.

Repeat the **Read/Spell/Write** routine. Mix the words and have children chorally say each one.

Monitor and *Differentiate*

✓ **Quick Check**

Can children isolate /i/ and match it to the letter *I*i?

Can children recognize and read the high-frequency word?

⬇

Small Group Instruction

If No → | Approaching | Reteach pp. T62-67
| ELL | Develop pp. T80-83

If Yes → | On Level | Review pp. T70-73
| Beyond Level | Extend pp. T76-77

→ # Shared Read

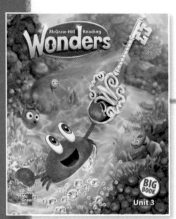

Reading/Writing Workshop Big Book

OBJECTIVES

 Read emergent-reader text with purpose and understanding. **RF.K.4**

 Read common high-frequency words by sight. **RF.K.3c**

ACADEMIC LANGUAGE

- *predict*
- Cognates: *predecir*

MINILESSON
10 Mins

Read "Can I Pat It?"

Model Skills and Strategies

Model Book Handling Demonstrate book handling. *This is how I hold a book. This is the front cover. I make sure that the book is not upside down so that I can see the words. This is how I turn the pages of the book. When I turn to each page, I stop to read the words on it.*

Model Concepts About Print Turn to the title page. Point out the question mark in the title. *This is a question mark. A question mark is used at the end of a sentence that asks something. This type of sentence is called a question.* Demonstrate how print moves from left to right and top to bottom.

Predict Read the title together. Ask children to describe the illustration. Ask children to predict what the story will be about.

Read Have children chorally read the story with you. Point to each word as you read it together. Help children sound out the decodable words and say the sight words. If children have difficulty, provide corrective feedback and guide them page by page using the student **Reading/Writing Workshop**.

Ask the following:

→ *Look at page 9. What does the girl like to pat?* (the dog)

→ *Look at page 12. What does the girl like?* (the fish)

→ *Look at page 13. Can she pat it?* (Possible answer: No. The fish is in water.)

Go Digital

"Can I Pat It?"

"Can I Pat It?"

READING/WRITING WORKSHOP, pp. 8–13

Rereading

Have small groups use the **Reading/Writing Workshop** to reread "Can I Pat It?" Then review the skills and strategies using the *Phonics* and *Words to Know* pages that come before the selection.

→ Remind children that as they reread, they can ask themselves questions and then find the answers in the words and pictures.

→ Have children use page 7 to review high-frequency word *to*.

→ Have children use page 6 to review that the letter *i* can stand for the sound /i/. Guide them to blend the sounds to read the words.

 Language Arts

Interactive Writing

Writing Trait: Sentence Fluency

Review Tell children that writers use complete sentences to share their ideas. *I can make a complete sentence for a rule about crossing the street:* We look both ways. *It is a complete sentence because it tells that someone or something is doing an action.*

Write a Sentence

Discuss Display and read aloud the lists of rules from Day 1. Guide children to pick a rule to write about, such as *follow the street signs*.

Model/Apply Grammar Tell children that you will work together to write a complete sentence about a rule for crossing the street. Remind children that sentences begin with a capital letter and end with a punctuation mark.

Ask: *What kinds of street signs tell you when it is safe to cross the street?* Record children's responses.

Write the following sentences and frames: *The light is red. We* _____. *The light is green. We* _____.

Read the sentences together, tracking the print. Model how to choose an action word to complete the second sentence in each pair. Ask: *What do you do when the light is red?* (stop) *What do you do when the light is green?* (walk) Point to the capital letters that start the sentences and the periods at the end.

Write Have children help you create a sentence about other rules for crossing the street, such as: *We walk with an adult. We pay attention.* Write the sentence frame: *We* _____.

Guide children to complete the sentence frame. Write the words. Share the pen with children and have them write the letters they know.

Go
Digital

Writing

I see a fish.

Grammar

OBJECTIVES

 CCSS Use a combination of drawing, dictating, and writing to compose information/ explanatory texts in which they name what they are writing about and supply some information about the topic. **W.K.2**

CCSS Print many upper- and lowercase letters. **L.K.1a**

• Recognize sentences

• Write a sentence

ACADEMIC LANGUAGE

• *sentence, punctuation*

• Cognates: *puntuación*

Grammar

5 Mins

Sentences

1 Review Remind children that a sentence tells about someone or something doing an action. A sentence begins with a capital letter and ends with a punctuation mark, such as a period. Say: *I can make a complete sentence about things I do with my friends. We play a game. Who is playing the game?* (We are.) *What is the action word?* (play) *My sentence tells that someone or something is doing an action. It is a complete sentence.*

→ Write the following groups of words:

> *take turns*
> *We take turns.*

Read the groups of words aloud and have children chorally repeat. Ask children which group of words is a complete sentence

2 Guided Practice Show **Photo Cards** for *dog, bird, jet,* and *man.* Ask children to name what they see. Have them create a sentence for each Photo Card, supplying an action word. Ask: *What can the dog do?* (run) *What could your sentence be?* Elicit a complete sentence, such as: *The dog can run.* Write it on chart paper without a capital letter or end punctuation. Ask children what needs to go at the beginning of the sentence and at the end.

3 Practice Have children work with a partner. Provide each pair with a Photo Card. Have partners think of a complete sentence about the item on the Photo Card. Help children write the sentences. Emphasize the initial capital letter and ending punctuation. Have partners share their sentences by reading them aloud.

Talk About It

Have partners work together to orally generate sentences about games they like to play. Have them tell about the rules in the games, using complete sentences.

ENGLISH LANGUAGE LEARNERS

Naming Objects Help children understand the name of the objects on the Photo Cards. Write the name of the object on a self-stick note and put it on the card. Say the name, pointing to the word on the note as you say it. Have the child repeat it, tracking the print as they speak. Provide a sentence frame for children to complete: *A dog can _____.*

Daily Wrap Up

- Discuss the Essential Question and encourage children to use the oral vocabulary words. *How can we cooperate and follow rules in traveling to and from school?*

- Prompt children to review and discuss the skills they used today. How do those skills help them?

Materials

Reading/Writing Workshop Big Book
UNIT 3

Interactive Read-Aloud Cards

Visual Vocabulary Cards
guard
prank
responsible

Photo Cards
bat	insect
cow	man
fan	mix
fish	pig
hat	six

Word-Building Cards

High-Frequency Word Cards
a
like
see
the
to
we

Response Board

🎵 **"Kim Hears an Insect"**

→ # Build the Concept

MINILESSON
10 Mins

Oral Language

OBJECTIVES

CCSS Actively engage in group reading activities with purpose and understanding. **RL.K.10**

CCSS Identify real-life connections between words and their use. **L.K.5c**

Develop oral vocabulary

ACADEMIC LANGUAGE
• *fable*
• Cognates: *fábula*

ESSENTIAL QUESTION

COLLABORATE

Remind children that this week they are talking and learning about following rules. Guide children to discuss the Essential Question using information from the **Big Book** and the weekly rhyme.

Remind children about the lamb in "Mary Had a Little Lamb" and the school rules. Say the rhyme and have children join in.

Oral Vocabulary

Review last week's oral vocabulary words, as well as *cooperate* and *rules* from Day 1. Then use the **Define/Example/Ask** routine to introduce *guard, prank,* and *responsible.*

Visual Vocabulary Cards

Oral Vocabulary Routine

Define: When you **guard** something, you watch over it and keep it safe.

Example: The policeman will guard the bank.

Ask: Why might you want to guard your backpack?

Define: When you play a **prank**, you do something to fool people.

Example: I played a prank by giving my brother a toy that popped out of a can and surprised him.

Ask: How might you feel if someone played a prank on you?

Define: **Responsible** people do what they are supposed to do.

Example: The responsible children put away the toys after playtime.

Ask: How can you be a responsible pet owner?

Listening Comprehension

Read the Interactive Read Aloud

MINILESSON 10 Mins

Genre: Fable

Tell children that you will be reading a fable. Explain that a *fable* is a fiction story that teaches a lesson. Display the **Interactive Read-Aloud Cards**.

Read the title. Point out that *cry* has more than one meaning. In this story, *cry* means to yell loudly.

Interactive Read-Aloud Cards

ELL ENGLISH LANGUAGE LEARNERS

Reinforce Meaning As you read "The Boy Who Cried Wolf" make meaning clear by pointing to specific people, places or objects in the illustrations, demonstrating word meanings, paraphrasing text, and asking children questions. For example, on Card 2, point to the sheep in the picture. Say *these animals are called sheep.*

Strategy: Visualize

Remind children that they can picture in their minds what is happening in the story. They can use information from the words and illustrations to help them create the picture using the **Think Aloud Cloud**.

Think Aloud I read that Gabriel was "bursting with excitement" waiting for his uncle. In my mind I can picture him smiling and walking quickly back and forth because he is so excited. Making a picture in my mind of the way characters look and do things will help me understand what happens as I keep reading.

Read "The Boy Who Cried Wolf." Pause to model using the strategy of visualizing.

Make Connections

COLLABORATE

Guide partners to connect "The Boy Who Cried Wolf" with *How Do Dinosaurs Go to School?* Discuss ways the characters in the stories cooperate with one another.

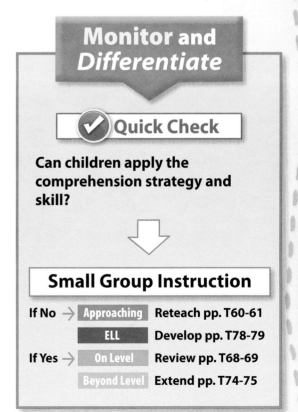

Monitor and *Differentiate*

✓ Quick Check

Can children apply the comprehension strategy and skill?

⬇

Small Group Instruction

If No →	**Approaching**	Reteach pp. T60-61
	ELL	Develop pp. T78-79
If Yes →	**On Level**	Review pp. T68-69
	Beyond Level	Extend pp. T74-75

→ # Word Work

Quick Review

Build Fluency: Sound Spellings: Show the following **Word-Building Cards:** *a, i, m, p, s, t.* Have children chorally say each sound. Repeat and vary the pace.

MINILESSON **5** Mins

Phonemic Awareness

Phoneme Isolation

Photo Card

OBJECTIVES

CCSS Isolate and pronounce the initial, medial vowel, and final sounds in three-phoneme words. **RF.K.2d**

CCSS Associate the long and short sounds with the common spellings for the five major vowels. **RF.K.3b**

Read and blend words with short *i*

❶ **Model** Show the **Photo Card** for *insect* and say the word. *Insect has the /i/ sound at the beginning: /i/, /i/,* insect. *Say the sound with me: /i/.* Tell children that now they will listen for the /i/ sound in the middle of words. Display the Photo Card for *pig.* Have children say the word *pig* with you. *Pig has the /i/ sound in the middle. Listen: /p/ /iii/ /g/,* pig. Emphasize the medial sound. *Let's say /iii/ because we hear the sound in the middle of* pig: /iii/.

❷ **Guided Practice/Practice** Say each of the following words and have children repeat. Have them say /i/ if they hear the sound in the middle of the word. Guide children with the first word.

big   mat   sit   pin   pass   fit   hip   Kim

Then show Photo Cards for *fish, cow, mix, six, hat, pig.*

Have children say the name of each picture with you. Ask them to raise their hands if they hear the /i/ sound in the middle of the word. Guide practice with the first word.

Photo Cards

♪ Review initial /i/. Play and sing "Kim Hears an Insect." Have children clap when they hear initial /i/. Demonstrate as you sing with them.

Go Digital

Phonemic Awareness

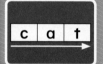
Phonics

Handwriting

Phonics

10 Mins

Word-Building Card

Review Short /i/ *i*

1 Model Display **Word-Building Card** *i*. *This is the letter* i. *The letter* i *stands for /iii/, the sound you hear in the middle of* pig. *Say the sound with me: /iii/. I will write the letter* i *because* pig *has /iii/ in the middle.*

2 Guided Practice/Practice Tell children that you will say some words that have /i/ in the middle and some words that do not. Have children say /i/ and write the letter *i* on their **Response Boards** when they hear /i/ in the middle of the word. Guide practice with the first word.

sit   school   bit   fin   fan   miss   kick

Blend Words with Short *i* and *m, s, t, p*

1 Model Display Word-Building Cards *s, i, t*. *This is the letter* s. *It stands for /s/. This is the letter* i. *It stands for /i/. This is the letter* t. *It stands for /t/. Let's blend the three sounds together: /siiit/. The word is* sit. Continue with *sip, tip, pit.*

2 Guided Practice/Practice Write the following words. Have children read each word, blending the sounds. Guide practice with the first word.

sip   tap   pit   map   sit   it

Write these sentences and prompt children to read the connected text, sounding out the decodable words: *We can tap it. I see the map. We like to sit and sip.*

Corrective Feedback

Sound Error Model the sound that children missed, then have them repeat. For example, say: *My turn.* Tap under the letter *i* in the word *sip* and ask: *Sound? What's the sound?* Return to the beginning of the word. Say: *Let's start over.* Blend the word again.

Extend the Lesson

Final Double Letters *s, t*

Place the Word-Building Cards *m, i, s, s* in a pocket chart and model blending and reading the word.

Point out that the two letters, *ss*, stand for one sound /s/. Have children blend and read the word *miss*. Continue with the word *mitt*.

YOUR TURN PRACTICE BOOK p. 80

→ # Word Work

Go Digital

Phonics

| the | is |
| you | do |

High-Frequency Word Routine

MINILESSON
5 Mins

Phonics

Photo Cards

Picture Sort

❶ **Model** Remind children that the letter *i* can stand for /i/. Place the **Word-Building Card** *i* on the left side of a pocket chart. *What is this letter?* (i) *What sound does this letter stand for?* (/i/)

Hold up the **Photo Card** for *mix*. Say: *Here is the picture for* mix. Mix *has the /i/ sound in the middle. Listen, /m/ /iii/ /ks/. I will place* mix *under the letter* i *because the letter* i *stands for /i/.*

Repeat for letter *a* using the Photo Card for *bat*.

❷ **Guided Practice/Practice** Display and name each Photo Card: *fan, fish, hat, man, pig, six.* Have children say the picture name and then say the sound in the middle of the word. Ask them to tell under which letter the Photo Card should be placed. Guide practice with the first word.

Photo Cards

High-Frequency Words

to

1 **Guided Practice** Display the **High-Frequency Word Card** *to*. Review the word using the **Read/Spell/Write** routine.

2 **Practice** Point to the High-Frequency Word Card *to* and have children read it. Repeat with last week's words *the, we, see, a, like*.

Build Fluency

Word Automaticity Write the following sentences. Read each sentence and then have children chorally read as you track the print. Repeat several times.

> *We like to sip it.*
> *I like to see the map.*
> *Tim can see a pit.*

Read for Fluency Distribute pages 81–82 of the **Your Turn Practice Book** and help children assemble their Take-Home Books. Chorally read the Take-Home book with children. Then have children reread the book to review high-frequency words and build fluency.

YOUR TURN PRACTICE BOOK pp. 81–82

Monitor and *Differentiate*

✓ Quick Check

Can children isolate medial /i/ and sort words by medial /i/*i* and /a/*a*?

Can children read and recognize the high-frequency word?

⬇

Small Group Instruction

If No →	**Approaching**	Reteach pp. T62-67
	ELL	Develop pp. T80-83
If Yes →	**On Level**	Review pp. T70-73
	Beyond Level	Extend pp. T76-77

→ # Language Arts

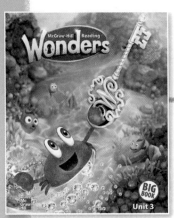

Reading/Writing Workshop Big Book

OBJECTIVES

CCSS Capitalize the first word in a sentence and the pronoun *I*. **L.K.2a**

CCSS Recognize and name end punctuation. **L.K.2b**

• Write a sentence
• Apply writing trait and grammar to writing

ACADEMIC LANGUAGE

• *punctuation*
• Cognates: *puntuación*

MINILESSON

10 Mins

Independent Writing

Writing Trait: Sentence Fluency

❶ Practice Tell children that today they will write a sentence about somebody following rules at home.

❷ Guided Practice Share the Readers to Writers page in the **Reading/Writing Workshop**. Read the model sentences aloud.

READING/WRITING WORKSHOP BIG BOOK, pp. 22–23

Write a Sentence

Model Write the following sentence frame: *I _____. I will write about a rule at home. Point to the word* I. *When you use the word* I, *you are telling about yourself. Point to the blank. Now I need to write about the rule that I follow at home.* Write "put my toys away" on the line. *This is a rule that I follow.* Read the sentence aloud, tracking the print.

Prewrite

Brainstorm Have children work with a partner. Ask them to think of other rules they might follow at home.

Go Digital

Present the Lesson

Writing

Grammar

Draft

Ask children to draw pictures of themselves following the rule at home. Guide children in writing the sentence frame. Help children write the rule they chose in the blank line.

Apply Writing Trait As children fill in their sentences, ask them to point to the action word and identify who is doing the action.

Apply Grammar Tell children to make sure that their sentence begins with a capital letter and ends with a punctuation mark, a period. Remind children that the word *I* is always a capital letter.

ENGLISH LANGUAGE LEARNERS

Identify Support children as they identify places they like to visit by having them point to pictures or draw pictures that show the place. Label the picture with the name of the place underneath. Then write a complete sentence that includes the place, such as *I go to the beach.*

Grammar
MINILESSON 5 Mins

Sentences

❶ Review Remind children that a sentence is a group of words we put together that tell about someone or something doing an action.

Write the sentence: *I feed the fish. Who is doing the action?* (I) *What is the action word?* (feed) Point to the capital letter. *How do I begin my sentence?* (with a capital letter) Remind children that the word *I* always begins with a capital letter. *How do I end my sentence?* Then point to the period.

COLLABORATE

❷ Guided Practice/Practice Ask children to name places they like to visit. Record responses writing some sentences as complete sentences without capitalization and periods and some as incomplete sentences, for example:
to the park, i like to go to the park; to the movies, i like to go to the movies

Point to an incomplete sentence. *What is missing from this sentence? The person doing the action or the action?* Point to a complete sentence and prompt children to share what comes at the beginning of a sentence and at the end. Have children help you correct each sentence. Rewrite the sentences with the changes.

Talk About It

COLLABORATE

Have partners work together to orally generate sentences about rules they follow at home. Have them tell about the rules, using complete sentences.

Daily Wrap Up

- Review the Essential Question and encourage children to discuss it, using the oral vocabulary words *cooperate* and *rule. How can we work together to follow the rules?*

- Prompt children to review and discuss the skills they used today. Guide them to give examples of how they used each skill.

LANGUAGE ARTS **T41**

Materials

Reading/Writing Workshop Big Book
UNIT 3

Reading/Writing Workshop
UNIT 3

Literature Big Book
How Do Dinosaurs Go to School?

Interactive Read-Aloud Cards

Word-Building Cards

Visual Vocabulary Cards

High-Frequency Word Cards
can
I
like
see
the
to
we

to

Photo Cards
baby   sing
bird   write
dolphin
horse
insect
juggle
kitten

Puppet

→ # Extend the Concept

MINILESSON
10 Mins

Oral Language

OBJECTIVES

CCSS Use words and phrases acquired through conversations, reading and being read to, and responding to texts. **L.K.6**

CCSS Recognize and produce rhyming words. **RF.K.2a**

Develop oral vocabulary

ESSENTIAL QUESTION

Remind children that this week they have been talking and reading about following rules in different places. Have them recite "Mary Had a Little Lamb" and think about the school rule. Then ask if they think the dinosaurs from *How Do Dinosaurs Go to School?* would be allowed at Mary's school. (Possible answer: No, because dinosaurs are animals. It would be against the rules.)

Phonological Awareness

Recognize Rhyme

Have children repeat these lines from the rhyme: "Its fleece was white as snow. The lamb was sure to go." Say *snow* and *go* and have children repeat. Tell children that *snow* and *go* rhyme because they sound the same at the end. *I will say two words. If they rhyme, I will raise my hand: bag, pen.* Say the following word pairs and have children raise their hands if they rhyme: *rule, tool; bus, bat; rock, sock; cap, fig; dog, log.*

Review Oral Vocabulary

Reread the Interactive Read Aloud Use the **Define/Example/Ask** routine to review the oral vocabulary words *cooperate, rules, guard, prank,* and *responsible.* Then have children listen as you reread "The Boy Who Cried Wolf." Then ask the following questions:

→ *What did Gabriel have to guard?* (sheep)

→ *Why did Gabriel play a prank on the villagers?*
(He was bored and wanted excitement.)

Go Digital

Visual Glossary

"The Boy Who Cried Wolf"

Category Words

Category Words: Action Words

❶ Explain/Model Chant the following jingle:

We jump, jump, jump in the air,
We skip, skip, skip over there!
We hop, hop, hop to the beat,
We dance, dance, dance with our feet!

→ Repeat the first line of the chant and ask children which words are actions, or words that name what someone or something does. (jump) Repeat the routine with the remaining lines, encouraging children to perform the action once they correctly identify the action word.

❷ Guided Practice Display the **Photo Cards** for *horse, dolphin, bird,* and *insect. How do these animals get from here to there?* Read the following sentences and have children identify the action words and perform the action.

Horses gallop.
Dolphins swim.
Birds fly.
Insects crawl.

→ Ask children to identify other words that describe what animals do. (Possible answers: dive, waddle, hop, climb)

LET'S MOVE!

Have children pretend that they are one of the animals on the Photo Cards. Encourage them to act out the animal's movements. Challenge them to make the sounds their animal makes at the same time.

ENGLISH LANGUAGE LEARNERS

Reinforce Meaning Point to the Photo Cards for *horse, dolphin, bird,* and *insect*. Help children identify other animals that gallop, swim, fly, and crawl. Have children repeat the action words in their native language and in English.

YOUR TURN PRACTICE BOOK p. 83

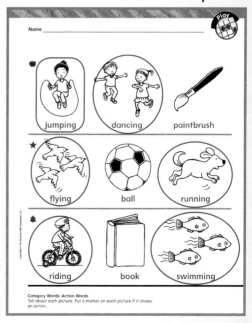

→ # Listening Comprehension

CLOSE READING

Literature Big Book

OBJECTIVES

CCSS With prompting and support, identify the reasons an author gives to support points in a text. **RI.K.8**

- Understand the characteristics of informational text
- Use the text feature, lists, to gather information
- Apply the comprehension strategy: Visualize
- Make connections across texts

ACADEMIC LANGUAGE

- *informational text, visualize*
- Cognates: *texto informativo, visualizar*

MINILESSON
10 Mins

Read "Be Safe"

Genre: Informational Text

Display "Be Safe" on pages 34–36 of the **Big Book** and read aloud the title. Explain to children that this informational text will give facts on how to stay safe.

Set a Purpose for Reading

Read aloud the first sentence on page 34. Tell children to listen as you read aloud to find out what rules can keep them safe on the way home from school. Continue reading the selection.

Strategy: Visualize

Remind children that good readers sometimes use the text and photos to make pictures in their minds of what is happening in a selection. Have children look at the picture on page 34.

Tell children that as you read the selection that they should try to make pictures in their minds. *What pictures do you see in your head about a busy street? Why would it be important to have rules to keep us safe?* (Possible answer: I see a lot of cars and people trying to cross the street. It is important to have rules so people know when to cross the street safely.)

Text Feature: Lists

Explain Point out the list on page 34 and read it aloud. Explain that sometimes informational text gives extra information in the form of a list. *This list gives us important information about walking rules. What does it tell us?* (look both ways; cross at the crosswalk)

Apply Turn to page 35 and have children point to the list. Read the list aloud and ask children to tell the important information that is given. (wear a helmet; stay on the bike path) Continue the same procedure with page 36 about riding in a car.

Go Digital

"How Do Dinosaurs Go to School?"

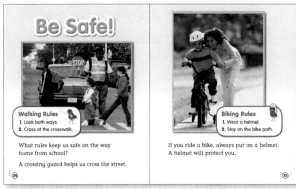

LITERATURE BIG BOOK   PAGES 34–35

VISUALIZE

Picture yourself riding on a bike. What things may make you stop suddenly? Why is it important to wear a helmet? (If you bumped into something, you might fall off the bike. A helmet will protect your head.)

LITERATURE BIG BOOK   PAGE 36

KEY DETAILS

Look at the photograph. What rules are the children following? (sitting in the back seat; wearing seat belts)

Retell and Respond

Have children discuss the selection by asking the following questions:

→ *How does a crossing guard keep us safe?* (A crossing guard helps us to cross the street.)

→ *What are some rules you should follow to stay safe on your way home from school?* (Answers will vary.)

Make Connections

Have children recall the selections they have read this week.

→ *The selections this week have told us about rules. How did the dinosaur show that he was responsible by following the rules?* (Possible answers: He raised his hand, helped out with classroom projects, and tidied his desk.)

Write About It Think about how Gabriel did not follow the rules. Write about how the story might have been different if he had followed the rules.

ENGLISH LANGUAGE LEARNERS

Reinforce Meaning As you read aloud the text, make the meaning clear by pointing to the details in the photographs and lists. Ask children questions and elicit language.

CONNECT TO CONTENT

Rules to Go By Review with children the rules they should follow when they are riding in a car (sit in the back seat, buckle your seat belt). Ask children to tell the rules for following traffic lights. Have children tell why it is important to follow rules.

→ # Word Work

Quick Review

Build Fluency: Sound Spellings: Show the following **Word-Building Cards:** *a, i, m, p, s, t.* Have children chorally say each sound. Repeat and vary the pace.

OBJECTIVES

CCSS Distinguish between similarly spelled words by identifying the sounds of the letters that differ. **RF.K.3d**

CCSS Read common high-frequency words by sight. **RF.K.3c**

- Blend phonemes to make words
- Blend letter sounds to make words

MINILESSON
5 Mins

Phonemic Awareness

Puppet

Phoneme Blending

❶ **Model** *The puppet is going to say the sounds in a word. Listen: /b/ /i/ /t/. It can blend these sounds together: /biiit/,* bit. *Now say the word with the puppet:* bit. *Repeat with* cat.

❷ **Guided Practice/Practice** Have children blend sounds to make words. *The puppet is going to say the sounds in a word. Listen to the puppet as it says each sound. Repeat the sounds, then blend them to say the word.* Guide practice with the first word.

/l/ /i/ /d/   /m/ /a/ /t/   /b/ /i/ /g/   /t/ /i/ /p/   /t/ /a/ /n/

MINILESSON
5 Mins

Phonics

Blend Words with Short *i, a,* and *s, p, t*

❶ **Guided Practice** Display **Word-Building Cards** *s, i, t.* Point to letter *s. This is the letter* s. *The letter* s *stands for /s/. Say /sss/. This is the letter* i. *The letter* i *stands for /i/. Listen as I blend the two sounds together: /sssiii/. Say /sssiii/. This is the letter* t. *The letter* t *stands for /t/. Listen as I blend the three sounds: /sssiiit/,* sit. *Now you say it. Let's change* i *to* a. *Use the same routine to blend* sat.

❷ **Practice** Write *tip, tap* and *pit, pat.* Have children blend the words. Point to *tip* and *tap.* Ask children which letters are the same. (t, p) Ask children to tell which letters are different. (i, a) Discuss the sound each letter stands for and how it changes the word. Repeat with *pit, pat.* Remind children that words are made up of vowels and consonants. The letters *i* and *a* are vowels and the letters *s, p,* and *t* are consonants.

Go Digital

Phonemic Awareness

Phonics

Handwriting

Visual Glossary

| the | is |
| you | do |

High-Frequency Word Routine

Dictation

Review Dictate these sounds for children to spell. Have them repeat the sound and then write the letter that stands for the sound.

/i/   /s/   /p/   /t/   /m/   /a/

Dictate the following words for children to spell: *it, sit, sip, tip, tap*. Model for children how to segment each word to scaffold the spelling.

When I say the word sit, *I hear three sounds: /s/ /i/ /t/. I know the letter* s *stands for /s/, the letter* i *stands for /i/, and the letter* t *stands for /t/. I will write the letters* s, i, t *to spell the word* sit.

When children finish, write the letters and words for them to self-correct.

MINILESSON **5 Mins**

High-Frequency Words

to

Visual Vocabulary Card

Practice Say the word *to* and have children write it. Then display the **Visual Vocabulary Card** *to* and follow the Teacher Talk routine on the back.

Build Fluency Build sentences in a pocket chart using the **High-Frequency Word Cards**, **Photo Cards** and teacher-made punctuation cards. Have children chorally read the sentences as you track the print. Then have them identify the word *to*.

I like *to* sing.
We like *to* see the baby.
We like *to* see the kitten.

| I | like | to | 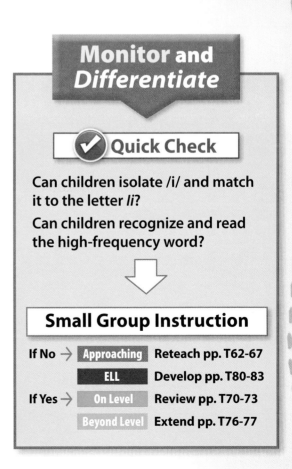 | . |

High-Frequency Words Practice

Have partners create sentences using the word *to*.

Monitor and *Differentiate*

✔ **Quick Check**

Can children isolate /i/ and match it to the letter *Ii*?

Can children recognize and read the high-frequency word?

⬇

Small Group Instruction

If No → **Approaching** Reteach pp. T62-67
ELL Develop pp. T80-83
If Yes → **On Level** Review pp. T70-73
Beyond Level Extend pp. T76-77

→ # Shared Read

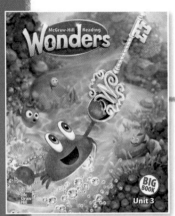

Reading/Writing Workshop Big Book

OBJECTIVES

CCSS Read emergent-reader texts with purpose and understanding. **RF.K.4**

CCSS Read common high-frequency words by sight. **RF.K.3c**

MINILESSON
10 Mins

Read "Tim Can Tip It"

Model Skills and Strategies

Model Book Handling Demonstrate book handling. *This is how I hold a book. This is the front cover. I make sure that the book is not upside down so that I can see the words. This is how I turn the pages of the book. When I turn to each page, I stop to read the words on it.*

Model Concepts About Print Point to the title page. *This is the title page. It has the title of the story, and it tells us the name of the author, or the person who wrote the story. It also tells us the name of the illustrator, or the person who drew the pictures.* Point out the spaces between the words in the title. Count the words in the title with children. Ask them to point to the last word.

Predict Read the title with children. Ask them to describe the illustration. *What do you think this story will be about? Why?*

Read Point out each rebus and discuss what it stands for. Then have children chorally read the story. Children should sound out the decodable words and say the sight words. Offer support as needed using the student **Reading/Writing Workshop**.

Ask the following:

→ *Look at page 16. What does Tim tip?* (the bag)

→ *Look at page 17. Who can eat the birdseed from the bag?* (the bird)

→ *Look at page 19. What does Tim pat?* (the cat)

Go Digital

"Tim Can Tip It"

"Tim Can Tip It"

Tim can tip the pal.

Tim can tip the bag.

Tim can see the bird tap.

Tim can see the cat tap.

Tim can sit **to** pat the cat.

READING/WRITING WORKSHOP, pp. 14–19

Rereading

COLLABORATE

Have small groups use the **Reading/Writing Workshop** to reread "Tim Can Tip It." Then review the skills and strategies using the *Phonics* and *Words to Know* pages that come before the selection.

→ Remind children that as they reread, they can ask themselves questions and then find the answers in the words and pictures.

→ Have children use page 7 to review high-frequency word *to.*

→ Have children use page 6 to review that the letter *i* can stand for the sound /i/. Guide them to blend the sounds to read the words.

ELL

ENGLISH LANGUAGE LEARNERS

Reinforce Vocabulary Display the **High-Frequency Word Cards** *I, can, the, see, like, to.* Point to classroom objects and groups of children as you use the high-frequency words in sentences such as the following: *I can see the big book. Do you see the big book?* (Yes, we see the big book.) *I like to read the big book. Do you like to read the big book?* (Yes, we like to read the big book.)

$\rightarrow$ # Language Arts

 MINILESSON **10 Mins**

Independent Writing

Write a Sentence

OBJECTIVES

CCSS With guidance and support from adults, respond to questions and suggestions from peers and add details to strengthen writing as needed. **W.K.5**

CCSS Capitalize the first word in a sentence and the pronoun *I*. **L.K.2a**

Revise sentences

ACADEMIC LANGUAGE

revise

Revise

Distribute the children's draft sentences with drawings from Day 3.

Apply Writing Trait Sentence Fluency Explain that as writers revise, they make sure their sentences are complete. Write the sentence: *I walk to school*. Read aloud the sentence. *Let's work together to make sure that I have a complete sentence. What is the action? Which word tells who is doing the action?* Then have children reread the sentences they wrote on Day 3 and check for the following:

→ What is the action? Who is doing it?

→ Does my sentence start with a capital letter?

→ Do I have a punctuation mark at the end of my sentence?

Apply Grammar Explain that the word *I* is always capitalized. *What is the name of the punctuation mark in your sentence?* Review that a sentence must start with a capital letter and end with a punctuation mark.

Peer Edit Have children work in pairs to do a peer edit, in which they read their partner's draft. Ask partners to check that their sentences are complete. Have children check that their sentences begin with a capital letter and end with a period. Provide time for children to make revisions to their sentences.

Final Draft

After children have edited their own papers and finished their peer edits, have them write their final draft.

Go
Digital

Writing

I see a fish.

Grammar

MINILESSON 5 Mins

Grammar

Sentences

1 Review Remind children that a complete sentence tells about someone or something doing an action. *What must every sentence begin with?* (a capital letter) *What must every sentence end with?* (a punctuation mark)

2 Guided Practice Display a sentence strip with a complete sentence, such as *She runs to the park.* Read the sentence aloud, tracking the print.

Cut the strip into three pieces so that one piece has the word *She*, another has the word *runs*, and the last has the words *to the park*. Display the pieces out of order. Ask children to help you put the strips back into the correct order to make a complete sentence. *What do you think the first word should be? Why do you think so?* Elicit that the word *she* tells who is doing the action, and it begins with a capital letter.

Have children continue to help you piece together the sentence. *Where does she run? What do we have at the beginning of the sentence?* (the capital letter *S*) *What do we have at the end of the sentence?* (a period)

3 Practice Make sentence strips for this sentence: *I help a friend.* Read the sentence aloud before you cut it into pieces. Provide pairs of children with strips of the sentence. Have partners work together to put the sentence back together. Ask partners to read aloud the sentence. *What is at the beginning of the sentence? Who is doing the action? What is the action? Who do I help? What is at the end?* Remind children that the word *I* is always a capital letter.

Talk About It

Have partners work together to orally generate sentences about rules they follow in the playground. Have them tell about the rules, using complete sentences.

ENGLISH LANGUAGE LEARNERS

Photo Cards and Sentences
Provide sentences that go with images on the **Photo Cards** for *baby, horse, juggle,* and *kitten.* As you say a sentence aloud, hold up a Photo Card as you say the action and the person or animal doing the action such as *The baby smiles.*

Daily Wrap Up

- Review the Essential Question and encourage children to discuss it, using the oral vocabulary words.

- Prompt children to discuss the skills they practiced and learned today. Guide them to share examples of each skill.

Go Digital

www.connected.mcgraw-hill.com
RESOURCES
Research and Inquiry

→ **Wrap Up the Week**
Integrate Ideas

RESEARCH AND INQUIRY

Rules to Go By

 OBJECTIVES

Participate in shared research and writing projects (e.g., explore a number of books by a favorite author and express opinions about them). **W.K.7**

ACADEMIC LANGUAGE

research

Make a Book

Tell children that today partners will do a research project to make a page for a school rule book. Review the steps in the research process below.

STEP 1 **Choose a Topic**

Prompt a discussion about why rules are necessary in the classroom, the hallways, the schoolyard, the cafeteria, and on the bus. Guide partners to choose a school rule.

STEP 2 **Find Resources**

Review how to locate and use resources. Direct children to research how rules were or were not followed in selections from the week. Have children use the Research Process Checklist online.

STEP 3 **Keep Track of Ideas**

Have children list their ideas by drawing pictures of the rules and writing words to describe the rules.

Collaborative Conversations

Take Turns Talking As children engage in partner, small group, and whole group discussions, encourage them to:

→ take turns talking.

→ listen carefully to the speaker.

→ ask others to share their ideas and opinions.

We walk in school.

STEP 4 Create the Project: Rule Book

Explain the characteristics of the project:

→ **Information** A book can give information. In this project, the book will give information about rules in school.

→ **Text** Each page of the rule book will have a sentence that tells the rule. Provide this sentence frame:

We _____ in school.

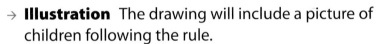

→ **Illustration** The drawing will include a picture of children following the rule.

Explain that each pair will choose one rule from their lists and write and illustrate a page for the book. The pages will be put together in a school rule book that everyone can share.

→ Guide children to write a sentence that begins with a capital letter and ends with a punctuation mark.

→ Prompt children to include details in their illustration.

ELL ENGLISH LANGUAGE LEARNERS SCAFFOLD

Beginning	Intermediate	Advanced/Advanced High
Use Sentence Frames Pair children with more fluent speakers. Use sentence frames to help children describe their rule and picture. For example: *My rule is about ____. The picture shows ____.*	**Discuss** Guide children to focus on why it is important to follow their rule. Have them describe their picture. Ask: *What might happen if we do not follow the rule? What happens when we follow the rule?*	**Describe** Prompt children to brainstorm lists of words, such as *cooperate*, which describe what happens when rules are followed in different places. Encourage them to think about how their choice of words could make their rule book page more interesting.

Materials

Reading/Writing Workshop Big Book
UNIT 3

Literature Big Book
How Do Dinosaurs Go to School?

Word-Building Cards

Visual Vocabulary Cards

rule
cooperate
to

High-Frequency Word Cards

a
like
see
the
we
to

Photo Cards

car	key	pig
cat	lock	saw
city	man	soap
fire	mop	tie
fish	nail	toe
hay	nest	vest
hippo	net	vine
inch	ox	web
insect	pie	

Response Board

"Kim Hears an Insect"

→ Integrate Ideas

TEXT CONNECTIONS

Connect to Essential Question

OBJECTIVES

 Participate in collaborative conversations with diverse partners about *kindergarten topics and texts* with peers and adults in small and larger groups. **SL.K.1**

 With prompting and support, compare and contrast the adventures and experiences of characters in familiar stories. **RL.K.9**

• Make connections among texts

• Make connections to the world

Text to Text

Remind children that all week they have been reading selections about rules in different places. Tell them that now they will connect the texts, or think about how the selections are alike and different. Model comparing *How Do Dinosaurs Go to School?* to another selection from the week.

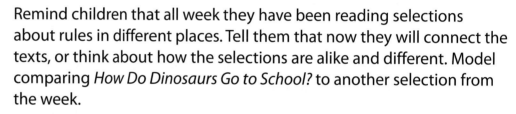 **Think Aloud** In *How Do Dinosaurs Go to School?* I learned about the school rules. In "Be Safe" I learned about rules that keep me safe on the way home from school. In the dinosaur story, I used illustrations to understand the school rules. In "Be Safe," I used photographs to learn about safety rules.

Guide children to compare the experiences of characters as they pertain to rules in "The Boy Who Cried Wolf" and *How Do Dinosaurs Go to School?* as well as other selections from the week.

Text to Self

Have children discuss the different rules that apply to them. Have them name a rule they follow at home and tell why it is important.

Text to World

Talk about the different rules children have within their community. For each rule presented, ask: *Why do we have this rule? Why is it important to you? Why is it important to other people?*

TALK ABOUT READING

OBJECTIVES

 Confirm understanding of a text read aloud or information presented orally or through other media by asking and answering questions about key details and requesting clarification if something is not understood. SL.K.2

Becoming Readers

Talk with children about the genres, strategy, and skill they have learned about this week. Prompt them to discuss how this knowledge helps them to read and understand selections.

→ Remind them that one genre they learned about is fantasy. Recall with them some of the characteristics of fantasy.

→ Discuss with them the strategy of visualizing. *How did picturing in your minds some of the things the dinosaurs were doing help you to understand the story* How Do Dinosaurs Go to School?

→ Talk about how children learned to look for key details in the illustrations and the text to help them understand the story. *Why is it important to look closely at the illustrations when you are reading a story?*

RESEARCH AND INQUIRY

SOCIAL STUDIES

OBJECTIVES

 Participate in shared research and writing projects (e.g., explore a number of books by a favorite author and express opinions about them). W.K.7

Wrap Up the Project

Guide partners to share the information about their rule and to point out details in their pictures. Encourage children to use words and phrases they learned this week. Have children use the Presenting and Listening checklists online.

Word Work

MINILESSON 5 Mins
Phonemic Awareness

OBJECTIVES

CCSS Spell simple words phonetically, drawing on knowledge of sound-letter relationships. **L.K.2d**

CCSS Read common high-frequency words by sight. **RF.K.3c**

• Categorize words with the same beginning sounds

• Blend sounds to read words with short *i*

Phoneme Categorization

❶ **Model** Display **Photo Cards** for *inch, man,* and *insect. Listen for which picture names begin with the same sound.* Say the picture names. Inch *and* insect *both begin with /i/.* Man *does not begin with /i/.* Man *does not belong.*

❷ **Guided Practice/Practice** Show children sets of Photo Cards. Name the pictures and have children repeat. Ask them to identify the picture in each set that does not begin with the same sound. Guide practice with the first set.

pig, pie, nail	saw, key, soap	mop, cat, car	tie, toe, web
fire, city, fish	vine, vest, lock	key, hay, hippo	nest, ox, net

MINILESSON 5 Mins
Phonics

Blend Words with Short *i, a,* and *s, p, t*

❶ **Guided Practice** Remind children that the letter *i* can stand for the sound /i/. Repeat for *a*. Display **Word-Building Cards** *i, t*. Point to the letter *i*. *The letter* i *stands for the sound /i/. Say /iii/. The letter* t *stands for /t/. Say /t/. Let's blend the sounds to make the word: /iiit/* it. *Now let's add* s *to the beginning.* Blend and read *sit* with children.

❷ **Practice** Write the words and sentences for children to read:

sip   tip   map

Pam can see Tim.   We like to sit.

I can tip it.   Tim sat at the mat.

Remove words from view before dictation.

 Review initial /i/*i*. Have children write the letter *i* on their **Response Boards**. Play and sing "Kim Hears an Insect." Have children hold up and show the letter *i* on their boards when they hear initial /i/. Demonstrate as you sing with children. Say the title of the song and ask children which word has /i/ in the middle. (Kim)

Go Digital

Phonemic Awareness

Phonics

Handwriting

the	is
you	do

High-Frequency Word Cards

Dictation

1 **Review** Dictate the following sounds for children to spell. As you say each sound, have children repeat it and then write the letter that stands for the sound.

/p/   /s/   /i/   /t/   /m/   /a/

2 Dictate the following words for children to spell. Model how to use **Sound Boxes** to segment each word to scaffold the spelling. *I will say a word. Repeat the word, then think about how many sounds are in the word. Use your Sound Boxes to count the sounds. Then write one letter for each sound you hear.*

sit   sip   tip   sat   pit   tap

Then, write the letters and words for children to self-correct.

MINILESSON 5 Mins

High-Frequency Words

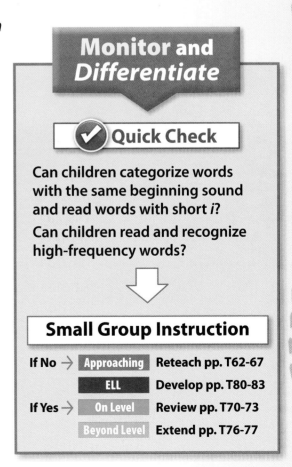

Visual Vocabulary Card

1 **Review** Display **Visual Vocabulary Card** *to*. Have children **Read/Spell/Write** the word. Then choose a Partner Talk activity.

Distribute **High-Frequency Word Cards** to children: *to, the, we, see, a, like*. Tell children that you will say some sentences. *When you hear the word that is on your card, stand and show your word card.*

I can *see* stars tonight.
Matt will read *the* book.
I ate *a* big breakfast this morning!
I *like* museums.
We sang songs today.
Jane wants *to* play outside.

2 **Build Fluency: Word Automaticity** Display High-Frequency Word Cards *the, we, see, a, like* and *to*. Point to each card, at random, and have children read the word as quickly as they can.

Monitor and *Differentiate*

✓ **Quick Check**

Can children categorize words with the same beginning sound and read words with short *i*?

Can children read and recognize high-frequency words?

⬇

Small Group Instruction

If No →	Approaching	Reteach pp. T62-67
	ELL	Develop pp. T80-83
If Yes →	On Level	Review pp. T70-73
	Beyond Level	Extend pp. T76-77

→ # Language Arts

OBJECTIVES

 Speak audibly and express thoughts, feelings, and ideas clearly. **SL.K.6**

 Capitalize the first word in a sentence and the pronoun *I*. **L.K.2a**

Present sentences

ACADEMIC LANGUAGE

• *present, publish*
• Cognates: *presente*

 MINILESSON 10 Mins

Independent Writing

Write a Sentence

Prepare

Tell children that they will present their finished sentences with drawings from Day 4 to the class. Hold up an example from Day 4 and read it aloud, tracking the print. *I read my sentence loud enough so that everyone can hear me. I read it slowly so that everyone can understand what I am saying.*

Present

Have children take turns standing up and reading their sentences aloud. Remind children to speak loudly and clearly. Encourage the rest of the class to be respectful, ask questions when appropriate, and listen carefully to others.

Evaluate

Have children discuss their own presentations and evaluate their performances using the presentation rubric. Use the teacher's rubric to evaluate children's writing.

Publish

After children have finished presenting, collect the sentences. Create a banner with the title "Rules At Home." Tape the banner to a wall. Display children's work under the banner. Read aloud some of the sentences, tracking the print. *This is an important rule. Why do you think it's important to follow?*

At the end of the unit, have children add their writing to their Writer's Portfolio. Then have them look back at their previous writing and discuss how they have changed as writers throughout the year.

Go Digital

Writing

I see a fish.

Grammar

Grammar

Write a Sentence

1 Review Remind children that a complete sentence tells about someone or something doing an action. A sentence begins with a capital letter and ends with a period. Write: *The boy skips to the park.* Have children tell what the action word is and who is doing the action. Point to the punctuation mark. *What is the name of this punctuation mark?*

2 Review Practice Write and read aloud these sentences:

I swing in the park.   *She slides in the park.*
He climbs in the park.   *We sing in the park.*

What is the action word? Who is doing the action? What is the name of the place? Have partners choose a sentence and copy it onto a sentence strip. Cut the sentences into three parts. Then have children mix up the order:

I / swing / in the park.
He / climbs / in the park.
She / slides / in the park.
We / sing/ in the park.

Ask partners to put the sentence strips in the correct order. Circulate and offer corrective feedback as needed.

Gather the sentence strips and store them in an envelope for a center or review activity.

Wrap Up the Week

- Review blending words with initial and medial /i/i. Remind children that a complete sentence tells about someone or something doing an action.

- Use the **High-Frequency Word Cards** to review the **Words to Know**.

- Remind children that a story is usually made up of complete sentences.

→ Approaching Level

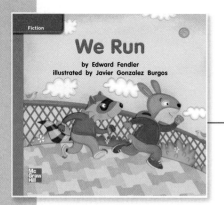

Leveled Reader

OBJECTIVES

 With prompting and support, ask and answer questions about key details in a text. **RL.K.1**

 With prompting and support, retell familiar stories, including key details. **RL.K.2**

Read emergent-reader texts with purpose and understanding. **RF.K.4**

Leveled Reader:
We Run

Go Digital

Leveled Reader

Before Reading

Preview and Predict

Read the title and the name of the author. Discuss the cover illustration. *What are the animals doing?* Turn to the title page and point out that it also has the title and the names of the author and illustrator. Preview the illustrations and identify the rebus pictures. Ask: *What do you think this story will be about?*

Review Genre: Fantasy

Remind children that fantasy is a kind of fiction where things happen that could never happen in real life. Ask: *How can you tell this book is fantasy?* (The animals are dressed in human clothes.)

Model Concepts of Print

Demonstrate book handling as children follow along with their books. *I hold the book so that the cover faces me and the words are right side up. I open the book by turning the cover. Then I turn each page as I read it.*

Review High-Frequency Words

Point out the word *to* on page 3, and read it with children. Have them look through the book and find the word on pages 5 and 7.

Essential Question

Set a purpose for reading: *Let's find out how the animals follow the rules in different places.*

During Reading

Guided Comprehension

As children read *We Run*, monitor and provide guidance by correcting blending and modeling the strategy and skill.

Strategy: Visualize

Remind children that as they read they can make pictures in their mind of what is happening in the story.

Skill: Key Details

Remind children that often the words in a story don't give all the information. They can learn important things that are happening in stories by looking for details in the illustrations. After reading ask: *What details did you find in the illustrations?*

Think Aloud The words on page 3 don't tell me where the friends are, but I can see in the illustration that they are on a playground. On pages 4 and 5 they are running on the playground and then run to the bars. From the illustration I can see that they are monkey bars.

Guide children to identify the details in the illustration on page 8 that tell where the animals are and why they are sitting quietly. Have children point to evidence in the pictures to support their statements.

After Reading

Respond to Reading

→ *Why do the animals run?* (They are on the playground.)

→ *Why aren't the animals running on the last page?* (The animals are in the classroom.)

→ *What would happen if everyone ran in the classroom?* (Possible answer: Too noisy, children might get hurt.)

→ *What are the rules in the classroom?* (Sit quietly.)

Retell

Have children take turns retelling the story. Help them make a personal connection. Ask: *What is your favorite activity on the playground?*

Model Fluency

Reread the story aloud, pausing after each page to have children chorally repeat.

Apply Have children practice reading with partners.

LITERACY ACTIVITIES

Have children complete the activities on the inside back cover of the reader.

Level Up

IF Children read *We Run* **Approaching Level** with fluency and correctly answer the Respond to Reading questions,

THEN Tell children that they will read another story about characters that play a game, but this time not all of them follow the rules.

• Have children page through *Go, Nat!* **On Level** as you introduce the game of baseball and the characters. Preview the illustration on page 8.

• Have children read the story, monitoring their comprehension and providing assistance as necessary.

→ Approaching Level

Phonological Awareness

TIER 2

RECOGNIZE RHYME

OBJECTIVES

 CCSS Recognize and produce rhyming words. **RF.K.2a**

 I Do Remind children that words that rhyme have the same ending sounds. Explain that the words *snow* and *go* have the same ending sound. Repeat the words, emphasizing the /ō/ sound in each.

 We Do Work with children to generate other words from "Mary Had a Little Lamb" that rhyme with *snow* and *go*, such as *bow* and *no*.

 You Do Say each of the following word pairs. Have children nod "yes" when they hear a rhyming pair and shake their heads "no" when the pair does not rhyme: *bear, pear; shoe, blue; fan, fat; fat, hat; pie, pin; pie, sky.*

PHONEME BLENDING

TIER 2

OBJECTIVES

 CCSS Isolate and pronounce the initial, medial vowel, and final sounds in three-phoneme words. **RF.K.2d**

 I Do *The puppet is going to say the sounds in a word. Listen:* /i/ /t/. *The puppet can blend these sounds together:* /iiit/, *it. Repeat with* tin.

 We Do *Now the puppet will say the sounds in the word with the puppet:* fin. *Say the sounds with the puppet:* /f/ /i/ /n/. *Let's blend the sounds together:* /fffiiinnn/, fin. *Repeat with* mitt.

 You Do Have the puppet say the following sounds. Ask children to blend the sounds and say the word: /l/ /i/ /t/ lit; /p/ /a/ /n/ pan; /h/ /i/ /p/ hip; /k/ /i/ /d/ kid; /r/ /i/ /p/ rip; /t/ /i/ /n/ tin; /k/ /a/ /p/ cap.

You may wish to review Phonological Awareness and Phonemic Awareness with **ELL** using this section.

Phonemic Awareness

PHONEME ISOLATION

OBJECTIVES

CCSS Isolate and pronounce the initial, medial vowel, and final sounds (phonemes) in three-phoneme (consonant-vowel-consonant, or CVC) words. **RF.K.2d**

 Display the *Insect* **Photo Card**. *This is an insect. The first sound I hear in insect is /i/.* Have children repeat the word with you, emphasizing the initial sound. Then isolate the first sound: /iii/. Repeat with the *Fish* Photo Card, emphasizing /i/ in the medial position.

 Display the *Inch* Photo Card. Name the photo and say the initial sound together: /i/. Repeat with the *Ink* Photo Card. Then repeat with the *Pig* Photo Card, emphasizing the medial /i/.

 Show the *Inchworm* Photo Card. Have children name it and say the initial sound. Repeat with the *Insect* Photo Card (initial position) and the *Chin* Photo Card (medial position).

PHONEME CATEGORIZATION

OBJECTIVES

CCSS Isolate and pronounce the initial, medial vowel, and final sounds in three-phoneme words. **RF.K.2d**

 Display the *Inchworm, Ink,* and *Leaf* Photo Cards. Say each picture name, emphasizing the intial sound. *Inchworm and ink begin with /i/. Say the sound with me: /i/. Leaf does not begin with /i/. Leaf does not belong.*

 Display the *Insect, Invitation,* and *Sock* Photo Cards. Have children say the name of each picture with you, emphasizing the beginning sound. *Which words begin with the same sound?* Repeat the routine with the *Pig, Six,* and *Toe* Photo Cards, emphasizing the medial sound.

 Display the *Ink, Inch,* and *Train* Photo Cards. Have children name each picture and tell which words have the same beginning sound. Repeat the routine with the Mix, *Wrist,* and *Plate* Photo Cards, emphasizing the medial sound.

ELL ENGLISH LANGUAGE LEARNERS

For the **ELLs** who need **phonics, decoding,** and **fluency** practice, use scaffolding methods as necessary to ensure students understand the meaning of the words. Refer to the Language Transfer Handbook for phonics elements that may not transfer in students' native languages.

Approaching Level

Phonics

SOUND-SPELLING REVIEW

TIER **2**

 OBJECTIVES
Demonstrate basic knowledge of one-to-one letter-sound correspondences by producing the primary or many of the most frequent sounds for each consonant.
RF.K.3a

 I Do Display **Word-Building Card** *i*. Say the letter name and the sound it stands for: i, /i/. Repeat for *m, a, p, s, t*.

 We Do Display the *Inchworm* **Photo Card** and together say the first letter in the word and the sound that it stands for.

You Do Display the *Insect, Ink,* and *Inch* Photo Cards one at a time, and have children say the first sound in the word and the letter that it stands for.

CONNECT *I* TO /i/

TIER **2**

OBJECTIVES
Demonstrate basic knowledge of one-to-one letter-sound correspondences by producing the primary or many of the most frequent sounds for each consonant. **RF.K.3a**

 I Do Display the *Inch* **Sound-Spelling Card**. *The letter* i *can stand for* /i/ *at the beginning of* inch. *What is this letter? What sound does it stand for? I will write* i *when I hear* /i/: *it, inch, bowl, duck*. Repeat with *mix, tap, pin, ran* for medial /i/.

 We Do *The word* is *begins with* /i/. *Let's write* i. Guide children to write *i* when they hear /i/: *if, go, inch, toast, into*. Repeat with *lip, hill, toe, win, tell* for medial /i/.

 You Do Say the following words and have children write the letter *i* if a word begins with /i/: *if, man, lap, igloo*. Repeat with *swim, lit, ran, fish* for medial /i/.

RETEACH

 OBJECTIVES
Associate the long and short sounds with the common spellings (graphemes) for the five major vowels. **RF.K.3b**

 I Do Display **Reading/Writing Workshop**, p. 6. *The letter* i *stands for the* /i/ *sound you hear at the beginning of* insect. Say *insect*, emphasizing /i/.

 We Do Have children name each picture in the apple row. Repeat the name, emphasizing /i/. Repeat for the star row, emphasizing the medial sound.

 You Do Guide children in reading the words in the tree row. Then have them read the words in the fish row, offering assistance as needed.

BLEND WORDS WITH SHORT *i*

OBJECTIVES

Know and apply grade-level phonics and word analysis skills in decoding words. **RF.K.3**

I Do Display **Word-Building Cards** *i, t. This is the letter* i. *It stands for /i/. This is the letter* t. *It stands for /t/. Listen as I blend both sounds: /iiit/,* it. *The word is* it. *Repeat for Tim.*

We Do *Now let's blend more sounds to make the word s*it. *Let's blend: /sssiiit/,* sit. Have children blend the sounds to read the word. Repeat with *pit*.

You Do Distribute sets of Word-Building Cards with *i, t, s,* and *p.* Write: *it, tip, sit, sip, pit.* Have children form the words and then blend and read the words.

BUILD WORDS WITH SHORT *i*

OBJECTIVES

Know and apply grade-level phonics and word analysis skills in decoding words. **RF.K.3**

I Do Display Word-Building Cards *i, t. These are the letters* i *and* t. *They stand for /i/, /t/. I will blend the sounds together: /iiit/,* it. *The word is* it.

We Do Distribute sets of Word-Building Cards for *i, t, s,* and *p.* Show how to make the word *it* and have children do the same. Place the letter *s* in front of *it* and have children do the same. *Let's blend: /sssiiit/,* sit. *Now we have read a new word,* sit.

You Do Have children change the *t* in *sit* to *p* and read the new word, *sip.* Have children change the *s* in *sip* to *t* and read the new word, *tip.* Point out that by changing one letter we make a new word.

BUILD FLUENCY WITH PHONICS

Sound/Spelling Fluency

Display the following Word-Building Cards: *m, a, s, p, t,* and *i.* Have children chorally say each sound. Repeat and vary the pace.

Fluency in Connected Text

Write the following sentences. *I can sip it; Tim can sit; Sam can see it.* Have children read the sentences and identify the words with /i/.

→ Approaching Level
High-Frequency Words

RETEACH WORDS

OBJECTIVES

 Read common high-frequency words by sight. **RF.K.3C**

 I Do Use the **High-Frequency Word Card** *to* with the **Read/Spell/Write** routine to reteach the high-frequency word *to*.

 We Do Have children turn to p. 7 of **Reading/Writing Workshop** and discuss the first photo. Then read aloud the first sentence. Reread the sentence with children. Then distribute index cards with the word *to* written on them. Have children match their word card with the word *to* in the sentence. Use the same routine for the other sentence on the page.

 You Do Write the sentence frame *I like to ___.* Have children copy the sentence frame on their **Response Boards**. Then have partners work together to read and orally complete the frame by talking about things they like to do.

Reteach previously introduced high-frequency words using the **Read/Spell/Write** routine.

REREAD FOR FLUENCY

OBJECTIVES

 Read emergent-reader texts with purpose and understanding. **RF.K.4**

I Do Turn to page 8, and read aloud the title. *Let's read the title together.* Page through the book. Ask children what they see in each picture. Ask children to find the word *to* on the pages.

We Do Then have children open their books and chorally read the story. Have children point to each word as they read. Provide corrective feedback as needed. After reading, ask children to recall what the boy liked.

 You Do Have children reread "Can I Pat It?" with a partner for fluency.

 Repeat for "Tim Can Tip It" on page 14. Have children find the word *to* on page 19.

Oral Vocabulary

REVIEW WORDS

OBJECTIVES

Identify real-life connections between words and their use. **L.K.5c**

Develop oral vocabulary: *cooperate, rules, guard, prank, responsible*

I Do Use the **Define/Example/Ask** routine to review words. Use the following definitions and provide examples:

cooperate	When you **cooperate** you work together with others.
rules	A **rule** is something that tells you what you can or can't do, such as the rules of a game.
guard	When you **guard** something, you watch over it and keep it safe.
prank	When you play a **prank**, you do something to fool people.
responsible	**Responsible** people do what they are supposed to do.

We Do Ask questions to build understanding. *How do you cooperate on the playground? What rules do we follow for a fire drill? How might a dog guard something? Show how you would feel if someone played a prank on you. Are you responsible when you remember to take a note home from school? Why?*

You Do Have children complete these sentence frames: *I am responsible when ___. It's important to follow rules because ___. We cooperate when we ___. I can guard ___. That's a funny prank because ___.*

Comprehension

SELF-SELECTED READING

OBJECTIVES

With prompting and support, ask and answer questions about key details in a text. **RL.K.1**

Apply the strategy and skill to reread text

Read Independently

Have children pick a fantasy story for sustained silent reading. Remind them that they can use illustrations and words to make a picture in their minds of what is happening in the story. Tell them to look for important details in the illustrations and words.

Read Purposefully

Have children identify an illustration that has an important detail. After reading, guide children to participate in a discussion about the story. Guide them to share their detail with the group and show the illustration. Have children share the pictures they made in their minds of the story.

→ On Level

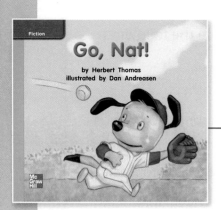

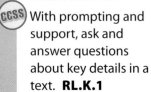

Leveled Reader

OBJECTIVES

 With prompting and support, ask and answer questions about key details in a text. **RL.K.1**

With prompting and support, retell familiar stories, including key details. **RL.K.2**

Leveled Reader:
Go, Nat!

Go Digital

Leveled Reader

Before Reading

Preview and Predict

Read the title and the name of the author and illustrator. Have children name the animal on the cover. Preview the illustrations and identify the rebus pictures. Explain that these animals are the characters in the story. Ask: *What do you think the book is about?* (a ball game)

Review Genre: Fantasy

Remind children that fantasy stories are made-up and the events cannot happen in real life. Ask: *How do you know that this story is fantasy?* (Animals don't play ball games in real life.) Have children point to evidence in the pictures to support their answers.

Model Concepts of Print

Say: *I read each word from left to right.* Have children follow along with their books as you read the sentence on page 2 aloud, tracking the print.

Review High-Frequency Words

Point out the word *to* on page 2, and read it with children. Have them look through the book and find the word on pages 4 and 6.

Essential Question

Set a purpose for reading: *Let's find out what rules Nat follows during the ball game.* Remind children to use the rebuses and illustrations as they read.

During Reading

Guided Comprehension

As children whisper read *Go, Nat!*, monitor and provide guidance by correcting blending and modeling the strategy and skill.

Strategy: Visualize

Review with children that as they read they can make pictures in their mind of what is happening in the story.

Skill: Key Details

Remind children that the illustrations show what is happening in the story and that often they give readers information that isn't in the text. After reading ask: *What details did you find in the pictures?*

Think Aloud On page 6, I read that Mouse hits the ball to Nat. I know that mice are very small. I bet Mouse can't hit the ball very far because he is so small. But then I look at the picture and I see that the ball is moving very fast. Mouse hit the ball very hard!

Guide children to use the pictures on pages 3, 5, 7, and 8 to find details about how Nat feels during the ball game. Have children point to evidence in the text or pictures to support their statements.

After Reading

Respond to Reading

→ *Does Nat ever catch the ball?* (Yes.) *How do you know?* (The picture on page 8 shows Nat burying the ball.)

→ *Who hits the ball the farthest?* (Mouse) *How do you know?* (The picture on pages 6 and 7 show Mouse hitting the ball the farthest.)

→ *Why do the animals tell Nat "no" at the end?* (Nat digs a hole to bury the ball.)

→ *What rule did Nat break?* (The "No Digging" rule.)

Retell

Have children take turns retelling the story. Help them make personal connections. Ask: *Would you play a ball game with Nat? Why or why not?*

Model Fluency

Read the sentences one at a time and have children chorally repeat.

Apply Have children practice reading with partners. Encourage them to read sentences with exclamation points with excitement.

LITERACY ACTIVITIES

Have children complete the activities on the inside back cover of the reader.

Level Up

IF Children can read *Go, Nat!* On Level with fluency and correctly answer the Respond to Reading questions,

THEN Tell children that they will read another story about characters that have fun together.

• Have children page through *The Birdhouse* Beyond Level and introduce unfamiliar words, such as hammer and nails.

• Have children read the story, monitoring their comprehension and providing assistance as necessary.

→ On Level

Phonemic Awareness

PHONEME ISOLATION

OBJECTIVES

CCSS Isolate and pronounce the initial, medial vowel, and final sounds (phonemes) in three-phoneme (consonant-vowel-consonant, or CVC) words. **RF.K.2d**

I Do Display the *Insect* **Photo Card**. *This is an* insect. *The first sound is* /i/. *Say it with me.* Repeat with the *Six* Photo Card and the medial sound /i/.

We Do Say *inch* and have children repeat it. *What is the first sound in* inch? Say the sound together. Repeat with *igloo, mitt, pin,* and *sip*.

You Do Say *if, map, pat, in, sad, is*. Have children tell the initial sound. Then say *it, pass, tip, sit, Tim* and have children tell the ending sound.

PHONEME BLENDING

OBJECTIVES

CCSS Demonstrate understanding of spoken words, syllables, and sounds (phonemes). **RFK.2**

I Do Place the *Inch, Fish, Mix, Pig,* and *Six* Photo Cards facedown. Choose a card but don't show it. Say the sounds in the word. *These are the sounds:* /p/ /i/ /g/. *I will blend the sounds:* /piiig/, pig. *The word is* pig. Show the picture.

We Do Choose another picture, and say the sounds in the word. Together say the sounds and blend the sounds to say the word. Then show the picture.

You Do Continue choosing Photo Cards. Say the sounds and have children blend the sounds and say the word.

PHONEME CATEGORIZATION

OBJECTIVES

CCSS Isolate and pronounce the initial, medial vowel, and final sounds (phonemes) in three-phoneme (consonant-vowel-consonant, or CVC) words. **RF.K.2d**

I Do Display the *Insect, Inchworm,* and *Koala* Photo Cards. *Listen:* insect, inchworm, koala. Emphasize the initial sounds. Insect *and* inchworm *begin with* /i/. Koala *does not begin with* /i/. Koala *does not belong.*

We Do Display the *Mop, Pea,* and *Mouse* Photo Cards. Have children name each picture with you. *Which word does not have the same beginning sound?*

You Do Continue the activity with these Photo Card sets: *Six, Sock, Tie; Tie, Mouse, Top; Map, Mouse, Pea; Paint, Sock, Pea.*

Phonics

REVIEW PHONICS

OBJECTIVES

 Associate the long and short sounds with common spellings (graphemes) for the five major vowels. **RF.K.3b**

 I Do Display **Reading/Writing Workshop**, p. 6. Point to the *Insect* **Sound-Spelling Card**. *What letter stands for the /i/ sound you hear at the beginning of* insect? *The letter is* i.

 We Do Have children say the name of each picture. Then ask them to identify the words with /i/ in the beginning and the words with /i/ in the middle.

 You Do Have children read each word. Repeat, asking them to raise their hands if they hear /i/ in the middle of the word and keeping their hands lowered if they hear /i/ in the beginning of the word.

PICTURE SORT

OBJECTIVES

Associate the long and short sounds with the common spellings (graphemes) for the five major vowels. **RF.K.3b**

Associate the short sound of a vowel with its common spelling.

 I Do Display **Word-Building Cards** *a* and *i* in a pocket chart. Then show the *Map* **Photo Card**. Say: /m/ /a/ /p/, *map*. Tell children that the sound in the middle is /a/. *The letter* a *stands for /a/. I will put the* map *card under the letter* a. Show the *Six* Photo Card. Say: /s/ /i/ /ks/, *six*. Tell children that the sound in the middle is /i/. *The letter* i *stands for /i/. I will put the* six *card under the* i.

 We Do Show the *Pig* Photo Card and say *pig*. Have children repeat. Then have them tell the sound they hear in the middle of *pig*. Ask them if they should place the photo under the *a* or the *i*.

 You Do Continue the activity using the *Bat, Chin, Fan, Fish, Hand, Hat, Man, Map, Mix, Pig,* and *Six* Photo Cards. Have children say the picture name and the sounds in the name. Then have them place the card under the *a* or *i*.

→ **On Level**

Phonics

BLEND WORDS WITH SHORT i

OBJECTIVES

(CCSS) Demonstrate basic knowledge of one-to-one letter-sound correspondences by producing the primary or many of the most frequent sounds for each consonant. **RF.K.3a**

 Write *s, i, t.* Say: *This is the letter* s. *It stands for /s/. Say it with me: /sss/. This is the letter* i. *It stands for /i/. Say it with me: /iii/. This is the letter* t. *It stands for /t/. Say it with me: /t/. I'll blend the sounds together to read the word:* /sssiiit/, sit.

 Write *if* and *pit*. Guide children to blend the words sound by sound to read each word.

 Write the following words and have children blend the words sound by sound to read each word.

tip   it   sip   Tim

High-Frequency Words

REVIEW WORDS

OBJECTIVES

(CCSS) Read common high-frequency words by sight. **RF.K.3c**

 Use the **High-Frequency Word Card** *to* with the **Read/Spell/Write** routine to review *to*.

 Have children turn to page 7 of **Reading Writing Workshop**. Discuss the photographs and read aloud the sentences. Point to the word *to* and have children read it. Then chorally read the sentences. Have children frame the word *to* in the sentences and read the word.

 Say the word *to*. Ask children to close their eyes, picture the word, and write it as they see it. Have children self-correct.

Reteach previously introduced high-frequency words using the **Read/Spell/Write** routine.

Fluency Point to the High-Frequency Word Cards *I, can, the, we, see, a, like* and *to* in random order. Have children chorally read. Repeat at a faster pace.

REREAD FOR FLUENCY

OBJECTIVES

Read emergent-reader texts with purpose and understanding. **RF.K.4**

 I Do Point to the title *Can I Pat It?* on p. 8 of **Reading/Writing Workshop 3** and tell children that this is a question. *When we read questions, our voice goes up at the end of the sentence.* Read the title and have them repeat with the same inflection. Work with them to read for accuracy and expression. Model reading p. 9: *When I read, "I like to pat it," I read all the way to the end of the sentence before pausing. This makes my reading sound natural, as if I were talking.*

 We Do Reread page 9. Then have children choral read the page with you. Continue choral reading the remainder of the pages.

You Do Have children reread *Can I Pat It?* Provide time to listen as children read the pages. Comment on their accuracy and expression and provide corrective feedback by modeling proper fluency.

Use the same routine for *Tim Can Tip It* on pages 14–19.

Comprehension

SELF-SELECTED READING

OBJECTIVES

With prompting and support, ask and answer questions about key details in a text. **RL.K.1**

Apply the strategy and skill to reread text.

Read Independently

Have children pick a fantasy story for sustained silent reading. Remind them that they can use illustrations and words to make a picture in their minds of what is happening in the story. They should also look for important details in the illustrations and words.

Read Purposefully

Have children identify an illustration that has an important detail. After reading, guide children to participate in a discussion. Guide them to share their detail with the group and show the illustration. Have them tell about the pictures they made in their minds of what was happening in the story.

→ Beyond Level

Leveled Reader

OBJECTIVES

CCSS With prompting and support, ask and answer questions about key details in a text. **RL.K.1**

CCSS With prompting and support, retell familiar stories, including key details. **RL.K.2**

Leveled Reader:
The Birdhouse

Before Reading

Preview and Predict

Ask children to point to and read the title as you name the author and the illustrator. Have them identify the front cover and the back cover. Point out the illustrations on the front and back covers. Ask: *What do you think the book will be about?* Have children page through the book and look at the illustrations. Did they confirm their predictions?

Review Genre: Fantasy

Have children recall that fantasy stories are made-up and the events cannot happen in real life. Ask: *Do you think this story can happen in real life? How do you know?* (Bears don't live in houses, drive trucks, or use tools.) Have children point to evidence to support their answers.

Essential Question

Remind students of the Essential Question: *What rules do we follow in different places?* Have children set a purpose for reading by asking: *What rules do you need to follow if you are building a birdhouse?*

During Reading

Guided Comprehension

As children whisper read *The Birdhouse*, monitor and provide guidance by correcting blending and modeling the strategy and skill. Stop periodically to ask open-ended questions, such as *How does the little bear help her father?*

Strategy: Visualize

Review with children that as they read, they can make pictures in their minds of what is happening in the story.

Leveled Reader

Skill: Key Details

Remind children that finding key details in the text and the illustrations will help them to understand what is happening in the story. Explain that in this book, the illustrations provide key details about the project the little bear is helping her father with.

Think Aloud On page 3, the words tell me that the bears are eating breakfast. When I look at the picture, I see that the father bear has a blue paper on the table. I think it is a plan for building a birdhouse. When I look at the picture on page 5, I see the little bear is holding the plan for the birdhouse.

Guide children to read the text and look for key details in the illustrations. On page 6, draw their attention to the goggles that the little bear is putting on to protect her eyes.

After Reading

Respond to Reading

→ *What rules do the father and daughter follow?* (Possible answers: Page 2—The father and daughter follow rules of politeness and are careful not to wake other family members. Page 4—They wear seat belts. The daughter sits in the back seat.)

→ *What does the daughter do to help to build the birdhouse?* (The daughter participates in planning, getting the wood, and building the birdhouse.)

→ *Do the father and daughter enjoy working together? How can you tell?* (Possible answers: Yes. The narrator (daughter) says she likes to work with her father. The illustrations show they are happy to be together.)

Retell

Have children take turns retelling the story. Help them make a personal connection by asking: *Would you enjoy being part of this family? Tell why or why not.*

Gifted and Talented

EVALUATING Have children recall all the different kinds of rules the father and daughter followed during the story. Challenge children to think why the bears followed the rules.

HAVE children put the different rules into categories, such as family rules, safety rules, and directions.

LITERACY ACTIVITIES

Have children complete the activities on the inside back cover of the reader.

Beyond Level

Phonics

OBJECTIVES

 Associate the long and short sounds with the common spellings (graphemes) for the five major vowels. **RF.K.3b**

 I Do Display **Reading/Writing Workshop**, p. 6. Point to the *Insect* **Sound-Spelling Card**. *What is the sound at the beginning of* insect? *What letter can stand for* /i/? *The letter is* i.

 We Do Have children say the name of each picture. Then ask children to share other words they know that begin with /i/.

You Do Have partners read each word. Ask them to write the words on their **Response Boards**, underlining the letter in each word that stands for /i/.

High-Frequency Words

OBJECTIVES

 Read emergent-reader texts with purpose and understanding. **RF.K.4**

I Do Use index cards to create High-Frequency Word Cards for *now* and *today*. Introduce the words using the **Read/Spell/Write** routine.

 We Do Display the **High-Frequency Word Cards** for *I, can, the, we, see, a, like,* and *to.* Have children help you complete the following sentence frames using the High-Frequency Word Cards: *We can ____ now. I can see some ____.*

 You Do Have partners write sentences using the High-Frequency Words *now* and *today* on their Response Boards. Have them read their sentences.

 Fluency Have children turn to pp. 8–13 and 14–19 in **Reading/Writing Workshop 3** and reread the stories *Can I Pat It?* and *Tim Can Tip It* for fluency.

Innovate Have children create a new page for *Can I Pat It?* using the same question. For *Tim Can Tip It,* have children complete the sentence frame *Tim can see the ____ tap* by suggesting other animals that might be in the garden.

Vocabulary

ORAL VOCABULARY: SYNONYMS

OBJECTIVES

 With guidance and support from adults, explore word relationships and nuances in word meanings. **L.K.5**

 I Do Review the meanings of the oral vocabulary words *guard* and *rules*. Explain that a synonym is a word that means almost the same thing as another word. *A synonym for* guard *is* protect. *When you protect someone, you help keep them safe.* The police officer will protect the people in town. *A synonym for* rules *is* laws. *Laws are regulations that say what you can and can't do.* Everyone must obey the laws in their community.

 We Do Write a few sentences together using the new words *protect* and *laws*. Read the sentences.

 You Do Have children work with a partner to come up with a question using one of the new words. Have partners share their questions with the group.

 Gifted and Talented **Extend** Have each child choose one person who works to protect us. Then ask each child to talk about his or her job and why following laws are important.

Comprehension

SELF-SELECTED READING

OBJECTIVES

 With prompting and support, ask and answer questions about key details in a text. **RL.K.1**

Apply the strategy and skill to reread text

Read Independently

Have children select a fantasy story for sustained silent reading. Remind them that key details from the illustrations can help them make a picture in their minds of what is happening in the story. Tell them to look for important details in the illustrations and words.

Read Purposefully

Before reading, have children choose an illustration that shows an important detail about the story. After reading, guide them to join a discussion. Ask how key details in the illustration they chose helped them to create a picture in their mind about what is happening in the story.

 Gifted and Talented **Independent Study** Have children create a book cover illustrating a memorable scene or a favorite character in the stories they read this week. Challenge them to include key details in their picture and write a few sentences stating their opinion about the story.

→ English Language Learners

Leveled Reader

OBJECTIVES

 With prompting and support, ask and answer questions about key details in a text. **RL.K.1**

With prompting and support, retell familiar stories, including key details. **RL.K.2**

Read emergent-reader texts with purpose and understanding. **RF.K.4**

Shared Read:
Go, Nat!

Go Digital

Leveled Reader

Before Reading

Preview and Predict

Read the title *Go, Nat!* Ask: *What's the title? Say it again.* Repeat with the author's name. Point to the cover and say: *I see a dog.* Point to the dog and say: *I see that the dog is wearing a baseball mitt. What else can you see?* Have children describe what they see in the picture. Then do a picture walk and identify the rebus pictures *Cat, Dog, Rabbit,* and *Mouse* and the labels. Use simple language to describe each picture.

Essential Question

Set a purpose for reading: *Let's find out what game the animals play and what rules they follow.* Encourage children to seek clarification when they encounter a word or phrase that does not make sense to them. Model asking for clarification: *I'm not sure where Nat is going. Can you show me?*

During Reading

Interactive-Question Response

Pages 2–3 Point to the illustration on page 2. *I see Cat. What is Cat holding?* (a baseball bat) *What is he doing?* (hitting a ball to Nat) *Let's reread the sentence that tells us what Cat is doing. Say the words with me: Cat hit it to Nat.* Point to the illustration on page 3. *I see Nat. What is Nat doing?* (trying to catch the ball) *What is he wearing?* (a baseball glove)

Tell your partner what Nat is doing. (trying to catch the ball)

Pages 4–5 Point to the illustration and label on page 4. *Who is hitting the ball?* (Rabbit) *Who is Rabbit hitting the ball to?* (Nat) *Let's reread the sentence that tells us who Rabbit hits the ball to. Say the words with me: Rabbit hit it to Nat.* Point to the text on page 5. *Let's reread to find out what Nat is doing. Say the words with me: Go, Nat, go! Where is Nat going?* (to catch the ball)

Pages 6–7 Point to the illustration and label on page 6. *What does Mouse look like?* (He is very small.) *Does Mouse hit the ball?* (yes) *Let's find the text that tells us that.* (Mouse hit the ball to Nat.) Point to the illustration on page 7. *I see that the ball is flying very high in the air. What does Nat do?* (tries to catch it) *How does Nat look?* (very tired)

Page 8 *What is Nat doing?* (digging a hole to bury the ball) *Why is Nat putting the ball into a hole?* (He is tired and does not want to play ball anymore.) *Let's reread the sentence. Say the words with me: No, Nat, no!* Point to the illustration: *Why do the animals say no to Nat?* (The sign says "No Digging," so Nat is breaking a rule.) *Talk with a partner about why Nat does not want to play ball anymore.*

After Reading

Respond to Reading

→ *Who hits the ball first?* (Cat) *Who do the animals hit the ball to?* (Nat)

→ *What does Nat do when Rabbit hits the ball to him?* (tries to catch it)

→ *What does Nat do when Mouse hits the ball to him?* (Nat digs a hole to bury the ball.)

→ *Why did Nat bury the ball?* (He is tired and does not want to play ball anymore.)

Retell

Let's retell the book together. What are the animals doing? (playing a ball game) *Who do the animals hit the ball to?* (Nat) *What does Nat do at the end of the book?* (digs a hole and puts the ball in it)

Model Fluency

Read the sentences one at a time as you track the print. Have children chorally repeat. Point out that your voice gets a little louder and shows excitement for sentences with exclamation points.

Apply Have children read with partners. Encourage them to read sentences with exclamation points with excitement.

Level Up

IF Children can read *Go, Nat!* **ELL Level** with fluency and correctly answer the Respond to Reading questions,

THEN Tell children that they will read a more detailed version of the story.

• Have children page through *Go, Nat!* **On Level** and conduct a picture walk to describe each picture in simple language.

• Have children read the story, monitoring their comprehension and providing assistance as necessary.

LITERACY ACTIVITIES

Have children complete the activities on the inside back cover of the reader.

→ English Language Learners
Vocabulary

PRETEACH ORAL VOCABULARY

OBJECTIVES

CCSS Speak audibly and express thoughts, feelings, and ideas clearly. **SL.K.6**

LANGUAGE OBJECTIVE

Preview vocabulary

 I Do Display the images from the **Visual Vocabulary Cards** and follow the routine to preteach the oral vocabulary words.

 We Do Display each image again and explain how it illustrates or demonstrates the word. Model using sentences to describe the image.

 You Do Display the words again and have children talk to a partner about how the pictures demonstrate the words.

Beginning	Intermediate	Advanced/High
Have partners repeat each word. Then have them pantomime the meanings of *cooperate* and *prank*.	Provide the following sentence frame: *I am responsible because* ____.	Ask partners to use one of the words in a sentence of their own.

PRETEACH ELL VOCABULARY

OBJECTIVES

CCSS Speak audibly and express thoughts, feelings, and ideas clearly. **SL.K.6**

LANGUAGE OBJECTIVE

Preview ELL vocabulary

I Do Display the images from the **Visual Vocabulary Cards** one at a time to preteach the ELL vocabulary words *catch* and *tired* and follow the routine. Say each word and have children repeat it. Define each word in English.

We Do Display each image again and incorporate the words in a short discussion about the images. Model using sentences to describe the image.

You Do Say the word *catch* again and have children repeat. Provide children opportunities to use the word in a sentence by providing this sentence starter: *I can catch* ____.

Beginning	Intermediate	Advanced/High
Have partners pantomime throwing and catching a ball. Have them say *catch* after they "catch the ball."	Have partners talk about different items they can catch.	Ask children to give additional examples of ways to complete the sentence frame: *I get tired when* ____.

High-Frequency Words

REVIEW WORDS

OBJECTIVES

CCSS Read common high-frequency words by sight (e.g., *the, of, to, you, she, my, is, are, do, does*). **RF.K.3c**

LANGUAGE OBJECTIVE

Review high-frequency words

 I Do Display the **High-Frequency Word Card** for *to*. Read the word. Use the **Read/Spell/Write** routine to teach the word. Have children write the word on their **Response Boards**.

 We Do Write the following sentence frame, which uses the week's high-frequency word: *We go to _____*. Track the print as children read and complete the sentence. If necessary, refer to the back of the **Visual Vocabulary Card** for support.

You Do Display a sentence that uses the high-frequency word *to*. Ask children to point to the word *to* and say it aloud. Then work with children to read and say the entire sentence aloud.

Beginning	Intermediate	Advanced/High
Say a sentence with the word *to* in it. Have children clap and say *to* when they hear the word.	Have partners create oral sentences using the word *to*.	Ask children to write the word *to* and use it in a sentence.

REVIEW CATEGORY WORDS

OBJECTIVES

CCSS Identify real-life connections between words and their use (e.g., note places at school that are colorful). **L.K.5c**

LANGUAGE OBJECTIVE

Use category words

 I Do Display the **Visual Vocabulary Card** for Movement Words and say the words. Define the words in English, and then in Spanish, if appropriate, identifying any cognates.

We Do Follow the routine on the card.

You Do Have children share other words that fit into the category.

Beginning	Intermediate	Advanced/High
Demonstrate the following: *walk, hop, clap,* and *wiggle*. Have children identify each movement.	Have partners talk about the different ways they can move.	Have children use the category words in oral sentences.

→ English Language Learners
Writing

SHARED WRITING

OBJECTIVES

Use a combination of drawing, dictating, and writing to narrate a single event or several loosely linked events, tell about the events in the order in which they occurred, and provide a reaction to what happened. **W.K.3**

LANGUAGE OBJECTIVE

Contribute to a shared writing project

 I Do Review the rules shown for "In a Library" and "Crossing the Street" from the Whole Group Shared Writing project for possible ideas for rules. Model writing a rule that you follow: *I talk quietly in the library.*

We Do Encourage children to choose a rule they would like to write about. Write the rule together, for example, *We walk in the hallway.*

You Do Help partners choose a rule and write a sentence about the rule they have chosen. Provide them with a sentence frame to get started. For example, *At the park, we _____.*

Beginning	Intermediate	Advanced/High
Ask children to dictate their rule aloud as you write it for them.	Provide partners with a more complex sentence frame, such as: *One rule we follow is ____.*	Challenge partners to write a sentence about a rule.

WRITING TRAIT: SENTENCE FLUENCY

OBJECTIVES

Use a combination of drawing, dictating, and writing to narrate a single event or several loosely linked events, tell about the events in the order in which they occurred, and provide a reaction to what happened. **W.K.3**

LANGUAGE OBJECTIVE

Recognize complete sentences

 I Do Explain that writers use complete sentences which includes a part that tells who or what is doing an action and a part about what that action is.

 We Do Point to the first sentence on p. 26 in the **Big Book** *How Do Dinosaurs Go to School?* Ask: *What is the action in the sentence? Who does the action?* Point out several sentences and have children locate the subject and action.

 You Do Have children write a sentence about a rule they follow. Have them look at the Big Book selection for ideas. Provide the frame: *We _____ at school.*

Beginning	Intermediate	Advanced/High
Ask children what they do in school. Repeat their responses in complete sentences.	Ask children to work with a partner to complete the sentence frame.	Have children complete the sentence frame and identify the subject and action.

Grammar

SENTENCES

OBJECTIVES

 Capitalize the first word in a sentence and the pronoun *I*. **L.K.2a**

LANGUAGE OBJECTIVE

Learn to recognize sentences

Language Transfers Handbook

In languages such as Cantonese, Haitian Creole, Hmong, Korean, and Vietnamese, there is no subject-verb agreement. Guide native speakers of these languages to add an -s to present tense verbs in third-person usage, such as *He enjoys school* instead of *He enjoy school*.

 I Do Review with children that a sentence has two parts. One part is who the sentence is about, the subject. The other part is what the person or thing does, the action. Explain that the first word in a sentence starts with a capital letter. The last word in the sentence is followed by a punctuation mark such as a period.

We Do Write the following sentences. Read the sentences and underline the capital letter at the beginning of each sentence. Have them say: *The first word is _____. It begins with a capital letter.*

We follow rules.

Tim can go to school.

I walk with you.

 You Do Say or write the following sentence frame:

Rules help because _____.

Pair children and have them orally complete the sentence frame by providing details from this week's readings. Circulate, listen in, and take note of each child's language use and proficiency.

Beginning	Intermediate	Advanced/High
Describe the rules discussed in the selections. Ask: *How does this rule help?* Guide children to complete the sentence frame.	Ask children to describe the illustrations in the selections to help them complete the sentence frame.	Ask children to complete the sentence frame without help, only looking back to the selection if necessary.

PROGRESS MONITORING

Weekly Assessment

Use your Quick Check observations and the assessment opportunities identified below to evaluate children's progress in key skill areas.

✓ TESTED SKILLS ⒸⒸⓈⓈ	Quick Check Observations	Pencil and Paper Assessment
PHONEMIC AWARENESS/ PHONICS /i/ (initial/medial) **RF.K.3b** **i**	Can children isolate /i/ and match it to the letter *Ii*?	Practice Book, pp. 77–78, 80
HIGH-FREQUENCY WORDS *to* **RF.K.3c** **to**	Can children recognize and read the high-frequency word?	Practice Book, pp. 81–82
COMPREHENSION Key Details **RL.K.1, RL.K.7**	As you read *How Do Dinosaurs Go to School?* with children, can they identify and discuss key details using the illustrations and the text?	Practice Book, p. 79

Quick Check Rubric

Skills	1	2	3
PHONEMIC AWARENESS/ PHONICS	Does not connect the sound /i/ with the letters *Ii*.	Usually connects the sound /i/ with the letters *Ii*.	Consistently connects the sound /i/ with the letters *Ii*.
HIGH-FREQUENCY WORDS	Does not identify the high-frequency word.	Usually recognizes the high-frequency word with accuracy, but not speed.	Consistently recognizes the high-frequency word with speed and accuracy.
COMPREHENSION	Does not identify key details using the illustrations and text.	Usually identifies key details using the illustrations and text.	Consistently identifies key details using the illustrations and text.

Go Digital! www.connected.mcgraw-hill.com

Using Assessment Results

✓ TESTED SKILLS	If ...	Then ...
PHONEMIC AWARENESS/ PHONICS	**Quick Check Rubric:** Children consistently score 1 or **Pencil and Paper Assessment:** Children get 0–2 items correct	... reteach tested Phonemic Awareness and Phonics skills using Lessons 16–17 in the *Tier 2 Phonemic Awareness Intervention Online PDFs* and Lesson 14 in the *Tier 2 Phonics/ Word Study Intervention Online PDFs.*
HIGH-FREQUENCY WORDS	**Quick Check Rubric:** Children consistently score 1	... reteach tested skills by using the High-Frequency Word Cards and asking children to read and spell the word. Point out any irregularities in sound-spellings.
COMPREHENSION	**Quick Check Rubric:** Children consistently score 1 or **Pencil and Paper Assessment:** Children get 0–1 items correct	... reteach tested skill using Lessons 10–12 in the *Tier 2 Comprehension Intervention Online PDFs.*

Response to Intervention

Use the children's assessment results to assist you in identifying children who will benefit from focused intervention.

Use the appropriate sections of the *Placement and Diagnostic Assessment* to designate children requiring:

 Tier 2 Intervention Online PDFs

 WonderWorks Intervention Program

→ Phonemic Awareness

→ Phonics

→ Vocabulary

→ Comprehension

→ Fluency

WEEKLY OVERVIEW

Literature Big Book

CLANG! CLANG! BEEP! BEEP! LISTEN TO THE CITY
BY ROBERT BURLEIGH
ILLUSTRATED BY BEPPE GIACOBBE

Listening Comprehension

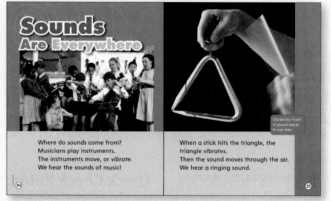

Clang! Clang! Beep! Beep! Listen to the City, 4–32
Genre Fiction

"Sounds Are Everywhere," 34–39
Genre Informational Text

Interactive Read-Aloud Cards

"The Turtle and the Flute"
Genre Fable

Oral Vocabulary

chat   listen
exclaimed   volume
familiar

Minilessons   ✓ TESTED SKILLS (CCSS)

✓ **Comprehension Strategy** .... Visualize, T95
✓ **Comprehension Skill** .... Key Details, T104

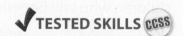

☞ **Go Digital**

www.connected.mcgraw-hill.com

Nathan Love

Essential Question
What are the different sounds we hear?

WEEK 2 →

Big Book and Little Book
Reading/Writing Workshop

Shared Reading

"Nat and Tip," 26–31
Genre Fiction

"Tim and Nan," 32–37
Genre Nonfiction

High-Frequency Word and, T99

Minilessons   ✔ TESTED SKILLS CCSS

✔ **Phonics** . . . . /n/n, T97
Writing Trait. . . . . Ideas, T100
Grammar . . . . Sentences, T101

Differentiated Text

Approaching   On Level   Beyond   **ELL**

TEACH AND MANAGE

What You Do

INTRODUCE

Weekly Concept

Sounds Around Us

**Reading/Writing Workshop
Big Book, 24–25**

TEACH AND APPLY

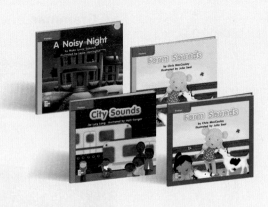

Listening Comprehension

Big Book
Clang! Clang! Beep! Beep! Listen to the City
Genre Fiction
Paired Read "Sounds are Everywhere"
Genre Informational Text

Minilessons
Strategy: Visualize
Skill: Key Details

Shared Reading

Reading/Writing Workshop
"Nat and Tip"
"Tim and Nan"

Minilessons
/n/n, High–Frequency Word: and
Writing, Grammar

 Go Digital

 Interactive Whiteboard

 Interactive Whiteboard

 Mobile

What Your Students Do

WEEKLY CONTRACT

PDF Online

PRACTICE AND ONLINE ACTIVITIES

Your Turn Practice Book, pp. 85–92

Leveled Readers

 Go Digital

Online To-Do List

Online Activities

Mobile

WEEK 2 →

DIFFERENTIATE

Small Group Instruction
Leveled Readers

 Mobile

INTEGRATE

Research and Inquiry
School Sound Chart, pp. T134–T135

Text Connections
Compare Sounds, p. T136

Talk About Reading
Becoming Readers, p. T137

 Online Research

WORKSTATION CARDS

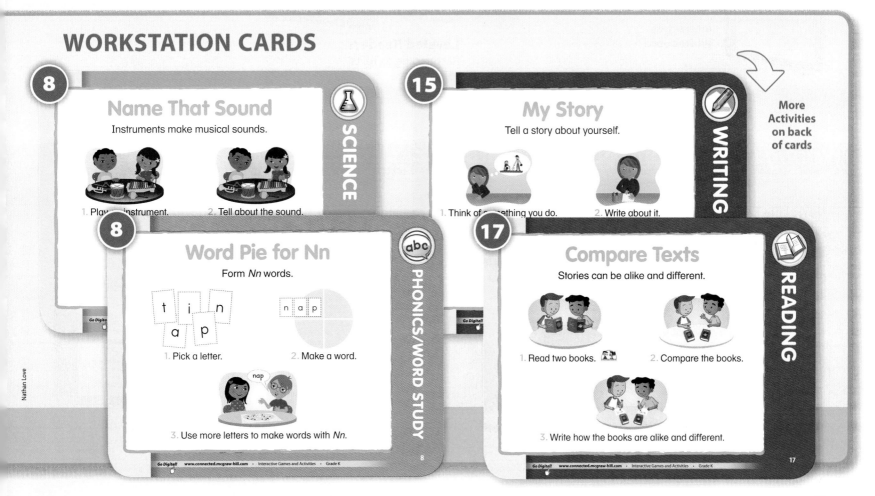

8 — **Name That Sound** — SCIENCE
Instruments make musical sounds.
1. Play an instrument. 2. Tell about the sound.

8 — **Word Pie for Nn** — PHONICS/WORD STUDY
Form *Nn* words.
1. Pick a letter. 2. Make a word.
3. Use more letters to make words with *Nn*.

15 — **My Story** — WRITING
Tell a story about yourself.
1. Think of something you do. 2. Write about it.

More Activities on back of cards

17 — **Compare Texts** — READING
Stories can be alike and different.
1. Read two books. 2. Compare the books.
3. Write how the books are alike and different.

Go Digital! www.connected.mcgraw-hill.com • Interactive Games and Activities • Grade K

Nathan Love

DEVELOPING READERS AND WRITERS

Write to Sources and Research

Respond to Reading, T95, T143, T151, T157, T161

Connect to Essential Question, T95, T127

Key Details, 104

Research and Inquiry, T134

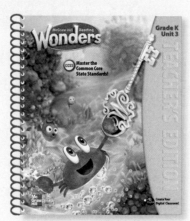

Teacher's Edition

Literature Big Book
Clang! Clang! Beep! Beep! Listen to the City
Paired Read: *"Sounds Are Everywhere"*

Leveled Readers
Responding to Texts

Interactive Whiteboard

Writing Process • Independent Writing

Narrative Text
Personal Narrative Sentences, T122–T123, T132, T140

Conferencing Routines
Peer Conferences, T132

Interactive Whiteboard

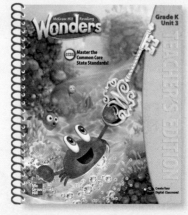

Teacher's Edition

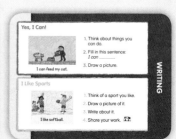

Leveled Workstation Card
My Story, Card 15

Writing Traits • Shared and Interactive Writing

Writing Trait:
Ideas
Personal Narrative
Sentences, T100, T114

Teacher's Edition

Sentences,
pp. 40–41

Reading/Writing Workshop

Interactive Whiteboard

Leveled Workstation Card
My Story, Card 15

Grammar and Spelling/Dictation

Grammar
Sentences, T101

Spelling/Dictation
Words with Short *a*, *i*, and *n*, *p*, *t*, *m*, T129, T139

Interactive Whiteboard

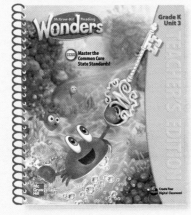

Teacher's Edition

Online Grammar Games   **Handwriting**

SUGGESTED LESSON PLAN

	DAY 1	**DAY 2**

READING

Whole Group

Teach and Model

Literature Big Book

Reading/ Writing Workshop

DAY 1

Build Background Sounds Around Us, T92
Oral Vocabulary Words listen, volume, T92
✓**Listening Comprehension**
• Genre: Fiction
• Strategy: Visualize, T95
Big Book *Clang! Clang! Beep! Beep! Listen to the City*
✓**Word Work**
Phonemic Awareness
• Phoneme Isolation, T96
Phonics
• Introduce /n/n, T97
Handwriting Nn, T98
High-Frequency Word and, T99

Practice *Your Turn* 85–86

DAY 2

Oral Language Sounds Around Us, T102
✓**Category Words** Sound Words, T103
✓**Listening Comprehension**
• Genre: Fiction
• Strategy: Visualize, T104
• Skill: Key Details
• Guided Retelling
• Model Fluency, T109
Big Book *Clang! Clang! Beep! Beep! Listen to the City*
✓**Word Work**
Phonemic Awareness
• Phoneme Blending, T110
Phonics
• Blend Words with /n/n, T111
High-Frequency Word and, T111
Shared Reading "Nat and Tip," T112–T113

Practice *Your Turn* 87

DIFFERENTIATED INSTRUCTION — Choose across the week to meet your student's needs.

Small Group

Approaching Level

Leveled Reader *City Sounds,* T142–T143
Phonological Awareness
Onset/Rime Blending, T144 TIER 2
Phonics Sound-Spelling Review, T146 TIER 2
High-Frequency Words Reteach Words, T148 TIER 2

Leveled Reader *City Sounds,* T142–T143
Phonemic Awareness
Phoneme Isolation, T144 TIER 2
Phonics Connect n to /n/, T146 TIER 2
High-Frequency Words
Reread for Fluency, T148 TIER 2

On Level

Leveled Reader *Farm Sounds,* T150–T151
Phonemic Awareness Phoneme Isolation, T152

Leveled Reader *Farm Sounds,* T150–T151
Phonemic Awareness Phoneme Blending, T152
Phonics Review Phonics, T153
High-Frequency Words Review Words, T154

Beyond Level

Leveled Reader *A Noisy Night,* T156–T157
Phonics Review, T158

Leveled Reader *A Noisy Night,* T156–T157
High-Frequency Words Review, T158

English Language Learners

Leveled Reader *Farm Sounds,* T160–T161
Phonological Awareness
Onset/Rime Blending, T144 TIER 2
Phonics Sound-Spelling Review, T146 TIER 2
Vocabulary Preteach Oral Vocabulary, T162
Writing Shared Writing, T164

Leveled Reader *Farm Sounds,* T160–T161
Phonemic Awareness
Phoneme Isolation, T144 TIER 2
Phonics Connect n to /n/, T146 TIER 2
Vocabulary Preteach ELL Vocabulary, T162

LANGUAGE ARTS

Whole Group

Writing and Grammar

Shared Writing
Writing Trait: Ideas, T100
Write a Personal Narrative Sentence, T100
Grammar Sentences, T101

Interactive Writing
Writing Trait: Ideas, T114
Write a Personal Narrative Sentence, T114
Grammar Sentences, T115

Nathan Love

DAY 3	**DAY 4**	**DAY 5** Review and Assess

READING

Oral Language Sounds Around Us, T116	**Oral Language** Sounds Around Us, T124	**Integrate Ideas**
Oral Vocabulary chat, exclaimed, familiar, T116	✓ **Category Words** Sound Words, T125	• Text Connections, T136
✓ **Listening Comprehension**	✓ **Listening Comprehension**	• Talk About Reading, T137
• Genre: Fable	• Genre: Informational Text	• Research and Inquiry, T137
• Strategy: Visualize, T117	• Strategy: Visualize, T126	✓ **Word Work**
• Make Connections, T117	• Text Features: Captions	**Phonemic Awareness**
Interactive Read Aloud "The Turtle and the Flute," T117	• Make Connections, T127	• Phoneme Categorization, T138
✓ **Word Work**	**Big Book** Paired Read: "Sounds Are Everywhere," T126	**Phonics**
Phonemic Awareness	✓ **Word Work**	• Read Words with Short *a, i* and, *p, n, t, m,* T138
• Phoneme Isolation, T118	**Phonemic Awareness**	**High-Frequency Word** and, T139
Phonics	• Phoneme Blending, T128	
• Blend Words with Short *a, i* and *t, p, n,* T119	**Phonics**	
High-Frequency Word and, T121	• Blend Words with Short *a, i* and *n, p, t,* T128	
	High-Frequency Word and, T129	
	Shared Reading "Tim and Nan," T130–T131	
	Integrate Ideas Research and Inquiry, T134–T135	
Practice *Your Turn* 88–90	**Practice** *Your Turn* 91	**Practice** *Your Turn* 92

DIFFERENTIATED INSTRUCTION

Leveled Reader *City Sounds,* T142–T143	**Leveled Reader** *City Sounds,* T142–T143	**Leveled Reader** Literacy Activities, T143
Phonemic Awareness Phoneme Blending, T145	**Phonemic Awareness** Phoneme Categorization, T145	**Phonemic Awareness** Phoneme Categorization, T145
Phonics Reteach, T146	**Phonics** Blend Words with /n/n, T147	**Phonics** Build Words with *n,* T147
High-Frequency Words Reteach Words, T148	**Oral Vocabulary** Review Words, T149	Build Fluency with Phonics, T147
		Comprehension Self-Selected Reading, T149
Leveled Reader *Farm Sounds,* T150–T151	**Leveled Reader** *Farm Sounds,* T150–T151	**Leveled Reader** Literacy Activities, T151
Phonemic Awareness Phoneme Categorization, T152	**Phonics** Blend Words with *n,* T154	**Comprehension** Self-Selected Reading, T155
Phonics Picture Sort, T153	**High-Frequency Words** Reread for Fluency, T155	
Leveled Reader *A Noisy Night,* T156–T157	**Leveled Reader** *A Noisy Night,* T156–T157	**Leveled Reader** Literacy Activities, T157
Vocabulary Oral Vocabulary: Synonyms, T159	**High-Frequency Words** Innovate, T158	**Comprehension** Self-Selected Reading, T159
Leveled Reader *Farm Sounds,* T160–T161	**Leveled Reader** *Farm Sounds,* T160–T161	**Leveled Reader** Literacy Activities, T161
Phonemic Awareness Phoneme Blending, T145	**Phonemic Awareness** Phoneme Categorization, T145	**Phonemic Awareness** Phoneme Categorization, T145
Phonics Reteach, T146	**Phonics** Blend Words with /n/n, T147	**Phonics** Build Words with *n,* T147
High-Frequency Words Review Words, T163	**High-Frequency Words** Review Category Words, T163	Build Fluency with Phonics, T147
Writing Writing Trait: Ideas, T164	**Grammar** Sentences, T165	

LANGUAGE ARTS

Independent Writing	**Independent Writing**	**Independent Writing**
Writing Trait: Ideas, T122	Writing Trait: Ideas, T132	Write a Personal Narrative Sentence
Write a Personal Narrative Sentence	Writing a Personal Narrative Sentence	Prepare/Present/Evaluate/Publish, T140
Prewrite/Draft, T122–T123	Revise/Final Draft, T132	**Grammar** Write a Personal Narrative Sentence, T141
Grammar Sentences, T123	**Grammar** Sentences, T133	

DIFFERENTIATE TO ACCELERATE

Qualitative   Quantitative
Reader and Task
TEXT COMPLEXITY

IF the text complexity of a particular section is too difficult for children

THEN see the references noted in the chart below for scaffolded instruction to help children Access Complex Text.

	Literature Big Book	**Reading/Writing Workshop**	**Leveled Readers**	

	Literature Big Book	**Reading/Writing Workshop**	**Leveled Readers**	
Quantitative	*Clang! Clang! Beep! Beep! Listen to the City* **Lexile** 630 Paired Selection: "Sounds Are Everywhere" **Lexile** 290	"Nat and Tip" **Lexile** 250 "Tim and Nan" **Lexile** 250	**Approaching Level** **Lexile** BR **Beyond Level** **Lexile** 190	**On Level** **Lexile** 280 **ELL** **Lexile** BR
Qualitative	What Makes the Text Complex? • **Connection of Ideas** Text within Illustrations, T104 **A C T** *See Scaffolded Instruction in Teacher's Edition, T104.*	What Makes the Text Complex? **Foundational Skills** • Decoding with *n*, T110–T111 • Identifying high-frequency words, T111	What Makes the Text Complex? **Foundational Skills** • Decoding with *n* • Identifying high-frequency words *and* *See Level Up lessons online for Leveled Readers.*	
Reader and Task	The Introduce the Concept lesson on pages T92–T93 will help determine the reader's knowledge and engagement in the weekly concept. See pages T94–T95, T105–T109, T126–T127 and T134–T137 for questions and tasks for this text.	The Introduce the Concept lesson on pages T92–T93 will help determine the reader's knowledge and engagement in the weekly concept. See pages T112–T113, T130–T131 and T134–T137 for questions and tasks for this text.	The Introduce the Concept lesson on pages T92–T93 will help determine the reader's knowledge and engagement in the weekly concept. See pages T142–T143, T150–T151, T156–T157, T160–T161 and T134–T137 for questions and tasks for this text.	

Nathan Love

Monitor and *Differentiate*

IF you need to differentiate instruction

THEN use the Quick Checks to assess children's needs and select the appropriate small group instruction focus.

✔ Quick Check

Comprehension Strategy Visualize, T117

Phonemic Awareness/Phonics /n/n, T99, T111, T121, T129, T139

High-Frequency Words *and*, T99, T111, T121, T129, T139

If No → **Approaching** **Reteach,** pp. T142–T149

ELL **Develop,** pp. T160–T165

If Yes → **On Level** **Review,** pp. T150–T155

Beyond Level **Extend,** pp. T156–T159

Level Up with Leveled Readers

IF children can read their leveled text fluently and answer comprehension questions

THEN work with the next level up to accelerate children's reading with more complex text.

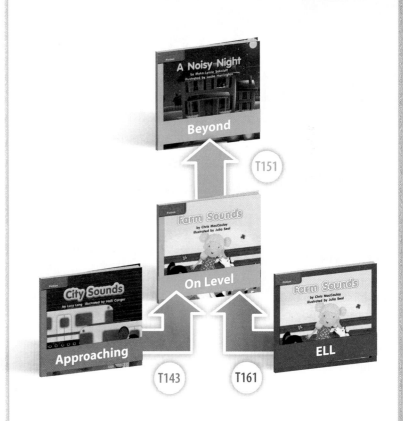

ENGLISH LANGUAGE LEARNERS
ELL SCAFFOLD

IF ELL students need additional support **THEN** scaffold instruction using the small group suggestions.

| Reading-Writing Workshop T93 "Keep Your Ears Open!" Integrate Ideas T135 | Leveled Reader T160–T161 *Farm Sounds* | Phonological Awareness Onset/Rime Blending, T144 Phoneme Isolation, T144 Phoneme Blending, T145 Phoneme Categorization, T145 | Phonics, /n/n, T146–T147 | Oral Vocabulary, T162 listen, volume, familiar, chat, exclaimed High-Frequency Word, T163 *and* | Writing Shared Writing, T164 Writing Trait: Ideas, T164 | Grammar T165 Sentences |

Note: Include ELL Students in all small groups based on their needs.

Materials

Reading/Writing Workshop Big Book UNIT 3

Literature Big Book *Clang! Clang! Beep! Beep! Listen to the City*

Visual Vocabulary Cards
listen
volume

Response Board

"Nellie's Nest"
"The Bus"

Photo Cards
berries   nut
horse   rabbit
kitten   sing
nest   vegetables
net   write
night

Nn
nest
Sound-Spelling Cards

and
High-Frequency Word Cards
a
and
can
I
like
see
we

I was able to picture in my mind…
Think Aloud Cloud

Reading/Writing Workshop Big Book

OBJECTIVES

CCSS Confirm understanding of a text read aloud or information presented orally or through other media by asking and answering questions about key details and requesting clarification if something is not understood. **SL.K.2**

CCSS Identify real-life connections between words and their use. **L.K.5c**

→ # Introduce the Concept

MINILESSON 10 Mins

Build Background

ESSENTIAL QUESTION

What are the different sounds we hear?

Read aloud the Essential Question. Tell children you are going to sing a song about sounds we hear and things we see on a bus.

The Bus

The people on the bus go up and down,

Up and down, up and down.

The people on the bus go up and down,

All through the town.

The wheels on the bus go 'round and 'round…

The lights on the bus go "Blink, blink, blink…"

The horn on the bus goes "Beep! Beep! Beep!…"

The wiper on the bus goes "Swish! Swish! Swish!…"

Sing the weekly song, "The Bus," with children. Ask: *What sound does the horn on the bus make?* (beep, beep, beep) Tell children that this week they will read to find out about sounds in many different places.

Oral Vocabulary Words

Use the **Define/Example/Ask** routine to introduce the oral vocabulary words **listen** and **volume**.

To introduce the theme of "Sounds Around Us," explain that children hear many sounds in many places. Ask them to name a sound they heard on the way to school today.

Go Digital

"Sounds Around Us"

Video

Visual Glossary

Oral Vocabulary Routine

<u>**Define:**</u> When you **listen**, you hear a sound.

<u>**Example:**</u> I listen to hear the sounds outside.

<u>**Ask:**</u> Why do you listen when the teacher reads a story?

<u>**Define:**</u> **Volume** is how loud or soft a sound is.

<u>**Example:**</u> The volume of the music was too loud.

<u>**Ask:**</u> What is the volume of a bell?

Visual Vocabulary Cards

Talk About It: Sounds Around Us

Guide children to name loud sounds they have heard in their town. Make a list of their responses. Display pages 24–25 of the **Reading/ Writing Workshop Big Book** and have children do the **Talk About It** activity with a partner.

Weekly Concept Sounds Around Us

Essential Question
What are the different sounds we hear?

Go Digital!

Keep Your Ears Open!

Talk About It
What sounds do these instruments make?

READING/WRITING WORKSHOP BIG BOOK, pp. 24–25

Collaborative Conversations

Add New Ideas As children engage in partner, small group, and whole group discussions, encourage them to:

→ Stay on topic.

→ Connect their own ideas to the ideas of others.

→ Connect their personal experience to the conversation.

ELL

ENGLISH LANGUAGE LEARNERS SCAFFOLD

Beginning

Use Visuals Explain that the photograph shows children playing musical instruments. Point out and name the instruments in the picture. Then ask yes/no questions such as these: *Is this a drum? Is this a shaker?* Allow children ample time to respond.

Intermediate

Describe Ask children to describe what is happening in the picture. Ask what instruments they see. *Who is playing the drum?* (the boy) Correct grammar and pronunciation as needed.

Advanced/Advanced High

Exemplify Have children elaborate on what is happening in the picture. Elicit more details to support children's answers.

→ # Listening Comprehension

Literature Big Book

Read the Literature Big Book

OBJECTIVES

CCSS Follow words from left to right, top to bottom, and page to page. **RF.K.1a**

CCSS Actively engage in group reading activities with purpose and understanding. **RL.K.10**

- Strategy: Visualize
- Connect Big Book to Weekly Concept

ACADEMIC LANGUAGE
events, illustrated

Connect to Concept: Sounds Around Us

Tell children that you will now read about many sounds in a town. *What sounds do you hear in your town?*

Concepts of Print

Directionality and Word Spacing Display the **Big Book** cover. Then page through the book from beginning to end, reminding children that we start at the front of the book and then turn pages until we get to the back of the book. Turn to pages 6–7. Point to the word *alarm* as you read it aloud. Then point to the space after *alarm. I see the word* alarm. *Then I see a space with no letters. Then I see the word* clock. *Words have spaces between them. That makes them easier to read.*

Genre: Fiction

Model *Clang! Clang! Beep! Beep! Listen to the City* is a fiction story. Remind children of these characteristics of fiction:

→ The events in the story are made up.

→ Many fiction stories have illustrations.

Story Words Preview these words before reading:

eardrum: an inside part of your ear that helps you hear
wrecking ball: a big ball that a machine swings to knock down old buildings

Set a Purpose for Reading

→ Identify and read aloud the title and the names of the author and illustrator.

→ Remind children that the author wrote the words in the story and the illustrator drew the pictures.

→ Ask children to listen as you read aloud the Big Book to find out about sounds in a city.

Go Digital

Clang! Clang! Beep! Beep! Listen to the City

Model Think Aloud Cloud

Strategy: Visualize

Explain Remind students that they can make pictures in their minds to help them understand what is happening in a story. Information from the text and illustrations can help them make these pictures in their minds.

Think Aloud When I look at the cover, I see cars and trucks driving on the road and I see tall buildings. I also see something that looks like a bus. I can read the title of the book: *Clang! Clang! Beep! Beep! Listen to the City*. I can picture what it would be like in a city with all the traffic around me. I make a picture in my mind of children on the bus, singing and talking. In my mind, I can see the driver honking the horn: Beep! Beep! This picture can help me understand the story.

Model As you read, use the **Think Aloud Cloud** to model the strategy.

Think Aloud On pages 8–9, I read that trash cans were knocking. The trash cans are on their sides on the ground now. I can picture in my mind the trash cans crashing into each other and making a loud noise.

Respond to Reading

After reading, prompt children to share what they learned about sounds in the city. Discuss the pictures they made in their minds as they listened to the story. Then have children draw a picture of something in their town that makes noise.

Make Connections

Use *Clang! Clang! Beep! Beep! Listen to the City* to discuss the sounds around us. Revisit the concept behind the Essential Question *What are the different sounds we hear?* by paging through the **Big Book**.

Write About It Have children write one example of how the city sounds in the story are similar or different from sounds in their neighborhood.

ENGLISH LANGUAGE LEARNERS SCAFFOLD

Beginning

Describe Display the cover of the book and describe the picture. Point out and name the different types of vehicles. Ask children what kinds of sounds the different vehicles might make. Then have them visualize the scene and imagine the sounds they would hear.

Intermediate

Discuss Ask children to visualize their favorite part in the story. Have them describe it and tell what they like about it. Is there anything about that part they don't like? Model correct pronunciation as needed.

Advanced/Advanced High

Express Ask children to visualize and describe a city scene that isn't in the book. Where is it? What is happening? What sounds do they hear? Correct their grammar and pronunciation as needed.

→ # Word Work

Quick Review

Review /i/, /t/: Ask children to tell the initial sound of the *Insect* and *Tie* Photo Cards.

Build Fluency: Sound-Spellings: Show the following **Word-Building Cards:** *a, i, m, p, s, t.* Have children chorally say each sound. Repeat and vary pace.

MINILESSON
5 Mins

Phonemic Awareness

OBJECTIVES

CCSS Isolate and pronounce the initial, medial vowel, and final sounds in three-phoneme words. **RF.K.2d**

CCSS Demonstrate basic knowledge of one-to-one letter-sound correspondences by producing the primary or many of the most frequent sounds for each consonant. **RF.K.3a**

Phoneme Isolation

① Model Introduce initial sound /n/. Display the **Photo Card** for *nest. Listen for the sound at the beginning of* nest. Nest *has the /n/ sound at the beginning. Say the sound with me: /nnn/.* Say these words and have children repeat: *nice, near, nap.* Emphasize the phoneme /n/.

Photo Card

♪ *Let's play a song. Listen for the words with /n/ at the beginning.* Play "Nellie's Nest," and have children listen for the /n/ sound. *Let's listen to the song again and clap when we hear words that begin with /n/.* Play or sing the letter song again, encouraging children to join in. Have children clap when they hear words that begin with /n/.

② Guided Practice/Practice Display and name each Photo Card: *nest, net, night, nut. Say each picture name with me. Tell me the sound at the beginning of the word.* Guide practice with the first word.

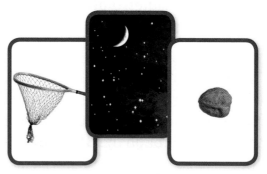
Photo Cards

ELL

ENGLISH LANGUAGE LEARNERS

Minimal Contrasts
Focus on articulation. Say /n/ and point out your mouth position. Have children repeat. Repeat for /m/. Have children say both sounds, noticing the differences. (The lips are slightly apart for /n/. The lips are closed for /m/.) Tell children that both sounds will stop if you pinch your nose.

ARTICULATION SUPPORT

Demonstrate the way to say /n/. Put your lips apart just a little bit. Push your tongue behind your top teeth. Use your voice and let the air go out through your nose. If you pinch your nose the /n/ sound will stop! Say *name, new, nice, note* and have children repeat. Stretch initial /n/.

MINILESSON
10
Mins

Phonics

Introduce /n/ *n*

Sound-Spelling Card

❶ **Model** Display the *Nest* **Sound-Spelling Card**. Say: *This is the Nest card. The sound is /n/. The /n/ sound is spelled with the letter* n. *Say the sound with me: /n/. This is the sound at the beginning of* nest. *Listen: /nnn/,* nest. *What is the name of this letter?* (n) *What sound does this letter stand for?* (/n/)

Display the song "Nellie's Nest" (see **Teacher's Resource Book** online). Read or sing the song with children. Reread the title and point out that the word *nest* begins with the letter *n*. Model placing a self-stick note below the *n* in *nest*.

❷ **Guided Practice/Practice** Read each line of the song. Stop after each line and ask children to place self-stick notes below words that begin with *N* or *n* and say the letter name.

ENGLISH LANGUAGE LEARNERS

Phoneme Variations in Language
In some languages, such as Cantonese, Korean, or Khmer, there is no direct transfer for the sound-symbol match for /n/. Emphasize the /n/ sound and demonstrate correct mouth position.

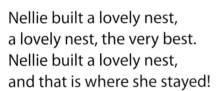

Nellie built a lovely nest,
a lovely nest, the very best.
Nellie built a lovely nest,
and that is where she stayed!

All her friends said fly away.
"Not today! Not today!
No, I cannot fly away.
Oh, no, I never will."

Nellie built a lovely nest,
a lovely nest, the very best.
Nellie built a lovely nest,
and that is where she stayed!

Corrective Feedback

Sound Error Model the sound /n/ in the initial position, then have children repeat the sound. Say: *My turn. Nest. /nnn/. Now it's your turn.* Have children say the word and isolate the initial sound.

YOUR TURN PRACTICE BOOK pp. 85–86

Word Work

MINILESSON
5 Mins

Handwriting: Write *Nn*

Go
Digital

❶ **Model** Say the handwriting cues below as you write and then identify the uppercase and lowercase forms of *Nn*. Then trace the letters on the board and in the air as you say /n/.

OBJECTIVES

CCSS Write a letter or letters for most consonant and short-vowel sounds. **L.K.2c**

CCSS Read common high-frequency words by sight. **RF.K.3c**

ACADEMIC LANGUAGE
uppercase, lowercase

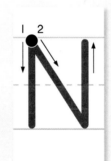
Straight down.
Go back to the
top. Slant down.
Straight up.

Straight down.
Around and
straight down.

Handwriting

the   is
you   do

High-Frequency Word Routine

❷ **Guided Practice/Practice**

→ Say the cues together as children trace both forms of the letter with their index fingers. Have children identify the uppercase and lowercase forms of the letter.

→ Have children write *N* and *n* in the air as they say /n/ multiple times.

→ Distribute **Response Boards**. Observe children's pencil grip and paper position, and correct as necessary. Have children say /n/ every time they write the letter *Nn*.

 Daily Handwriting

Throughout the week teach uppercase and lowercase letters *Nn* using the Handwriting models. At the end of the week, have children use the **Your Turn Practice Book** page 92 to practice handwriting.

MINILESSON
5 Mins

High-Frequency Words

and

1 Model Display the **High-Frequency Word Card** *and.* Use the **Read/Spell/Write** routine to teach the word.

and

High-Frequency Word Cards

→ **Read** Point to the word *and* and say the word. Say: *This is the word* and. *Say it with me:* and. *I hear buses* and *trucks in the city.*

→ **Spell** *The word* and *is spelled a-n-d. Spell it with me.* As children spell the word, remind them that the letter *a* stands for the /a/ sound they hear at the beginning of *and.* The letter *n* has the same /n/ sound as in *nap.*

→ **Write** *Let's write the word in the air as we say each letter: a-n-d.*

→ Have partners create sentences using the word.

2 Guided Practice/Practice Build sentences using High-Frequency Word Cards, **Photo Cards**, and teacher-made punctuation cards. Have children point to the high-frequency word *and.* Use these sentences.

> I like berries and vegetables.
> I can write and sing.
> We see a rabbit and kitten.

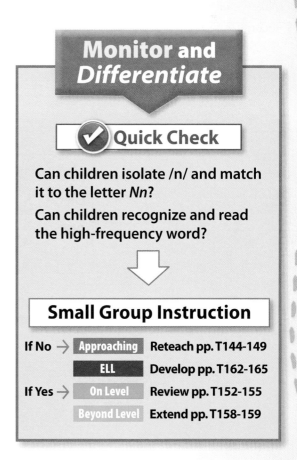

Monitor and *Differentiate*

✔ Quick Check

Can children isolate /n/ and match it to the letter *Nn*?

Can children recognize and read the high-frequency word?

⬇

Small Group Instruction

If No →	**Approaching**	Reteach pp. T144–149
	ELL	Develop pp. T162–165
If Yes →	**On Level**	Review pp. T152–155
	Beyond Level	Extend pp. T158–159

WHOLE GROUP
DAY 1

→ # Language Arts

 MINILESSON
10 Mins

Shared Writing

Writing Trait: Ideas

1 Model Remind children that a sentence tells about someone or something doing an action. Tell children that they can write sentences to tell about things they observe. *You use your senses to observe. You see, hear, touch, taste, and smell many different things.*

→ Display the **Photo Card** for *horse*. Write and read aloud: *I see a brown horse. The sentence tells what I see. I can use sentences to give details about what I see. I see that the horse is brown.*

2 Guided Practice/Practice Write and read aloud: *I see a green crayon.* Help children name the sense word (see) and the details word (green). *What does the word* green *describe?* (the crayon)

Write a Personal Narrative Sentence

Focus and Plan Tell children that this week they will learn how to write a sentence to tell about sounds they hear.

 COLLABORATE **Brainstorm** Have children name some sounds they hear outdoors, at home, and at school. Create a three-column chart to write some of their ideas. *What do you hear when you're outdoors? What do you hear in school? What do you hear in your home?*

Outdoors	School	Home
birds chirping	teachers talking	parents cooking
cars moving	children singing	vacuum cleaner running
dogs barking	blocks falling	music playing

Write Model writing a sentence using an idea from the list. *I can take one of the sounds we hear and write about it:* I hear music playing at home. Continue modeling other sentences. Read aloud the sentences with children.

OBJECTIVES

 CCSS With guidance and support from adults, recall information from experiences or gather information from provided sources to answer a question. **W.K.8**

 CCSS Capitalize the first word in a sentence and the pronoun *I*. **L.K.2a**

 CCSS Recognize and name end punctuation. **L.K.2b**

• Make a chart
• Recognize sentences

ACADEMIC LANGUAGE
sentence, senses, capital letter, period

 # Go
Digital

Writing

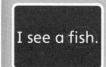

I see a fish.

Grammar

Grammar

MINILESSON 5 Mins

Sentences

1 Model Remind children that a sentence is a group of words that tells a complete thought. *A sentence has a naming part (noun) that says who or what does something and an action part that says what action the person or thing does.* Review that a sentence always begins with a capital letter and ends with a period.

→ Write and read aloud: *The boy eats ice cream. Who is the person in the sentence?* (the boy) *What is the action word?* (eats)

2 Guided Practice/Practice Write and read aloud: *a pencil; I touch a pencil.* Work together to identify which group of words is a sentence and which is not. Have children tell who is doing the action in the sentence (I) and what the action is. (touch a pencil)

Model how to form sentences from groups of words. Write and read aloud: *the lion. We can add to the words* the lion *to make a sentence.* Write: *The lion roars.* Read the sentence aloud as you point to each word. *This group of words is a sentence because it forms a complete thought about the lion. The lion is doing an action. What is the lion doing?* Point to the beginning and end of the sentence as you say: *The sentence begins with a capital letter and ends with a mark called a period.*

Provide another incomplete sentence, such as *the big truck.* Have children think of ways to complete the sentence.

Talk About It

Have partners work together to orally generate sentences about sounds an animal can make. Challenge them to create complete sentences that names an animal and tells the sound the animal makes.

ENGLISH LANGUAGE LEARNERS SCAFFOLD

Beginning

Explain Tell children that a sentence has a naming part and an action part. Write and read: *The dog barks. This is a complete sentence because it tells that an animal is doing something. What is the animal? What does the dog do?* Restate children's responses in order to develop their oral language proficiency.

Intermediate

Practice Write and read: *The cat meows; the boy; the dog sits; the girl.* Have partners identify the complete sentences. Ask them to circle the naming word and action word in each complete sentence. Allow children ample time to respond.

Advanced/Advanced High

Practice Write and read aloud: *A cat; I see a cat; A girl laughs; A boy.* Have children identify the complete sentences. Guide children in adding words to the incomplete sentences to make them complete sentences. Clarify children's responses as needed by providing vocabulary.

Daily Wrap Up

- Review the Essential Question and encourage children to discuss it, using the new oral vocabulary words. *What sounds do we hear at school?*

- Prompt children to share the skills they learned. *How might they use those skills?*

Materials

Reading/Writing Workshop Big Book
UNIT 3

Literature Big Book
Clang! Clang! Beep! Beep! Listen to the City

Visual Vocabulary Cards
listen
volume

Response Board

Word-Building Cards

Photo Cards
farm

Sound-Spelling Cards

Puppet

and
High-Frequency Word Cards
a
like
to

Retelling Cards

"The Bus"

→ Build the Concept

MINILESSON
10 Mins

Oral Language

OBJECTIVES

CCSS Use words and phrases acquired through conversations, reading and being read to, and responding to texts. **L.K.6**

CCSS Blend and segment onsets and rimes of single-syllable spoken words. **RF.K.2c**

CCSS Identify real-life connections between words and their use (e.g., note places at school that are colorful). **L.K.5c**

Develop oral vocabulary

ACADEMIC LANGUAGE
• *vocabulary*
• Cognates: *vocabulario*

ESSENTIAL QUESTION

What are the different sounds we hear?

Remind children that this week they are learning about the sounds around us. Point out that there are sounds everywhere—at home, on the way to school, and at school. Ask children to tell about a sound they have heard both at home and at school.

With children, sing "The Bus." Ask: *What is your favorite sound in the song?*

> ### Phonological Awareness
> **Onset and Rime Blending**
> Say the word *bus*. Repeat the word, segmenting and then blending the onset and rime, /b/ /us/, bus. Have children repeat. Then segment and blend *wheels* (/w/ /ēlz/, wheels) and *down* (/d/ /oun/, down) and have children repeat. Ask children to blend other words from the song, such as /b/ /ēp/, *beep* and /t/ /oun/, *town*.

Review Oral Vocabulary

Use the **Define/Example/ Ask** routine to review the oral vocabulary words **listen** and **volume**. Prompt children to use the words in sentences.

Visual Vocabulary Cards

Category Words: Sound Words

1 Model Use the **Big Book** *Clang! Clang! Beep! Beep! Listen to the City* to introduce these sound words. Page through the book and discuss which things make sounds. Turn to page 5. Ask children what is making the *tick-tick* sound. (clock) *What is making the* zzzz *sound.* (boy) Continue with page 7, *ting-a ling;* page 9, *thunk, clunk;* pages 10–11, *rumble, rattle;* pages 12–13, *flutter, coo;* page 15, *clang;* pages 16–17, *scritch, scratch, hop;* pages 18–19, *ring;* pages 22–23, *beep;* page 25, *kapow;* page 29, *zzzz, tick.*

Explain that these are sound words, and that they describe the noises that people, animals, and things make.

2 Guided Practice/Practice Sing the following verse from "Old MacDonald Had a Farm." Ask children to listen for sound words.

Old MacDonald had a farm, E-I-E-I-O.
And on his farm he had a cow, E-I-E-I-O.
With a moo moo here and a moo moo there,
Here a moo, there a moo, everywhere a moo moo.
Old MacDonald had a farm, E-I-E-I-O.

What sound word do you hear in the song? (moo) *What makes that sound?* (a cow) Work with children to name other farm animals and the sounds they make: duck, *quack;* pig, *oink;* cat, *meow;* sheep, *baa.* Then sing the song again, substituting the new words for *moo* and *cow.*

LET'S MOVE!

Divide children into small groups. Have each group choose a sound word they will say aloud together. Then have each group march in a circle around the room. Tell children to call out their sound word as they march. Have the children who are not marching tell what makes the sound.

ENGLISH LANGUAGE LEARNERS

Identify Display a page from the Big Book. Help children identify the sounds that go with the illustrations. Point to an illustration and ask: *What sound does a pigeon make? A pigeon says coo, coo.* Then have children make the sound in their native languages.

→ # Listening Comprehension

CLOSE READING

Literature Big Book

___

OBJECTIVES

CCSS With prompting and support, ask and answer questions about key details in a text. **RL.K.1**

CCSS With prompting and support, retell familiar stories, including key details. **RL.K.2**

___

• Strategy: Visualize
• Skill: Key Details

___

ACADEMIC LANGUAGE

• *fiction*
• Cognates: *ficción*

 MINILESSON 15 Mins

Reread Literature Big Book

Genre: Fiction

Display *Clang! Clang! Beep! Beep! Listen to the City*. Remind children that fiction stories are made up. Guide them in recalling that the events in fiction did not happen in real life. *How do you know that Clang! Clang! Beep! Beep! Listen to the City is fiction?* Have children point to evidence in the text and the pictures to show that this is a fiction story. (Possible answer: The illustrations are drawn and look make-believe. If they were photographs, I might think these things really happened.)

Strategy: Visualize

Remind children that good readers use the words and pictures in a story to make pictures in their own minds. *As we reread, you can make pictures in your mind about the many ways sounds are made in the city.*

Skill: Key Details

Guide children in recalling that they can learn important details in a story by looking for information in the text and illustrations. Remind them that illustrations sometimes give details that are not in the author's words. *Details from illustrations can help you make a picture in your mind of what is happening in a story.* As you read, have children listen for evidence in the text to find details.

Go Digital

Clang! Clang! Beep! Beep! Listen to the City

Retelling Cards

A C T
Access Complex Text

Connections of Ideas In this book, text within illustrations is used to identify sounds. Guide children to recognize that this information is in the pictures and it is important to understanding the story.

→ On pages 10–11, point out how the words *RUMBLE* and *RATTLE* make up the track for the elevated train. As time allows, help children recognize that the shape of the words on the page often helps to explain the sounds they make.

LITERATURE BIG BOOK **PAGES 4–5**

KEY DETAILS

Think Aloud I can see the boy sleeping. I also see that it is getting light outside. I think he will wake up soon and get out of bed.

pp. 4–5

Point to the letters above the boy's head. Point out that the illustrator used ZZZZZ to represent snoring.

LITERATURE BIG BOOK **PAGES 6–7**

ASK AND ANSWER QUESTIONS

Think Aloud I was right about the boy waking up. Now, I wonder: What will he do next?

pp. 6–7

stinging: I wonder why the boy's ears are stinging. I don't see a bug stinging his ears. I can see that the alarm clock is making a loud noise. I think the noise from the alarm clock is hurting the boy's ears. That's what stinging means on this page.

LITERATURE BIG BOOK **PAGES 8–9**

VISUALIZE

Think Aloud I can picture in my mind what the boy is seeing and hearing when the workers grab the trash cans and dump the trash into the truck. In my mind, I can see the trash cans flipping over and rolling on the ground after the workers put them down, and I can hear the truck: *GROO CLUNK! THUNK THUNK.*

Listening Comprehension

CLOSE READING
ELL

LITERATURE BIG BOOK   PAGES 10–11

VISUALIZE

Think Aloud I can picture in my mind riding on the train and looking out the window. In my mind I can imagine the rumbling and the shaking. It is very excting. This helps me understand how the boy might be feeling.

pp. 10–11

roar: Point out that a tiger and a lion can roar, but the word *roar* can also tell how other loud noises sound.

LITERATURE BIG BOOK   PAGES 12–13

CONCEPTS OF PRINT

Point out the space between words as you read the sentence on page 12.

pp. 12–13

Coo. Coo. Coo! As bird sounds are represented differently in different languages, make sure children understand that the birds are making this sound. Then invite children to share the way they tell about bird sounds in languages they speak at home.

LITERATURE BIG BOOK   PAGES 14–15

KEY DETAILS

Think Aloud I read that the bridge arms are lifting. Details in the picture help me understand why. I see the two parts of the bridge are going up to let the tall boats pass.

pp. 14–15

bridge arms: Demonstrate: *I can see that the two parts of the bridge look like arms as they lift up.*

LITERATURE BIG BOOK   PAGES 16–17

CONCEPTS OF PRINT

Ask a volunteer to point out the spaces between the words on page 16.

LITERATURE BIG BOOK   PAGES 18–19

VISUALIZE

What can you picture in your mind to help you understand how the boy might feel standing in the crowd? (Possible answer: I can picture lots of people around me, making it hard to see very far.)

LITERATURE BIG BOOK   PAGES 20–21

ASK AND ANSWER QUESTIONS

Think Aloud   The boy and his mother are in traffic and the ambulance is making a loud noise. On the cover the cars were all making the "Beep, beep!" noise too. I wonder if the cars will make this noise in the story.

pp. 20–21

traffic streaming: Explain that traffic moves along like the water flowing in a stream.

siren screaming: Explain that the siren makes a loud noise that sounds like someone screaming.

LITERATURE BIG BOOK   PAGES 22–23

HIGH-FREQUENCY WORDS

Have children identify and read the high-frequency word *and* on this page. Help them echo the hyphenated phrase that contains *and: in-and-outing.*

pp. 22–23

beep: Some languages use words other than *beep* to represent the sound of a car horn. To clarify the meaning of *beep,* display an illustration of a car steering wheel with a horn. Push against the horn as you say: *Beep! Beep!*

LITERATURE BIG BOOK   PAGES 24–25

KEY DETAILS

Explain to children that sometimes old buildings are knocked down, but only when they are empty. Point out the workers in the picture and the warning markers to make sure everyone stays safe.

Listening Comprehension

LITERATURE BIG BOOK   PAGES 26–27

KEY DETAILS

Think Aloud I read that the sun is sinking. This means the sun is setting and it is the end of the day. That must be why the family in the picture is getting ready to eat dinner.

pp. 26–27

blinking: Demonstrate blinking with your eyes and then blink the classroom lights.

LITERATURE BIG BOOK   PAGES 28–29

KEY DETAILS

How is this picture like the picture at the beginning of the story? If necessary, turn back to pages 4–5 to refresh children's memories. (The boy is in bed in both pictures.) *How is this picture different from the picture at the beginning of the story?*

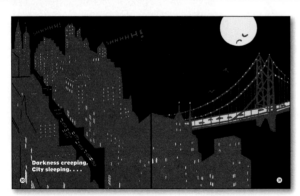

LITERATURE BIG BOOK   PAGES 30–31

VISUALIZE

Look at the sounds "Shhhhh! Shhhhh!" in the picture. Can you picture in your mind the people in the city who are making the "Shhhhh!" sound? Where are they? Why do you think they are saying "Shhhhh!"? (They want to sleep.)

pp. 30–31

creeping: Explain that if something is creeping it is moving slowly and quietly. Model by delicately and slowly tip-toeing across the room. Say: *I am creeping. When the darkness is creeping it means that it is slowly getting dark.*

LITERATURE BIG BOOK PAGE 32

AUTHOR'S PURPOSE

Why do you think the author wrote this story? (Possible answers: He wanted to share fun sounds. He wanted to help us think about how many sounds we can hear in a city.)

Guided Retelling

Tell children that they will use the **Retelling Cards** to retell the story.

→ Display Retelling Card 1. Based on children's needs, use either the Modeled, Guided or ELL retelling prompts. The ELL prompts contain support for English Language Learners based on levels of language acquisition. Repeat with the rest of the cards, using the prompts as a guide. Encourage them to include key details about sounds.

→ Discuss the story. Choose a scene from the book and have children discuss how the boy looked—and how he probably felt—when he heard certain sounds. Have children defend their comments.

→ Invite children to choose a favorite part of the story and act it out. Encourage them to make the sounds from the scene.

Model Fluency

Turn to page 25 and track the print with your finger as you read aloud: *Ka Pow!* Use appropriate intonation for an exclamation mark. Point to the exclamation mark, and say: *This end mark is called an exclamation mark. When I read a sentence that ends in an exclamation mark, I say the sentence in a strong way. Listen:* Ka Pow! On page 13, demonstrate intonation for a period and an exclamation mark: *Coo. Coo. Coo!*

Retelling Cards

Text Evidence

Explain Remind children that when they answer a question, they need to show where in the story (both words and pictures) they found the answer.

Discuss *How do you know it is nighttime at the end of the story?* (The picture on pages 30–31 looks dark. The author writes "Darkness creeping, City sleeping….")

YOUR TURN PRACTICE BOOK p. 87

→ # Word Work

Quick Review

Build Fluency: Sound-Spellings: Show the following **Word-Building Cards:** *a, i, m, n, p, s, t*. Have children chorally say each sound. Repeat several times.

MINILESSON **5** Mins

Phonemic Awareness

Puppet

Phoneme Blending

OBJECTIVES

CCSS Demonstrate basic knowledge of one-to-one letter-sound correspondences by producing the primary or many of the most frequent sounds for each consonant. **RF.K.3a**

CCSS Read common high-frequency words by sight. **RF.K.3c**

❶ **Model** Use the puppet to demonstrate how to blend phonemes to make words. *The puppet is going to say sounds in a word, /n/ /e/ /t/. It can blend those sounds to make a word: /nnneeet/,* net. *When the puppet blends the sounds together, it makes the word* net. *Listen as it blends more sounds to make a word.* Model phoneme blending with the following.

/n/ /a/ /p/, nap   /n/ /ī/ /s/, nice   /n/ /i/ /p/, nip

❷ **Guided Practice/Practice** *The puppet is going to say the sounds in a different word: /n/ /o/ /t/. Say the sounds. Let's blend the sounds and say the word with the puppet: /nnnooot/,* not. Tell children to listen as the puppet says the sounds in words. Have them repeat the sounds, and then blend them to say the word.

/n/ /a/ /p/, nap   /n/ /o/ /d/, nod   /n/ /u/ /t/, nut

MINILESSON **5** Mins

Phonics

Nn
nest

Sound-Spelling Card

ENGLISH LANGUAGE LEARNERS

High-Frequency Words: Build Meaning Reinforce the use of the word *and* by saying these sentences and demonstrating them.

• He *and* I are going to the door.

• Monday *and* Tuesday are weekdays.

• Pick up a book *and* a pen.

• Write your name *and* the date.

Review /n/*n*

❶ **Model** Display the *Nest* **Sound-Spelling Card**. *This is the letter* n. *The letter* n *stands for the sound /n/ as in the word* nest. *What is the letter?* (n) *What sound does the letter* n *stand for?* (/n/)

❷ **Guided Practice/Practice** Have children listen as you say some words. Ask them to write the letter *n* on their **Response Boards** if the word begins with /n/. Do the first two words with children.

sip   noise   niece   happy
man   nut   never   nephew

Go Digital

Phonemic Awareness

Phonics

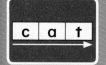

High-Frequency Word Routine

Handwriting

Blend Words with /n/ *n*

❶ Model Remind children that the letter *n* stands for /n/. Display **Word-Building Cards** *n, a,* and *p* in a pocket chart. Point to the letter *n*. *This is the letter* n. *The letter* n *stands for /n/. Say /n/. This is the letter* a. *Letter* a *stands for /a/. Say /a/. This is the letter* p. *The letter* p *stands for /p/. Say /p/. Listen as I blend the three sounds together: /nnnaaap/. Blend the sounds with me to read the word.*

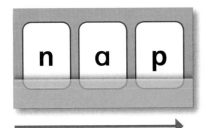

❷ Guided Practice/Practice Change Word-Building Card *a* to *i*. Point to the letter *n* and have children say the sound. Point to *i* and have children say the sound. Point to *p* and have children say the sound. Move your hand from left to right under the word, have children blend and read the word *nip*. Repeat for the word *Nat*.

MINILESSON
5 Mins

High-Frequency Words

and

❶ Guided Practice Display the **High-Frequency Word Card** *and*. Use the **Read/Spell/Write** routine to teach the word. Ask children to close their eyes, picture the spelling of the word in their minds, and then write it the way they see it. Have children self-correct by checking the High-Frequency Word Card.

and

High-Frequency Word Card

❷ Practice Add the High-Frequency word *and* to the word bank.

→ Have partners create sentences using the word.

→ Have children count the number of letters in the word and then write the word again.

Cumulative Review Review words, *to, like, a.*

→ Repeat the **Read/Spell/Write** routine. Then mix the words and have children chorally say each one.

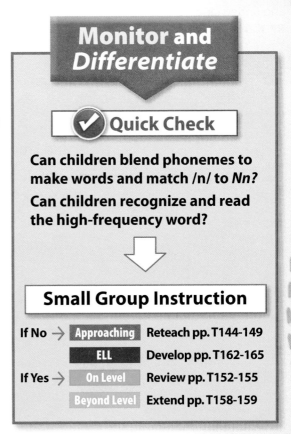

Monitor and *Differentiate*

✓ **Quick Check**

Can children blend phonemes to make words and match /n/ to *Nn*?

Can children recognize and read the high-frequency word?

Small Group Instruction

If No →	Approaching	Reteach pp. T144-149
	ELL	Develop pp. T162-165
If Yes →	On Level	Review pp. T152-155
	Beyond Level	Extend pp. T158-159

→ # Shared Read

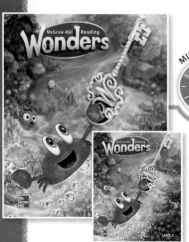

Reading/Writing Workshop Big Book and Reading/Writing Workshop

---

OBJECTIVES

CCSS Read common high-frequency words by sight.
RF.K.3c

CCSS Read emergent-reader texts with purpose and understanding.
RF.K.4

ACADEMIC LANGUAGE
• predict
• Cognates: *predecir*

MINILESSON
10 Mins

Read "Nat and Tip"

Model Skills and Strategies

Model Book Handling Demonstrate book handling. *This is the front cover of the book.* Then display the back cover. *This is the back cover of the book.* Model turning the pages of the book.

Model Concepts About Print Point to a word in the story. Then point to the spaces between the words. *Words are separated by spaces.* Have a volunteer come up to the **Big Book** and point to a single word in a sentence. Remind children that a word is made up of different letters and sounds and has meaning.

Predict Read the title together. Encourage children to describe the illustration. Invite them to predict where the story takes place and what it will be about.

Read Have children chorally read the story with you. Point to each word as you read it together. Help children sound out the decodable words and say the sight words. If children have difficulty, provide corrective feedback and guide them page by page using the student **Reading/Writing Workshop**.

Ask the following:

→ *Look at pages 26–27. If you were Nat, what sounds might you hear in the park?* (Possible answers: Tip barking; children might be shouting and laughing as they play soccer.)

→ *Look at page 30. What do Nat and Tip see and hear?* (Possible answer: A worker is hammering a nail into a fence.)

→ *Look at page 31. What do Nat and Tip hear?* (Nat and Tip hear another dog barking.)

Go Digital

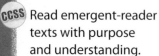

"Nat and Tip"

"Nat and Tip"

READING/WRITING WORKSHOP, pp. 26–31

Rereading

Have small groups use the **Reading/Writing Workshop** to reread "Nat and Tip." Then review the skills and strategies using the *Phonics* and *Words to Know* pages that come before the selection.

→ As they reread, have children look closely at the illustrations and think about what they would see and hear if they were at a park. If necessary, guide the discussion by suggesting something that they might see and hear.

→ Have children use page 25 to review the high-frequency word *and*.

→ Have children use page 24 to review that the letter *n* can stand for the sound /n/. Guide them to identify and name each picture that begins or ends with the sound /n/. Guide them to blend the sounds to read the words.

Language Arts

 MINILESSON 10 Mins

Interactive Writing

OBJECTIVES

 CCSS Use a combination of drawing, dictating, and writing to narrate a single event or several loosely linked events, tell about the events in the order in which they occurred, and provide a reaction to what happened. **W.K.3**

CCSS Capitalize the first word in a sentence and the pronoun *I*. **L.K.2a**

CCSS Recognize and name end punctuation. **L.K.2b**

• Recognize sentences

• Write a sentence

ACADEMIC LANGUAGE

• *sentence, details, observe*

• Cognates: *detalles, observar*

Writing Trait: Ideas

Review Remind children that they can share interesting details about things through writing. They can write complete sentences to share details.

Write and read aloud: *I hear children playing outdoors. I see pink flowers outdoors. I feel happy outdoors. I can write sentences about things I observe. I can use sentences to share details about what I observe. I can tell how I feel.*

Write a Personal Narrative Sentence

Discuss Display the chart of sounds that children hear in different places and the sample sentence from Day 1. Read each sound on the chart aloud. Read where children hear each sound. Choose another sound from the chart to write about, such as *dogs barking*.

Model/Apply Grammar Tell children that you will work together to write a sentence using something you hear outdoors. Remind children that they can use writing to share interesting details.

Write and read this sentence frame: *I hear _____ outdoors. What detail can I add to finish the sentence?* (dogs barking) Write the words in the sentence frame and read aloud: *I hear dogs barking outdoors.* Point out the capital letter at the beginning of the sentence and the period at the end of the sentence.

Write and read: *I hear _____ outdoors. I feel _____ outdoors.* Model how to write a sentence about how you might feel about hearing a certain sound. *I hear musicians outdoors. I feel like dancing.* Read the completed sentences aloud together, tracking the print.

Write Have children write about another sound they hear outdoors. Challenge them to tell how they feel when they hear a certain sound. Guide children to complete the sentence frames. Write the words. Share the pen with children and have them write the letters they know.

MINILESSON 5 Mins

Grammar

Sentences

1 Review Remind children that a sentence tells about someone or something doing an action. A sentence always begins with a capital letter and ends with a punctuation mark. Remind children that when they use the word *I*, they are telling about themselves. The word *I* is always a capital letter. Write and read aloud: *I smell a rose. How do you know that this is a complete sentence?* (It begins with a capital letter and ends with a period. It tells a complete thought.)

→ Write and read aloud:

> i see a gray cat
> sam hears a dog howl
> tess tastes the candy

Ask children to circle the letters that should be capitalized. Have children place a period to show the end of each sentence.

2 Guided Practice Write the following sentence parts in two columns: (Column 1) *My little sister; Your bird; Dan's mom;* (Column 2) *chirps loudly; plays with dolls; is a doctor.* Ask children to draw a line from each sentence beginning (Column 1) to the correct sentence ending (Column 2). Rewrite each complete sentence and read it aloud. Have children point to the capital letter and end punctuation in each sentence.

3 Practice Have children work with a partner. Make two sentence strips: *i hear a bell; i taste a fruit.* Cut each sentence strip in half: *i hear/a bell; i taste/a fruit.* Give each pair of children the sentence strips. Have children work together to tape the sentence strips together to form complete sentences. Help children read their sentences and add proper capitalization and punctuation.

Talk About It

Have partners work together to orally generate complete sentences. Encourage them to tell about things they see and hear in the park.

ENGLISH LANGUAGE LEARNERS

Describe in Sentences Display the **Photo Card** of the *farm.* Have children study the picture. Ask them to tell what they see in the picture, using sentences. Provide a sentence frame for children to complete: *I see a _____.* For example: *I see a barn.* Write suggested sentences on the board and read them chorally. Clarify children's responses as needed by providing vocabulary.

Daily Wrap Up

- Discuss the Essential Question and encourage children to use the oral vocabulary words. *What sounds have you heard today?*

- Prompt children to review and discuss the skills they used today. How do those skills help them?

Materials

Reading/Writing Workshop Big Book
UNIT 3

Interactive Read-Aloud Cards

Visual Vocabulary Cards
exclaimed
chat
familiar

Photo Cards
chin	nut
fan	pen
green	queen
man	spoon
nail	sun
nest	train
nine	vest
nose	web
nurse	wolf

Word-Building Cards

High-Frequency Word Cards
and
to

Think Aloud Cloud

Response Board

♪ **"Nellie's Nest"**

→ Build the Concept

MINILESSON
10 Mins
Oral Language

OBJECTIVES

CCSS With prompting and support, compare and contrast the adventures and experiences of characters in familiar stories. **RL.K.9**

CCSS Identify real-life connections between words and their use. **L.K.5c**

Develop oral vocabulary

ACADEMIC LANGUAGE
• *fable*
• Cognates: *fábula*

ESSENTIAL QUESTION

Remind children that this week they are talking and learning about the different sounds we hear as we go from place to place. Guide children to discuss the Essential Question using information from the **Big Book** and the weekly rhyme.

Remind children about the sounds the bus made in "The Bus." Sing the song and have children join in.

Oral Vocabulary

Review last week's oral vocabulary words, as well as *listen* and *volume* from Day 1. Then use the **Define/Example/Ask** routine to introduce *exclaimed, chat,* and *familiar.*

Oral Vocabulary Routine

Define: Exclaimed means "to have spoken suddenly in surprise, anger or excitement."

Example: "You used my bike without asking me," Lisa exclaimed to her sister.

Ask: Have you ever exclaimed something in excitement? Give an example.

Define: When you **chat,** you talk about something in a friendly way.

Example: I chat with my mom about my day at school.

Ask: When do you chat with a neighbor?

Define: Something that you know well is **familiar** to you.

Example: Our classroom is very familiar to us.

Ask: What other place at school is familiar to you?

Vocab...
Define...
Examp...
Ask:

Visual Vocabulary Cards

Go Digital

Visual Glossary

"The Turtle and the Flute"

Think Aloud Cloud

Listening Comprehension

Read the Interactive Read Aloud

Genre: Fable

Tell children you will be reading a tale, which is like a fable. Remind them that a *fable* is a fiction story that teaches a lesson. Display the **Interactive Read-Aloud Cards**.

Read the title. Point out that this story comes from the country of Brazil in South America. Explain that a flute is a musical instrument.

Interactive Read-Aloud Cards

Strategy: Visualize

Guide children in recalling that good readers visualize as they read. Explain that this means you make pictures in your mind to help you see and feel what is happening in a story. They can use the words and pictures in the story to help them create these pictures. Use the **Think Aloud Cloud** to model visualizing.

Think Aloud At the beginning of the tale, I read that the animals were swaying and humming to Turtle's music. In my mind I pictured Toad moving from side to side and Macaw bouncing on the branches of the tree. I could see Turtle hopping and jumping. And I could hear Tapir whistling to the beautiful flute music. These pictures help me better understand what is happening in the story.

Read "The Turtle and the Flute." Pause to model the strategy.

Make Connections

Guide partners to connect "The Turtle and the Flute" with *Clang! Clang! Beep! Beep! Listen to the City*. Discuss the ways both stories describe different sounds we hear as we go from place to place. *How are the sounds in each story different?*

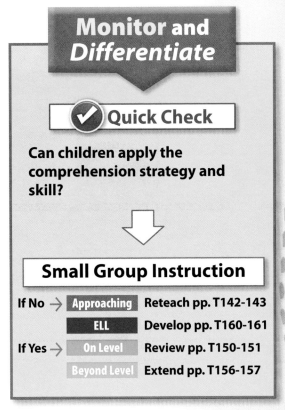

ELL

ENGLISH LANGUAGE LEARNERS

Reinforce Meaning As you read "The Turtle and the Flute," make meaning clear by pointing to specific characters, places, or objects in the illustrations, demonstrating word meanings, paraphrasing text, and asking children questions. For example, on Card 1, point to Turtle in the picture. Say: *This animal is a turtle.* Repeat with the toad, tapir, and macaw.

Monitor and *Differentiate*

✓ Quick Check

Can children apply the comprehension strategy and skill?

⬇

Small Group Instruction

If No →	**Approaching**	Reteach pp. T142–143
	ELL	Develop pp. T160–161
If Yes →	**On Level**	Review pp. T150–151
	Beyond Level	Extend pp. T156–157

→ # Word Work

Quick Review

Build Fluency: Sound-Spellings: Show the following **Word-Building Cards:** *a, i, m, n, p, s, t.* Have children chorally say each sound. Repeat and vary the pace.

MINILESSON 5 Mins

Phonemic Awareness

OBJECTIVES

CCSS Isolate and pronounce the initial, medial vowel, and final sounds in three-phoneme words. **RF.K.2d**

CCSS Demonstrate basic knowledge of one-to-one letter-sound correspondences by producing the primary or many of the most frequent sounds for each consonant. **RF.K.3a**

Phoneme Isolation

Photo Card

❶ **Model** Display the *Nest* **Photo Card** and say the word. Nest *has the /n/ sound at the beginning: /nnn/, nest. Say the sound with me: /n/.* Tell children that now they will listen for the /n/ sound at the end of words. Display the *Man* Photo Card. Have children say the word *man* with you. Man *has the /n/ sound at the end. Listen /m/ /a/ /nnn/,* man. Emphasize the ending sound. *Let's say /nnn/ because we hear the sound at the end of* man: */nnn/.*

❷ **Guided Practice/Practice** Say each of the following words and have children repeat. Have them say /n/ if they hear the /n/ sound at the end of the word. Guide children with the first word.

spoon   pig   tune   Jan   fly   brown   pan   boy

Then show Photo Cards for *chin, fan, queen, sun, vest, web, wolf.* Have children say the name of each picture with you. Ask them to tell whether or not they hear the /n/ sound at the end of the word.

♪ Review initial /n/. Play "Nellie's Nest." Have children clap when they hear initial /n/. Demonstrate as you sing with them.

Photo Cards

Go Digital

Phonemic Awareness

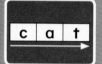

c a t

Phonics

Handwriting

Phonics

MINILESSON **10 Mins**

n

Word-Building Card

Review /n/ *n*

❶ **Model** Display **Word-Building Card** *n. This is the letter* n. *The letter* n *stands for /nnn/, the sound you hear at the end of* man. *Say the sound with me: /nnn/. I will write the letter* n *because* man *has /nnn/ at the end.*

❷ **Guided Practice/Practice** Tell children that you will say some words that end with /n/ and some words that do not. Have children say /n/ and write the letter *n* on their **Response Boards** when they hear /n/ at the end of the word. Guide practice with the first word.

fan   play   pan   sun   door   train   plan

Blend Words with Short *a, i* and *t, p, n*

❶ **Model** Display Word-Building Cards *n, a, p. This is the letter* n. *It stands for /n/. This is the letter* a. *It stands for /a/. This is the letter* p. *It stands for /p/. Let's blend the three sounds together: /nnnaaap/. The word is* nap. Continue with *nip, pin, pan.*

❷ **Guided Practice/Practice** Write the following words. Have children read each word blending the sounds. Guide practice with the first word.

nap   tan   tin   nip   pin   Nan

Write these sentences and prompt children to read the connected text, sounding out the decodable words: *We can sit. I see the tan pin. I can see Tim.*

Corrective Feedback

Sound Error Model the sound that children missed, then have them repeat. For example, say: *My turn.* Tap under the letter *n* in the word *tan* and ask: *Sound? What's the sound?* Return to the beginning of the word. Say: *Let's start over.* Blend the word again.

YOUR TURN PRACTICE BOOK p. 88

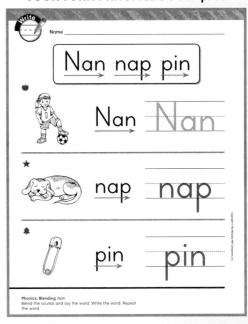

→ Word Work

 MINILESSON
5 Mins

Phonics

Photo Cards

Picture Sort

OBJECTIVES

CCSS Read common high-frequency words by sight. **RF.K.3c**

Sort picture names by initial and final /n/*n*

ACADEMIC LANGUAGE
sort

1 Model Remind children that the letter *n* stands for /n/. Place **Word-Building Card** *n* at the top of a pocket chart.

Hold up the *Nest* **Photo Card**. Nest *has /n/ at the beginning of the word. Listen: /nnn/,* nest. Place the Photo Card for *nest* on the left side of the pocket chart. Repeat the routine with final /n/ using the *Fan* Photo Card and place it on the right side of the pocket chart.

2 Guided Practice/Practice Say the picture name of the following Photo Cards and then have children sort them by initial and final /n/: *green, nail, nine, nose, nurse, nut, pen, spoon, train.* Have them tell if the card should be placed under the *Nest* Photo Card for initial /n/ or the *Fan* Photo Card for final /n/. Point out to children that *nine* has /n/ at both the beginning and end of the word.

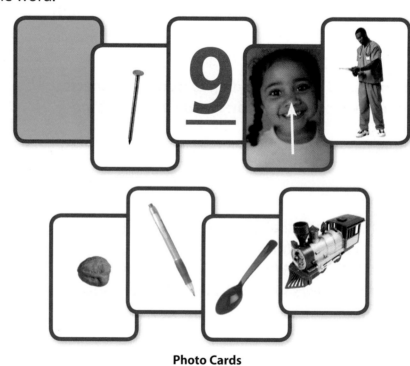

Photo Cards

Go Digital

Phonics

High-Frequency Word Routine

High-Frequency Words

and

1 Guided Practice Display the **High-Frequency Word Card** *and*. Review the word using the **Read/Spell/Write** routine.

2 Practice Point to the High-Frequency Word Card *and*. Have children read it. Repeat with last week's word *to*.

Build Fluency

Word Automaticity Write the following sentences and have children chorally read aloud as you track the print. Repeat several times.

> Tip *and* Nat like to nap.
> We like the pan *and* the tin.
> I see the pan *and* the pin.
> We can see Tim *and* Sam.

Read for Fluency Chorally read the Take-Home Book in the **Your Turn Practice Book**, pages 89–90, with children. Then have children reread the book to review high-frequency words and build fluency.

YOUR TURN PRACTICE BOOK pp. 89–90

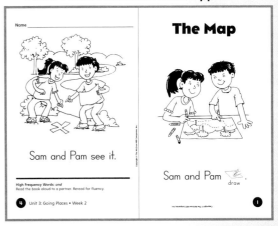

Monitor and *Differentiate*

✔ Quick Check

Can children isolate initial and final /n/ and match it to *Nn*?

Can children read and recognize the high-frequency word?

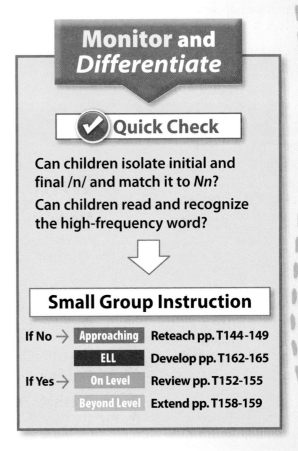

Small Group Instruction

If No →	**Approaching**	Reteach pp. T144-149
	ELL	Develop pp. T162-165
If Yes →	**On Level**	Review pp. T152-155
	Beyond Level	Extend pp. T158-159

→ # Language Arts

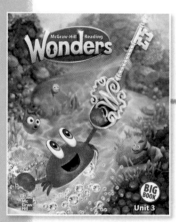

Reading/Writing Workshop Big Book

OBJECTIVES

CCSS Use a combination of drawing, dictating, and writing to narrate a single event or several loosely linked events, tell about the events in the order in which they occurred, and provide a reaction to what happened. **W.K.3**

CCSS Capitalize the first word in a sentence and the pronoun *I*. **L.K.2a**

CCSS Recognize and name end punctuation. **L.K.2b**

• Write a sentence
• Apply writing trait and grammar to writing

ACADEMIC LANGUAGE

sentence, details, capital letter, period

MINILESSON
10 Mins

Independent Writing

Writing Trait: Ideas

1 Practice Tell children that today they will write sentences to tell about different things they hear outdoors, in school, or at home.

2 Guided Practice Share the Readers to Writers page in the **Reading/Writing Workshop Big Book**. Read the model sentences aloud.

CCSS Readers to Writers

Read Together

Ideas

Look at the sentence that Sara wrote. The sentence tells about a sound she hears at home.

Sara's model

I hear Emma crying at home.

Look at the sentence that Tony wrote. The sentence tells about what Tony hears in the city.

Tony's model

I hear a car in the city.

READING/WRITING WORKSHOP BIG BOOK, pp. 40–41

Write a Personal Narrative Sentence

Model Ask children to clap their hands. Write and read aloud: *I hear children clapping. I heard you clapping, so I wrote a sentence to tell what I heard. I can add details to the sentence by telling where I heard the clapping.* Write and read aloud: *I hear children clapping at school.*

Prewrite

Have children think of other sounds they can make, such as tapping and laughing. Write and read aloud their responses, tracking the print.

 Brainstorm Have children work with a partner. Ask them to think about sounds they hear in school.

We share toys.

Present the Lesson

Writing

I see a fish.

Grammar

Draft

Guide children in writing the sentence frame: *I hear _____ at school.* Help children write the name of one of the sounds.

Apply Writing Trait As children complete their sentence frames, ask them to point to the word in the sentence that tells a detail about what they heard and where they heard it. Ask children how the sound made them feel.

Apply Grammar Remind children the word *I* always begins with a capital letter. Point out that the end punctuation is called a period.

ENGLISH LANGUAGE LEARNERS

Use Visuals Have children draw to illustrate the smell of things they like (flowers, cookies, fruits, and so on). Write the sentence frame: *I like to smell ____.* Guide children in writing the sentence frame below their drawing. Help them write the name of the object to complete the sentence frame.

MINILESSON 5 Mins

Grammar

Sentences

❶ Review Draw a picture of a slice of pizza. Write and read aloud: *I smell pizza. Is this a complete sentence?* (yes) *How do you know?* (It tells a complete thought.) *This is a sentence, so it starts with a capital letter and ends with a mark. The end mark in this sentence is called a* period. Circle the capital letter and period. Write: *a pizza. Is this a complete sentence?* (no) *How do you know?* (It does not tell a complete thought. It does not have a part about the person or thing doing an action.)

❷ Guided Practice/Practice Have children identify smells they like, such as flowers and foods. Write some of their responses as complete sentences without capitalization and periods and some as incomplete sentences, such as *roses outdoors, the smell of cookies, i like the smell of cookies.*

Read aloud the sentences. Ask children to point to the sentences that are complete. Ask what is missing from the incomplete sentences. *What can you add to these words to make them a sentence?* Have children help you correct each sentence and rewrite the sentences with the changes.

Talk About It

Have partners work together to orally generate sentences with things they like the smell of. Encourage children to tell why they like that particular scent.

Daily Wrap Up

- Review the Essential Question and encourage children to discuss it, using the oral vocabulary words *listen* and *volume.* *What happens when you turn the volume up? When you turn it down?*

- Prompt children to review and discuss the skills they used today. Guide them to give examples of how they used each skill.

Materials

Reading/Writing Workshop Big Book
UNIT 3

Reading/Writing Workshop
UNIT 3

Literature Big Book
Clang! Clang! Beep! Beep! Listen to the City

Interactive Read-Aloud Cards

Word-Building Cards

Puppet

Visual Vocabulary Cards
and

High-Frequency Word Cards
and
like
to
we

Photo Cards

bear	horse
bird	man
boy	owl
cook	phone
dog	tiger
fly	turkey
girl	watch
helicopter	

→ Extend the Concept

MINILESSON
10 Mins

Oral Language

OBJECTIVES

CCSS Use words and phrases acquired through conversations, reading and being read to, and responding to texts. **L.K.6**

CCSS Blend and segment onsets and rimes in single-syllable spoken words. **RF.K.2c**

Develop oral vocabulary

ESSENTIAL QUESTION

Remind children that this week they have been talking and reading about the sounds we hear as we go from place to place. Have them sing "The Bus" and think about the sounds the bus makes. Ask what sound the birds make in *Clang! Clang! Beep! Beep! Listen to the City*.

Phonological Awareness

Onset/Rime Blending

Sing again: *The horn on the bus goes "Beep! beep! beep!" Say the word* horn *with me*: horn. *Listen to the beginning and end sounds*: /h/ /ôrn/. *We blend the sounds to say* horn. *We can change the beginning sound from* /h/ *to* /t/, *to say* torn: /t/ /ôrn/. *Say* torn. Repeat with *born* and *corn*. Guide children to blend each beginning and end sound: /b/ /ôrn/ (born) and /k/ /ôrn/ (corn).

Review Oral Vocabulary

Reread the Interactive Read Aloud Use the **Define/Example/Ask** routine to review the oral vocabulary words *listen, volume, exclaimed, chat,* and *familiar*. Then have children listen as you reread "The Turtle and the Flute." Ask the following questions:

→ *Which place was familiar to Turtle?* (the banks of the river)

→ *As the children played with the flute, Turtle decided to do something. What was it?* (Turtle decided to escape.)

Go Digital

Visual Glossary

"The Turtle and the Flute"

Category Words

Category Words: Sound Words

❶ Explain/Model Chant the following jingle:

> A train can CHOO.
> A cow can MOO.
> A lion can ROAR.
> My grandma can SNORE!

Repeat each line of the jingle and ask children to identify the sound word. Remind them that sound words describe noises that people, animals, and things make. Ask children which one of the five senses is used with sound words. (hearing)

❷ Guided Practice Display and name the **Photo Cards** for *bear, bird, fly, helicopter, horse, owl, phone, tiger, turkey,* and *watch.* Have partners select a Photo Card. Ask partners to think of a sound that the animal or object on the Photo Card makes. Then have partners share with the class.

To extend the lesson, say the following names of objects or animals and have children say the sound that it makes: *cat, dog, fan, water drops coming out of a faucet, frog, wind, rain, car horn,* and *eating a carrot.*

LET'S MOVE!

Have children dramatize the lines from the jingle. Encourage them to use sound words as they act out each line.

YOUR TURN PRACTICE BOOK p. 91

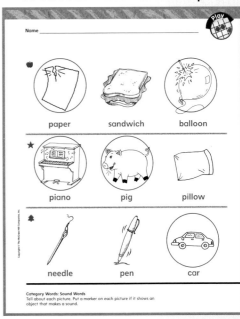

Name _____

paper   sandwich   balloon

piano   pig   pillow

needle   pen   car

Category Words: Sound Words
Tell about each picture. Put a marker on each picture if it shows an object that makes a sound.

→ # Listening Comprehension

 CLOSE READING

Literature Big Book

MINILESSON
10 Mins

Read "Sounds Are Everywhere"

Genre: Informational Text

Display "Sounds Are Everywhere" on pages 34–39 of the **Big Book** and read aloud the title. Explain to children that this informational text will tell about how sounds are made.

Set a Purpose for Reading

Read aloud the question on page 34. Tell children to listen as you continue reading the selection to learn more about sounds.

Strategy: Visualize

Remind children that good readers make pictures in their minds to visualize as they read. Have children look at page 35. *What else can you picture in your mind that makes a ringing sound?* (telephone, bells)

Text Feature: Captions

Explain Point to the photograph and caption on page 35. *Captions give more information about photographs. This caption tells more about vibrations.* Read aloud the caption and have children echo read.

Apply Turn to page 36. Have a volunteer point to the caption. Read the caption aloud with children. Repeat the procedure for page 37.

Go Digital

"Clang! Clang! Beep! Beep! Listen to the City"

OBJECTIVES

CCSS With prompting and support, describe the relationship between illustrations and the text in which they appear (e.g., what person, place, thing, or idea in the text an illustration depicts). **RI.K.7**

- Understand the characteristics of informational text
- Use the text feature captions to understand the photographs
- Apply the comprehension strategy: Visualize
- Make connections across texts

ACADEMIC LANGUAGE

- *visualize, captions*
- Cognates: *visualizar*

LITERATURE BIG BOOK   **PAGES 34–35**

KEY DETAILS

Look at the photograph on page 34. What musical instruments do you see? (clarinet, violin, guitar, flute, cello) *Look at the photograph on page 35. What do the rounded lines show?* (sound vibrations or sound waves)

LITERATURE BIG BOOK   **PAGES 36–37**

VISUALIZE

Look at the photograph on page 36. Close your eyes and make a picture of how the audience is reacting to the music. What do you see them doing? (Possible answers: People are happy and dancing. They are clapping their hands.)

LITERATURE BIG BOOK   **PAGES 38–39**

KEY DETAILS

How are the people in the photograph on page 39 making sounds? (hitting the tambourines; clapping their hands)

ENGLISH LANGUAGE LEARNERS

Reinforce Meaning As you read aloud the text, make the meaning clear by pointing to details in the photographs. Ask children questions and elicit language.

Retell and Respond

Have children discuss the selection by asking the following questions:

→ *How do you make sounds with a triangle?* (hit it with a stick)

→ *How do you make sounds on a drum?* (beat your hands on the drum)

Make Connections

Have children recall the selections they have read this week.

→ *What sound did the city subway make?* (roar)

Write About It Write about how Turtle made sounds. Draw a picture.

CONNECT TO CONTENT

Making Sounds Remind children that when an object is struck, such as a drum, it makes a vibration. The vibration is a sound that moves through the air. Have partners use objects to make different sounds.

STEM

→ # Word Work

Quick Review

Build Fluency: Sound-Spellings: Show the following **Word-Building Cards:** *a, i, m, n, p, s, t.* Have children chorally say each sound. Repeat and vary the pace.

MINILESSON
5 Mins

Phonemic Awareness

Puppet

Phoneme Blending

❶ **Model** *The puppet is going to say the sounds in a word. Listen: /n/ /a/ /p/. It can blend these sounds together: /nnnaaap/, nap. Now say the word with the puppet: nap. Repeat with man.*

❷ **Guided Practice/Practice** Have children blend sounds to form words. *The puppet is going to say the sounds in a word. Listen as it says each sound. Repeat the sounds, then blend them to say the word.* Guide practice with the first word.

/n/ /i/ /p/	/t/ /a/ /n/	/s/ /i/ /t/	/m/ /a/ /p/	/n/ /a/ /p/
/p/ /i/ /n/	/r/ /u/ /n/	/k/ /a/ /t/	/m/ /ā/ /k/	/h/ /a/ /t/

Go Digital

Phonemic Awareness

MINILESSON
5 Mins

Phonics

Phonics

Blend Words with Short *a, i,* and *n, p, t*

❶ **Guided Practice** Display **Word-Building Cards** *n, a, p.* Point to the letter *n. This is the letter* n. *The letter* n *stands for /n/. Say /n/. This is the letter* a. *The letter* a *can stand for /a/. Say /a/. Let's blend the two sounds together: /nnnaaa/. This is the letter* p. *The letter* p *stands for /p/. Let's blend the three sounds: /nnnaaap/,* nap. *Let's change* a *to* i. Use the same routine to blend the word *nip.*

❷ **Practice** Write *nap, nip* and *tan, tin.* Have children blend the words. Point to *nap* and *nip.* Ask children which letters are the same. (*n, p*) Ask children to tell which letters are different. (*a, i*) Discuss the sound each letter stands for and how it changes the word. Repeat with *tan* and *tin.*

Handwriting

Visual Glossary

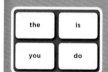
High-Frequency Word Routine

Dictation

Review Dictate the following sounds for children to spell. Have them repeat the sound and then write the letter that stands for the sound.

/n/   /t/   /m/   /a/   /i/   /p/

Dictate the following words for children to spell: *nap, nip, man, pan, pin*. Model for children how to segment each word to scaffold the spelling.

When I say the word nap, *I hear three sounds: /n/ /a/ /p/. I know the letter* n *stands for /n/. The letter* a *stands for /a/, and the letter* p *stands for /p/. I will write the letters* n, a, p *to spell the word* nap.

When children finish, write the letters and words for them to self-correct.

High-Frequency Words

**MINILESSON
5 Mins**

and

Visual Vocabulary Card

Practice Say the word *and*. Then have children write it. Display the **Visual Vocabulary Card** *and*. Follow the Teacher Talk routine on the back.

Build Fluency Build sentences in the pocket chart using the **High-Frequency Word Cards**, **Photo Cards**, and teacher-made punctuation cards. Have children chorally read the sentences as you track the print. Then have them identify the word *and*.

> The owl *and* I like night.
> I like to mix a pear *and* a peach.
> We can see the pig *and* the cow.
> I like the night *and* the moon.

Have partners orally create sentences using the word *and*.

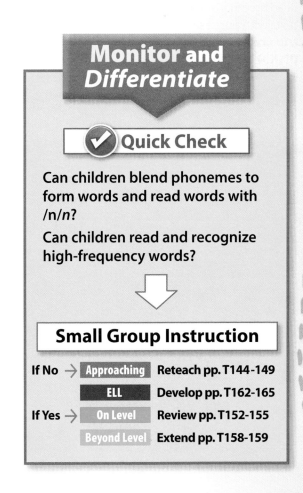

Monitor and *Differentiate*

✔ **Quick Check**

Can children blend phonemes to form words and read words with /n/n?

Can children read and recognize high-frequency words?

⬇

Small Group Instruction

If No →	Approaching	Reteach pp. T144-149
	ELL	Develop pp. T162-165
If Yes →	On Level	Review pp. T152-155
	Beyond Level	Extend pp. T158-159

→ # Shared Read

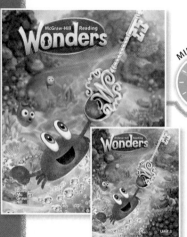

Reading/Writing Workshop Big Book and Reading/Writing Workshop

---

OBJECTIVES

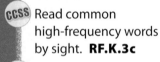

CCSS Read common high-frequency words by sight. **RF.K.3c**

CCSS Read emergent-reader texts with purpose and understanding. **RF.K.4**

MINILESSON
10 Mins

Read "Tim and Nan"

Model Skills and Strategies

Model Book Handling Demonstrate book handling. *This is how I hold a book. This is the front cover. I make sure that the book is not upside down so that I can see the words. This is how I turn the pages of the book. When I turn to each page, I stop to read the words on it.*

Model Concepts About Print Read the first page of the selection on page 33. Point to each word as you read. *A sentence is made up of many words. Let's count the words in this sentence.* Point to a space between two words. *Each word is separated by a space.* Have a volunteer come up to the **Big Book** and point to a word in the sentence and then to the spaces around it.

Predict Read the title and ask children to describe the photograph. *Where does this selection take place? What do you think it will be about?*

Read Point out each rebus and discuss what it stands for. Then have children chorally read the story. Children should sound out the decodable words and say the sight words. Offer support as needed using the student **Reading/Writing Workshop**.

Ask the following:

→ *Look at page 33. What are Tim and Nan looking at?* (a hen)

→ *Look at page 34. What do Tim and Nan hear?* (They hear the sound of a tractor.)

→ *Look at page 37. What sound does a pig make?* (oink, oink)

Go Digital

"Tim and Nan"

"Tim and Nan"

READING/WRITING WORKSHOP, pp. 32–37

Rereading

Have small groups use the **Reading/Writing Workshop** to reread "Tim and Nan." Then review the skills and strategies using the *Phonics* and *Words to Know* pages that come before the selection.

→ As children reread each page, encourage them to tell about what they might see and hear on a farm. Have them tell how the photographs in the selection help them.

→ Have children use page 25 to review the high-frequency word *and*.

→ Have children use page 24 to review that the letter *n* can stand for the sound /n/. Encourage them to identify and name each picture that begins or ends with the sound /n/. Guide children to blend the sounds to read the words.

ELL

ENGLISH LANGUAGE LEARNERS

Reinforce Vocabulary Display the **High-Frequency Word Cards** *and, to, like, we.* Point to classroom objects and groups of children as you use the high-frequency words in sentences such as the following: *I like red and blue. Do you like red and blue?* (Yes, we like red and blue.) *We have many desks in our classroom. Do we have many desks in our classroom?* (Yes, we have many desks in our classroom.) *I go to the window to see. Do you go to the window to see?* (Yes, we go to the window to see.)

Language Arts

 Independent Writing

MINILESSON
10 Mins

Writing a Personal Narrative Sentence

Revise

Distribute the children's draft sentences from Day 3.

Apply Writing Trait Ideas Explain that as writers revise, they add details to their sentences. These details tell more about their experiences. Write and read aloud: *I hear a bird. I can make this sentence better by adding details. Let's work together to tell what I hear the bird doing and where the bird is.*

Write: *I hear the bird chirping outdoors.* Then have children reread the sentences they wrote on Day 3 and check for the following:

→ Did I write about something I hear?

→ Did I describe what I hear?

→ Does my sentence tell where I hear the sound?

→ Does my sentence begin with a capital letter and end with a period?

Apply Grammar Read aloud again: *I hear the bird chirping outdoors.* Have children circle the punctuation mark at the end of the sentence and the capital letter at the beginning of the sentence.

 Peer Edit Have children work in pairs to do a peer edit, in which they read their partner's draft. Ask partners to check that their sentences are complete and that they begin with a capital letter and end with a period. Have children make sure the sentences tell what sound is heard and where. Provide time for children to make revisions to their sentences.

Final Draft

After children have edited their own papers and finished their peer edits, have them write their final draft. Explain that they should try to write letters carefully. Suggest that children use a finger as they write to keep the words evenly spaced. Make sure children do not have too much or too little space between letters within a word. Conference with children to provide guidance as they work.

 Go Digital

Writing

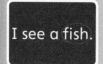
I see a fish.

Grammar

Grammar

MINILESSON
10 Mins

Sentences

1 Review Remind children that a sentence tells a complete thought. *What does every sentence begin with?* (a capital letter) *What does a sentence end with?* (a mark)

2 Guided Practice Display the **Photo Card** for *cook.* Read the label on the Photo Card. Tell children that you are going to work together to write a sentence about the cook.

Write and read aloud this sentence frame: *The cook _____ in the kitchen.* Have children help you complete the sentence frame by adding the action. *What does the cook do? What words can we use to make this a complete sentence?* (works, tastes food, cleans up, picks up a pot) Write a sentence that children dictate, such as *The cook makes dinner in the kitchen.* Ask children which letter should be capitalized and where the period should go.

3 Practice Display the Photo Cards for *bear, boy,* and *girl.* Read the label on each card aloud as you track the print.

Write this sentence frame and read it aloud: *The girl sees _____ at home.* Have children work with a partner to choose something the girl might see at home. (a cat) Have children work together to write and complete the sentence frame with the correct word. *Who is the sentence about?* (the girl) *What does the girl do?* (see a cat)

Repeat the activity with these sentence frames: *The bear sees _____ outdoors. The boy sees _____ at school.* Have children name the person or animal doing the action and the action in each sentence.

Talk About It

Have partners work together to orally generate complete sentences telling about something they like to do. Encourage them to tell why they like to do that particular activity.

ENGLISH LANGUAGE LEARNERS

Picture Cards and Sentences
Provide sentences that go with images on the Photo Cards for *dog, horse, man.* As you say a sentence aloud, hold up a Photo Card as you say the person or thing doing the action, such as *The dog barks.*

Daily Wrap Up

- Review the Essential Question and encourage children to discuss it, using the oral vocabulary words.

- Prompt children to discuss the skills they practiced and learned today. Guide them to share examples of each skill.

Go Digital

www.connected.mcgraw-hill.com
RESOURCES
Research and Inquiry

→ # Wrap Up the Week
Integrate Ideas

RESEARCH AND INQUIRY

Sounds Around Us

OBJECTIVES

CCSS Participate in shared research and writing projects (e.g., explore a number of books by a favorite author and express opinions about them). **W.K.7**

CCSS With guidance and support from adults, recall information from experiences or gather information from provided sources to answer a question. **W.K.8**

ACADEMIC LANGUAGE
research

Make a Sound Chart

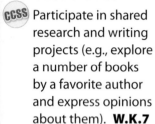

Tell children that today, they will do a research project with a partner to make a chart of the different sounds they hear at school. Review the steps in the research process below.

STEP 1 Choose a Topic

Prompt a discussion about the different sounds that children hear in school, such as the school bell. Guide children to understand that things that make sound vibrate. Demonstrate by having a volunteer play a triangle instrument. Have pairs choose something that makes a sound.

STEP 2 Find Resources

Talk about locating and using resources. Point out that children can research the sounds classroom objects make. Remind them that they need to observe their object making the sound. Have children use the Research Process Checklist online.

STEP 3 Keep Track of Ideas

Have children collaborate and note their ideas for different sounds around the school by drawing pictures or writing words.

Collaborative Conversations

Be Open to All Ideas As children engage in discussions with their partner, in a small group, and as a whole class, tell them to:

→ listen carefully because all ideas, questions, and comments are important.

→ ask a question if something is unclear.

→ respect the opinions of others.

→ give their opinions, even if they are different from those of other people.

STEM

We heard the phone in the classroom.

STEP 4 **Create the Project:**
School Sound Chart

Explain the characteristics of the project:

→ **Information** The class sound chart will give information about sounds that can be heard in school.

→ **Text** Each drawing of the sound will have a sentence that tells about it. Provide this sentence frame:

We heard _____ in the _____ .

→ **Illustration** The drawing of the sound will show the object making the sound.

Explain that pairs will choose a sound from their list and draw the object making the sound. Then they will write a sentence about the sound. The pages will be put together to make a chart of school sounds.

→ Guide children to include the object that makes the sound in their sentence.

→ Encourage children who can write more about their object and its sound to do so.

→ Encourage children to add details to their drawings. Demonstrate how to draw lines that show something is making a sound.

 ENGLISH LANGUAGE LEARNERS
SCAFFOLD

Beginning	Intermediate	Advanced/Advanced High
Practice Have more fluent partners help children practice talking about the sounds they heard. Partners should help each other talk about the object that makes the sound.	**Demonstrate Understanding** Prompt children to tell not just what they hear but where and/or when they hear it. These students might benefit from a sentence frame such as this: *We hear ____ when we ____.*	**Demonstrate Command** Encourage children to include details when they talk about their sound. Lead them toward describing words that help other children "hear" the sound.

Materials

Reading/Writing Workshop Big Book
UNIT 3

Literature Big Book *Clang! Clang! Beep! Beep! Listen to the City*

Interactive Read-Aloud Cards

Word-Building Cards

Visual Vocabulary Cards

High-Frequency Word Cards
and
can
I
like
see
the
to
we
and

Photo Cards
ant
insect
invitation
light
man
mouse
nail
nest

newspaper
night
nine
nose
nurse
nut
plate
seal
soup
toe

Response Board

"Nellie's Nest"

→ Integrate Ideas

TEXT CONNECTIONS

Connect to Essential Question

OBJECTIVES

 With prompting and support, compare and contrast the adventures and experiences of characters in familiar stories. **RL.K.9**

 Participate in collaborative conversations with diverse partners about *kindergarten topics and texts* with peers and adults in small and larger groups. **SL.K.1**

- Make connections among texts
- Make connections to the world

Text to Text

Remind children that all week they have been reading selections about sounds. Tell them that now they will connect the texts, or think about how the selections are alike or different. Model comparing *Clang! Clang! Beep! Beep! Listen to the City* with another selection from the week.

 Think Aloud In *Clang! Clang! Beep! Beep! Listen to the City*, I read about all of the city noises that the boy hears. In "Sounds Are Everywhere" I read about noises that we can make with musical instruments. Those noises were very different from the city noises. But in both stories, the illustrations helped me see the objects that were making the noises.

Guide children to compare the characters and the sounds they read about in "The Turtle and the Flute," "Sounds Are Everywhere," *Clang! Clang! Beep! Beep! Listen to the City*, and other selections from the week.

Text to Self

Talk about the different sounds children read about in the selections. Have children tell which of those sounds they have heard.

Text to World

Ask children what sounds they hear at home or in other places in the community. *What special sounds do you hear in certain places?*

TALK ABOUT READING

OBJECTIVES

 CCSS Confirm understanding of a text read aloud or information presented orally or through other media by asking and answering questions about key details and requesting clarification if something is not understood. **SL.K.2**

Becoming Readers

Talk with children about the genres, strategy, and skill they have learned about this week. Prompt them to discuss how this knowledge helps them to read and understand selections.

→ Remind children that they learned about fiction this week. Prompt them to recall some characteristics of fiction.

→ Talk about the strategy of visualizing. *When you read* Clang! Clang! Beep! Beep! Listen to the City, *how did picturing things in your mind help you understand the story?*

→ Note that children learned to look for key details in the words and illustrations to help them understand the text. *What did you learn from looking closely at an illustration in one of this week's selections?*

RESEARCH AND INQUIRY

OBJECTIVES

 CCSS Participate in shared research and writing projects (e.g., explore a number of books by a favorite author and express opinions about them). **W.K.7**

Wrap Up the Project

 Guide partners to share information about their chosen sound and to point out details in their illustrations. Encourage children to use words and phrases they learned this week. Have children use the Presenting and Listening checklists online.

STEM

→ # Word Work

Quick Review
Build Fluency: Sound-Spellings: Show the following **Word-Building Cards:** *a, i, m, n, p, s, t.* Have children chorally say each sound. Repeat and vary the pace.

MINILESSON 5 Mins

Phonemic Awareness

OBJECTIVES

CCSS Isolate and pronounce the initial, medial vowel, and final sounds in three-phoneme words. **RF.K.2d**

CCSS Spell simple words phonetically, drawing on knowledge of sound-letter relationships. **L.K.2d**

CCSS Read common high-frequency words by sight. **RF.K.3c**

Phoneme Categorization

1 Model Display the **Photo Cards** for *nut, nest, man. Listen for which picture names begin with the same sound.* Say the picture names. Nut *and* nest *both begin with /n/.* Man *does not begin with /n/.* Man *does not belong.*

2 Guided Practice/Practice Show children sets of Photo Cards. Name the pictures and have children repeat. Have them identify the picture in each set that does not begin with the same sound. Guide practice with the first set of words.

nail, toe, night	nose, soup, nine	plate, nurse, nut
man, light, mouse	nut, seal, newspaper	insect, ant, invitation

MINILESSON 5 Mins

Phonics

Read Words with Short *a, i* and *p, n, t, m*

1 Guided Practice Remind children that the letter *n* stands for /n/. Repeat for *p* and *a.* Display **Word-Building Cards** *n, a, p.* Point to the letter *n. The letter* n *stands for the sound /n/. Say /nnn/. The letter* a *stands for the sound /a/. Say /aaa/. The letter* p *stands for /p/. Say /p/. Let's blend the sounds to make the word: /nnnaaap/* nap. *Let's replace the* n *with* t. Blend and read *tap* with children.

2 Practice Write the words and sentences for children to read:

nap   nip   pan   pin

I can nap.	We like the pin.
Nan can see Nat and Pam.	We can see the mat.

Remove words from view before dictation.

♪ Review initial /n/ *n.* Have children write the letter *n* on their **Response Boards.** Play and sing "Nellie's Nest." Have children hold up and show the letter *n* on their boards when they hear initial /n/. Demonstrate as you sing with children.

Go Digital

Phonemic Awareness

Phonics

Handwriting

High-Frequency Word Cards

Dictation

❶ **Review** Dictate the following sounds for children to spell. As you say each sound, have children repeat it and then write the letter on their **Response Boards** that stands for the sound.

/a/   /m/   /s/   /n/   /t/   /i/   /p/

❷ **Dictate** the following words for children to spell. Model for children how to use sound boxes to segment each word to scaffold spelling. *I will say a word. You will repeat the word, then think about how many sounds are in the word. Use your sound boxes to count the sounds. Then write one letter for each sound you hear.*

nip   nap   tin   tan   man   nap   pan

Then write the letters and words for children to self-correct.

MINILESSON
5 Mins

High-Frequency Words

and

Visual Vocabulary Card

❶ **Review** Display **Visual Vocabulary Card** *and*. Have children **Read/Spell/Write** the word. Then choose a Partner Talk activity.

Distribute one of the following **High-Frequency Word Cards** to children: *and, I, like, to, can, the, see, we, to*. Tell children that you will say some sentences. *When you hear the word that is on your card, stand and hold up the word card.*

Sam *and* Pam *like to* read.
Mat *and* Tim *can* spell *the* word.
I can see the cat *and* dog.
We went to the park *and the* store.
We can see the sky *and the* water.
I like to talk *to* Pam *and* Sam.

❷ **Build Fluency: Word Automaticity** Display High-Frequency Word Cards *and, I, like, to, can, the, see, we, to*. Point to each card, at random, and have children read the word as quickly as they can.

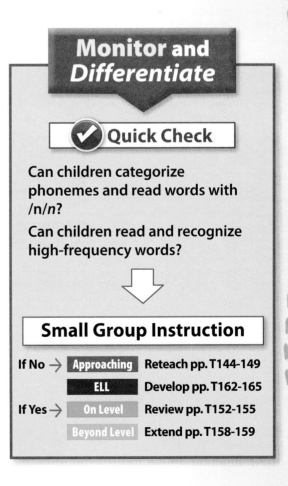

Monitor and *Differentiate*

✓ Quick Check

Can children categorize phonemes and read words with /n/n/?

Can children read and recognize high-frequency words?

Small Group Instruction

If No →	**Approaching**	Reteach pp. T144-149
	ELL	Develop pp. T162-165
If Yes →	**On Level**	Review pp. T152-155
	Beyond Level	Extend pp. T158-159

→ # Language Arts

MINILESSON
10 Mins

Independent Writing

Writing Trait: Ideas

Prepare

Tell children that they will present their finished sentences from Day 4 to the class. Hold up an example from Day 4 and read it aloud, tracking the print. *I read my sentence loudly so that everyone could hear me. I read my sentence clearly so that everyone could understand what I was saying. I described what I heard.*

Present

Have children take turns standing up and reading their sentences aloud. Remind children to speak slowly and clearly. Encourage the rest of the class to listen carefully to the person speaking and to be respectful by looking at the speaker while he or she is talking.

Evaluate

Have children discuss their own presentations and evaluate their performances, using the presentation rubric. Use the teacher's rubric to evaluate children's writing.

Publish

After children have finished presenting, collect the sentences. Bind them together with yarn or a metal ring. Put the sentences in the reading area for children to read on their own. Have children add their writing to their Writer's Portfolio. Then have them look back at their previous writing and discuss how they have changed as writers throughout the year.

OBJECTIVES

CCSS Follow agreed-upon rules for discussions (e.g., listening to others and taking turns speaking about the topics and texts under discussion. **SL.K.1a**

CCSS Speak audibly and express thoughts, feelings, and ideas clearly. **SL.K.6**

CCSS Recognize and name end punctuation. **L.K.2b**

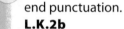

Make a presentation

ACADEMIC LANGUAGE
present, sentence, publish

Go
Digital 🖑

Writing

I see a fish.

Grammar

Grammar

Write a Personal Narrative Sentence

1 Review Remind children that a sentence tells about someone or something doing an action. Write and read aloud this sentence: *I hear a goose honk outdoors. Who is the sentence about?* (I) *What do I do?* (hear a goose) *Is this a sentence? How do you know?* (Yes. It tells a complete thought.) What mark do we use at the end of this sentence? (a period)

2 Review Practice Write the following sentence frames and read them aloud:

> Jeff hears _____ outdoors.
> Tanya hears _____ outdoors.
> I hear _____ outdoors.

Have children work with a partner to complete each sentence. Have them name the person doing the action and what the person is doing in each sentence. Then have children make up their own complete sentences. Circulate and offer corrective feedback as needed.

Wrap Up the Week

- Review blending words with initial and final /n/ *n*.
- Remind children that a sentence is a group of words that tells a complete thought.
- Use the High-Frequency Word Cards to review the Words to Know.
- Remind children that they can write sentences to share interesting details about what they know.

Approaching Level

Leveled Reader

OBJECTIVES

 With prompting and support, ask and answer questions about key details in a text. **RL.K.1**

 With prompting and support, retell familiar stories, including key details. **RL.K.2**

 Demonstrate understanding of the organization and basic features of print. **RF.K.1**

Read emergent-reader texts with purpose and understanding. **RF.K.4**

Leveled Reader:
City Sounds

Before Reading

Preview and Predict

Point to and read the title and the names of the author and illustrator. Discuss the cover illustration and things in the illustration that make sounds. Ask: *What do you think this story is about?* Preview the rest of the illustrations and identify the rebus pictures.

Review Genre: Fiction

Remind children that fiction stories are made-up. They have characters that are made-up, but that could exist in real life. Have children point to the characters in the pictures.

Model Concepts of Print

Demonstrate turning the pages and following the text with your finger from top to bottom and from the left page to the right page. Point to a single word and explain that words are separated from each other by spaces.

Review High-Frequency Words

Point to the high-frequency word *and* on each page. Ask children to find the word on pages 4 and 5.

Essential Question

Set a purpose for reading: *What kinds of sounds do you hear in a city? Let's find out about different sounds we hear in the city.* Remind children to use the rebuses and illustrations as they read.

During Reading

Guided Comprehension

As children read *City Sounds,* monitor and provide guidance by correcting blending and modeling the strategy and skill.

Go Digital

Leveled Reader

Strategy: Visualize

Remind children that as they read they can make pictures in their mind of what is happening in the story.

Skill: Key Details

Remind children that they can learn about key details by looking at the illustrations and reading the text. After reading, ask: *What details about the story did you learn from the pictures?*

Think Aloud I can learn a lot by looking at the illustration and reading the words on page 2. The text says: "Dan and I hear cars." I can look at the picture and see that Dan and his brother are the characters in the story. They are walking with their parents in the city. These are key details. I will use these details to understand the rest of the story.

Guide children to identify and point to the details in the illustration on page 3. Tell them that the dogs are shown in the picture and on the rebus. This means that the dogs are a key detail in the story.

After Reading

Respond to Reading

→ *What are three things that Dan and the main character hear in the city?* (cars, dogs, buses, drums, trains, boats, birds)

→ *On which page can you find key details about trains?* (page 6)

→ *Look at the pictures. What does the family think of the sounds of the city?* (Possible answer: They like the sounds. The sounds help the family enjoy the city.) *How do you know?* (expressions on their faces)

Retell

Have children take turns retelling the story. Help them make a personal connection by asking: *Have you ever been to a city? What sounds did you hear?*

Model Fluency

Read the story aloud, having children choral read with you.

Apply Have children practice reading aloud as they point to each word and rebus.

LITERACY ACTIVITIES

Have children complete the activities on the inside back cover of the reader.

Level Up

IF Children read *City Sounds* **Approaching Level** with fluency and correctly answer the Respond to Reading questions,

THEN Tell children that they will read another story about the sounds that we hear as we go from place to place.

• Have children page through *Farm Sounds* **On Level** as you preview what children know about the sounds on a farm.

• Have children read the story, monitoring their comprehension and providing assistance as necessary.

→ Approaching Level

Phonological Awareness

ONSET/RIME BLENDING

OBJECTIVES

 Blend and segment onsets and rimes of single-syllable spoken words. **RF.K.2c**

 I Do Demonstrate onset and rime blending. *The puppet can say the first sound in bus: /b/. The next sounds are /us/. Have the puppet blend the sounds:* /b/ /us/, bus.

 We Do *Listen as the puppet says the two parts of another word:* /n/ /ap/, nap. *Repeat the parts and blend the sounds after the puppet says them again:* /n/ /ap/, nap.

 You Do Ask children to blend the sounds to make a word. Have the puppet say the following: /l/ /īts/ (lights); /h/ /ôrn/ (horn); and /w/ /īpərs/ (wipers).

PHONEME ISOLATION

OBJECTIVES

 Isolate and pronounce the initial, medial vowel, and final sounds (phonemes) in three-phoneme words. **RF.K.2d**

I Do Display the *Net* **Photo Card**. *This is a net. The first sound I hear in* net *is /nnn/*. Repeat the word, emphasizing the initial sound. Repeat with the *Chin* Photo Card, emphasizing /n/ in the final position.

 We Do Display the *Nest* Photo Card. Name the photo and say the initial sound together: /n/. *What is the first sound in* nest? (/n/) Say the sound together. Repeat with the *Night* Photo Card. Then repeat with the *Fan* Photo Card, emphasizing final /n/.

 You Do Display the *Nine* Photo Card. Have children name it and say the initial and final sound. (/n/) Repeat with the *Nose* Photo Card (initial position) and the *Pen* Photo Card (final position).

You may wish to review Phonological Awareness and Phonemic Awareness with **ELL** using this section.

PHONEME BLENDING

OBJECTIVES

 Isolate and pronounce the initial, medial vowel, and final sounds (phonemes) in three-phoneme words. RF.K.2d

 I Do *The puppet is going to say the sounds in a word. Listen:* /n/ /e/ /t/. *The puppet can blend these sounds together:* /nnneeet/, net. Repeat with *ten.*

 We Do *Now the puppet is going to say the sounds in another word:* /n/ /u/ /t/. *Say the sounds with the puppet:* /n/ /u/ /t/. *Let's blend the sounds together:* /nnnuuut/, nut. Repeat with *nip* and *man.*

 You Do Have children blend sounds to form words. *I will say the sounds in a word. You will repeat the sounds, blend them and say the word. Listen:* /m/ /a/ /n/, /mmmaaannn/, man.

/n/ /a/ /p/, nap	/n/ /ī/ /s/, nice	/n/ /o/ /d/, nod
/t/ /i/ /n/, tin	/p/ /a/ /n/, pan	/k/ /a/ /n/, can

PHONEME CATEGORIZATION

OBJECTIVES

 Isolate and pronounce the initial, medial vowel, and final sounds (phonemes) in three-phoneme words. RF.K.2d

 I Do Display the *Net* **Photo Card** and say the word. Net *has the* /n/ *sound at the beginning:* /nnnet/. *Say the sound with me:* /n/. *I will say three words; two begin with* /n/, *and one does not:* nick, pin, not. Emphasize and extend the beginning sounds and then point out that *nick* and *not* begin with /n/.

We Do Say: *new, next, big.* Guide children to choose which two words begin with the same sound and which word does not.

You Do Say additional groups of words. Have children tell which words in each group begin with the same sound and which word does not.

pen, pig, nap	top, mop, ten	sip, no, sat	in, if, sit

ELL ENGLISH LANGUAGE LEARNERS

For the **ELLs** who need **phonics**, **decoding**, and **fluency** practice, use scaffolding methods as necessary to ensure children understand the meaning of the words. Refer to the Language Transfers Handbook for phonics elements that may not transfer in children's native languages.

→ Approaching Level
Phurics

Phonics

SOUND-SPELLING REVIEW

TIER 2

OBJECTIVES

CCSS Associate the long and short sounds with the common spellings (graphemes) for the five major vowels. **RF.K.3b**

 I Do Display **Word-Building Card** *n*. Say the letter name and the sound it stands for: *n, /n/*. Repeat for *m, a, s, p,* and *t*.

 We Do Display Word-Building Cards one at a time and together say the letter name and the sound that each letter stands for.

 You Do Display Word-Building Cards one at a time and have children say the letter name and the sound that each letter stands for.

CONNECT *n* TO /n/

TIER 2

OBJECTIVES

CCSS Demonstrate basic knowledge of one-to-one letter-sound correspondences by producing the primary or many of the most frequent sounds for each consonant. **RF.K.3a**

 I Do Display the *Nest* **Sound-Spelling Card**. *The letter* n *can stand for /n/ at the beginning of* nest. *What is this letter? What sound does it stand for? I will write* n *when I hear /n/ in these words:* nine, pick, nest, pen, melt.

 We Do *The word* nose *begins with /n/. Let's write* n. Guide children to write *n* when they hear a word that begins or ends with /n/. Say: *net, sun, near, inch, apple, neck, pan.*

 You Do Say the following words and have children write the letter *n* if a word begins or ends with /n/: *name, never, Sam, pink, noise, more, tin, salt, number.*

RETEACH

OBJECTIVES

CCSS Know and apply grade-level phonics and word analysis skills in decoding words. **RF.K.3**

 I Do Display **Reading/Writing Workshop**, p. 24. *The letter* n *stands for the /n/ sound you hear at the beginning of* nest. Say *nest,* stretching /n/.

 We Do Have children name each picture in the apple row. Repeat the name, emphasizing /n/. Repeat for the star row, emphasizing the final sound.

 You Do Guide children in reading the words in the tree row. Then have them read the words in the fish row, offering assistance as needed.

BLEND WORDS WITH /n/n

OBJECTIVES

 Demonstrate basic knowledge of one-to-one letter-sound correspondences by producing the primary or many of the most frequent sounds for each consonant. **RF.K.3a**

 I Do Display **Word-Building Cards** n, a, p, t, and i. *This is the letter* n. *It stands for* /n/. *This is the letter* i. *It stands for* /i/. *This is the letter* p. *It stands for* /p/. *Listen as I blend all three sounds:* /nnniiip/, nip. *The word is* nip. *Repeat for* pin.

 We Do *Now let's blend more sounds to make words. Let's blend* /nnnaaap/, nap. Have children blend to read the word. Repeat for *tin*.

 You Do Distribute sets of Word-Building Cards with n, a, p, t, and i. Write: *nap, pan, nip, pin, tin, tan*. Have children form the words and then blend and read the words.

BUILD WORDS WITH n

OBJECTIVES

Demonstrate basic knowledge of one-to-one letter-sound correspondences by producing the primary or many of the most frequent sounds for each consonant. **RF.K.3a**

 I Do Display Word-Building Cards n, a, and p. *These are letters* n, a, *and* p. *They stand for* /n/, /a/, /p/. *I will blend* /n/, /a/, /p/ *together:* /nnnaaap/, nap. *The word is* nap.

 We Do Distribute sets of Word-Building Cards with n, a, p, and t. Show how to make the word *an* and have children do the same. Place the letter *t* in front of it and have children do the same. *Let's blend* /taaannn/, tan. *Now we have read a new word,* tan.

 You Do Have children change the *t* in *tan* to *p* and read the new word, *pan*. Have children change the *n* in *pan* to *t* and read the new word, *pat*. Point out that by changing one letter we make a new word.

BUILD FLUENCY WITH PHONICS

Sound/Spelling Fluency

Display the following **Word-Building Cards**: *m, a, s, p, t, i,* and *n*. Have children chorally say each sound. Repeat and vary the pace.

Fluency in Connected Text

Write the following sentences. *Tim and Nat like to nap. We can see the pit. The can is tin.* Have children read the sentences and identify the words with /n/.

→ Approaching Level
High-Frequency Words

RETEACH WORDS

TIER 2

OBJECTIVES
 Read common high-frequency words by sight. **RF.K.3c**

 I Do Use the **High-Frequency Word Card** *and* with the **Read/Spell/Write** routine to reteach the high-frequency word *and*.

 We Do Have children turn to p. 25 of **Reading/Writing Workshop** and discuss the first photo. Then read aloud the first sentence. Reread the sentence with children. Then distribute index cards with the word *and* written on them. Have children match their word cards with the word *and* in the sentence. Use the same routine for the other sentence on the page.

You Do Write the sentence frame *We can ___ and ___* . Have children copy the sentence frame on their **Response Boards**. Then have partners work together to read and orally complete the frame by talking about two things they can do. Reteach previously introduced high-frequency words using the **Read/Spell/Write** routine.

REREAD FOR FLUENCY

TIER 2

OBJECTIVES
 Read emergent-reader texts with purpose and understanding. **RF.K.4**

 I Do Turn to p. 26, and read aloud the title. *Let's read the title together.* Page through the book. Ask children what they see in each picture. Ask children to find the word *and* on the pages.

 We Do Then have children open their books and chorally read the story. Have children point to each word as they read. Provide corrective feedback as needed. After reading, ask children to recall something that Nat and Tip like to do.

 You Do Have children reread "Nat and Tip" with a partner for fluency.

Repeat for "Tim and Nan" on p. 32. Have children find the word *and* on p. 35.

Oral Vocabulary

REVIEW WORDS

OBJECTIVES

 Identify real-life connections between words and their use. **L.K.5c**

Develop oral vocabulary: *listen, volume, exclaimed, chat, familiar*

 I Do Use the **Define/Example/Ask** routine to review words. Use the following definitions and provide examples:

listen — When you **listen**, you hear a sound.

volume — **Volume** is how loud or soft a sound is.

exclaimed — **Exclaimed** means to have spoken suddenly in surprise, anger or excitement.

chat — When you **chat**, you talk about something in a friendly way.

familiar — Something that you know well is **familiar** to you.

 We Do Ask questions to build understanding. *What sounds do you like to listen to? What had the loudest volume you ever heard? When was the last time you exclaimed with anger? When do you chat with friends? Why do you often feel comfortable in a familiar place?*

You Do Have children complete these sentence frames: *I like to listen to ___. I turned down the volume when ___. I exclaimed with joy when ___. I chat with my teacher about ___. I went back to a familiar place when ___.*

Comprehension

SELF-SELECTED READING

OBJECTIVES

 With prompting and support, ask and answer questions about key details in a text. **RL.K.1**

Apply the strategy and skill to reread the text.

Read Independently

Help children select an illustrated story for sustained silent reading. Remind children that they can use illustrations to help them understand what is happening in the story. Remind children that they can make pictures in their minds about the characters and events in the story.

Read Purposefully

Before reading, have children point out an interesting illustration. Tell them that as they read, they should think about how the picture helps them understand what is happening in the story. After reading, guide them in a discussion. Ask: *Which detail in the illustration helped you understand something about the story? What pictures did you make in your mind as you read?*

→ On Level

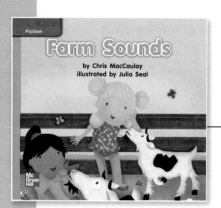

Leveled Reader

OBJECTIVES

CCSS With prompting and support, ask and answer questions about key details in a text. **RL.K.1**

CCSS With prompting and support, retell familiar stories, including key details. **RL.K.2**

CCSS Demonstrate understanding of the organization and basic features of print. **RF.K.1**

CCSS Read emergent-reader texts with purpose and understanding. **RF.K.4**

Leveled Reader:
Farm Sounds

Go Digital

Leveled Reader

Before Reading

Preview and Predict

Point to and read the title and the names of the author and illustrator. Ask: *What sounds might you hear on a farm?* Preview each illustration and identify the rebus picture. Ask: *What do you think this book will be about?*

Review Genre: Fiction

Remind children that fiction stories have made-up characters and events. Ask: *Where does this story take place?* (on a farm) *Who are the characters?* (two girls)

Model Concepts of Print

Hold up the book and open it to pages 2–3. Ask: *When I read a book, I have to know where to start. Can anyone tell me where I should start to read these words on these pages?* Have a child volunteer trace his or her finger over the text in the order it should be read—from the left page to the right page, from top to bottom.

Review High-Frequency Words

Point out the word *and* on page 2. Have children go through the rest of the book and point to the word *and* on each page.

Essential Question

Set a purpose for reading: *What sounds do you think you would hear on a farm? Let's read the book to find out.*

During Reading

Guided Comprehension

As children whisper-read *Farm Sounds*, monitor and provide guidance by correcting blending and modeling the strategy and skill.

Strategy: Visualize

Remind children that as they read they can make pictures in their mind of what is happening in the story.

Skill: Key Details

Remind children that they cannot know every detail about a story just by reading the text. They must also look at the illustrations to learn about key details in the story. After reading, ask: *What details about the story did you learn from the pictures?*

Think Aloud By looking at the pictures in the book, I can tell what the farm looks like and what things on the farm make noises. I can see the girls listening by putting their hands to their ears. This helps me understand what the characters are doing.

Guide children to use the illustrations to help name the animals that the girls can hear on the farm. Explain that each of the animals they name is a key detail that helps them understand the story.

After Reading

Respond to Reading

→ *What are the names of the characters in the story?* (Nan and Lin)

→ *What sounds on the farm are not made by animals?* (the trucks and bells)

→ *What do you think the trucks do on the farm?* (Possible answer: They deliver things to and from the farm.)

→ *Why are there bells in the story?* (The girls are being called to dinner.)

Retell

Have children take turns retelling the story. Help them make personal connections by asking: *Have you ever been to a farm? What sounds did you hear?*

Model Fluency

Read the sentences one at a time and have children chorally repeat. Emphasize the last word of each sentence to point out the importance of each sound that Nan and Lin hear.

Apply Have children practice reading with partners. Encourage them to emphasize the last word in each sentence.

LITERACY ACTIVITIES

Have children complete the activities on the inside back cover of the reader.

Level Up

Level-up lessons available online.

IF Children read *Farm Sounds* On Level with fluency and correctly answer the Respond to Reading questions,

THEN Tell children that they will read another story about sounds that we hear as we go from place to place.

• Have children page through *A Noisy Night* Beyond Level as you emphasize unfamiliar words such as *clank* and *crickets*.

• Have children read the story, monitoring their comprehension and providing assistance as necessary.

On Level

Phonemic Awareness

PHONEME ISOLATION

OBJECTIVES

 Isolate and pronounce the initial, medial vowel, and final sounds (phonemes) in three-phoneme words. **RF.K.2d**

 I Do Display the *Net* **Photo Card**. *This is* net. *The first sound is* /nnn/. *Say it with me. Say* net. *The first sound in* net *is* /nnn/. *Say the sound with me.* Repeat with the *Sun* Photo Card, emphasizing /n/ in the final position.

 We Do Say *not* and have children repeat it. *What is the first sound in* not? *Say the sound together. What is the last sound in* fun? Repeat with *nut, nose, fan.*

You Do Say *news, nine, map,* and *test.* Have children tell the initial sound in each word. Then have them tell the final sound in *can, pin, bus,* and *rip.*

PHONEME BLENDING

OBJECTIVES

 Isolate and pronounce the initial, medial vowel, and final sounds (phonemes) in three-phoneme words. **RF.K.2d**

 I Do Place the *Nut, Nest, Net, Man,* and *Pen* Photo Cards facedown. Choose a card. Do not show it to children. *These are the sounds in the word:* /n/ /u/ /t/. *I will blend the sounds:* /nnnuuut/, nut. *The word is* nut. Show the picture.

 We Do Choose another picture and say the sounds in the word. Together say the sounds and blend the sounds to say the word. Then show the picture.

 You Do Continue choosing Photo Cards. Say the sounds and have children blend the sounds and say the words. Then show the Photo Card.

PHONEME CATEGORIZATION

OBJECTIVES

 Demonstrate understanding of spoken words, syllables, and sounds (phonemes). **RF.K.2**

 I Do Display the *Nail, Newspaper,* and *Paint* Photo Cards. *Listen:* nail, newspaper, paint. Emphasize the initial sounds. Nail *and* newspaper *begin with* /n/. Paint *does not belong.*

 We Do Display the *Rock, Nest,* and *Nurse* Photo Cards. Have children name each picture with you. *Which word does not have the same beginning sound?*

 You Do Continue the activity with these Photo Card sets: *Night, Pea, Nine; Invitation, Insect, Camel; Pillow, Pizza, Fire.*

Phonics

REVIEW PHONICS

OBJECTIVES

 Demonstrate basic knowledge of one-to-one letter-sound correspondences by producing the primary or many of the most frequent sounds for each consonant. **RF.K.3a**

 I Do Display **Reading/Writing Workshop**, p. 24. Point to the *Nest* **Sound-Spelling Card**. *What letter stands for the* /n/ *sound you hear at the beginning of* nest? *The letter is* n.

We Do Have children say the name of each picture. Then ask them to identify words with /n/ in the beginning and words with /n/ at the end.

 You Do Have children read each word. Repeat, asking them to tap their noses if they hear /n/ at the beginning of the word, and raise their hands if they hear /n/ at the end of the word.

PICTURE SORT

OBJECTIVES

 Demonstrate basic knowledge of one-to-one letter-sound correspondences by producing the primary or many of the most frequent sounds for each consonant. **RF.K.3a**

I Do Display **Word-Building Cards** *n* and *t* in a pocket chart. Then show the *Nut* **Photo Card**. Say /n/ /u/ /t/, *nut.* Tell children that the sound at the beginning is /n/. *The letter* n *stands for* /n/. *I will put* nut *under the letter* n. Show the *Top* Photo Card. Say /t/ /o/ /p/, *top.* Tell children that the sound at the beginning is /t/. *The letter* t *stands for* /t/. *I will put the Photo Card for* top *under the* t.

 We Do Show the Photo Card for *Nose* and say *nose.* Have children repeat. Then have them tell the sound they hear at the beginning of *nose.* Ask them if they should place the photo under the *n* or the *t.*

 You Do Continue the activity using Photo Cards *Nurse, Newspaper, Night, Nail, Nine, Teeth, Tiger, Turkey, Toys,* and *Toe.* Have children say the picture name and the initial sound. Then have them place the Photo Card under the *n* or *t.*

→ **On Level**

Phonics

BLEND WORDS WITH *n*

OBJECTIVES
CCSS Demonstrate basic knowledge of one-to-one letter-sound correspondences by producing the primary or many of the most frequent sounds for each consonant. **RF.K.3a**

 Use **Word-Building Cards** or write *n*, *a*, and *p*. *This is the letter* n. *It stands for /n/. Say it with me: /nnn/. This is the letter* a. *It stands for /a/. Say it with me: /aaa/. This is the letter* p. *It stands for /p/. Say it with me: /p/. I'll blend the sounds together to read the word: /nnnaaap/,* nap.

 Write *pan* and *tan*. Guide children to blend the words sound by sound to read each word.

 Write the following words and have children blend the words sound by sound to read each word.

nip   pin   nap   tin   tan

High-Frequency Words

REVIEW WORDS

OBJECTIVES
CCSS Read common high-frequency words by sight. **RF.K.3c**

 Use **High-Frequency Word Card** *and* with the **Read/Spell/Write** routine to review *and*.

 Have children turn to p. 25 of **Reading/Writing Workshop**. Discuss the photographs and read aloud the sentences. Point to the word *and*. Have children read it. Then chorally read the sentences. Have children frame the word *and* in the sentences and read the word.

 Say the word *and*. Ask children to close their eyes, picture the word, and write it as they see it. Have children self-correct.

Reteach previously introduced high-frequency words using the **Read/Spell/Write** routine.

Fluency Point to **High-Frequency Word Cards** *I, can, the, we, see, a, like, to, and* in random order. Have children chorally read. Repeat at a faster pace.

High-Frequency Words

OBJECTIVES

 Read emergent-reader texts with purpose and understanding. **RF.K.4**

 I Do Read the title on p. 26 of **Reading/Writing Workshop**. Point to the sentence on p. 28. Ask children to identify the end mark. (period) *When we see a period, we should pause because we reached the end of a sentence.* Have children read for accuracy and expression. Model reading: *When I read, "Nat and Tip like to sip," I read to the end of the sentence before pausing. This makes my reading sound natural, as if I were talking.*

 We Do Read p. 27. Then have children chorally read the page with you. Continue choral reading the remainder of the pages.

 You Do Have children read "Nat and Tip." Provide time to listen as children read the pages. Comment on their accuracy and expression and provide corrective feedback by modeling proper fluency.

Use the same routine for "Tim and Nan" on pp. 32–37.

Comprehension

OBJECTIVES

With prompting and support, ask and answer questions about key details in a text. **RL.K.1**

Apply the strategy and skill to reread the text.

Read Independently

Have children select an illustrated story for sustained silent reading. Remind them that the illustrations can help them understand key details in the story. Guide children in recalling that illustrations and story details can help them visualize what is happening in the story. It can also help them to understand how the characters feel.

Read Purposefully

Before reading, ask children to point out an illustration that shows an important detail they would like to learn more about. Tell children that as they read, they should make pictures in their minds to help them understand illustrations and words. After reading, invite children to explain how the illustration helped them understand the story. Then have them explain how they visualized as they read.

→ **Beyond Level**

Leveled Reader

OBJECTIVES

CCSS With prompting and support, ask and answer questions about key details in a text. **RL.K.1**

CCSS With prompting and support, retell familiar stories, including key details. **RL.K.2**

CCSS With prompting and support, identify characters, settings, and major events in a story. **RL.K.3**

Visualize story events to better comprehend the text.

Leveled Reader: *A Noisy Night*

Leveled Reader

Before Reading

Preview and Predict

Ask children to point to the title and the names of the author and illustrator as you read them aloud. Have children think about what they see in the picture on the cover. Prompt them by asking: *Where do you think this story takes place? How do you know? What noises do you think the boy might hear at night?* Have children look at the illustrations inside the book. Ask: *Now that you have seen the pictures, would you like to change your prediction about what you think the boy hears?*

Review Genre: Fiction

Tell children that this book is fiction. Ask if they can recall what fiction is. Explain that fiction is a story with made-up characters and settings. Ask: *Who is the main character of this story?* Children may point to or name the boy. *What is the setting of the story?* (the boy's home at night)

Essential Question

Remind children of the Essential Question: *What are the different sounds we hear?* Have children set a purpose for reading by asking: *Let's read to find out the kinds of noises a boy in a town hears at night.*

During Reading

Guided Comprehension

Have children whisper-read *A Noisy Night*. Remind them to blend sounds and use picture clues. Model how to use the strategy and skill for children.

Strategy: Visualize

Remind children that good readers visualize as they read, which means that they picture what's happening in their minds. Explain that readers can visualize sounds as well.

Skill: Key Details

Review with children that the illustrations show what is happening in the story. Point out that illustrations often give readers more information than is in the text. After reading ask: *What details did you find in the pictures?*

Think Aloud The text on page 3 tells me that it is a noisy night and that the birds are calling. The picture on page 3 shows me the front yard of Ned's house. There are birds flying around. Through the open window I can see Ned in his bed. Now I know that Ned's window faces the street.

Have children use the pictures on pages 4, 5, 6, and 7 to find details about why it is a noisy night.

After Reading

Respond to Reading

→ *Which words in the story help you understand what noises Ned hears at night?* (call, honk, sing, clank, bark)

→ *Why is it so noisy as Ned tries to go to sleep?* (He is a young boy and he must go to bed when things are still happening outside.)

→ *Why do you think that Ned is able to fall asleep even with all this noise outside his window?* (He may be used to the noises every night outside his window. He may also be very tired and the noises don't keep him from falling to sleep.)

Retell

Have children take turns retelling the story. Help them make a personal connection by asking: *What sounds do you hear as you go to bed at night?*

Gifted and Talented

EVALUATING Have children think about what kinds of noises someone who lives in the country might hear at night. Challenge children to verbalize the similarities and differences between country noises and city noises.

HAVE children make a Venn diagram to compare the country and city noises.

LITERACY ACTIVITIES

Have children complete the activities on the inside back cover of the reader.

→ Beyond Level

Phonics

REVIEW

OBJECTIVES

 Demonstrate basic knowledge of one-to-one letter-sound correspondences by producing the primary or many of the most frequent sounds for each consonant. **RF.K.3a**

 I Do Display **Reading/Writing Workshop**, p. 24. Point to the *Nest* **Sound-Spelling Card**. *What is the sound at the beginning of* nest? *What letter stands for* /n/? *The letter is* n.

 We Do Have children say the name of each picture. Then ask children to share other words they know that begin with /n/.

 You Do Have partners read each word. Ask them to write the words on their **Response Boards**, underlining the letter in each word that stands for /n/.

High-Frequency Words

REVIEW

OBJECTIVES

 Read common high-frequency words by sight. **RF.K.3c**

 I Do Use index cards to create **High-Frequency Word Cards** for *eat* and *again*. Introduce the words using the **Read/Spell/Write** routine.

 We Do Display the High-Frequency Word Cards for *I, can, the, we, see, a, like, to,* and *and*. Have children help you complete the following sentence frames using the High-Frequency Word Cards: *We can eat the ___. I can see the ___ again.*

 You Do Have partners write sentences using the High-Frequency Words *eat* and *again* on their **Response Boards**. Have them read their sentences.

Fluency Have children turn to pp. 26–31 and 32–37 in **Reading/Writing Workshop** and reread the stories "Nat and Tip" and "Tim and Nan" for fluency.

Innovate Have children create a new page for "Nat and Tip" using the sentence frame *Nat and Tip like ___.* For "Tim and Nan" have children complete *Tim and Nan see ___.* by writing one thing that the characters in the story saw.

Vocabulary

ORAL VOCABULARY: SYNONYMS

OBJECTIVES

 With guidance and support from adults, explore word relationships and nuances in word meaning. **L.K.5**

Develop oral vocabulary: Synonyms

 I Do Review the meanings of the oral vocabulary words *listen* and *familiar*. Explain that a synonym is a word that means almost the same thing as another word.

A synonym for listen *is* hear. *When you* hear *something, you know what it sounds like.* He saw the storm clouds and waited to hear thunder.

A synonym for familiar *is* well-known. *When something is well-known, you have seen or heard it often.* That is a well-known song.

 We Do Think of a few sentences together using the new words *hear* and *well-known*. Say the sentences.

 You Do Have partners think of two or three sentences that include the words *hear* and *well-known*. Ask partners to share their sentences to the group.

Gifted and Talented **Extend** Challenge children to use new words *hear* and *well-known* to interview a partner. Have the interview be about sounds we hear.

Comprehension

SELF-SELECTED READING

OBJECTIVES

 With prompting and support, ask and answer questions about key details in a text. **RL.K.1**

Apply the strategy and skill to reread the text.

Read Independently

Have children select an illustrated story for sustained silent reading. Remind them that illustrations often show key story details, and that visualizing can help them understand the illustrations and details in the text.

Read Purposefully

Before reading, ask children to point to an illustration that shows an important detail. Remind them to look for details as they read. After reading, ask children to display the illustration and explain how details helped them understand the story. Then have them point out another illustration or passage and explain how visualizing helped them understand the story.

Gifted and Talented **Independent Study** Have children use the selections they read this week to think about sounds. Have them make a chart showing noisy sounds, such as traffic, and nice sounds, such as music.

English Language Learners

Leveled Reader

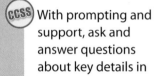

OBJECTIVES

 With prompting and support, ask and answer questions about key details in a text. **RL.K.1**

With prompting and support, retell familiar stories, including key details. **RL.K.2**

Read emergent-reader texts with purpose and understanding. **RF.K.4**

Shared Read: *Farm Sounds*

Go Digital

Leveled Reader

Before Reading

Preview and Predict

Read the title *Farm Sounds*. Ask: *What's the title? Say it again.* Repeat with the author's and illustrator's names. Point to the cover and say: *I see a farm. What animals are on this farm?* Have children name the animals they see in the picture. Then do a picture walk and identify the rebus pictures: cows, trucks, hens, pigs, horses, goats, and bells. Tell children that *hen* is another word for chicken. Then point to the labels. Ask: *What does a cow sound like? What noise does a truck make?*

Essential Question

Set a purpose for reading: *What sounds do you think you would hear on a farm? Let's read the book to find out what sounds we might hear.* Encourage children to ask questions and seek clarifications about what they read and see in the pictures. Remind them that illustrations can help them understand the text better.

During Reading

Interactive Question Response

Pages 2–3 Point to the illustration on page 2. Model the language pattern used in the text. Say: *I see cows. Can you point to the cows? The girls are Nan and Lin.* Point to the girls. Ask: *What sounds do Nan and Lin hear? Yes, Nan and Lin hear cows. Let's read that sentence aloud.* Point to the illustration on page 3. Ask: *What do Nan and Lin hear on this page? That's right. Nan and Lin hear trucks. Let's read this sentence together.*

Pages 4–5 Point to the illustration and label on page 4. *These are hens. They are female chickens. How can you tell Nan and Lin are listening to the hens?* (They hold their hands to their ears to listen.) Read aloud the sentence with children as they point to each word in the sentence. Point to the label on page 5. Say: *Point to the pigs. What sound do pigs make? What do the girls think of the sound?* (They like it. They think it is funny.) *Let's read the sentence together.*

Pages 6–7 Point to the illustration and label on page 6. *What do the girls see on this page?* (horses) *What sound do horses make? Let's read this page.* Look at page 7 with children. Ask: *What is this animal?* (goat) *Point to the word that says* goat. *Let's read this page together.*

Page 8 Point to the illustration. *What is the woman doing in the picture?* (ringing bells) *Why is she ringing the bells?* (to call the girls to come eat) *Point to the word that says* bells. *Now let's read this page together.*

After Reading

Respond to Reading

→ *Who are the characters in the story?* (Nan and Lin) *Where are they?* (on a farm)

→ *What kinds of animals do they hear in the story?* (cows, hens, pigs, horses, goats)

→ *What is the last sound they hear?* (bells) *What is the sound for?* (to call them for lunch)

Retell

Let's retell the book together. What are the girls doing? (listening to sounds on a farm) *What sounds do they hear?* (They hear animals and trucks and a bell on the farm.) *What happens at the end of the book?* (They go eat lunch.)

Model Fluency

Read the sentences one at a time as you track the print. Have children chorally repeat. Ask children to point to each rebus as they say the word that corresponds to it.

Apply Have children read with partners. Encourage them to point to each rebus as they say the word it corresponds to.

Level Up

IF Children read *Farm Sounds* **ELL Level** with fluency and correctly answer the Respond to Reading questions,

THEN Tell children that they will read a more detailed version of the story.

• Have children page through *Farm Sounds* **On Level** and conduct a picture walk to describe each picture in simple language.

• Have children read the story, monitoring their comprehension and providing assistance as necessary.

LITERACY ACTIVITIES

Have children complete the activities on the inside back cover of the reader.

English Language Learners
Vocabulary

PRETEACH ORAL VOCABULARY

OBJECTIVES
 Speak audibly and express thoughts, feelings, and ideas clearly. **SL.K.6**

LANGUAGE OBJECTIVE
Preview vocabulary

 I Do Display the images from the **Visual Vocabulary Cards** and follow the routine to preteach the oral vocabulary words.

 We Do Display each image again and explain how it illustrates or demonstrates the word. Model using sentences to describe the image.

 You Do Display the words again and have children talk to a partner about how each picture demonstrates the word.

Beginning	Intermediate	Advanced/High
Have partners repeat each word. Then have them pantomime the meanings of *listen* and *chat*.	Provide the following sentence frame: *I listen to ____.*	Ask partners to use the words in a sentence.

PRETEACH ELL VOCABULARY

OBJECTIVES
 Speak audibly and express thoughts, feelings, and ideas clearly. **SL.K.6**

LANGUAGE OBJECTIVE
Preview ELL vocabulary

 I Do Display the images from the **Visual Vocabulary Cards** one at a time to preteach the ELL vocabulary words *noise* and *ear*, then follow the routine. Say each word and have children repeat it. Define each word in English.

 We Do Display each image again and incorporate the words in a short discussion. Model using sentences to describe the image.

 You Do Display the words again and have children say each word. Ask children to talk about how different *noises* sound to their *ear*. Use the following sentence starter to help them think of ideas: *I hear a ____ noise.*

Beginning	Intermediate	Advanced/High
Have children point to a partner's ear and say "ear." Then have them cover their ears and say "noise."	Have pairs work together to talk about things that make noise.	Ask children to make a sentence of their own that incorporates both words.

High-Frequency Words

REVIEW WORDS

OBJECTIVES

Read common high-frequency words by sight (e.g., *the, of, to, you, she, my, is, are, do, does*). **RF.K.3c**

LANGUAGE OBJECTIVE

Review high-frequency words

 I Do Display the **High-Frequency Word Card** for *and*. Read the word. Use the **Read/Spell/Write** routine to teach the word. Have children write the word on their **Response Boards**.

We Do Write the following sentence frame using the word *and* as well as words from previous weeks: *I like _____ and _____*. Model reading and completing it by using examples of things you like. Ask children to repeat. If necessary, refer to the back of the **Visual Vocabulary Card** for support.

 You Do Ask children to work with a partner to complete the sentence frame.

Beginning	Intermediate	Advanced/High
Help children to say the word *and* and write it on paper.	Ask children to find and read aloud the word *and* in any classroom book.	Have partners create a new sentence using the word *and*.

REVIEW CATEGORY WORDS

OBJECTIVES

Identify real-life connections between words and their use (e.g., note places at school that are colorful). **L.K.5c**

LANGUAGE OBJECTIVE

Use category words

 I Do Display and name the following **Photo Cards**: *fan, fly, helicopter, phone, watch*. Define the words in English, and then in Spanish, if appropriate, identifying any cognates.

 We Do Tell children that each of the things on the Photo Cards makes a sound. Display the *Fan* Photo Card and demonstrate by making a rattling sound. Have children repeat. Continue with the remaining Photo Cards.

 You Do Then show children **Photo Cards** for *kitten, bird, cow, goat, pig, horse*, and *sheep*, and help children identify the sound each animal makes.

Beginning	Intermediate	Advanced/High
Ask children to name each animal after you say the corresponding animal sound.	Have partners name the sounds they hear and tell what is making the sound.	Have children use sound words in sentences.

→ English Language Learners
Writing

SHARED WRITING

OBJECTIVES

 Use a combination of drawing, dictating, and writing to narrate a single event or several loosely linked events, tell about the events in the order in which they occurred, and provide a reaction to what happened. **W.K.3**

LANGUAGE OBJECTIVE

Contribute to a shared writing project

 I Do Explain to children that they will work together to write a sentence about a sound they hear. Review the words in the chart from the Whole Group Shared Writing project as the possible sounds children might hear outdoors, at school, and at home.

We Do With children, choose a sound they hear at school. Write a shared sentence, for example, *We hear children laughing.*

You Do Ask partners to work together to write about a sound they hear. Have them use the sentence frame *I hear _____.*

Beginning	Intermediate	Advanced/High
Help children express the sentence in their own words before beginning to write it.	Ask partners to complete the following sentence frame: *I hear ____ when I ____.*	Have partners work to write a sentence on their own.

WRITING TRAIT: IDEAS

OBJECTIVES

 Use a combination of drawing, dictating, and writing to narrate a single event or several loosely linked events, tell about the events in the order in which they occurred, and provide a reaction to what happened. **W.K.3**

LANGUAGE OBJECTIVE

Use ideas in writing

 I Do Explain that good writing starts with good ideas. Explain to children that they can get ideas about their writing from the things they read.

 We Do Point to the **Big Book** selection *Clang! Clang! Beep! Beep! Listen to the City.* Remind children that the story tells about different sounds that people hear. Ask: *What noises can you hear in a city?* Point out events from the story that will help give children ideas about sounds.

 You Do Have children write a sentence to tell about sounds that they hear. Provide them with the sentence frame *The sounds I hear are _____.*

Beginning	Intermediate	Advanced/High
Identify things that make sounds in the Big Book selection. Then help them complete the sentence frame. Have them say the sentence.	Ask children to copy and complete the sentence frame with a partner.	Ask children to complete the sentence frame. Challenge them to write another sentence about sounds.

Grammar

SENTENCES

OBJECTIVES

CCSS Produce and expand complete sentences in shared language activities. **L.K.2f**

LANGUAGE OBJECTIVE

Recognize and form complete sentences

Language Transfers Handbook

Native speakers of Cantonese may tend to omit prepositions when they form sentences because the Cantonese language does not use prepositions in the way that English does. Children may say *I like come school* instead of *I like to come to school*. Guide children to use prepositions as needed.

 I Do Review that a sentence has two parts: who or what the sentence is about and what that person or thing does. Say *We hear the rain*. Tell children that this is a complete sentence. It tells who (we) and what happens (hear the rain).

 We Do Say the following phrase. Work with children to tell if it has both parts to make a complete sentence. Say *makes noise*. Ask children if this sentence has both parts (*who* and *what happens*). Work with children to make the sentence complete. For example: *The dog makes noise*.

 You Do Say the following and have children determine if it is a complete sentence. If it is a phrase, have children supply information to make the sentence complete. Take note of each child's language use and proficiency.

is loud
I hear
Sounds can be loud or soft.
the horn of the ship

Beginning	Intermediate	Advanced/High
Ask children what are sounds they hear. Guide children to use complete sentences when answering.	Ask children to complete the frame: *I hear____*. Remind children to use end punctuation.	With little or no help, ask children to complete the frame: *Listen to ____* Have them read their sentence aloud.

PROGRESS MONITORING

Weekly Assessment

Use your Quick Check observations and the assessment opportunities identified below to evaluate children's progress in key skill areas.

✓ TESTED SKILLS [CCSS]	Quick Check Observations	Pencil and Paper Assessment
PHONEMIC AWARENESS/ PHONICS /n/ (initial/final) **RF.K.3b** [n]	Can children isolate /n/ and match it to the letter *Nn*?	Practice Book, pp. 85–86, 88
HIGH-FREQUENCY WORDS *and* **RF.K.3c** [and]	Can children recognize and read the high-frequency word?	Practice Book, pp. 89–90
COMPREHENSION Key Details **RL.K.1, RL.K.7**	As you read *Clang! Clang! Beep! Beep! Listen to the City* with children, can they identify and discuss key details using the illustrations and the text?	Practice Book, p. 87

Quick Check Rubric

Skills	1	2	3
PHONEMIC AWARENESS/ PHONICS	Does not connect the sound /n/ with the letters *Nn*.	Usually connects the sound /n/ with the letters *Nn*.	Consistently connects the sound /n/ with the letters *Nn*.
HIGH-FREQUENCY WORDS	Does not identify the high-frequency word.	Usually recognizes the high-frequency word with accuracy, but not speed.	Consistently recognizes the high-frequency word with speed and accuracy.
COMPREHENSION	Does not identify key details using the illustrations and text.	Usually identifies key details using the illustrations and text.	Consistently identifies key details using the illustrations and text.

Go Digital! www.connected.mcgraw-hill.com

Using Assessment Results

TESTED SKILLS	If ...	Then ...
PHONEMIC AWARENESS/ PHONICS	**Quick Check Rubric:** Children consistently score 1 or **Pencil and Paper Assessment:** Children get 0–2 items correct	... reteach tested Phonemic Awareness and Phonics skills using Lessons 16–17 and 27–29 in the *Tier 2 Phonemic Awareness Intervention Online PDFs* and Lesson 16 in the *Tier 2 Phonics/Word Study Intervention Online PDFs.*
HIGH-FREQUENCY WORDS	**Quick Check Rubric:** Children consistently score 1	... reteach tested skills by using the High-Frequency Word Cards and asking children to read and spell the word. Point out any irregularities in sound-spellings.
COMPREHENSION	**Quick Check Rubric:** Children consistently score 1 or **Pencil and Paper Assessment:** Children get 0–1 items correct	... reteach tested skill using Lessons 10–12 in the *Tier 2 Comprehension Intervention Online PDFs.*

Response to Intervention

Use the children's assessment results to assist you in identifying children who will benefit from focused intervention.

Use the appropriate sections of the *Placement and Diagnostic Assessment* to designate children requiring:

 Tier 2 Intervention Online PDFs

 WonderWorks Intervention Program

→ Phonemic Awareness

→ Phonics

→ Vocabulary

→ Comprehension

→ Fluency

WEEKLY OVERVIEW

Literature Big Book

Listening Comprehension

Please Take Me for a Walk, 5–34
Genre Fantasy

"A Neighborhood," 36–40
Genre Informational Text

Interactive Read-Aloud Cards

"Field Trips"
Genre Informational Text

Oral Vocabulary

intelligent	routine
local	volunteer
neighborhood	

Minilessons ✔ TESTED SKILLS CCSS

✔ **Comprehension Strategy** .... Visualize, T177

✔ **Comprehension Skill** .... Character, Setting, Events, T186

☞ **Go** Digital

www.connected.mcgraw-hill.com

Nathan Love

THE PLACES WE GO

Essential Question
What places do you go to during the week?

WEEK 3 →

Shared Reading

"We Go to See Nan," 44–49
Genre Fiction

"Can We Go?" 50–55
Genre Nonfiction

High-Frequency Word and, T181

Minilessons ✔TESTED SKILLS CCSS

✔ **Phonics** .... /k/c, T179
Writing Trait .... Sentence Fluency, T182
Grammar .... Sentences, T183

Differentiated Text

Approaching   **On Level**   **Beyond**   **ELL**

TEACH AND MANAGE

What You Do

INTRODUCE

Weekly Concept

The Places We Go

**Reading/Writing Workshop
Big Book, 42–43**

TEACH AND APPLY

Listening Comprehension

Big Book
Please Take Me for a Walk
Genre Fantasy
Paired Read "A Neighborhood"
Genre Informational Text

Minilessons
Strategy: Visualize
Skill: Character, Setting, Events

Shared Reading

Reading/Writing Workshop
"We Go to See Nan"
"Can We Go?"

Minilessons
/k/c, High-Frequency Word: go
Writing, Grammar

 Go Digital

 Interactive Whiteboard

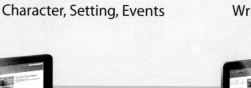 Interactive Whiteboard

 Mobile

What Your Students Do

WEEKLY CONTRACT

PDF Online

PRACTICE AND ONLINE ACTIVITIES

Your Turn Practice Book, pp. 93–100

Leveled Readers

Go Digital

Online To-Do List

Online Activities

 Mobile

WEEK 3 →

DIFFERENTIATE

Small Group Instruction
Leveled Readers

We Can Go

Going by Cab
by Chris MacCauley illustrated by Robin Boyer

Cal's Busy Week

Going by Cab
by Chris MacCauley illustrated by Robin Boyer

Mobile

INTEGRATE

Research and Inquiry
Page for a Class Book, pp. T216–T217

Text Connections
Compare Places, p. T218

Talk About Reading
Becoming Readers, p. T219

**Online
Research**

WORKSTATION CARDS

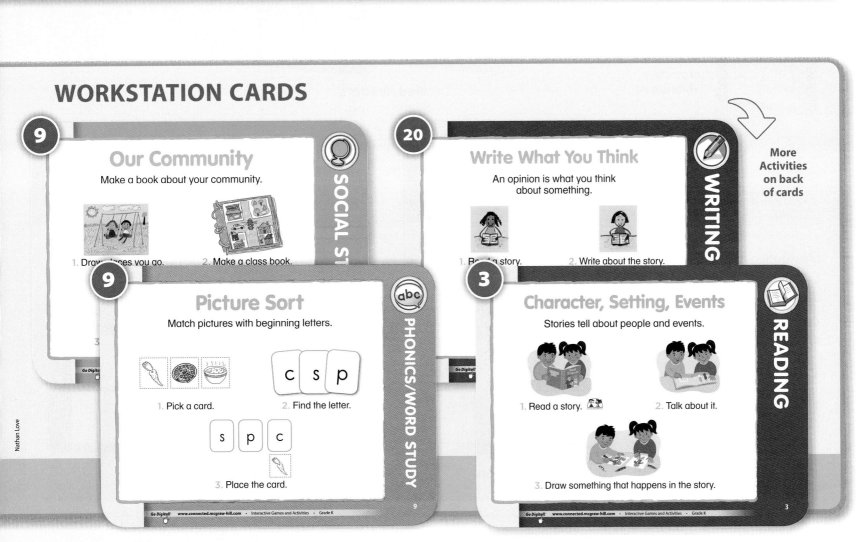

9

Our Community
Make a book about your community.

1. Draw places you go.   2. Make a class book.

SOCIAL ST...

9

Picture Sort
Match pictures with beginning letters.

| c | s | p |

1. Pick a card.   2. Find the letter.

| s | p | c |

3. Place the card.

PHONICS/WORD STUDY

9

Go Digital! www.connected.mcgraw-hill.com • Interactive Games and Activities • Grade K

20

Write What You Think
An opinion is what you think
about something.

1. Read a story.   2. Write about the story.

WRITING

**More
Activities
on back
of cards**

3

Character, Setting, Events
Stories tell about people and events.

1. Read a story.   2. Talk about it.

3. Draw something that happens in the story.

READING

3

Go Digital! www.connected.mcgraw-hill.com • Interactive Games and Activities • Grade K

Nathan Love

DEVELOPING READERS AND WRITERS

Write About Reading • Analytical Writing

Write to Sources and Research

Respond to Reading, T177, T225, T233, T239, T243

Connect to Essential Question, T177, T209

Character, Setting, Events, 186

Research and Inquiry, T216

Teacher's Edition

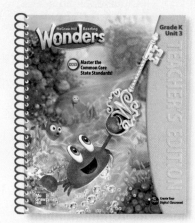

Literature Big Book
Please Take Me for a Walk
Paired Read: *"A Neighborhood"*

Interactive Whiteboard

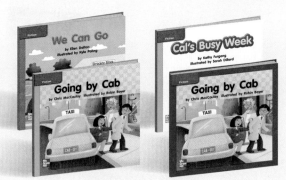

Leveled Readers
Responding to Texts

Writing Process • Independent Writing

Opinion

Opinion Sentences, T204–T205, T214, T222

Conferencing Routines

Peer Conferences, T214

Interactive Whiteboard

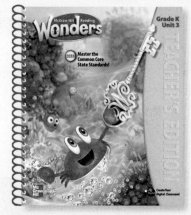

Teacher's Edition

Leveled Workstation Card
Write What You Think, Card 20

Writing Traits • Shared and Interactive Writing

Writing Trait:
Sentence Fluency
Opinion Sentences, T182, T196

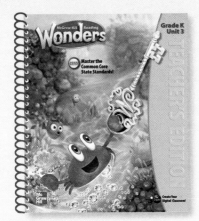
Teacher's Edition

Sentences, p. 58

Reading/Writing Workshop

Interactive Whiteboard

Leveled Workstation Card
Write What You Think, Card 20

Grammar and Spelling/Dictation

Grammar
Sentences, T183

Spelling/Dictation
Words with Short *a* and *c, n, p, t,* T210, T220

Interactive Whiteboard

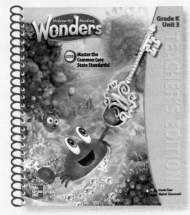
Teacher's Edition

Online Grammar Games

Handwriting

SUGGESTED LESSON PLAN

	DAY 1	**DAY 2**
✓ **TESTED SKILLS** CCSS		

READING

Whole Group — Teach and Model

Literature Big Book

Reading/ Writing Workshop

DAY 1

Build Background The Places We Go, T174
Oral Vocabulary Words neighborhood, routine, T174
✓ **Listening Comprehension**
• Genre: Fantasy
• Strategy: Visualize, T177
Big Book *Please Take Me for a Walk*
✓ **Word Work**
Phonemic Awareness
• Phoneme Isolation, T178
Phonics:
• Introduce /k/c, T179
Handwriting Cc, T180
High-Frequency Word go, T181

Practice *Your Turn* 93–94

DAY 2

Oral Language The Places We Go, T184
✓ **Category Words** Sequence Words, T185
✓ **Listening Comprehension**
• Genre: Fantasy
• Strategy: Visualize, T186
• Skill: Character, Setting, Events
• Guided Retelling
• Model Fluency, T191
Big Book *Please Take Me for a Walk*
✓ **Word Work**
Phonemic Awareness
• Phoneme Blending, T192
Phonics
• Review /k/c, T192
High-Frequency Word go, T193
Shared Reading "We Go to See Nan," T194–T195

Practice *Your Turn* 95

DIFFERENTIATED INSTRUCTION — Choose across the week to meet your student's needs.

Small Group

Approaching Level

DAY 1

Leveled Reader *We Can Go,* T224–T225
Phonological Awareness Count and Pronounce Syllables, T226 (TIER 2)
Phonics Sound-Spelling Review, T228 (TIER 2)
High-Frequency Words Reteach Words, T230 (TIER 2)

DAY 2

Leveled Reader *We Can Go,* T224–T225
Phonemic Awareness Phoneme Isolation, T226 (TIER 2)
Phonics Connect c to /k/, T228 (TIER 2)
High-Frequency Words Reread for Fluency, T230 (TIER 2)

On Level

DAY 1

Leveled Reader *Going by Cab,* T232–T233
Phonemic Awareness Phoneme Isolation, T234

DAY 2

Leveled Reader *Going by Cab,* T232–T233
Phoneme Awareness Phoneme Blending, T234
Phonics Review Phonics, T235
High-Frequency Words Review Words, T236

Beyond Level

DAY 1

Leveled Reader *Cal's Busy Week,* T238–T239
Phonics Review, T240

DAY 2

Leveled Reader *Cal's Busy Week,* T238–T239
High-Frequency Words Review, T240

English Language Learners

DAY 1

Leveled Reader *Going by Cab,* T242–T243
Phonological Awareness Count and Pronounce Syllables, T226 (TIER 2)
Phonics Sound-Spelling Review, T228 (TIER 2)
Vocabulary Preteach Oral Vocabulary, T244
Writing Shared Writing: T246

DAY 2

Leveled Reader *Going by Cab,* T242–T243
Phonemic Awareness Phoneme Isolation, T226 (TIER 2)
Phonics Connect c to /k/, T228 (TIER 2)
Vocabulary Preteach ELL Vocabulary, T244

LANGUAGE ARTS

Whole Group — Writing and Grammar

DAY 1

Shared Writing
Writing Trait: Sentence Fluency, T182
Write an Opinion Sentence, T182
Grammar Sentences, T183

DAY 2

Interactive Writing
Writing Trait: Sentence Fluency, T196
Write an Opinion Sentence, T196
Grammar Sentences, T197

Nathan Love

DAY 3	DAY 4	DAY 5 Review and Assess

READING

Oral Language The Places We Go, T198

Oral Vocabulary intelligent, local, volunteer, T198

✓ **Listening Comprehension**
• Genre: Informational Text
• Strategy: Visualize, T199
• Make Connections, T199

Interactive Read Aloud "Field Trips," T199

✓ **Word Work**
Phonemic Awareness
• Phoneme Blending, T200
Phonics
• Blend Words with *c, p, n, t, s, m, a*, T201
High-Frequency Word go, T203

Practice *Your Turn* 96–98

Oral Language The Places We Go, T206

✓ **Category Words** Sequence Words, T207

✓ **Listening Comprehension**
• Genre: Informational Text
• Strategy: Visualize, T208
• Text Feature: Maps
• Make Connections, T209

Big Book Paired Read: "A Neighborhood," T208

✓ **Word Work**
Phonemic Awareness
• Phoneme Identity, T210
Phonics
• Blend Words with *c, p, t, n* and Short *a*, T210
High-Frequency Word go, T211
Shared Reading "Can We Go?" T212–T213
Integrate Ideas Research and Inquiry, T216–T217

Practice *Your Turn* 99

Integrate Ideas
• Text Connections, T218
• Talk About Reading, T219
• Research and Inquiry, T219

✓ **Word Work**
Phonemic Awareness
• Phoneme Segmentation, T220
Phonics
• Read Words with Short *a* and *c, n, p, t*, T220
High-Frequency Word go, T221

Practice *Your Turn* 100

DIFFERENTIATED INSTRUCTION

Leveled Reader *We Can Go*, T224–T225
Phonological Awareness
Phoneme Blending, T227
Phonics Reteach, T228
High-Frequency Words Reteach Words, T230

Leveled Reader *We Can Go*, T224–T225
Phonemic Awareness
Phoneme Segmentation, T227
Phonics Blend Words with /k/c, T229
Oral Vocabulary Review Words, T231

Leveled Reader Literacy Activities, T225
Phonemic Awareness
Phoneme Segmentation, T227
Phonics Build Words with *c*, T229
Build Fluency with Phonics, T229
Comprehension Self-Selected Reading, T231

Leveled Reader *Going by Cab*, T232–T233
Phonemic Awareness
Phoneme Segmentation, T234
Phonics Word Sort, T235

Leveled Reader *Going by Cab*, T232–T233
Phonics Blend Words with *c*, T236
High-Frequency Words Reread for Fluency, T237

Leveled Reader Literacy Activities, T233
Comprehension Self-Selected Reading, T237

Leveled Reader *Cal's Busy Week*, T238–T239
Vocabulary Oral Vocabulary: Synonyms, T241

Leveled Reader *Cal's Busy Week*, T238–T239
High-Frequency Words Innovate, T240

Leveled Reader Literacy Activities, T239
Comprehension Self-Selected Reading, T241

Leveled Reader *Going by Cab*, T242–T243
Phonological Awareness
Phoneme Blending, T227
Phonics Reteach, T228
High-Frequency Words Review Words, T245
Writing Writing Trait: Ideas, T246

Leveled Reader *Going by Cab*, T242–T243
Phonemic Awareness Phoneme Segmentation, T227
Phonics Blend Words with /k/c, T229
High-Frequency Words
Review Category Words, T245
Grammar Sentences, T247

Leveled Reader Literacy Activities, T243
Phonemic Awareness
Phoneme Segmentation, T227
Phonics Build Words with *c*, T229
Build Fluency with Phonics, T229

LANGUAGE ARTS

Independent Writing
Writing Trait: Sentence Fluency, T204
Write an Opinion Sentence
Prewrite/Draft, T204–T205
Grammar Sentences, T205

Independent Writing
Writing Trait: Sentence Fluency, T214
Write an Opinion Sentence
Revise/Final Draft, T214
Grammar Sentences, T215

Independent Writing
Writing an Opinion Sentence
Prepare/Present/Evaluate/Publish, T222
Grammar Sentences, T223

DIFFERENTIATE TO ACCELERATE

 A C T Scaffold to **A**ccess **C**omplex **T**ext

Qualitative · Quantitative
Reader and Task
TEXT COMPLEXITY

IF ▶ the text complexity of a particular section is too difficult for children

THEN ▶ see the references noted in the chart below for scaffolded instruction to help children Access Complex Text.

Literature Big Book	Reading/Writing Workshop	Leveled Readers	

Quantitative

Please Take Me for a Walk **Lexile** 260	"We Go to See Nan" **Lexile** 140	**Approaching Level** **Lexile** BR	**On Level** **Lexile** 160
Paired Selection: "A Neighborhood" **Lexile** 330	"Can We Go?" **Lexile** 60	**Beyond Level** **Lexile** 110	**ELL** **Lexile** BR

Qualitative

What Makes the Text Complex?	What Makes the Text Complex? **Foundational Skills**	What Makes the Text Complex? **Foundational Skills**
• **Sentence Structure and Organization** Sentences Across Pages, T186 **A C T** *See Scaffolded Instruction in Teacher's Edition, T186.*	• Decoding with *c*, T192–T193 • Identifying high-frequency words, T193	• Decoding with *c* • Identifying high-frequency words *go* *See Level Up lessons online for Leveled Readers.*

Reader and Task

The Introduce the Concept lesson on pages T174–T175 will help determine the reader's knowledge and engagement in the weekly concept. See pages T176–T177, T187–T191, T208–T209 and T216–T219 for questions and tasks for this text.	The Introduce the Concept lesson on pages T174–T175 will help determine the reader's knowledge and engagement in the weekly concept. See pages T194–T195, T212–T213 and T216–T219 for questions and tasks for this text.	The Introduce the Concept lesson on pages T174–T175 will help determine the reader's knowledge and engagement in the weekly concept. See pages T224–T225, T232–T233, T238–T239, T242–T243 and T216–T219 for questions and tasks for this text.

Nathan Love

BR = Epitome of a beginning reader   ***Go Digital!*** www.connected.mcgraw-hill.com

Monitor and *Differentiate*

IF you need to differentiate instruction

THEN use the Quick Checks to assess children's needs and select the appropriate small group instruction focus.

✓ Quick Check

Comprehension Strategy Visualize, T199

Phonemic Awareness/Phonics /k/c, T181, T193, T203, T211, T221

High-Frequency Words *go*, T181, T193, T203, T211, T221

If No → **Approaching** **Reteach,** pp. T224–T231

 ELL **Develop,** pp. T242–T247

If Yes → **On Level** **Review,** pp. T232–T237

 Beyond Level **Extend,** pp. T238–T241

Level Up with Leveled Readers

IF children can read their leveled text fluently and answer comprehension questions

THEN work with the next level up to accelerate children's reading with more complex text.

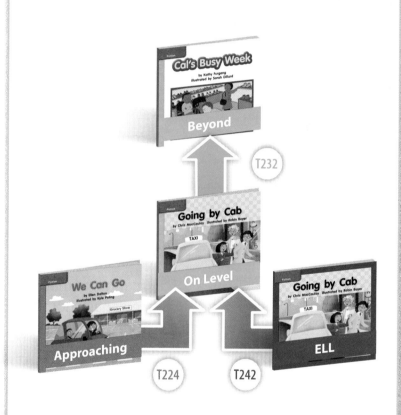

ENGLISH LANGUAGE LEARNERS
SCAFFOLD

IF ELL students need additional support **THEN** scaffold instruction using the small group suggestions.

| Reading-Writing Workshop T175 "Let's Go!" Integrate Ideas T217 | Leveled Reader T242–T243 *Going by Cab* | Phonological Awareness Count and Pronounce Syllables, T226 Phoneme Isolation, T226 Phoneme Blending, T227 Phoneme Segmentation, T227 | Phonics, /k/c, T228–T229 | Oral Vocabulary, T244 routine, neighborhood, local, volunteer, intelligent High-Frequency Word, T245 *go* | Writing Shared Writing, T246 Writing Trait: Sentence Fluency, T246 | Grammar T247 Sentences |

Note: Include ELL Students in all small groups based on their needs.

Materials

Reading/Writing Workshop Big Book
UNIT 3

Literature Big Book
Please Take Me For a Walk

Visual Vocabulary Cards

neighborhood
routine

Response Board

Photo Cards

bus
camera
car
comb
corn
helicopter

Sound-Spelling Cards

camel

go

High-Frequency Word Cards

can
go

Think Aloud Clouds

"Can Your Camel Do the Can-Can?"

Reading/Writing Workshop Big Book

OBJECTIVES

CCSS Confirm understanding of a text read aloud or information presented orally or through other media by asking and answering questions about key details and requesting clarification if something is not understood. **SL.K.2**

CCSS Identify real-life connections between words and their use. **L.K.5c**

→ # Introduce the Concept

MINILESSON
10 Mins

Build Background

ESSENTIAL QUESTION

What places do you go to during the week?

Read aloud the Essential Question. Tell children you are going to read a poem about a place to go—the market. Explain that a market is a place to buy food and other items. Some markets are outdoors, but most are inside.

To Market, To Market

To market, to market, to buy a fat pig,
Home again, home again, jiggety jig.
To market, to market, to buy a fine hog,
Home again, home again, joggety jog.

Recite "To Market, To Market" with children. Then ask: *Where did the person in the poem go after leaving the market?* (home) Tell children that this week they will read to find out about the many different places they might go in their neighborhood.

Oral Vocabulary Words

Use the **Define/Example/Ask** routine to introduce the oral vocabulary words **routine** and **neighborhood**.

To introduce the theme of "The Places We Go," explain that we go to many places during the week. *Where did you go yesterday after school?*

Go Digital

"The Places We Go"

Video

Visual Glossary

Oral Vocabulary Routine

<u>Define:</u> A **routine** is the way you do things all the time.

<u>Example:</u> My routine on Monday is to get up, have breakfast, and go to school.

<u>Ask:</u> What is your routine on Saturday?

<u>Define:</u> A **neighborhood** is part of a town.

<u>Example:</u> Houses and stores are in my neighborhood.

<u>Ask:</u> What is in the neighborhood near our school?

Visual Vocabulary Cards

Talk About It: The Places We Go

Guide children to name places where they like to go in their town. List their responses. Display page 42 of the **Reading/Writing Workshop Big Book** and have children do the **Talk About It** activity with a partner.

Weekly Concept The Places We Go

Essential Question
What places do you go to during the week?
Go Digital!

Let's Go!

Talk About It
Why is this boy at this place?

READING/WRITING WORKSHOP BIG BOOK, pp. 42–43

Collaborative Conversations

Listen Carefully As children engage in partner, small group, and whole group discussions, encourage them to:

→ Look at the person who is speaking.

→ Listen to the words they are saying.

→ Respect others by not interrupting them.

→ Repeat classmates' ideas to check understanding.

ELL

ENGLISH LANGUAGE LEARNERS SCAFFOLD

Beginning

Use Visuals Explain that the boy in the picture is getting a haircut. The barber is cutting the boy's hair and his dad is standing with him. *Is the boy happy to be getting a haircut? Is the dad's hair short or long?* Allow children ample time to respond.

Intermediate

Describe Ask children to describe what is happening in the picture. Ask them to tell where the boy and his dad are. *Who else is in the picture?* Correct grammar and punctuation as needed.

Advanced/Advanced High

Discuss Have children elaborate on places they go in their neigborhood. *When was the last time you got a haircut? Where did you go?* Elicit more details to support children's answers.

→ # Listening Comprehension

Literature Big Book

OBJECTIVES

 With prompting and support, name the author and illustrator of a story and define the role of each in telling the story. **RL.K.6**

 Actively engage in group reading activities with purpose and understanding. **RL.K.10**

- Strategy: Visualize
- Connect Big Book to Weekly Concept

ACADEMIC LANGUAGE
sentence, period

 MINILESSON 10 Mins

Read the Literature Big Book

Connect to Concept: The Places We Go

Tell children that you will now read about many places people go in a neighborhood. Ask: *What is one place you went over the weekend?*

Concepts of Print

Directionality and Sentences Display page 5 of the **Big Book**. Track the print as you read the sentence aloud. Remind children that we read from left to right. *All of these words together make a sentence.* Next, point to the period and say: *This is an end mark called a period. Every sentence needs an end mark.* On page 6, point to the word *I*. Say: *This is the word* I. *The word* I *is always a capital letter.*

Genre: Fantasy

Model *Please Take Me for a Walk* is a fantasy story. Remind children of these characteristics of fantasy:

→ The events are made up.

→ Some events, like animals talking, could never happen in real life.

> **Story Words** Preview these words before reading:
>
> **butcher:** someone who gets meat ready to sell and then sells it
> **greengrocer:** someone who sells fresh fruits and vegetables
> **retrieve:** get and bring back

Set a Purpose for Reading

→ Read aloud and identify the title and the name of the author/illustrator. Ask: *What does the author do?* (writes the words) *What does the illustrator do?* (creates the pictures)

→ Point out that the same person wrote the words and created the pictures for this story.

→ Ask children to listen as you read aloud the Big Book to find out the places where the dog would like to go and the people the dog would like to visit.

Go Digital

Please Take Me For a Walk

I was able to picture in my mind...

Think Aloud Cloud

Strategy: Visualize

Explain Remind children that they can use the words and pictures in the story, as well as their own experiences, to make pictures in their minds. These pictures will help them understand what is happening in a story.

Think Aloud When I look at the cover, I see a dog holding a leash. He wants to go for a walk. I've seen dogs walking in my neighborhood, and I've walked in my neighborhood. In my mind I can picture places the dog might go with its owner like the park and stores. While I read, I will make more pictures in my mind to help me understand the story.

Model As you read, use the **Think Aloud Cloud** to model the strategy.

Think Aloud On page 11, I read: "Some neighbors like to pet me." I see a girl from the neighborhood reaching out to pet the dog. I can make a picture in my mind of the dog jumping up and trying to grab the cookie. I can picture the child pulling the cookie back and laughing. I can imagine the skateboards on the sidewalk and see the dogs running by. I think this looks like fun. I think that is why the dog wants to go for a walk!

Respond to Reading

After reading, prompt children to name the places the dog has gone and would like to go again. Point out that the author repeats "Please take me for a walk" over and over as the dog begs to go places he has been and has enjoyed before. Discuss the pictures that children made in their minds as they listened to the story. Then have children draw a picture of one of the scenes that they visualized. Encourage them to describe what is happening in their pictures.

Make Connections

Use *Please Take Me for a Walk* to discuss the places we go. Revisit the concept behind the Essential Question *What places do you go to during the week?* by paging through the **Big Book**.

Write About It Write about one of the places the dog in the story would like to go. Tell what he wants to do when he gets there.

→ # Word Work

MINILESSON 5 Mins

Phonemic Awareness

Phoneme Isolation

Photo Card

1 Model Introduce initial sound /k/. Display the *Camel* **Photo Card.** *Listen for the sound at the beginning of* camel. Camel *has the /k/ sound at the beginning. Say the sound with me: /k/.* Say these words and have children repeat: *can, cap, cat.* Emphasize the phoneme /k/.

♪ *Let's play a song. Listen for the words with /k/ at the beginning.* Play "Can Your Camel Do the Can-Can?" Have children listen for the /k/ sound. *Let's listen to the song again and clap when we hear words that begin with /k/.* Play and sing the letter song again, encouraging children to join in. Have children clap when they hear a word that begins with /k/.

2 Guided Practice/Practice Display and name each Photo Card: *camera, car, comb, corn. Say each picture name with me. Tell me the sound at the beginning of the word.* Guide practice with the first word.

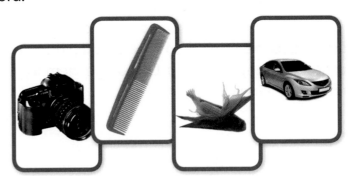
Photo Cards

OBJECTIVES

CCSS Isolate and pronounce the initial, medial vowel, and final sounds in three-phoneme words. **RF.K.2d**

CCSS Demonstrate basic knowledge of one-to-one letter-sound correspondences by producing the primary or many of the most frequent sounds for each consonant. **RF.K.3a**

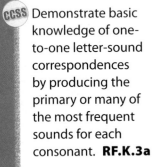

ENGLISH LANGUAGE LEARNERS

Pronunciation
Display and have children name Photo Cards from this lesson to reinforce phonemic awareness and word meanings. Point to a card. *What do you see?* (a car) *What is the sound at the beginning of the word* cow? (/k/) Repeat using Photo Cards with words that begin with /k/.

ARTICULATION SUPPORT

Demonstrate the way to say /k/. Open your mouth. Put your tongue against the back and top of your mouth. Hold your breath. Now, let a little air out as you lower your tongue. Say *cool, cane, cat* and have children repeat. Emphasize initial /k/.

Phonics

10 Mins
MINILESSON

Cc

camel

Sound-Spelling Card

Introduce /k/c

① Model Display the *Camel* **Sound-Spelling Card**. Say: *This is the Camel* card. *The sound is /k/. The /k/ sound can be spelled with the letter* c. *Say the sound with me: /k/. This is the sound at the beginning of the word* camel. *Listen: /k/, /k/, /k/,* camel. *What is the name of this letter?* (c) *What sound does this letter stand for?* (/k/)

Display the song "Can Your Camel Do the Can-Can?" (see **Teacher's Resource Book** online). Read or sing the song with children. Reread the title and point out that the words *can, camel* and *can-can* all begin with the letter *c*. Model placing a self-stick note below the *c* in *can, can-can* and *camel*.

② Guided Practice/Practice Read each line of the song. Stop after each line and ask children to place self-stick notes below words that begin with *C* or *c* and say the letter name.

ELL

ENGLISH LANGUAGE LEARNERS

Phoneme Variations in Language In some languages, including Cantonese, Hmong, Korean, and Khmer, there is no direct transfer for /k/ spelled *c*. Emphasize the /k/ sound in words such as *cake, cat, cab, cap*. Point out that /k/ can be spelled with the letter *c*.

Can Your Camel Do the Can-Can?

Can your camel do the can-can?
Can she do the can-can?
Can your camel do the can-can?
Can she do the can-can?
Yes, she does the can-can.
Yes, she does the can-can.
Yes, she does the can-can, tra-la-la!

Corrective Feedback

Sound Error Model the sound /k/ in the initial position, then have children repeat the sound. Say: *My turn. Camel. /k/, /k/, /k/. Now it's your turn.* Have children say the word and isolate the initial sound.

YOUR TURN PRACTICE BOOK pp. 93–94

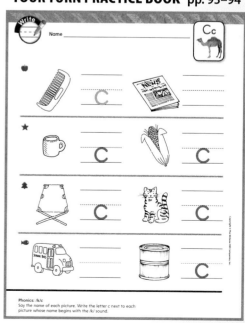

→ Word Work

Handwriting: Write Cc

OBJECTIVES

CCSS Write a letter or letters for most consonant and short-vowel sounds. **L.K.2c**

CCSS Read common high-frequency words by sight. **RF.K.3c**

ACADEMIC LANGUAGE

uppercase, lowercase

❶ **Model** Say the handwriting cues below as you write and then identify the upper and lowercase forms of *Cc*. Then trace the letters on the board and in the air as you say /k/.

Circle back and around, then stop.

Circle back and around, then stop.

❷ **Guided Practice/Practice**

→ Say the cues together as children trace both forms of the letter with their index fingers. Have them identify the uppercase and lowercase forms of the letter.

→ Have children write *C* and *c* in the air as they say /k/ multiple times.

→ Distribute **Response Boards**. Observe children's pencil grip and paper position, and correct as necessary. Have children say /k/ every time they write the letter *Cc*.

 Daily Handwriting

Throughout the week teach uppercase and lowercase letters *Cc* using the Handwriting models. At the end of the week, have children use the **Your Turn Practice Book** p. 100 to practice handwriting.

Go Digital

Handwriting

| the | is |
| you | do |

High-Frequency Word Routine

MINILESSON
5 Mins

High-Frequency Words

go

go

High-Frequency Word Card

1 Model Display the **High-Frequency Word Card** *go.* Use the **Read/Spell/Write** routine to teach the word.

→ **Read** Point to the word *go* and say the word. *This is the word* go. *Say it with me:* go. *I want to* go *for a walk.*

→ **Spell** *The word* go *is spelled g-o. Spell it with me.*

→ **Write** *Let's write the word in the air as we say each letter: g-o.*

→ Have partners create sentences using the word.

COLLABORATE

2 Guided Practice/Practice Build sentences using the High-Frequency Word Cards, **Word-Building Cards**, **Photo Cards**, and teacher-made punctuation cards. Have children point to the high-frequency word *go.* Use these sentences.

Also online

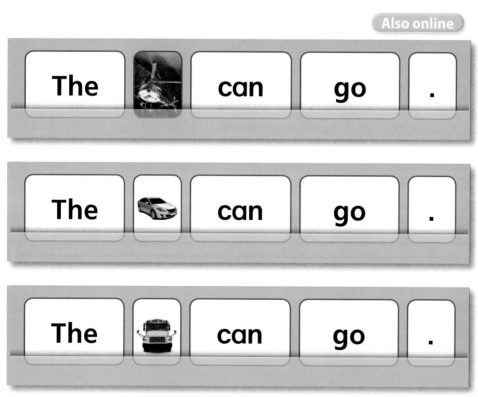

High-Frequency Words Practice

Monitor and *Differentiate*

✓ **Quick Check**

Can children isolate /k/ and match it to the letter *Cc*?

Can children recognize and read the high-frequency word?

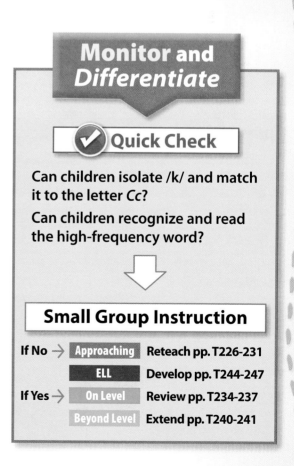

Small Group Instruction

If No →	**Approaching**	Reteach pp. T226–231
	ELL	Develop pp. T244–247
If Yes →	**On Level**	Review pp. T234–237
	Beyond Level	Extend pp. T240–241

→ # Language Arts

 MINILESSON **10** Mins

Shared Writing

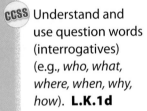
OBJECTIVES

CCSS With guidance and support from adults, recall information from experiences or gather information from provided sources to answer a question. **W.K.8**

CCSS Understand and use question words (interrogatives) (e.g., *who, what, where, when, why, how*). **L.K.1d**

CCSS Recognize and name end punctuation. **L.K.2b**

• Make a chart
• Recognize sentences

ACADEMIC LANGUAGE

• *sentence, opinion*
• Cognates: *opinión*

Writing Trait: Sentence Fluency

❶ **Model** Tell children that a sentence can be used to tell an opinion. *An opinion is how you feel about something. I think skipping is fun. This is something I like to do. It is my opinion.*

→ Ask a volunteer to do an action that she or he thinks is fun, such as jumping, hopping, or skipping. Write and read aloud: *[NAME] likes to _____.* Fill in the action and read aloud the sentence. *This is a complete sentence that tells how [name] feels about something.*

❷ **Guided Practice/Practice** Write and read aloud: *Malia likes to play soccer.* Guide children in naming who is doing the action. *The word* like *tells you how Malia feels about playing soccer.*

Write an Opinion Sentence

Focus and Plan Tell children that this week they will learn how to write a sentence to share an opinion.

Brainstorm Have children name some places they like to go to during the week. Create a list of some of their ideas.

> **Places We Go**
>
> school
> library
> park
> store

Write Model writing a sentence using an idea from the list. *I can take one of the places from the list and write about it:* I like to go to school. *This sentence tells about a place I like to go to during the week.* Model writing sentences about other places you like to go to during the week. Use the other examples on the list. Read aloud the sentences with children.

Grammar

5 Mins · MINILESSON

Sentences

❶ Model Remind children that a sentence always begins with a capital letter and ends with a mark. *Many sentences end with a period. Some sentences ask a question, so they end with a question mark.* Write: *Who plays baseball? Dan plays baseball.*

→ Read aloud: *Who plays baseball? This sentence is asking about someone. It is a question sentence. All questions must have a question mark at the end. I know it is a question sentence because it starts with the word* who. *Many questions start with the words* who, what, when, where, why, *or* how.

→ Read aloud: *Dan plays baseball. This is a complete sentence because it tells about somebody doing an action. It answers the question sentence. The sentence tells who plays baseball. It begins with a capital letter and ends with a period.*

❷ Guided Practice/Practice Write and read aloud the words: *rides the bike. We can add words to* rides the bike *to make a question sentence.* Write: *Who rides the bike?* Guide children in thinking of an answer sentence to the question, such as *The girl rides the bike.* Read the sentence aloud as you point to each word. Encourage children to think of other answer sentences for the question.

Talk About It

COLLABORATE

Have partners work together to orally generate question and answer sentences. Encourage them to pick something in the school to ask a question about, such as *Where is the library? The library is down the hall.*

ELL

ENGLISH LANGUAGE LEARNERS SCAFFOLD

Beginning

Explain Write question and answer sentences, such as: *What is your name? My name is Luz.* Read aloud sentences with children. Point to each sentence. *Is this a question sentence? Is this an answer sentence?* Restate children's responses in order to develop their oral language proficiency.

Intermediate

Practice Tell children to ask a question, such as *What is your favorite color?* Write and read aloud children's questions. Answer each question. Model pronunciation as needed.

Advanced/Advanced High

Practice Have children pick a famous person they would like to learn more about. Have them dictate a question that they would like to ask that person. Write the question on a sentence strip. Model correct pronunciation as needed.

Daily Wrap Up

- Review the Essential Question and encourage children to discuss it, using the new oral vocabulary words. *What places do you go to during the week?*

- Prompt children to share the skills they learned. *How might they use those skills?*

Materials

Reading/Writing Workshop Big Book
UNIT 3

Literature Big Book
Please Take Me For a Walk

Visual Vocabulary Cards
routine
neighborhood

Response Board

Word-Building Cards

Cc
camel
Sound-Spelling Cards

go
High-Frequency Word Cards
and
go
like
to

Retelling Cards

Puppet

→ Build the Concept

MINILESSON
10 Mins

Oral Language

Go Digital

OBJECTIVES

CCSS Count, pronounce, blend, and segment syllables in spoken words. **RF.K.2b**

CCSS Use words and phrases acquired through conversations, reading and being read to, and responding to texts. **L.K.6**

CCSS Identify real-life connections between words and their use (e.g., note places at school that are colorful). **L.K.5c**

Develop oral vocabulary

ACADEMIC LANGUAGE

• *syllable, vocabulary*

• Cognates: *sílaba, vocabulario*

ESSENTIAL QUESTION

What places do you go to during the week?

Remind children that this week they are learning about the places we go. Ask them to tell about places they have gone in the neighborhood near school.

With children, recite "To Market, To Market." *What might you buy at a market?*

Visual Glossary

Category Words

Phonological Awareness
Count and Pronounce Syllables

After children recite the rhyme, say the word *market*, clapping out the syllables. Have children repeat. *The word* market *has two parts. How many parts does* market *have?* (two) Have children clap and say *market* with you. Repeat this routine with *jiggety* (three parts), *home* (one part), and *again* (two parts).

Review Oral Vocabulary

Use the **Define/Example/Ask** routine to review the oral vocabulary words **routine** and **neighborhood**. Prompt children to use the words in sentences.

Vocab
Define
Examp
Ask:

Visual Vocabulary Cards

Category Words: Sequence Words

❶ Model Use the **Big Book** *Please Take Me for a Walk* to discuss sequence words. Explain that sequence words tell the order in which things happen. Introduce the words *first, next, then, last, before,* and *after*. Turn to pages 14–15 and point to each illustration. *The dog wants to say hello to different people in town. First, he says hello to the florist. Next, he says hello to the greengrocer. Then, he says hello to the baker. Last, he says hello to the bookseller.*

→ Ask children questions using the sequence words *before* and *after*. *Who does the dog say hello to* before *the baker?* (the greengrocer) *Who does he say hello to* after *the baker?* (the bookseller)

❷ Guided Practice/Practice Say the following sentences. Ask children to listen for sequence words.

> *First, we walk into the classroom.*
> *Next, we put away our coats.*
> *Then, we sit in a circle.*
> *Last, we talk about our day.*

→ Repeat each sentence and ask children to raise their hands when they hear a sequence word.

LET'S MOVE!

Give simple directions that include sequence words: First, *jump in place.* Next, *put your hands on your hips.* Then, *do a jumping jack.* Last, *sit in your chair.*

ENGLISH LANGUAGE LEARNERS

Explain Demonstrate washing your hands. As you show each step, say: First, *I rub soap on my hands.* Next, *I turn on the water.* Then, *I rinse my hands.* Last, *I dry my hands.* Have children mirror your actions as they repeat the words with you.

→ **Listening Comprehension** CLOSE READING

Literature Big Book

OBJECTIVES

CCSS With prompting and support, ask and answer questions about key details in a text. **RL.K.1**

CCSS With prompting and support, identify characters, settings, and major events in a story. **RL.K.3**

• Strategy: Visualize
• Skill: Character, Setting, Events

ACADEMIC LANGUAGE
characters, setting, events

 MINILESSON **15** Mins

Reread Literature Big Book

Genre: Fantasy

Display *Please Take Me for a Walk*. Guide children in recalling that fantasy stories are made up and could never happen in real life. *How do you know that* Please Take Me for a Walk *is fantasy?* Have children point to evidence in the text and the pictures to show that this is a fantasy. (The dog is talking, but real dogs cannot talk.)

Strategy: Visualize

Guide children in recalling that good readers use the words and pictures in a story to make pictures in their minds. This helps them understand what is happening. Say: *As we reread, you can make pictures in your mind about the places in the neighborhood.*

Skill: Character, Setting, Events

Tell children that the characters in a story are the people or animals the story is about. *Who is the main character in this story?* (the dog) The setting is where the story happens. *What is the setting of this story? Where does it take place?* (the dog's neighborhood) Explain that events are the things that happen in a story. *What events happen in this story?* (The dog visits places in the neighborhood.) Explain: *Thinking about character, setting, and events can help you understand and enjoy a story.* As you read, have children listen for evidence in the text that will help them understand the character, setting, and events.

 **A C T**
Access Complex Text

Sentence Structure and Organization In this book, some sentences begin on one spread and end on the next. This could be confusing to young readers. Explain: *Sometimes, an author might start a sentence on one page and finish it on the next page.*

→ Read aloud pages 26–27: *I want to feel the wind lift my ears and the sun warm my belly.* Point out that there is no period after *ears* on page 26—but there is a period after *belly* on page 27 to show the end of the sentence.

Go Digital

Please Take Me For a Walk

Retelling Cards

LITERATURE BIG BOOK PAGE 5

CHARACTER

What character do you see on this page? What can you tell about him? (Possible answer: The dog. He looks friendly and excited, and he wants to go for a walk.)

p. 5

walk: English language learners might recognize *walk* as a verb but be confused by *walk* as a noun. Have them repeat with you: *We walk.* Then point to the leash in the illustration. Pretend to clip it onto a dog's collar and then pull it as you say: *I take the dog for a walk.*

LITERATURE BIG BOOK   PAGES 6–7

PHONICS

Reread the sentence on page 6 and ask: *Which word has the beginning sound /k/?* (cat) What letter makes the /k/ sound? (c)

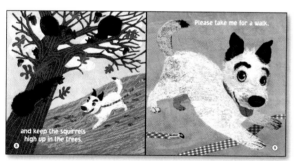

LITERATURE BIG BOOK   PAGES 8–9

VISUALIZE

Think Aloud I read that the dog likes to keep squirrels up high in the tree. In my mind I can picture the dog running to the tree and jumping at the squirrels, and I can picture him barking. He is very excited. I think the squirrels are probably scared of the dog.

LITERATURE BIG BOOK   PAGES 10–11

SETTING

What is the setting? How do you know? (A street and sidewalks in a neighborhood. I can see the neighborhood houses and people in the illustrations. I also heard the words *the people on my street.*)

pp. 10–11

greet: When I greet someone, I say "hello" to them. I might also wave to them, hug them, or shake their hand. Ask children how they greet friends and family.

Listening Comprehension

CLOSE READING
ELL

LITERATURE BIG BOOK   **PAGES 12–13**

CHARACTER

Think Aloud I see the boy crying. I think he is scared of the dog. The dog looks a little sad. I think he doesn't want to scare the boy. He is a nice dog.

LITERATURE BIG BOOK   **PAGES 14–15**

SETTING

What different settings do you see on this page? (a flower shop, a grocery store, a bakery, a bookstore)

pp. 14–15

florist, greengrocer, baker, bookseller: Explain that a florist sells flowers, a greengrocer sells fruit and vegetables, a baker sells bread and cakes, and a bookseller sells books.

LITERATURE BIG BOOK   **PAGES 16–17**

KEY DETAILS

The dog says that the butcher is its special friend. Why do you think he says that? (The butcher gives bones to the dog. I can see the dog carrying the bone in the picture.)

LITERATURE BIG BOOK   **PAGES 18–19**

CONCEPTS OF PRINT

Have a volunteer point to the word *I*. Remind children that the word *I* is always a capital letter. Explain that the letter *i* in *kids* and *in* is lowercase, so it is not a word.

pp. 18–19

shooting hoops: Help children understand that the idiom *shooting hoops* means "playing basketball." Pantomime throwing a basketball toward a hoop, saying: *I'm shooting hoops.*

LITERATURE BIG BOOK   PAGES 20–21

CONCEPTS OF PRINT

Have a child track the print from left to right as you read aloud the sentence on page 21. Tell the child to point to the end mark. *What is the name of this end mark?* (period)

pp. 20–21

chess: Point to the chessboard, and explain that this is a game that two people play together. It has a board and pieces.

LITERATURE BIG BOOK   PAGES 22–23

PHONICS

What words begin with the /k/ sound? What letter makes that sound? (could, catch, the letter *c*)

LITERATURE BIG BOOK   PAGES 24–25

EVENTS

What are some events that have happened so far in the story? (Possible answer: The dog has been asking for someone to take him for a walk. He has been thinking about all the places he wants to go in the neighborhood.)

LITERATURE BIG BOOK   PAGES 26–27

VISUALIZE

How is the dog feeling? What pictures can you make in your mind to help you figure this out? (Possible answers: I can picture in my mind the wind pushing his ears up. I can picture the sun high in the sky making him warm. I think the dog feels good.)

pp. 26–27

belly: Explain that *belly* means "stomach." Point to the dog's belly on page 27 as you say *belly.* Then point to your own stomach and say *belly.* Have children point to their own bellies.

Listening Comprehension

LITERATURE BIG BOOK   **PAGES 28–29**

CHARACTER

There are many dogs in the illustration on these pages. Can you find the dog that is the main character in this story? Have a volunteer point to the dog with the red leash.

LITERATURE BIG BOOK   **PAGES 30–31**

CHARACTER

How does the dog seem to feel in this illustration? Which detail in the illustration helps you figure it out? (Possible answer: The dog looks a little scared. There are a lot of other dogs. Some of them are big. The dog is not sure he is safe. I can tell by his eyes.)

LITERATURE BIG BOOK   **PAGES 32–33**

EVENTS

Why is the dog happy now? What is happening? (All of the dogs on the page are looking at their owners and smiling. The main dog is smiling and looking toward someone who I can't see but who is holding the leash. I think he is happy.)

pp. 32–33

leash: Explain that a leash is like a rope that people use to keep their dogs from running away. Point out the leashes in the illustration.

LITERATURE BIG BOOK   **PAGE 34**

AUTHOR'S PURPOSE

Why do you think the author wrote this story? (Possible answer: She wanted the reader to see places to go in a neighborhood, and she wanted to show a fun story about a dog.)

p. 34

best friend: A best friend is a very, very good friend who you like to spend a lot of time with.

Guided Retelling

Tell children that they will use the **Retelling Cards** to retell the story.

→ Display Retelling Card 1. Based on children's needs, use either the Modeled, Guided or ELL retelling prompts. The ELL prompts contain support for English Language Learners based on levels of language acquisition. Repeat with the rest of the cards, using the prompts as a guide.

→ Discuss the story. Choose a place in the book and have children discuss how the dog felt. Have children defend their comments.

→ Invite children to choose a favorite part of the story and act it out.

Model Fluency

→ Turn to pages 26–27. Point out that we should read aloud words the way the characters would say them. *I can tell from the words and pictures that the dog feels really happy when the wind lifts his ears and the sun warms his belly. I'll read the words the way this character would say them.* With an expression of contentment and happiness, read aloud: *I want to feel the wind lift my ears and the sun warm my belly.* Have children echo. Then invite volunteers to say the words the way the dog would say them.

Retelling Cards

Text Evidence

Explain Remind children that when they answer a question, they need to show where in the story (both words and pictures) they found the answer.

Discuss *We saw the dog go to many places in the neighborhood. Do people in the neighborhood like the dog? How do you know? Show details in the book that make you think this.*

YOUR TURN PRACTICE BOOK p. 95

→ **Word Work**

MINILESSON **5** Mins

Phonemic Awareness

Puppet

Go Digital

Phonemic Awareness

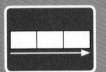
Phonics

High-Frequency Word Routine

Handwriting

Phoneme Blending

❶ **Model** Use the puppet to demonstrate how to blend phonemes to make words. *The puppet is going to say sounds in a word, /k/ /a/ /t/. It can blend those sounds to make a word: /kaaat/, cat. When the puppet blends the sounds together, it makes the word cat. Listen as the puppet blends more sounds to make a word.* Model phoneme blending with the following.

/k/ /a/ /p/, cap   /k/ /a/ /n/, can   /k/ /ou/, cow

❷ **Guided Practice/Practice** *The puppet is going to say the sounds in a different word: /k/ /a/ /n/. Say the sounds. Let's blend the sounds and say the word with the puppet: /kaaan/, can.*

Tell children to listen as the puppet says the sounds in words. Have them repeat the sounds, and then blend them to say the word.

/k/ /ā/ /m/, came   /k/ /ā/ /k/, cake
/k/ /u/ /t/, cut   /k/ /ō/ /m/, comb

MINILESSON **5** Mins

Phonics

Cc
camel
Sound-Spelling Card

Review /k/c

❶ **Model** Display the *Camel* **Sound-Spelling Card**. *This is the letter* c. *The letter* c *can stand for the sound /k/ as in the word* camel. *What is the letter?* (c) *What sound can the letter* c *stand for?* (/k/)

❷ **Guided Practice/Practice** Have children listen as you say some words. Ask them to write the letter *c* on their **Response Boards** if the word begins with /k/. Do the first two words with children.

cab   cage   nice   man
call   cold   came   enjoy

OBJECTIVES

CCSS Demonstrate basic knowledge of one-to-one letter-sound correspondences by producing the primary or many of the most frequent sounds for each consonant. **RF.K.3a**

CCSS Read common high-frequency words by sight. **RF.K.3c**

Blend phonemes to make words

ENGLISH LANGUAGE LEARNERS

High-Frequency Words: Build Meaning Reinforce the use of the word *go* by saying these sentences and demonstrating them.

• We will *go* for a walk.
• Sam and I like to *go* to the park.
• Nan will *go* to the store.
• We *go* to school.

Blend Words with /k/c

❶ Model Remind children that the letter *c* can stand for /k/. Place the **Word-Building Cards** *c, a,* and *t* in a pocket chart. Point to the letter *c*. Say: *This is the letter* c. *The letter* c *can stand for /k/. Say /k/. This is the letter* a. *The letter* a *stands for /a/. Say /a/. This is the letter* t. *The letter* t *stands for /t/. Say /t/. Listen as I blend the three sounds together: /kaaat/. Now blend the sounds with me to read the word.*

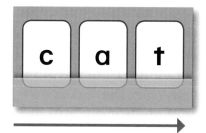

❷ Guided Practice/Practice Point to the letter *c* and have children say the sound. Point to the letter *a* and have children say the sound. Point to the letter *t* and have children say the sound. Then move your hand from left to right under the word and have children blend and read *cat*. Repeat with the word *can*.

MINILESSON
5 Mins

High-Frequency Words

go

❶ Guided Practice Display the **High-Frequency Word Card** *go*. Use the **Read/Spell/Write** routine to teach the word. Ask children to close their eyes, picture the spelling of the word in their minds, and then write it the way they see it. Have children self-correct by checking the High-Frequency Word Card.

| go |

High-Frequency Word Cards

❷ Practice Add the high-frequency word *go* to the word bank.

→ Have partners create sentences using the word.

→ Have children count the number of letters in the word and then write the word *go* again.

Cumulative Review Review words: *and, to, like.*

→ Repeat the **Read/Spell/Write** routine. Mix the words and have children chorally say each one.

Monitor and *Differentiate*

✓ **Quick Check**

Can children blend phonemes to make words and match /k/ to *Cc*?

Can children recognize and read the high-frequency word?

⬇

Small Group Instruction

If No →	Approaching	Reteach pp. T226–231
	ELL	Develop pp. T244–247
If Yes →	On Level	Review pp. T234–237
	Beyond Level	Extend pp. T240–241

→ Shared Read

Read "We Go to See Nan"

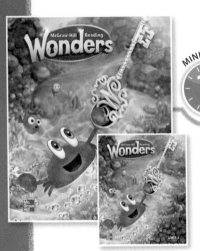

Reading/Writing Workshop Big Book and Reading/Writing Workshop

 OBJECTIVES

CCSS Read common high-frequency words by sight. **RF.K.3c**

CCSS Read emergent-reader texts with purpose and understanding. **RF.K.4**

ACADEMIC LANGUAGE
- *predict*
- Cognates: *predecir*

Model Skills and Strategies

Model Book Handling Demonstrate book handling. Display the front cover of the book. *This is the front cover of the book. Model turning the pages of the book. When I'm finished reading one page, I turn the page to read the next one. I continue doing this until I reach the end of the book.* Display the back cover of the book. *This is the back cover of the book.*

Model Concepts About Print Turn to page 45 and read the sentence. *This is a sentence. A sentence is made up of a group of related words.* Point to the period. *A period is one kind of mark that comes at the end of a sentence.* Then point to the word *I* in the sentence. *I is a pronoun. It takes the place of a person's name. The pronoun I is always a capital letter.*

Predict Read the title together. Invite children to look closely at the pictures on pages 44 and 45 and predict where the boy and girl are going. Then have children tell what they think the boy and girl will do there.

Read Have children chorally read the story with you. Point to each word as you read it together. Help children sound out decodable words and say the sight words. If children have difficulty, provide corrective feedback and guide them page by page using the student **Reading/Writing Workshop**.

Ask the following:

→ *Look at page 46. What does Cam like to do at the bookstore?* (She likes to pat the cat.)

→ *Look at page 47. What are the sister and brother looking at?* (a book about cats)

→ *Look at page 49. What is the cat looking at?* (the pictures in the book about cats)

Go Digital

"We Go to See Nan"

"We Go to See Nan"

READING/WRITING WORKSHOP, pp. 44–49

Rereading

Have small groups use the **Reading/Writing Workshop** to reread "We Go to See Nan." Then review the skills and strategies using the *Phonics* and *Words to Know* pages that come before the selection.

→ Have children visualize what they might see if they visited a bookstore. As they reread the story, have them tell about what the bookstore is like and what the characters do while they are there.

→ Have children use page 43 to review the high-frequency word *go*.

→ Have children use page 42 to review that the letter *c* can stand for the sound /k/. Guide them to identify and name each picture that begins with the sound /k/. Guide them to blend the sounds to read the words.

→ # Language Arts

MINILESSON 10 Mins

Interactive Writing

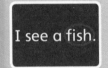
OBJECTIVES

 CCSS Use a combination of drawing, dictating, and writing to compose opinion pieces in which they tell a reader the topic or the name of the book they are writing about and state an opinion or preference about the topic or book (e.g., *My favorite book is . . .*). **W.K.1**

CCSS Understand and use question words (interrogatives) (e.g., *who, what, where, when, why, how*). **L.K.1d**

 CCSS Recognize and name end punctuation. **L.K.2b**

- Recognize sentences
- Write a sentence

ACADEMIC LANGUAGE

- *opinion*
- Cognates: *opinión*

Writing Trait: Sentence Fluency

Review Remind children that they can share opinions about things through writing. Write and read aloud these sentences: *I like to go for a walk. I do not like to walk in the rain. I can write complete sentences to share my opinions, or feelings, about going for a walk. Both sentences start with a capital letter and end with a period.*

Write an Opinion Sentence

Discuss Display the list of places children go to during the week and the sample sentence from Day 1. Read aloud each place on the list. *Where do you like to go?* Encourage children to add more places to the list.

Model/Apply Grammar Tell children that you will work together to write a sentence telling about a favorite place they go to during the week and what they do there.

Write and read the following sentence frame: *I like to _____ in the _____.* Guide children in describing what they like to do in the park. Write their responses in the first blank and write *park* in the second blank, such as *I like to play in the park.* Read aloud the sentence chorally with children. Point out the capital letter at the beginning of the sentence and the period at the end of the sentence.

Write Have children help you write about a favorite thing they do when they go to a friend's house. Write the sentence frame: *I like to _____ at my friend's house.*

Guide children to complete the sentence frame. Write the words. Share the pen with children and have them write the letters they know. Read aloud the sentences chorally with children.

Grammar

MINILESSON 5 Mins

Sentences

① **Review** Write and read the following sentences as shown, with incorrect capitalization and no end punctuation:

> who is your friend
> i go to the movies
> how old is Tim

Ask children to circle the letters that should be capitalized. Have children identify the sentence that tells about somebody doing an action. Ask them to place a period at the end of the sentence. Then have children identify the sentences that are questions. Ask them to place a question mark at the end of each question sentence.

② **Guided Practice** On two index cards, write a large period. On two more index cards, write a large question mark. Write and read aloud the following sentences without end punctuation: *Which pencil is yours; His name is Pete; Who is going to the store; My sister is nice.* Ask children to tape the proper end punctuation index card at the end of each sentence. Read the sentences aloud with children.

③ **Practice** Have children work with a partner. Give each pair a sentence strip that has one of the following words at the beginning of the strip: *Who, What, When, Where, Why,* and *How.* Ask children to think of a question sentence they can write that starts with the word they were given. Help children write their sentences as needed. Help children read their sentences to the class.

Talk About It

Have partners work together to orally generate questions about why they like a particular place, such as *Why do you like the park?* Encourage children to give a reason why they like a place.

ENGLISH LANGUAGE LEARNERS

Use Visuals Have children choose a **Photo Card** at random. Ask children a question about the card. For example: *What color is the bear?* Write the question on a sentence strip. Have children dictate an answer, such as *The bear is brown.* Write the answer on a sentence strip. Have children read the questions and answers with you.

Daily Wrap Up

- Discuss the Essential Question and encourage children to use the oral vocabulary words. *What places in your neighborhood did you go to yesterday?*

- Prompt children to review and discuss the skills they used today. How do those skills help them?

Materials

Reading/Writing Workshop Big Book
UNIT 3

Interactive Read-Aloud Cards

Visual Vocabulary Cards
local
intelligent
volunteer

Photo Cards
car   nest
comb   net
corn   night
cow   nine
cube   nut

Word-Building Cards

a b c

and

High-Frequency Word Cards
and
go

I was able to picture in my mind...
Think Aloud Cloud

Response Board

Puppet

♪ **"Can Your Camel Do the Can-Can?"**

→ Build the Concept

MINILESSON
10 Mins

Oral Language

OBJECTIVES

 Actively engage in group reading activities with purpose and understanding. **RI.K.10**

 Identify real-life connections between words and their use. **L.K.5c**

Develop oral vocabulary

ACADEMIC LANGUAGE
• *informational text*
• Cognates: *texto informativo*

ESSENTIAL QUESTION

COLLABORATE

Remind children that this week they are talking and learning about places we go to during the week. Guide children to discuss the Essential Question using information from the **Big Book** and the weekly rhyme.

Remind children that the market, or store, in "To Market, To Market" is one place we often go during the week. Say the rhyme and have children join in.

Oral Vocabulary

Review last week's oral vocabulary words, as well as *routine* and *neighborhood* from Day 1. Then use the **Define/Example/Ask** routine to introduce *local, intelligent,* and *volunteer.*

Oral Vocabulary Routine

Define: A **local** place is in your town or community.

Example: The local bakery is around the corner from school.

Ask: What is your favorite local store?

Define: A person who is **intelligent** is very smart.

Example: Marta asked an intelligent question about sea animals.

Ask: What can help you become more intelligent?

Define: When you **volunteer**, you offer to do a job without getting paid.

Example: I volunteer to help clean up the park in my neighborhood.

Ask: How could you volunteer to help at school?

Vocabulary
Define
Example
Ask:

Visual Vocabulary Cards

Go Digital

Visual Glossary

"Field Trips"

I was able to picture in my mind...
Think Aloud Cloud

Listening Comprehension

Read the Interactive Read Aloud

MINILESSON
10 Mins

Genre: Informational Text

Tell children that you will be reading an informational text. Remind them that *informational text* gives true information, or facts, about a topic. Display the **Interactive Read-Aloud Cards**.

Interactive Read-Aloud Cards

Read the title. Explain that when children go on a field trip, they leave school to see and learn about a new place.

Strategy: Visualize

Remind children that good readers visualize as they read. They make pictures in their minds to help them see, feel, and understand what is happening. *You can use information from the words and photographs to help you visualize.* Use the **Think Aloud Cloud** as you model visualizing.

Think Aloud I read that aquarium workers sometimes show how animals are fed. I pictured in my mind a big dolphin jumping out of the water to grab a fish. I picture the water splashing, and I hear the dolphin making loud, high sounds. This helps me understand what happens as I keep reading.

Continue reading "Field Trips," pausing to model the strategy. Afterwards, encourage children to share things they visualized while you read.

Make Connections

COLLABORATE

Guide partners to connect "Field Trips" with *Please Take Me for a Walk.* Discuss the places that were visited in each selection. Have children tell whether they visit any of these places during the week. *What kind of worker was in both selections?* (a mail carrier)

ELL

ENGLISH LANGUAGE LEARNERS

Reinforce Meaning As you read "Field Trips," make meaning clear by pointing to specific people, places, or objects in the photographs, demonstrating word meanings, paraphrasing text, and asking children questions. For example, on Card 3, point to a firefighter. Say: *This is a firefighter. This person works to stop fires.*

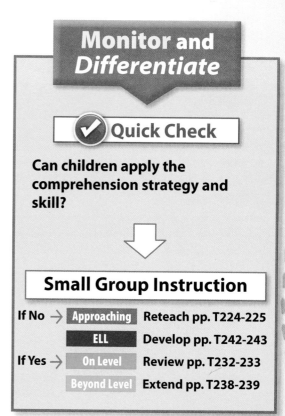

Monitor and *Differentiate*

✓ Quick Check

Can children apply the comprehension strategy and skill?

⬇

Small Group Instruction

If No → | Approaching | Reteach pp. T224–225
| ELL | Develop pp. T242–243
If Yes → | On Level | Review pp. T232–233
| Beyond Level | Extend pp. T238–239

Word Work

Quick Review
Build Fluency: Sound-Spellings: Show the following **Word-Building Cards:** *a, c, i, m, n, p, s, t.* Have children chorally say each sound. Repeat and vary the pace.

OBJECTIVES

CCSS Isolate and pronounce the initial, medial vowel, and final sounds in three-phoneme words. **RF.K.2d**

CCSS Demonstrate basic knowledge of one-to-one letter-sound correspondences by producing the primary or many of the most frequent sounds for each consonant. **RF.K.3a**

MINILESSON 5 Mins

Phonemic Awareness

Puppet

Phoneme Blending

❶ Model Use the puppet to demonstrate how to blend phonemes to make words. *The puppet is going to say sounds in a word: /k/ /a/ /p/. It can blend those sounds to make a word: /k/, /k/, /kaaap/, cap. When the puppet blends the sounds together, it makes the word cap. Listen as the puppet blends more sounds to make a word.* Model phoneme blending with the following:

/k/ /u/ /p/, cup   /k/ /ō/ /n/, cone   /k/ /a/ /n/, can

❷ Guided Practice/Practice *The puppet is going to say the sounds in a different word. Listen as it says each sound: /k/ /a/ /m/ /p/. Let's blend these sounds together and then say the word: /kaaamp/, camp.*

Tell children that the puppet is going to say the sounds in words. Have them repeat the sounds, then blend them to say the word.

/k/ /ā/ /m/, came	/k/ /ā/ /p/, cape	/k/ /u/ /p/, cup
/k/ /ō/ /t/, coat	/k/ /a/ /s/ /t/, cast	/k/ /a/ /t/, cat
/d/ /o/ /g/, dog	/h/ /a/ /z/, has	/l/ /i/ /p/, lip

 Review initial /k/. Play "Can Your Camel Do the Can-Can?" Have children clap when they hear initial /k/. Demonstrate as you sing with them.

Go Digital

Phonemic Awareness

Phonics

Handwriting

Phonics

MINILESSON
5 Mins

Word-Building Card

Review /k/c

❶ Model Display **Word-Building Card** c. *This is the letter* c. *The letter* c *can stand for /k/, the sound you hear at the beginning of* camel. *Say the sound with me. /k/, /k/, /k/. I will write the letter* c *because* camel *has /k/, /k/, /k/ at the beginning.*

❷ Guided Practice/Practice Tell children that you will say some words that begin with /k/ and some words that do not. Have children say /k/ and write the letter *c* on their **Response Boards** when they hear /k/ at the beginning of the word. Guide practice with the first word.

cat	fan	came	cannot	sun
door	car	exit	cow	cape

Blend Words with *c, p, n, t, s, m, a*

❶ Model Display Word-Building Cards *c, a, p*. *This is the letter* c. *It stands for /k/. This is the letter* a. *It stands for /a/. This is the letter* p. *It stands for /p/. Let's blend the three sounds together: /k/ /a/ /p/, /kaaap/. The word is* cap. *Continue with* can *and* cat.

❷ Guided Practice/Practice Write the following words. Have children read each word, blending the sounds. Guide practice with the first word.

cat   map   mat   can   cap

Write these sentences and prompt children to read the connected text, sounding out the decodable words. *I like the cap. I see the can. We like the cat.*

Corrective Feedback

Sound Error Model the sound that children missed, then have them repeat. For example, say: *My turn.* Tap under the letter *c* in the word *can* and ask: *Sound? What's the sound?* Return to the beginning of the word. Say: *Let's start over.* Blend the word again.

YOUR TURN PRACTICE BOOK p. 96

→ # Word Work

OBJECTIVES
CCSS Read common high-frequency words by sight. **RF.K.3c**

Sort objects by initial /k/c or /n/n

ACADEMIC LANGUAGE
sort

MINILESSON
5 Mins

Phonics

Photo Cards

Picture Sort

1 Model Remind children that the letter *c* can stand for /k/. Place **Word-Building Card** *c* on the left side of a pocket chart. *What is this letter?* (c) *What sound does this letter stand for?* (/k/) Repeat the routine for letter *n*.

Hold up the *Cow* **Photo Card**. *Here is the picture for* cow. *Cow has the /k/ sound at the beginning. I will place* cow *under the letter* c *because the letter* c *stands for /k/.*

Use the same routine for the letter *n* and the *Net* Photo Card.

2 Guided Practice/Practice Say the picture name of the following Photo Cards and have children sort the Photo Cards by initial /k/ and initial /n/: *car, comb, corn, cube, nest, night, nine, nut.* Have them say the sound in the beginning of the word and tell under which letter the Photo Card should be placed.

Photo Cards

Go Digital

Phonics

High-Frequency Word Routine

High-Frequency Words

go

1 Guided Practice Display the **High-Frequency Word Card** *go*. Review the word using the **Read/Spell/Write** routine.

2 Practice Point to the High-Frequency Word Card *go* and have children read it. Repeat with last week's word *and*.

Build Fluency

Word Automaticity Write the following sentences and have children chorally read aloud as you track the print. Repeat several times.

> We can go.
> Sam can go in.
> We can go to see Sam.
> I can see Nan go.

3 Read for Fluency Chorally read the Take-Home Book in the **Your Turn Practice Book**, pages 97–98, with children. Then have children reread the book to review high-frequency words and build fluency.

YOUR TURN PRACTICE BOOK pp. 97–98

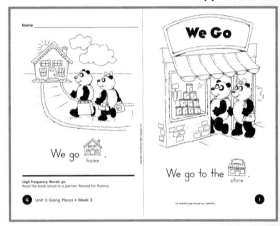

Monitor and *Differentiate*

✓ Quick Check

Can children blend phonemes to make words and sort words with /k/c?

Can children read and recognize the high-frequency word?

⬇

Small Group Instruction

If No →	**Approaching**	Reteach pp. T226–231
	ELL	Develop pp. T244–247
If Yes →	**On Level**	Review pp. T234–237
	Beyond Level	Extend pp. T240–241

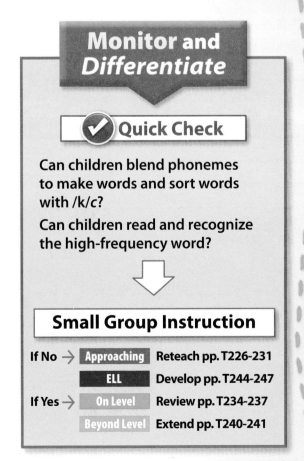

→ # Language Arts

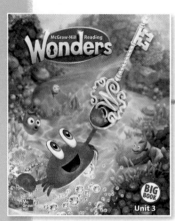

Reading/Writing Workshop Big Book

OBJECTIVES

 CCSS Use a combination of drawing, dictating, and writing to compose opinion pieces in which they tell a reader the topic or the name of the book they are writing about and state an opinion or preference about the topic or book (e.g., *My favorite book is . . .*). **W.K.1**

 CCSS Recognize and name end punctuation. **L.K.2b**

Write a sentence

ACADEMIC LANGUAGE

• opinion, sentence, period
• Cognates: opinión

 MINILESSON **10** Mins

Independent Writing

Writing Trait: Sentence Fluency

❶ Practice Tell children that today they will write sentences to tell about their favorite place and what they do when they are there. Write and read: *I like going to the fair. I like to go on rides at the fair.*

❷ Guided Practice Share the Readers to Writers page in the **Reading/Writing Workshop**. Read the model sentences aloud.

READING/WRITING WORKSHOP BIG BOOK, p. 58

Write an Opinion Sentence

Model Write: *I like to _____ at the library. One place I like to go to is the library. I read books when I go there. I will write a sentence telling about it.* Complete the sentence: *I read books at the library. I can draw a picture to show what I do at the library.* Draw a picture of a person reading a book at a library.

Prewrite

 Brainstorm Have children work with a partner. Ask them to choose their favorite place and tell the partner what they like to do there.

Go Digital

Present the Lesson

Writing

Grammar

Draft

Guide children in writing this sentence frame: *I* _____ *at the* _____. Help children write the name of their favorite place and what they like to do there. Have children draw a picture to illustrate their sentence.

Apply Writing Trait As children write their sentence frames, ask them to explain how they know that their sentences are complete.

Apply Grammar Tell children that the word *I* always begins with a capital letter. Make sure children remember to end their sentences with a period.

Grammar

Sentences

① Review Remind children that question sentences end with a question mark. Place a board eraser on a desk. Write and read: *Where is the eraser? What kind of sentence is this? How do you know? This is a question sentence. It starts with the word* what *and ends with a question mark.* Circle the capital letter and the question mark.

② Guided Practice/Practice Ask a volunteer to put a different item on the desk. Have children dictate a question about that item. For example: *Where is the book?* Write the question. Have children point to the question word at the beginning of the sentence and the question mark at the end.

Then have children dictate an answer to the question, such as *The book is on the desk.* Write the answer and have children point out the period at the end of the sentence.

Give each child a sentence strip that has a question sentence or an answer sentence written on it, but with no end punctuation, such as *Where is the ball; I catch the ball.*

Help children read the sentences. Ask children to write the correct end punctuation on the sentence strip.

Talk About It

Have partners work together to orally generate question and answer sentences. Encourage them to ask questions about what they did yesterday.

ENGLISH LANGUAGE LEARNERS

Oral Language Support children as they create questions and answers about items in the classroom. Provide sentence frames for children to complete: *Where is the* _____? *The* _____ *is on the* _____. Repeat correct answers slowly and clearly to the class.

Daily Wrap Up

- Review the Essential Question and encourage children to discuss, using the oral vocabulary words *routine* and *neighborhood*. *Where do you like to go to in your neighborhood?*

- Prompt children to review and discuss the skills they used today. Guide them to give examples of how they used each skill.

Materials

Reading/Writing Workshop Big Book
UNIT 3

Reading/Writing Workshop
UNIT 3

Literature Big Book
Please Take Me for a Walk

Interactive Read-Aloud Cards

Word-Building Cards

Visual Vocabulary Cards
go

High-Frequency Word Cards
a
and
can
go
I
see
the
to
we

go

Photo Cards
ball   cow
boy   farm
camel   giraffe
camera   girl
car   house
carrots   umbrella
city   wrist
comb

→ Extend the Concept

MINILESSON
10 Mins

Oral Language

OBJECTIVES

CCSS Use words and phrases acquired through conversations, reading and being read to, and responding to texts. **L.K.6**

CCSS Count, pronounce, blend, and segment syllables in spoken words. **RF.K.2b**

Develop oral vocabulary

ESSENTIAL QUESTION

Remind children that this week they have been talking and reading about the places we go during the week. Have them recite "To Market, To Market." *Why would you go to a market?* Then ask them to name the different workers that the dog saw in *Please Take Me for a Walk*.

Phonological Awareness

Count and Pronounce Syllables
Listen: mar-ket. *The word* market *has two parts.* Have children clap while saying the word. *Let's say and count the parts of another word from the rhyme:* again. Have children join as you say and clap: *a-gain.* Ask: *How many parts does* again *have?* (two) Repeat with the following words: *library* (3), *playground* (2), *store* (1), *neighborhood* (3).

Review Oral Vocabulary

Reread the Interactive Read Aloud Use the **Define/Example/Ask** routine to review the oral vocabulary words *routine, neighborhood, local, intelligent,* and *volunteer.* Then have children listen as you reread "Field Trips." Then ask the following questions:

→ *What might you see on a field trip to an aquarium?* (fish and plants; how the animals are fed)

→ *Why do people volunteer to fight fires?* (They want to keep the town safe.)

Go Digital

Visual Glossary

"Field Trips"

Category Words

Category Words: Sequence Words

1 Explain/Model Say the following and have children listen for the sequence words. Explain that sequence words can be used to tell the order in which things happen and can also be used to give directions. Ask children to listen to these directions and to raise their hands with you when they hear a sequence word.

Before *you begin, get everything you need.* First, *take two slices of bread.* Then, *spread peanut butter on one slice of bread.* Next, *spread jelly on the other slice of bread.* Last, *put the two slices of bread together with the peanut butter and jelly facing each other.*

2 Guided Practice Tell children to listen to the following and raise their hands when they hear a sequence word.

→ First, *buy or pick the blueberries.* Then, *bring them home.* Next, *put them in a strainer.* Last, *wash the blueberries.* After, *eat them and enjoy.*

→ First, *I went to the grocery store* before *the library.* Then, *I borrowed a book from the library.* Next, *I bought bread at the bakery.* Last, *I walked home.* After, *I took a nap.*

Have partners work together to tell each other about their day using sequence words.

For example: *First*, I woke up. *Then* I ate breakfast. *Next*, I got dressed. *Last*, I went to school.

Have children share with the class.

LET'S MOVE!

Divide the class into groups of four. Give each group a set of instructions: First, *go to the computer table. Clay, you go* before *Maria. Maria, you go* next. *Charlie, you go* after *Maria. Cara, you go* last. Continue until each group has had a chance to follow your instructions.

ELL

ENGLISH LANGUAGE LEARNERS

Demonstrate Understanding
Write or display the numbers 1, 2, and 3 separately in different corners of the classroom. Call on children one at a time and give them the following directions: First, *stand by the number 1.* Next, *stand by the number 2.* Last, *stand by the number 3.*

YOUR TURN PRACTICE BOOK p. 99

→ Listening Comprehension

CLOSE READING

Literature Big Book

OBJECTIVES

CCSS With prompting and support, describe the relationship between illustrations and the text in which they appear (e.g., what person, place, thing, or idea in the text an illustration depicts). **RI.K.7**

- Understand the characteristics of informational text
- Use the text feature map to gather information
- Apply the comprehension strategy: Visualize
- Make connections across texts

ACADEMIC LANGUAGE

- *map, picture key*
- Cognates: *mapa*

MINILESSON
10 Mins

Read "A Neighborhood"

Genre: Informational Text

Display "A Neighborhood" on pages 36–40 of the **Big Book** and read aloud the title. Explain to children that this informational text tells about real places in a neighborhood.

Set a Purpose for Reading

Read aloud the first two sentences on page 36. Tell children to listen as you continue reading the selection so they can learn about places in a neighborhood.

Strategy: Visualize

Remind children that good readers make pictures in their minds as they read. Point to the map on page 36. *Look at the pictures on the map of the different neighborhood places. How do these places look in your neighborhood?* (Answers will vary.)

Text Feature: Map

Explain Point to the map key on page 36. *We can look at a map key to find out what places are shown on the map. We look for the pictures of these places on the map to see where they are located in the neighborhood.*

Apply Point to the library on the map key and read aloud the label. Ask a volunteer to point to the library on the picture map. Repeat the procedure with the school, the park, and the fire station.

Go Digital

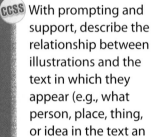

"Please Take Me for a Walk"

LITERATURE BIG BOOK   PAGES 36–37

TEXT FEATURE

Look at the map on page 36. What place is to the right of the fire station? (the library) *What place is to the left of the school?* (the park)

LITERATURE BIG BOOK   PAGES 38–39

HIGH-FREQUENCY WORDS

Have children identify and read the high-frequency word *go* on page 38.

LITERATURE BIG BOOK   PAGE 40

VISUALIZE

The photographs on the page show what children do in different places in a school. Picture in your head the things you do in these places. What do you see? (Possible answers: jumping rope at the playground; listening to a story in the library; painting in class)

ENGLISH LANGUAGE LEARNERS

Reinforce Meaning As you read aloud the text, make the meaning clear by pointing to details in the photographs and map. Ask children questions and elicit language.

Retell and Respond

Have children discuss the selection by asking the following questions:

→ *Where can you go to play with friends?* (to the playground)

→ *What can you do at the library?* (borrow books to read)

Make Connections

Have children recall the selections they have read this week.

→ *Who are two people the dog wanted to see on his walk?* (Possible answers: butcher, florist, baker, bookseller)

Write About It Write about one of the fun places you would like to visit from "Field Trips." Draw a picture.

CONNECT TO CONTENT

A Neighborhood Map Review with children the neighborhood places on the map. Have children draw a picture map of places in their neighborhood. Display the maps for children to compare the places they chose.

→ # Word Work

Quick Review
Build Fluency: Sound-Spellings: Show the following **Word-Building Cards:** *a, c, i, m, n, p, s, t.* Have children chorally say each sound. Repeat and vary the pace.

MINILESSON
5 Mins

Phonemic Awareness

OBJECTIVES

CCSS Distinguish between similarly spelled words by identifying the sounds of the letters that differ. **RF.K.3d**

CCSS Read common high-frequency words by sight. **RF.K.3c**

- Blend phonemes to make words
- Blend letter sounds to make words

Phoneme Identity

1 Model Display the **Photo Cards** for *camera, camel, car. I will say three picture names:* camera, camel, car. *Repeat these words with me. Which sound is the same in* camera, camel, *and* car? Camera, camel, *and* car *all begin with* /k/. *Repeat the activity with* carrots, cow, *and* comb. *Listen to these words:* carrots, cow, comb. *Say the words with me. Which sound is the same in* carrots, cow, *and* comb? Carrots, cow, *and* comb *all begin with the* /k/ *sound.*

Photo Card

2 Guided Practice/Practice *Listen to these words. Repeat the words and then say the sound that is the same.* Guide children with the first set of words.

cat, can, could	map, mad, my	cow, cup, come
inch, it, into	cape, coat, count	new, now, nickel
dog, dish, dip	fun, fox, fit	goat, get, gift

MINILESSON
5 Mins

Phonics

Blend Words with *c, p, t, n* and Short *a*

1 Guided Practice Display **Word-Building Cards** *c, a, n.* Point to the letter *c.* Say: *This is the letter* c. *The letter* c *stands for* /k/. *Say* /k/. *This is the letter* a. *The letter* a *stands for* /a/. *Let's blend the two sounds together:* /kaaa/. *This is the letter* n. *The letter* n *stands for* /n/. *Let's blend the three sounds:* /kaaannn/, can. *Let's change the* n *to* t. Use the same routine to blend the word *cat.*

2 Practice Write *cap, cat, can.* Have children blend and read the words. Ask children which letters are the same. (c, a) Ask children to tell which letters are different. (p, t, n) Discuss the sound each letter stands for and how it changes the word.

Go Digital

Phonemic Awareness

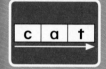
c a t

Phonics

Handwriting

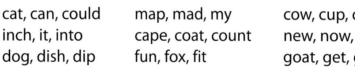

Visual Glossary

| the | is |
| you | do |

High-Frequency Word Routine

Dictation

Review Dictate these sounds for the children to spell. Have them repeat the sound and then write the appropriate letter. Repeat several times.

/k/   /n/   /i/   /t/   /p/   /s/   /a/   /m/

Dictate the following words for children to spell: *cap, can, cat.* Model for children how to segment each word to scaffold the spelling.

When I say the word cap, *I hear three sounds: /k/ /a/ /p/. I know the letter* c *stands for /k/, the letter* a *stands for /a/, and the letter* p *stands for /p/. I will write the letters* c, a, p *to spell the word* cap.

When children finish, write the letters and words for them to self-correct.

High-Frequency Words

MINILESSON 5 Mins

Visual Vocabulary Card

Practice Say the word *go* and have children write it. Display the **Visual Vocabulary Card** *go*. Use the Teacher Talk routine on the back of the card.

Build Fluency Build sentences in the pocket chart using the **High-Frequency Word Cards**, **Photo Cards**, and teacher-made punctuation cards. Have children chorally read the sentences as you track the print. Then have them identify the word *go*.

> *I can go to the farm.*
>
> *We can go to the house.*

Also online

| Go | to | the | | . |

High-Frequency Words Practice

Have partners orally create sentences using the word *go*.

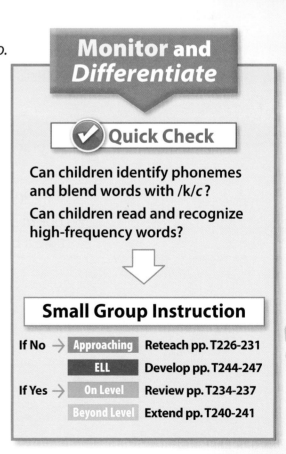

Monitor and *Differentiate*

✓ Quick Check

Can children identify phonemes and blend words with /k/c ?

Can children read and recognize high-frequency words?

⬇

Small Group Instruction

If No →	**Approaching**	Reteach pp. T226–231
	ELL	Develop pp. T244–247
If Yes →	**On Level**	Review pp. T234–237
	Beyond Level	Extend pp. T240–241

→ # Shared Read

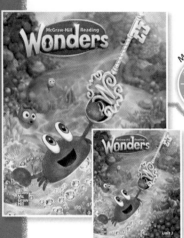

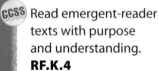

Reading/Writing Workshop Big Book and Reading/Writing Workshop

OBJECTIVES

CCSS Read common high-frequency words by sight. **RF.K.3c**

CCSS Read emergent-reader texts with purpose and understanding. **RF.K.4**

MINILESSON **10** Mins

Read "Can We Go?"

Model Skills and Strategies

Model Book Handling Demonstrate book handling. Display the front cover of the book. *This is the front cover of the book.* Display the back cover of the book. *This is the back cover of the book.* Model turning the pages of the book.

Model Concepts About Print Open the book, turn to page 51, and read the sentence. Then point to the period. *A period is a mark at the end of the sentence. It tells us to stop because the sentence has ended.* Invite volunteers to point to periods at the ends of other sentences in the **Big Book**.

Predict Read the title and ask children to repeat it. Encourage them to describe the photograph. *What do you think the selection will be about?*

Read Point out each rebus and discuss what it stands for. Then have children chorally read the story. Help children sound out the decodable words and say the sight words. Offer support as needed using the student **Reading/Writing Workshop**.

Ask the following:

→ *Look at page 51. What is this place called? What can you do there?* (a library; read books)

→ *Look at page 53. What can you buy here?* (Possible answers: different fruits and vegetables)

→ *Look at page 55. What is one way you can get from place to place?* (take a bus)

Go Digital

"Can We Go?"

"Can We Go?"

READING/WRITING WORKSHOP, pp. 50–55

Rereading

Have small groups use the **Reading/Writing Workshop** to reread "Can We Go?" Then review the skills and strategies using the *Phonics* and *Words to Know* pages that come before the selection.

→ As children reread the selection, have them name the places that were pictured in the story. Encourage them to think about what it would be like to visit each place.

→ Have children use page 43 to review the high-frequency word *go*.

→ Have children use page 42 to review that the letter *c* can stand for the sound /k/. Encourage them to identify and name each picture that begins with the sound /k/. Guide them to blend the sounds to read the words.

ENGLISH LANGUAGE LEARNERS

Reinforce Vocabulary Display the **High-Frequency Word Cards** *go, and, see, a, can*. Point to pictures posted in the classroom and groups of children as you use the high-frequency words in sentences such as the following: *I like to go to the beach. Do you like to go to the beach?* (Yes, we like to go to the beach.) *I can jump high. Can you jump high?* (Yes, we can jump high.) *I see a backpack. Can you see a backpack?* (Yes, we can see a backpack.) *This ball is green and round. What can you tell about the ball?* (The ball is green and round.)

→ # Language Arts

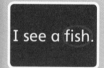
MINILESSON 10 Mins — Independent Writing

Write an Opinion Sentence

Revise

Distribute children's draft sentences with drawings from Day 3.

Apply Writing Trait Sentence Fluency Explain that as writers revise, they make sure their sentences are complete and make sense. Write this sentence: *I like to go to Grandma's house.* Read the sentence aloud. *I use the sentence to tell about a place I like to go to. Let's work together to tell what I like to do while at my grandma's house. I like to bake cookies at Grandma's house.* Then have children reread the sentences they wrote on Day 3 and check for the following:

→ Did I write about my favorite place to go?

→ Did I tell what I do there?

→ Did I write a complete sentence?

Apply Grammar Explain that writers use sentences to tell about something or to ask a question. Write the sentence *I like to bake cookies at Grandma's house* and read it aloud. *Does this sentence tell about somebody doing something or is it a question sentence? How do you know?* (It tells what someone does.) Have children add the period at the end of the sentence.

Peer Edit Have children work in pairs to do a peer edit, in which they read their partner's draft. Ask partners to check that the sentences are complete, begin with a capital letter, and end with a period. Have children make sure the picture they drew matches the sentence. Provide time for children to make revisions to their sentences.

Final Draft

After children have edited their own papers and finished their peer edits, have them write their final draft. Explain that they should try to write letters and punctuation marks carefully. Make sure children do not have too much or too little space between letters within a word. Conference with children to provide guidance as they work.

OBJECTIVES

CCSS Use a combination of drawing, dictating, and writing to compose opinion pieces in which they tell a reader the topic or the name of the book they are writing about and state an opinion or preference about the topic or book (e.g., *My favorite book is . . .*). **W.K.1**

CCSS Understand and use question words (interrogatives) (e.g., *who, what, where, when, why, how*). **L.K.1d**

CCSS Recognize and name end punctuation. **L.K.2b**

Revise sentences

ACADEMIC LANGUAGE
• *revise, sentence*
• Cognates:
  revisar

MINILESSON 10 Mins

Grammar

Sentences

1 **Review** Remind children that sentences that tell about someone or something doing an action ends with a period. Question sentences end with a question mark. Write and read aloud this sentence: *How old is your sister? What kind of sentence is this?* (question sentence) *How do you know?* (The sentence asks a question and starts with *How.*)

2 **Guided Practice** Display the **Photo Card** for *girl*. Read the label on the Photo Card. Tell children that you are going to work together to write a question sentence about the girl.

Ask children to think about what they would like to know about the girl. Write their ideas on the board. Have children use one of the ideas to write a question about the girl, such as *How old is the girl?* Write the question and read it aloud.

3 **Practice** Display the Photo Cards for *ball, boy,* and *giraffe*. Read aloud the label on each card as you track the print.

Have children work with a partner and choose one Photo Card. Have children work together to think of a question about the item on the Photo Card. Help children write the question on a sentence strip and add a question mark at the end of the sentence.

Talk About It

Have partners work together to orally generate questions about a place in their neighborhood. Encourage children to think about a place they would like to find out more about.

ENGLISH LANGUAGE LEARNERS

Picture Cards and Sentences
Provide questions that go with images on the Photo Cards for *umbrella* and *wrist*. Hold up a Photo Card as you ask a question, such as *What color is the umbrella?* or *Where is your wrist?*

Daily Wrap Up

- Review the Essential Question and encourage children to discuss it, using the oral vocabulary words.

- Prompt children to discuss the skills they practiced and learned today. Guide them to share examples of each skill.

Go Digital

www.connected.mcgraw-hill.com
RESOURCES
Research and Inquiry

→ ## Wrap Up the Week
Integrate Ideas

RESEARCH AND INQUIRY SOCIAL STUDIES

The Places We Go

Make a Class Book

 Tell children that today they will do a research project with a partner about the places they go during the week. Explain that they will create a page for a class book about the places people go. Review the steps in the research process below.

STEP 1 Choose a Topic

Guide partners to talk about the places they go. Encourage children to think about places in their school and community where they both have been, such as the library.

STEP 2 Find Resources

Talk about locating and using resources. Direct children to review the selections from the week. Guide children to use Internet resources. Have children use the Research Process Checklist online.

STEP 3 Keep Track of Ideas

Direct children to note their ideas by drawing pictures or writing words. They may also use pictures from the local paper or the Internet. Help children with the names of places if they need assistance.

Collaborative Conversations

Add New Ideas As children engage in discussions with a partner, in a small group, and with the whole class, encourage them to:

→ stay on topic.

→ connect their own ideas to things their partner or classmates have said.

→ connect their personal experiences or prior knowledge to the conversation.

We go to the library to read.

STEP 4 **Create the Project:**
Page for a Class Book

Explain the characteristics of the project:

→ **Information** A book can give information. This book will give information about the places the children go to during the week.

→ **Text** The pages of the book will include words that tell about each place. Provide this sentence frame:

We go to the _____ *to* _____ *.*

→ **Illustration** Tell children that the page will include a picture of their chosen place.

Explain that each pair will create one page of a book. Suggest that children use the computer to write sentences about their place. They can print out the page and place their picture above their words.

→ Guide children to complete the sentence frame.

→ Encourage children who can write more about their chosen place to do so.

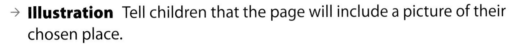

ENGLISH LANGUAGE LEARNERS
SCAFFOLD

Beginning	Intermediate	Advanced/Advanced High
Identify Details As partners work on their picture, help children identify and repeat the names of objects or details in the picture.	**Demonstrate Understanding** Guide children to include details and information about *how* they go to the place they show in their picture. When they share their work, have them answer this question: *How do you get to this place?*	**Describe** Prompt children to include details in their picture and to tell about how the place looks, smells, and "feels." For example, is it an exciting place or a quiet place?

Materials

Reading/Writing Workshop Big Book
UNIT 3

Literature Big Book *Please Take Me for a Walk*

a b c
Word-Building Cards

Visual Vocabulary Cards
go

go
High-Frequency Word Cards
a
and
can
go
I
like
see
the
to
we

Response Board

♪ **"Can Your Camel Do the Can-Can?"**

→ Integrate Ideas

TEXT CONNECTIONS

Connect to Essential Question

OBJECTIVES

 With prompting and support, compare and contrast the adventures and experiences of characters in familiar stories. **RL.K.9**

 Participate in collaborative conversations with diverse partners about kindergarten topics and texts with peers and adults in small and larger groups. **SL.K.1**

- Make connections among texts
- Make connections to the world

Text to Text

Remind children that all week they have been reading about places they go to during the week. Tell them that now they will connect the texts, or think about how the selections are alike and different. Model comparing *Please Take Me for a Walk* with another selection they read this week.

 Think Aloud In *Please Take Me for a Walk,* the dog went to many places. My own neighborhood has some of those places—such as a bakery and a bookstore and a schoolyard. In "Going by Cab," I also saw some places just like the ones in my neighborhood: a store and the park. Both the illustrations and the photos in the selections showed places that are familiar to me.

Guide children to compare the places characters and people go in the various selections from the week, including the Leveled Readers.

Text to Self

Ask children to tell about a place they read about that they have been to before. Then ask: *What place did we read about that you have never been to?*

Text to World

Talk about the places children go to, and how those places make up a community. Help children see that stores, schools, parks, police stations, and so on are parts of many communities.

TALK ABOUT READING

OBJECTIVES

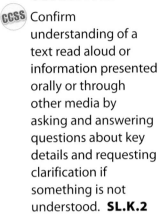 Confirm understanding of a text read aloud or information presented orally or through other media by asking and answering questions about key details and requesting clarification if something is not understood. **SL.K.2**

Becoming Readers

Talk with children about the genres, strategy, and skill they have learned about this week. Prompt them to discuss how this knowledge helps them to read and understand selections.

→ Point out that one genre children learned about this week is fiction. Have them recall some characteristics of fiction.

→ Talk about the strategy of visualizing. *Remember that you pictured in your mind some of the places the dog wanted to go to in* Please Take Me for a Walk. *What else did you picture in your mind this week to help you understand a selection?*

→ Remind children that they learned about character, setting, and events in stories. Review *Please Take Me for a Walk* and prompt children to identify the characters and setting and to recall events.

RESEARCH AND INQUIRY

OBJECTIVES

 Participate in shared research and writing projects (e.g., explore a number of books by a favorite author and express opinions about them). **W.K.7**

Wrap Up the Project

Guide partners to share their pictures about the places they go to and to point out details in their illustrations. Encourage children to use words and phrases they learned this week. Have children use the Presenting and Listening checklists online.

→ # Word Work

Phonemic Awareness

Phoneme Segmentation

OBJECTIVES

CCSS Isolate and pronounce the initial, medial vowel, and final sounds in three-phoneme words. **RF.K.2d**

CCSS Spell simple words phonetically, drawing on knowledge of sound-letter relationships. **L.K.2d**

CCSS Read common high-frequency words by sight. **RF.K.3c**

Blend words with the same beginning sounds

❶ **Model** Use the **Sound Boxes** on the reverse side of the **Response Board** and markers. *Listen as I say a word:* can. *Say the word with me. Say the sounds with me:* /k/ /a/ /n/. *There are three sounds in* can. *I'll place a marker in each box for each sound:* /k/ /a/ /n/. *Repeat with* an. *Point out that there are only two sounds.*

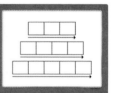

Sound Box

❷ **Guided Practice/Practice** Distribute Sound Boxes and markers. Say the word. Have children repeat the word and say each sound as they place a marker in a box. Then have them tell the number of sounds in the word. Guide practice with the first word.

cat /k/ /a/ /t/	no /n/ /ō/	coat /k/ /ō/ /t/
nut /n/ /u/ /t/	camp /k/ /a/ /m/ /p/	cold /k/ /ō/ /l/ /d/

Phonics

Read Words with Short *a* and *c, n, p, t*

❶ **Guided Practice** Display **Word-Building Cards** *c, a, p*. Point to the letter *c*. *The letter* c *stands for the sound* /k/. *Say* /k/. *The letter* a *stands for* /a/. *Say* /a/. *The letter* p *stands for* /p/. *Say* /p/. *Let's blend the sounds to make a word:* /kaaap/ cap. *Now let's replace the* c *with* n. Blend and read *nap* with children.

❷ **Practice** Write the words and sentences for children to read:

cat   can   cap

I can pat the cat.	I like the cap.
We can see the cat.	Tim and Sam can go.

Remove words from view before dictation.

♪ Review /k/c. Have children write *c* on their Response Boards. Play and sing "Can Your Camel Do the Can-Can"? Have children hold up their boards when they hear /k/. Demonstrate as you sing with children.

Go Digital

Phonemic Awareness

Phonics

Handwriting

High-Frequency Word Cards

Dictation

❶ Review Dictate the following sounds for children to spell. As you say each sound, have children repeat it and then write the letter on their **Response Boards** that stands for the sound.

/k/   /a/   /s/   /n/   /t/   /p/

❷ Dictate the following words for children to spell. Model for children how to use sound boxes to segment each word to scaffold the spelling. *I will say a word. You will repeat the word, then think about how many sounds are in the word. Use your sound boxes to count the sounds. Then write one letter for each sound you hear.*

tap   cap   sat   cat   pan   can

Then write the letters and words for children to self-correct.

High-Frequency Words

go

Visual Vocabulary Card

❶ Review Display **Visual Vocabulary Card** *go*. Have children **Read/Spell/Write** the word. Use the Partner Talk activity on the back of the card.

Distribute one of the following **High-Frequency Word Cards** to children: *go, I, and, like, to, can, the, we, a*. Tell children that you will say some sentences. Say: *When you hear the word that is on your card, stand and hold up your word card.*

Sam *and* Pam *can go* home.
I can go to the store.
We like to go to school.
Nat will *go* on *a* trip.
Will you *go* with me *to the* park?
I like to go fishing.

❷ Build Fluency: Word Automaticity Display High-Frequency Word Cards *go, a, and, like, to, can, the, see, we, to, I*. Point to each card, at random, and have children read the word as quickly as they can.

Monitor and *Differentiate*

✓ Quick Check

Can children segment words into sounds and read words with /k/c?

Can children read and recognize high-frequency words?

⬇

Small Group Instruction

If No →	**Approaching**	Reteach pp. T226-231
	ELL	Develop pp. T244-247
If Yes →	**On Level**	Review pp. T234-237
	Beyond Level	Extend pp. T240-241

$\rightarrow$ # Language Arts

Independent Writing

Writing an Opinion Sentence

Prepare

Tell children that they will present their finished sentences and drawings from Day 4 to the class. Hold up an example from Day 4 and read it aloud, tracking the print. *I read my sentence loudly so that everyone could hear me. I read my sentence clearly so that everyone could understand what I was saying. I described clearly what I drew in my picture.*

Present

Have children take turns standing up, reading their sentences aloud, and describing their drawings. Remind children to speak slowly and clearly. Encourage the rest of the class to listen carefully to the person speaking and to be respectful by raising a hand to ask a question.

Evaluate

Have children discuss their own presentations and evaluate their performances, using the presentation rubric. Use the teacher's rubric to evaluate children's writing.

Publish

After children have finished presenting, collect the sentences. Create a bulletin board display with the heading "Our Favorite Places." Display the sentences and drawings on the bulletin board. Have children use a meter stick or pointer to point to each sentence as the class reads it aloud. Have children add their writing to their Writer's Portfolio. Then have them look back at their previous writing and discuss how they have changed as writers throughout the year.

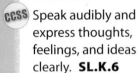

Go
Digital

Writing

I see a fish.

Grammar

OBJECTIVES

CCSS Speak audibly and express thoughts, feelings, and ideas clearly. **SL.K.6**

CCSS Understand and use question words (interrogatives) (e.g., *who, what, where, when, why, how*). **L.K.1d**

CCSS Capitalize the first word in a sentence and the pronoun *I*. **L.K.2a**

CCSS Recognize and name end punctuation. **L.K.2b**

Make a presentation

ACADEMIC LANGUAGE
• *present, sentence, publish*
• Cognates: *presente*

MINILESSON
5 Mins

Grammar

Sentences

1 **Review** Remind children that a sentence tells a complete thought. A sentence tells that someone or something is doing an action. A question sentence asks a question.

Write and read aloud: *What is your favorite sport? I like to play football. Which sentence is a question sentence? How do you know?* (It asks a question and starts with the word *What.*) *Which sentence tells about someone and an action they do? How do you know?* (It tells what the person likes to play.) Have children point out the capital letter at the beginning of each sentence and the end mark at the end of each sentence.

Have students dictate more answers to the question *What is your favorite sport?* Have children add the correct end punctuation to each sentence.

2 **Review/Practice** Write the following sentences and read them aloud:

> jenny is my friend
> who is David's friend

COLLABORATE

Have children work with a partner to capitalize the letter in each sentence. Have children add the correct end punctuation to each sentence and tell you whether the sentence is a question sentence or a sentence that tells something about somebody.

Wrap Up the Week

- Review blending words with initial /k/c.
- Remind children that a sentence is a group of words that tells a complete thought or asks a question.
- Use the **High-Frequency Word Cards** to review the **Words to Know**.
- Remind children that they can write sentences to share their opinions.

→ Approaching Level

Leveled Reader

OBJECTIVES

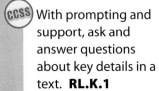 With prompting and support, ask and answer questions about key details in a text. **RL.K.1**

With prompting and support, retell familiar stories, including key details. **RL.K.2**

 With prompting and support, identify characters, settings, and major events in a story. **RL.K.3**

Read emergent-reader texts with purpose and understanding. **RF.K.4**

Leveled Reader:
We Can Go

Before Reading

Preview and Predict

Read the title and the names of the author and illustrator. Discuss the cover illustration. Ask: *What places do you think the boy will go? How will he get there?* Point to the title and the names of the author and illustrator on the title page. Discuss the illustration. Ask: *What is happening in this illustration?* Preview the illustrations and rebus pictures.

Review Genre: Fiction

Remind children that fiction stories have made-up characters and events. Ask: *Who is a character in this story?*

Model Concepts of Print

Model for children how to read each line of text from left to right and continue again on the next line from left to right. Ask children to use their fingers to show you the direction they would read the text on page 2.

Review High-Frequency Words

Point to the high-frequency word *go* on each page. Ask children to say the word aloud each time they point to it on a new page.

Essential Question

Set a purpose for reading: *Let's read the book to find out where the boy goes.* Remind children to use the rebuses and illustrations as they read to help them with unfamiliar words.

During Reading

Guided Comprehension

As children read, monitor and provide guidance by correcting blending and modeling the strategy and skill for children.

Go
Digital

Leveled Reader

Strategy: Visualize

Remind children that as they read they can make pictures in their mind of what is happening in the story. This can help them to understand what they are reading.

Skill: Character, Setting, Events

Remind children that stories have characters that can be animals or people. The events in the story are the things the characters do. Explain that the setting is the time and the place where the story happens.

Think Aloud I need to use more than the words of the story to help me understand who the characters are and what the setting is. On page 2, the illustration tells me that one of the characters is a boy. His mother is bringing him to his friend's house. The setting is outside the friend's house. I will use the illustrations as I read to help me figure out the characters, setting, and the events in the story.

Guide children to identify the characters, events, and setting as they read the story. Point out that the setting changes on each page.

After Reading

Respond to Reading

→ *Where does the boy go on his bike?* (to the park)

→ *How do the boy and his family go on the lake?* (in a boat)

→ *In what way are all the things that "can go" in the story alike?* (They can move people from place to place.)

Retell

Have children take turns retelling the story. Help them make a personal connection by asking: *Where are some places that you go during a week? How do you get there?*

Model Fluency

Read the story aloud, and pause after each page as children chorally repeat after you.

Apply Have children practice reading with a partner.

LITERACY ACTIVITIES

Have children complete the activities on the inside back cover of the reader.

Level Up

IF Children read *We Can Go* Approaching Level with fluency and correctly answer the Respond to Reading questions,

THEN Tell children that they will read another story about places people go during the week.

- Have children page through *Going By Cab* On Level as you preview where people go in cabs.

- Have children read the story, monitoring their comprehension and providing assistance as necessary.

→ # Approaching Level
Phonological Awareness

COUNT AND PRONOUNCE SYLLABLES

TIER 2

OBJECTIVES
Count, pronounce, blend, and segment syllables in spoken words. **RF.K.2b**

 I Do Reread the poem "To Market, To Market." Say *market*, separating it into syllables and clapping with each syllable.

 We Do Repeat the word *market*, clapping the syllables, and have children join in. *How many parts does* market *have?* (two) Have children say *market* with you, listening for two parts.

 You Do Repeat routine with *jiggety* (3), *again* (2), and *pig* (1). Ask children to clap and count the syllables in each word, guiding them as necessary.

PHONEME ISOLATION

TIER 2

OBJECTIVES
Isolate and pronounce the initial, medial vowel, and final sounds (phonemes) in three-phoneme words. **RF.K.2d**

 I Do Display the *Car* **Photo Card**. *This is a car. The first sound I hear in* car *is* /k/. Repeat the word, emphasizing the initial sound.

 We Do Display the *Cow* **Photo Card**. Name the photo and say the initial sound together: /k/. *What is the first sound in* cow? (/k/) Repeat with the *Comb* Photo Card.

 You Do Display the *Corn* Photo Card. Have children name it and say the initial sound. Repeat with the *Camera, Cowboy,* and *Cook* Photo Cards.

You may wish to review Phonological Awareness and Phonemic Awareness with **ELL** using this section.

PHONEME BLENDING

OBJECTIVES

 CCSS Isolate and pronounce the initial, medial vowel, and final sounds (phonemes) in three-phoneme words. **RF.K.2d**

 I Do *The puppet is going to say the sounds in a word. Listen: /k/ /ō/ /m/. The puppet can blend these sounds together: /kōōōmmm/, comb. Repeat with cow.*

 We Do *Now the puppet is going to say the sounds in another word. Say the sounds with the puppet: /k/ /uuu/ /t/. Let's blend the sounds together: /kuuut/, cut. Repeat with cap and core.*

 You Do Have children blend sounds to form words. Practice together: /k/ /ooo/ /t/, *cot.* Then have children practice blending the following sounds to say the words.

/k/ /a/ /t/ cat   /k/ /u/ /p/ cup   /k/ /ō/ /d/ code   /k/ /a/ /n/ can

PHONEME SEGMENTATION

OBJECTIVES

CCSS Demonstrate understanding of spoken words, syllables, and sounds (phonemes). **RF.K.2**

 I Do Use **Sound Boxes** and markers. *Listen as I say a word:* cat. *There are three sounds in the word* cat: /k/ /a/ /t/. *I'll place a marker in one box for each sound I hear in* cat: /k/ /a/ /t/. Repeat with the word *at.* Point out that there are only two sounds in *at.*

 We Do Distribute Sound Boxes and markers. *Let's listen for the number of sounds in more words. Listen as I say a word:* cone. *Say the word with me:* cone. *Say the sounds with me:* /k/ /ō/ /n/. *Let's place a marker in one box for each sound. There are three sounds in* cone. Repeat with *can.*

You Do Repeat the practice with the following words:

cap /k/ /a/ /p/   comb /k/ /ō/ /m/   cot /k/ /o/ /t/   cab /k/ /a/ /b/

ELL ENGLISH LANGUAGE LEARNERS

For the **ELLs** who need **phonics**, **decoding**, and **fluency** practice, use scaffolding methods as necessary to ensure students understand the meaning of the words. Refer to the Language Transfer Handbook for phonics elements that may not transfer in students' native languages.

→ Approaching Level

Phonics

SOUND-SPELLING REVIEW

TIER 2

OBJECTIVES

CCSS Demonstrate basic knowledge of one-to-one letter-sound correspondences by producing the primary or many of the most frequent sounds for each consonant. **RF.K.3a**

 I Do Display the **Word-Building Card** *n*. Say the letter name and the sound it stands for: *n, /n/*. Repeat for *m, a, s, p, t,* and *i*.

 We Do Display the *Nest* **Photo Card**. Together say the first letter in the word and the sound that it stands for. Repeat with the *Mop, Apple, Sock, Pen, Toe,* and *Ink* Photo Cards.

 You Do Display the *Ant, Mouse, Nose, Seal, Pizza, Table,* and *Insect* Photo Cards one at a time and have children say the first letter in the word and the sound that it stands for.

CONNECT c TO /k/

TIER 2

OBJECTIVES

 CCSS Demonstrate basic knowledge of one-to-one letter-sound correspondences by producing the primary or many of the most frequent sounds for each consonant. **RF.K.3a**

 I Do Display the *Camel* **Sound-Spelling Card**. *The letter* c *can stand for /k/ at the beginning of camel. What is this letter? What sound does it stand for? I will write* c *when I hear /k/ in these words:* cat, cobra, boy, can, lemon.

 We Do *The word* cat *begins with /k/. Let's write* c. Guide children to write *c* when they hear a word that begins with /k/: *canary, work, comb, cord, dinner*.

 You Do Say the following words and have children write the letter *c* if a word begins with /k/: *camera, horse, brother, can't, cab, fix, ice*.

RETEACH

OBJECTIVES

 CCSS Know and apply grade-level phonics and word analysis skills in decoding words. **RF.K.3**

 I Do Display **Reading/Writing Workshop**, p. 42. The letter *c* stands for the /k/ sound you hear at the beginning of *camel*. Say *camel*, emphasizing /k/.

 We Do Have children name each picture in the apple row. Repeat the name, emphasizing /k/. Repeat for the star row.

 You Do Guide children in reading the words in the tree row, offering assistance as needed.

BLEND WORDS WITH /k/c

OBJECTIVES

CCSS Demonstrate basic knowledge of one-to-one letter-sound correspondences by producing the primary or many of the most frequent sounds for each consonant. **RF.K.3a**

 I Do   Display **Word-Building Cards** c, a, and p. *This is the letter* c. *It stands for* /k/. *This is the letter* a. *It stands for* /a/. *This is the letter* p. *It stands for* /p/. *Listen as I blend all three sounds:* /kaaap/, cap. *The word is* cap. Repeat for *can*.

 We Do   Use Word-Building Cards c, a, t. *Together, let's blend the sounds and say the word:* /kaaat/, cat. Repeat with cap.

You Do   Distribute sets of Word-Building Cards with c, a, n, p, t. Write *cap, can, cat*. Have children form the words and then blend and read the words.

BUILD WORDS WITH c

OBJECTIVES

CCSS Add or substitute individual sounds (phonemes) in simple, one-syllable words to make new words. **RF.K.3e**

 I Do   Display Word-Building Cards c, a, and n. *These are letters* c, a, *and* n. *They stand for* /k/, /a/, *and* /n/. *I will blend* /k/, /a/, /n/ *together:* /kaaannn/, can. *The word is* can.

 We Do   Distribute sets of Word-Building Cards with c, a, n, p, and t. Show how to make the word *can* and have children do the same. Replace the letter *n* at the end of it with *p* and have children do the same. *Let's blend* /kaaap/, cap. *Now we have read a new word*, cap.

 You Do   Have children change the *p* in *cap* to *t* and read the new word, *cat*. Point out that by changing one letter we make a new word.

BUILD FLUENCY WITH PHONICS

Sound/Spelling Fluency

Display the following **Word-Building Cards**: *m, a, s, p, t, i, n,* and *c*. Have children chorally say each sound. Repeat and vary the pace.

Fluency in Connected Text

Write the following sentences. *Pat and Nat like the cat. Cam can see Pam and Tim*. Have children read the sentences and identify the words with /k/.

Approaching Level

High-Frequency Words

RETEACH WORDS

OBJECTIVES

 Read common high-frequency words by sight. **RF.K.3c**

 I Do Use **High-Frequency Word Card** *go* with the **Read/Spell/Write** routine to reteach the high-frequency word *go*.

 We Do Have children turn to p. 43 of **Reading/Writing Workshop** and discuss the first photo. Then read aloud the first sentence. Reread the sentence with children. Then distribute index cards with the word *go* written on them. Have children match their word cards with the word *go* in the sentence. Use the same routine for the other sentence on the page.

 You Do Write the sentence frame *We go to the ___ .* Have children copy the sentence frame on their **Response Boards**. Then have partners work together to read and orally complete the frame by talking about where they go to have fun. Reteach previously introduced high-frequency words using the **Read/Spell/Write** routine.

REREAD FOR FLUENCY

OBJECTIVES

 Read emergent-reader texts with purpose and understanding. **RF.K.4**

 I Do Turn to p. 44 and read aloud the title. *Let's read the title together.* Page through the book. Ask children what they see in each picture. Ask children to find the word *go* on pp. 45 and 48.

 We Do Then have children open their books and chorally read the story. Have children point to each word as they read. Provide corrective feedback as needed. After reading, ask children to recall who Cam and her brother like to visit.

 You Do Have children reread "We Go to See Nan" with a partner for fluency.

Repeat for "Can We Go?" on p. 50. Have children find the word *go* on p. 53.

Oral Vocabulary

REVIEW WORDS

OBJECTIVES

 Identify real-life connections between words and their use. **L.K.5c**

Develop oral vocabulary: *routine, neighborhood, local, intelligent, volunteer*

 Use the **Define/Example/Ask** routine to review words. Use the following definitions and provide examples:

routine	A **routine** is the way you do things all the time.
neighborhood	A **neighborhood** is a part of a town.
local	A **local** place is in your town or community.
intelligent	A person who is **intelligent** is very smart.
volunteer	When you **volunteer**, you offer to do a job without getting paid.

 Ask questions to build understanding. *What is your routine for lunch at school? Where is the library in your neighborhood? Why is it important to have a local fire station? How does going to school make you more intelligent? How could you volunteer to help your teacher at school?*

You Do Have children complete these sentence frames: *My routine before bed is ___. My neighborhood has many ___. Our local market sells ___. When we read books we become intelligent because ___. People should volunteer because ___.*

Comprehension

SELF-SELECTED READING

OBJECTIVES

 With prompting and support, ask and answer questions about key details in a text. **RL.K.1**

Apply the strategy and skill to reread the text.

Read Independently

Help children select an illustrated story for sustained silent reading. Remind them that they can use illustrations and story details to make pictures in their minds as they read. This will help them understand how places and characters look, as well as how the characters feel.

Read Purposefully

Before reading, have children identify a character they would like to learn more about. After reading, guide them in a discussion about the character. Have children explain what they learned about the character.

→ On Level

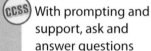

Leveled Reader

 OBJECTIVES

CCSS With prompting and support, ask and answer questions about key details in a text. **RL.K.1**

CCSS With prompting and support, retell familiar stories, including key details. **RL.K.2**

CCSS With prompting and support, identify characters, settings, and major events in a story. **RL.K.3**

CCSS Read emergent-reader texts with purpose and understanding. **RF.K.4**

Leveled Reader:
Going by Cab

Leveled Reader

Before Reading

Preview and Predict

Point to and read the title and the names of the author and illustrator. Make sure children understand that cabs drive people to places they need to go to. Ask: *Have you ever ridden in a cab? What was it like?* Have children tell what places they think the cabs will go to in this book. Preview the illustrations and help them confirm or change their predictions.

Review Genre: Fiction

Remind children that fiction stories are made-up and that they have characters, events, and a setting. Ask: *Where does this story take place?*

Model Concepts of Print

Point to the sentence on page 2. Say: *This is a sentence. It starts with a capital letter and ends with a period.* Point to each word and each space between words in the sentence.

Review High-Frequency Words

Point out the word *go* on page 2. Have children look through the rest of the book and point to the word *go* on each page. Ask children to use the word *go* in a sentence of their own.

Essential Question

Set a purpose for reading: *Let's read the book to find out what places the cabs go to during a week.*

During Reading

Guided Comprehension

As children whisper-read *Going by Cab*, monitor and provide guidance by correcting blending and modeling the strategy and skill.

Strategy: Visualize

Remind children that as they read they can make pictures in their mind of what is happening in the story. This can help them understand what they read.

Skill: Character, Setting, Events

Review with children that fiction stories have characters, events, and settings. Point out that the settings in this story are the places the cabs go.

Think Aloud On page 4, I can see a boy and his grandmother. They are in a zoo setting and they are getting out of the cab. These settings, events, and characters are important to the story. They help me understand what is happening.

Guide children to explain what is happening on other pages in the book. Ask children to talk about the characters, what they are doing, and where they are.

After Reading

Respond to Reading

→ *What kind of car is driving the characters around in this book?* (a cab)

→ *What are some places that people in the book go to ?* (Possible answers: store, beach, zoo, park, vet, movie, game)

→ *Who does the cab take to the beach?* (a family)

→ *What other places could a cab go?* (Possible answers: home, school)

Retell

Have children take turns retelling the story. Help them make personal connections by asking: *What places do you go to during the week? How do you get there? Have you ever taken a cab with an adult?*

Model Fluency

Read the sentences one at a time, emphasizing the last word, and have children chorally repeat each sentence.

Apply Have children practice reading with partners.

LITERACY ACTIVITIES

Have children complete the activities on the inside back cover of the reader.

Level Up

IF Children read *Going by Cab* `On Level` with fluency and correctly answer the Respond to Reading questions,

THEN Tell children that they will read another story about places people go during the week.

- Have children page through *Cal's Busy Week* `Beyond Level` as you point out the name of each day of the week.

- Have children read the story, monitoring their comprehension and providing assistance as necessary.

On Level

Phonemic Awareness

PHONEME ISOLATION

OBJECTIVES

 Isolate and pronounce the initial, medial vowel, and final sounds (phonemes) in three-phoneme words. **RF.K.2d**

I Do Display the *Car* **Photo Card**. *This is a* car. *The first sound is* /k/. *Say it with me. Say* car. *The first sound in* car *is* /k/. *Say the sound with me.*

We Do Say *cube* and have children repeat it. *What is the first sound in* cube? *Say the sound together.* Repeat with *cut, mouse, cave, pan,* and *ask.*

You Do Say *car, cold, new, insect, pick,* and *team* and have children tell the initial sound in each word.

PHONEME BLENDING

OBJECTIVES

 Isolate and pronounce the initial, medial vowel, and final sounds (phonemes) in three-phoneme words. **RF.K.2d**

I Do Place the *Car, Comb, Cook, Corn,* and *Cow* Photo Cards facedown. Choose a card. Do not show the card to children. *These are the sounds in the word* comb: /k/ /ō/ /m/. *I will blend the sounds:* /kōōōm/, comb. Show the picture.

We Do Choose another picture and say the sounds in the word. Together say and blend the sounds to say the word. Then show the picture.

You Do Continue choosing Photo Cards. Say the sounds and have children blend the sounds and say the word. Then show the Photo Card.

PHONEME SEGMENTATION

OBJECTIVES

 Isolate and pronounce the initial, medial vowel, and final sounds (phonemes) in three-phoneme words. **RF.K.2d**

I Do Use **Sound Boxes** and markers. *Listen to the sounds in the word* coat: /k/ /ō/ /t/. *There are three sounds in the word* coat. *Listen as I say the word again and place a marker in one box for each sound.*

We Do Distribute Sound Boxes and markers. *Listen as I say a word:* /k/ /a/ /b/, cab. *Let's place a marker in one box for each sound. There are three sounds in* cab.

You Do Repeat the practice with *cook, camp, cut,* and *cat.*

Phonics

REVIEW PHONICS

OBJECTIVES

 Demonstrate basic knowledge of one-to-one letter-sound correspondences by producing the primary or many of the most frequent sounds for each consonant. **RF.K.3a**

 I Do Display **Reading/Writing Workshop**, p. 42. Point to the *Camel* **Sound-Spelling Card**. *What letter stands for the /k/ sound you hear at the beginning of camel? The letter is* c.

 We Do Have children say the name of each picture. Then ask them to identify the words that begin with /k/.

 You Do Have children read each word. Repeat, asking them to touch their noses if they hear /k/ at the beginning of the word.

PICTURE SORT

OBJECTIVES

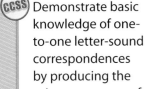 Demonstrate basic knowledge of one-to-one letter-sound correspondences by producing the primary or many of the most frequent sounds for each consonant. **RF.K.3a**

I Do Display **Word-Building Cards** *c* and *p* in a pocket chart. Then show the *Comb* **Photo Card**. Say: /k/ /ō/ /m/, *comb*. Tell children that the beginning sound is /k/. *The letter* c *stands for* /k/. *I will put* comb *under the letter* c. Show the *Pig* Photo Card. Say: /p/ /i/ /g/, *pig*. Tell children that the beginning sound is /p/. *The letter* p *stands for* /p/. *I will put the Photo Card for* pig *under the* p.

 We Do Show the *Cow* Photo Card and say *cow*. Have children repeat. Then have them tell the sound they hear at the beginning of *cow*. Ask them if they should place the photo under the letter *c* or *p*.

 You Do Continue using the *Camel, Camera, Car, Cook, Corn, Cube, Paint, Pea, Peach, Pear,* and *Pitcher* Photo Cards. Have children say the picture name and the initial sound. Then have them place the Photo Card under the *c* or *p*.

On Level

Phonics

BLEND WORDS WITH *c*

 OBJECTIVES
Demonstrate basic knowledge of one-to-one letter-sound correspondences by producing the primary or many of the most frequent sounds for each consonant. **RF.K.3a**

 I Do Use **Word-Building Cards** or write *c, a, n*. This is the letter c. It stands for /k/. Say it with me: /k/. This is the letter a. It stands for /a/. Say it with me: /aaa/. This is the letter n. It stands for /n/. Say it with me: /nnn/. I'll blend the sounds together to read the word: /kaaannn/, can.

 We Do Write *cap* and *cat*. Guide children to blend the words sound by sound to read each word.

 You Do Write the following words and have children blend the words sound by sound to read each word.

cap   can   cat

High-Frequency Words

REVIEW WORDS

OBJECTIVES
Read common high-frequency words by sight. **RF.K.3c**

 I Do Use **High-Frequency Word Card** *go* with the **Read/Spell/Write** routine to review *go*.

 We Do Have children turn to p. 43 of **Reading/Writing Workshop**. Discuss the photographs and read aloud the sentences. Point to the word *go* and have children read it. Then chorally read the sentences. Have children frame the word *go* in the sentences and read the word.

 You Do Say the word *go*. Ask children to close their eyes, picture the word, and write it as they see it. Have children self-correct.

Reteach previously introduced high-frequency words using the **Read/Spell/Write** routine.

Fluency Point to the **High-Frequency Word Cards** *I, can, the, we, see, a, like, the, to, and, go* in random order. Have children chorally read. Repeat at a faster pace.

High-Frequency Words

REREAD FOR FLUENCY

OBJECTIVES

 Read emergent-reader texts with purpose and understanding. **RF.K.4**

 I Do Point to the title "We Go to See Nan" on p. 44 of **Reading/Writing Workshop**. Tell children that when we see a period, we should pause because we have reached the end of a sentence. Work with children to read for accuracy and expression. Model reading a page: *When I read, "Cam and I go to see Nan." I read all the way to the end of the sentence before pausing. This makes my reading sound natural, as if I were talking.*

 We Do Reread p. 45. Then have children chorally read the page with you. Continue choral reading the remainder of the pages.

 You Do Have children read "We Go to See Nan." Provide time to listen as children read the pages. Comment on their accuracy and expression and provide corrective feedback by modeling proper fluency.

Use the same routine for "Can We Go?" on pp. 50–55.

Comprehension

SELF-SELECTED READING

OBJECTIVES

With prompting and support, ask and answer questions about key details in a text. **RL.K.1**

Apply the strategy and skill to reread the text.

Read Independently

Have children select an illustrated story for sustained silent reading. Remind them that illustrations can help them understand characters, setting, and events in a story. Tell them that key details can help them visualize story events, as well as understand the characters' feelings.

Read Purposefully

Before reading, ask children to identify a character or setting they would like to learn more about. Tell them that as they read, they should make pictures in their minds to help them understand the characters, setting, and events. After reading, invite children to explain what they learned about the character or setting. Invite them to explain how they visualized to guide their understanding of characters, setting, and events.

Beyond Level

Leveled Reader

OBJECTIVES

 With prompting and support, retell familiar stories, including key details. **RL.K.2**

 With prompting and support, identify characters, settings, and major events in a story. **RL.K.3**

With prompting and support, describe the relationship between the illustrations and the story in which they appear (e.g., what moment in a story an illustration depicts). **RL.K.7**

Leveled Reader:
Cal's Busy Week

Go Digital

Leveled Reader

Before Reading

Preview and Predict

Ask children to follow along in their books as you point to and read the title and the names of the author and illustrator. Preview the illustrations on the cover and the title page and ask children who they think Cal is. Ask: *What things do you do during the week after school? What things do you think Cal might do?* Preview the illustrations with children, asking them to tell what they see Cal doing in each one.

Review Genre: Fiction

Remind children that a fiction story is a made-up story. Point out that fiction stories have a beginning, middle, and end and that different things happen to the characters. Ask: *How can you tell this book is fiction?* (It has illustrations of the character doing different things.)

Essential Question

Remind children of the Essential Question: *What places do you go to during the week?* Have children set a purpose for reading: *Let's read to see the places that Cal goes to during the week.*

During Reading

Guided Comprehension

Have children whisper-read *Cal's Busy Week*. If they come across unfamiliar words, suggest that they blend sounds in the word, and use picture clues. Model the strategy and skill for children as needed.

Strategy: Visualize

Remind children that as they read, it helps to picture the story in their minds. Visualizing what they read can help them to better understand what is going on in the story.

Skill: Character, Setting, Events

Review with children that fiction stories have characters, events, and settings. Explain that the events are the things that happen to Cal. Point out that the settings in this story are the places that Cal goes during the week.

Think Aloud On page 3, the text tells me that Cal is getting a haircut. This is an event that is happening to Cal. The illustration shows me that the setting is a barber shop and the characters are Cal, the barber cutting Cal's hair, and Cal's mother. I will keep looking at the illustrations as I read so that I can see the characters and the places that Cal goes during his busy week.

Guide children to use the illustrations and text on pages 4, 5, and 6 to find out more about the other places that Cal goes. Have children point to evidence in the text or illustrations to support their statements.

After Reading

Respond to Reading

→ *How can we tell that the events in the story take place on different days of the week?* (Each page names a different day of the week; The book is called Cal's Busy Week.)

→ *What did Cal do on Wednesday?* (He went shoe shopping.)

→ *How do you think Cal feels on Friday?* (tired) *How do you know?* (He looks tired in the illustration, and he just wants to go to bed and read.)

Retell

Have children take turns retelling the story. Help them make a personal connection by asking: *Where are places you like to go? Where are places you have to go?*

Gifted and Talented

EVALUATING Have children think about places they go during the week. Challenge children to explain what this week has been like for them after school.

HAVE children make a drawing or comic strip to show what they did on each day so far this week and the places they have been to.

LITERACY ACTIVITIES

Have children complete the activities on the inside back cover of the reader.

Beyond Level

Phonics

 OBJECTIVES

Demonstrate basic knowledge of one-to-one letter-sound correspondences by producing the primary or many of the most frequent sounds for each consonant. **RF.K.3a**

 I Do Display **Reading/Writing Workshop**, p. 42. Point to the *Camel* **Sound-Spelling Card**. *What is the sound at the beginning of* camel? *What letter can stand for* /k/? *The letter is* c.

 We Do Have children say the name of each picture. Then ask children to share other words they know that begin with /k/.

 You Do Have partners read each word. Ask them to write the words on their **Response Boards**, underlining the letter in each word that stands for /k/.

High-Frequency Words

 OBJECTIVES

Read common high-frequency words by sight. **RF.K.3c**

 I Do Create **High-Frequency Word Cards** for *walk* and *there*. Introduce the words using the **Read/Spell/Write** routine.

 We Do Display the High-Frequency Word Cards for *I, can, the, we, see, a, like, to, and, go*. Have children help you complete the following sentence frames using the High-Frequency Word Cards: *We can walk to the ___. I can go and see ___ there.*

 You Do Have partners write sentences using the high-frequency words *walk* and *there* on their **Response Boards**. Have them read their sentences.

Fluency Have children turn to pp. 44–49 and 50–55 in **Reading/Writing Workshop** and reread the stories "We Go to See Nan" and "Can We Go?" for fluency.

Innovate Have children create a new page for "We Go to See Nan," writing about something else the characters might have seen at the bookstore. For "Can We Go?" have children complete *Can we go to the ___?* by adding a new place in the neighborhood to visit.

Vocabulary

ORAL VOCABULARY: SYNONYMS

OBJECTIVES

 With guidance and support from adults, explore word relationships and nuances in word meanings. **L.K.5**

Develop oral vocabulary: Synonyms

 I Do Review meanings of the oral vocabulary words *routine* and *neighborhood*. *A synonym is a word that means almost the same thing as another word.*

A synonym for routine *is* schedule. *Your schedule is the activities you do every day.* Our schedule has recess at 10:30 every day.

A synonym for neighborhood *is* community. *Your community is the place where you live.* Most people in my community live in apartment buildings.

 We Do Think of a few sentences together that include the new words *schedule* and *community*. Say the sentences aloud.

 You Do Have partners describe their daily schedules. They should tell about a place in the community where they go to meet their schedule. Ask them to share their schedules with the group.

Extend Have partners plan a weekly schedule of places to visit in the community. For example, Monday, the park; Tuesday, the library, etc. Have partners use the words *schedule* and *community* as they share with the group.

Comprehension

SELF-SELECTED READING

OBJECTIVES

 With prompting and support, ask and answer questions about key details in a text. **RL.K.1**

Apply the strategy and skill to reread the text.

Read Independently

Have children select an illustrated story for sustained silent reading. Remind them that visualizing as they read can help them understand more about the characters, setting, and events in a story.

Read Purposefully

Before reading, ask children to identify a character or setting they think is important, or will help them understand the story's plot. After reading, ask children to share the character or setting they identified, and explain how it helped them better understand and enjoy the story. Then have them point out an illustration or passage within the story and explain how they used it to visualize during reading.

 Independent Study Have children write a few sentences describing what they found surprising or interesting about neighborhoods. Ask them to create an illustration about what they wrote.

→ English Language Learners

Leveled Reader

OBJECTIVES

 With prompting and support, ask and answer questions about key details in a text. **RL.K.1**

 With prompting and support, retell familiar stories, including key details. **RL.K.2**

 Read emergent-reader texts with purpose and understanding. **RF.K.4**

Shared Read:
Going by Cab

Before Reading

Preview and Predict

Point to the cab on the cover of the book. Say: *This is a cab. People ride in cabs. Cabs take people to different places*. Point to the title and read it aloud. Walk children through each page, identifying the rebus pictures and talking about the illustrations. Model the language pattern. Ask: *Where do cabs go? Yes, cabs go to the store*. Make sure that children understand each of the rebus words in English.

Essential Question

Set a purpose for reading: *Let's read the book to find out where cabs go*. Model asking a question: *I see a cab and people on page 3. Where are they?* Point out the labels and ask children to look at the illustrations to help them understand the story.

During Reading

Interactive Question Response

Pages 2–3 Point to the illustration and label on page 2. *The cab is at the store. Who gets out of the cab?* Encourage children to use complete sentences as they respond: *The man and the woman get out of the cab.* If necessary, model the response and ask children to repeat. Read the sentence with children, pointing to each word. Point to the illustration on page 3. Say: *The cab is at the beach. Who gets out of the cab?* (The family gets out of the cab.) *Tell your partner what else you see in the picture. Let's read the sentence that tells where cabs go.*

Pages 4–5 Point to the illustration and label on page 4. *This is a zoo. Who gets out of the cab?* (The boy and the woman get out of the cab.) Make sure children understand what the English word *zoo* means. Point to the text on page 5. *Let's read the sentence that tells where cabs go*. Read the sentence. Then ask: *What can people do at a park?* (They can play, bike, and have fun.)

Go Digital

Leveled Reader

Pages 6–7 Point to the illustration and label on page 6. *This is a vet. A vet is a doctor for animals. A vet takes care of sick animals. Who gets out of the cab here?* (A girl and her mom get out of the cab.) *Why do you think the girl and her mom are at the vet?* (Their cat might be sick.) Read the sentence with children as they point to each word. Point to the van-sized cab in the illustration on page 7. Ask: *How is this cab different from the other cabs?* (It is bigger.) *Where are these people going in the cab?* (to the movies) *What does the label say?* (movie) *Let's read the sentence that tells where cabs go.*

Page 8 Point to the illustration. *Why are there so many cabs in this picture?* (They are at a big event, or big game.) *What kind of game is it?* (a baseball game) *Point to something in the picture that helps you know this. Talk to a partner about other kinds of games people might go to.*

After Reading

Respond to Reading

→ *What is a cab?* (It is a car that takes you where you want to go.)

→ *What are some places that people in the story go?* (Possible answers: store, beach, zoo, park, vet, movie, game)

→ *What are two places in the story where people will see animals?* (the zoo and the vet)

Retell

Let's retell the book together. What kind of car brings people places? (cab) *Where do people go in a cab?* (to the store, beach, zoo, park, vet, movie, and game)

Model Fluency

Read the sentences one at a time as you track the print. For the first few pages, ask children to chorally repeat each word after you. For the rest of the book, have them chorally repeat each complete sentence after you say it aloud.

Apply Have children read with partners. Encourage them to point to each rebus as they say the word it corresponds to.

Level Up

Level-up lessons available online.

IF Children read *Going by Cab* **ELL Level** with fluency and correctly answer the Respond to Reading questions,

THEN Tell children that they will read a more detailed version of the story.

• Have children page through *Going by Cab* **On Level** and conduct a picture walk to describe each picture in simple language.

• Have children read the story, monitoring their comprehension and providing assistance as necessary.

LITERACY ACTIVITIES

Have children complete the activities on the inside back cover of the reader.

→ English Language Learners
Vocabulary

PRETEACH ORAL VOCABULARY

OBJECTIVES

 Speak audibly and express thoughts, feelings, and ideas clearly. **SL.K.6**

LANGUAGE OBJECTIVE

Preview vocabulary

 I Do Display images from the **Visual Vocabulary Cards** and follow the routine to preteach the oral vocabulary words.

 We Do Display each image again and explain how it illustrates or demonstrates the word. Model using sentences to describe the image.

 You Do Display the words again and have partners talk about how the picture demonstrates the word.

Beginning	Intermediate	Advanced/High
Have partners repeat each word. Then have them pantomime a *routine* that they do to get ready for school.	Provide sentence starters for the words. Have partners repeat and complete each sentence.	Ask partners to make their own vocabulary cards that illustrate each word.

PRETEACH ELL VOCABULARY

OBJECTIVES

 Speak audibly and express thoughts, feelings, and ideas clearly. **SL.K.6**

LANGUAGE OBJECTIVE

Review ELL vocabulary

 I Do Display the **Visual Vocabulary Cards** one at a time to preteach the ELL vocabulary words *fare* and *traffic* and follow the routine. Say each word and have children repeat it. Define each word in English.

 We Do Display each image again and incorporate the word in a short discussion of the image. Model using sentences to describe the image.

 You Do Display the word *traffic* again and have children say the word. Provide children with opportunities to use the word *traffic* in a sentence by providing this sentence starter: *When there is a lot of traffic, _____.*

Beginning	Intermediate	Advanced/High
Have children draw a picture of traffic. Ask questions about the drawing to elicit language.	Have partners talk about the various types of transportation where they pay a fare.	Ask children to use each word in an oral sentence of their own. Provide guidance if necessary.

High-Frequency Words

REVIEW WORDS

OBJECTIVES

 Read common high-frequency words by sight (e.g., *the, of, to, you, she, my, is, are, do, does*). **RF.K.3c**

LANGUAGE OBJECTIVE

Review high-frequency words

 I Do Display the **High-Frequency Word Card** for *go*. Read the word. Use the **Read/Spell/Write** routine to teach the word. Have children write the word on their **Response Boards**.

 We Do Write the following sentence frame, which uses this week's high-frequency word: *I go to* _____. Track print as children read and complete the sentence.

 You Do Display a sentence that uses the high-frequency word *go*. Ask children to point to the word *go* and say it aloud. Then work with children to read the entire sentence aloud.

Beginning	Intermediate	Advanced/High
Ask children to say the word *go* aloud and write it on paper.	Ask children to use the word *go* in an oral sentence of their own.	Have children make and illustrate their own word card for the word *go*.

REVIEW CATEGORY WORDS

OBJECTIVES

Identify real-life connections between words and their use (e.g., note places at school that are colorful). **L.K.5c**

LANGUAGE OBJECTIVE

Use category words

 I Do Write and say the words that are related to this week's content words about sequence: *first, next, then,* and *last*. Define the words in English, and then in Spanish if appropriate, identifying any cognates.

 We Do Ask children to repeat the words after you. Use the words to describe simple things you did throughout the day.

 You Do Draw, use pictures, or use the **Big Book** *Please Take Me for a Walk* to show sequence. Ask children to point to the pictures in order and say *first, next,* or *last* as they point to each picture.

Beginning	Intermediate	Advanced/High
Have children follow instructions in sequence: First, stand up. Then raise your right hand, etc.	Have partners use the sequence words in a sentence or two to tell what they did today.	Have partners tell each other what they do after school using sequence words.

→ English Language Learners
Writing

SHARED WRITING

OBJECTIVES

CCSS Use a combination of drawing, dictating, and writing to narrate a single event or several loosely linked events, tell about the events in the order in which they occurred, and provide a reaction to what happened. **W.K.3**

LANGUAGE OBJECTIVE

Contribute to a shared writing project

I Do Review the words *school, library, park,* and *store* from the Whole Group Shared Writing project as ideas for places to go. Model writing a sentence that shares an opinion about a place: *I think the park is pretty.*

We Do Ask children to choose an idea from the list in the Whole Group Activity. Have them help write a shared sentence, such as *We think the store is fun.*

You Do Have children use the following sentence frame to write about what they think of the place they have chosen: *I think _____ is _____.* Have children write the sentence. Read it aloud and have children repeat after you.

Beginning	Intermediate	Advanced/High
Guide children to orally complete the sentence. Write the sentence. Then have children say their sentence.	Ask children to work in pairs to complete the sentence frame. Offer help when needed.	Ask children to write more than one answer to the sentence frame or to think of a sentence on their own.

WRITING TRAIT: SENTENCE FLUENCY

OBJECTIVES

CCSS Use a combination of drawing, dictating, and writing to narrate a single event or several loosely linked events, tell about the events in the order in which they occurred, and provide a reaction to what happened. **W.K.3**

LANGUAGE OBJECTIVE

Recognize complete sentences

I Do Tell children that they can get information and ideas for their writing from the books they read and the things they see in real life.

We Do Point to the **Big Book** selection *Please Take Me for a Walk.* Remind children that the story tells about the places someone goes. Ask: *Where did you walk today?* Point out places from the story that help give children ideas about places they go.

You Do Have children write a sentence about where they go. Provide them with the sentence frame *I go to the _____.*

Beginning	Intermediate	Advanced/High
Help children complete the sentence frame with places in their school, such as *hall, desk, gym,* or *playground.*	Ask partners to talk about places they have gone this week. Restate their responses in complete sentences.	Have children complete the sentence frame and describe specific places they have been and where they like to go.

Grammar

SENTENCES

OBJECTIVES

 Recognize and name end punctuation. **L.K.2b**

LANGUAGE OBJECTIVE

Recognize and form complete sentences

ELL Language Transfers

Languages such as Cantonese, Haitian Creole, Hmong, Korean, and Vietnamese do not use subject-verb agreement. As a result, these speakers may omit -s in the present tense, third-person agreement, such as in the sentence *He like pizza.* Guide children to understand subject-verb agreement when speaking in sentences.

I Do Review that a sentence begins with a capital letter and ends with a punctuation mark such as a period. Write: *we go to the park* Read the sentence. Ask children to help you correct the sentence by capitalizing the *w* in *we* and adding a period. Correct the sentence and reread it.

We Do Write the following sentences. Read each sentence. Then guide children to circle the first letter of the sentence and underline the end punctuation.

We go to the store!

I like to walk in the park.

Where do you like to go?

You Do Use the following sentence frame:

Some people go to _____.

Pair children and have them complete the sentence frame by providing details from this week's readings. Circulate, listen in, and take note of each child's language use and proficiency.

Beginning	Intermediate	Advanced/High
Guide children to use illustrations from this week's readings to think of ways they can complete the sentence frame.	Remind children of the features of a sentence. Have pairs check that each other's sentences start with a capital and end with a punctuation mark.	Ask children to complete the sentence frame with little or no help, and then read the sentence aloud.

PROGRESS MONITORING

Weekly Assessment

Use your Quick Check observations and the assessment opportunities identified below to evaluate children's progress in key skill areas.

✓ TESTED SKILLS CCSS	Quick Check Observations	Pencil and Paper Assessment
PHONEMIC AWARENESS/ PHONICS **k** /k/ (initial) **RF.K.3a**	Can children isolate /k/ and match it to the letter *Cc*?	Practice Book, pp. 93–94, 96
HIGH-FREQUENCY WORDS *go* **go** **RF.K.3c**	Can children recognize and read the high-frequency word?	Practice Book, pp. 97–98
COMPREHENSION Character, Setting, Events **RL.K.3**	As you read *Please Take Me for a Walk* with children, can they identify and discuss character, setting, and events in the text?	Practice Book, p. 95

Quick Check Rubric

Skills	1	2	3
PHONEMIC AWARENESS/ PHONICS	Does not connect the sound /k/ with the letters *Cc*.	Usually connects the sound /k/ with the letters *Cc*.	Consistently connects the sound /k/ with the letters *Cc*.
HIGH-FREQUENCY WORDS	Does not identify the high-frequency word.	Usually recognizes the high-frequency word with accuracy, but not speed.	Consistently recognizes the high-frequency word with speed and accuracy.
COMPREHENSION	Does not identify character, setting, or events in the text.	Usually identifies character, setting, and events in the text.	Consistently identifies character, setting, and events in the text.

Go Digital! www.connected.mcgraw-hill.com

Using Assessment Results

TESTED SKILLS	If ...	Then ...
PHONEMIC AWARENESS/ PHONICS	**Quick Check Rubric:** Children consistently score 1 or **Pencil and Paper Assessment:** Children get 0–2 items correct	... reteach tested Phonemic Awareness and Phonics skills using Lessons 16–17 in the *Tier 2 Phonemic Awareness Intervention Online PDFs* and Lesson 29 in the *Tier 2 Phonics/ Word Study Intervention Online PDFs.*
HIGH- FREQUENCY WORDS	**Quick Check Rubric:** Children consistently score 1	... reteach tested skills by using the High-Frequency Word Cards and asking children to read and spell the word. Point out any irregularities in sound-spellings.
COMPREHENSION	**Quick Check Rubric:** Children consistently score 1 or **Pencil and Paper Assessment:** Children get 0–1 items correct	... reteach tested skill using Lessons 22–30 in the *Tier 2 Comprehension Intervention Online PDFs.*

Response to Intervention

Use the children's assessment results to assist you in identifying children who will benefit from focused intervention.

Use the appropriate sections of the *Placement and Diagnostic Assessment* to designate children requiring:

 Tier 2 Intervention Online PDFs

 WonderWorks Intervention Program

→ Phonemic Awareness

→ Phonics

→ Vocabulary

→ Comprehension

→ Fluency

SUMMATIVE ASSESSMENT

Unit Assessment

✔ COMPREHENSION:	✔ HIGH-FREQUENCY WORDS:	✔ PHONEMIC AWARENESS:	✔ PHONICS:	✔ CATEGORY WORDS:
• Key Details **RL.K.1, RL.K.7** • Character, Setting, Events **RL.K.3**	• *to, and, go* **RF.K.3c**	• Phoneme Isolation **RF.K.2b, RF.K.2d** • Phoneme Blending **RF.K.2b** • Phoneme Identification **RF.K.2b**	• i (medial) **RF.K.3b** • n (initial/final) **RF.K.3a** • c (initial) **RF.K.3a**	• Sequence **L.K.5c** • Sound **L.K.5a**

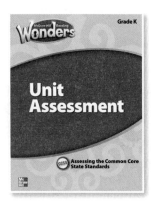

Use Multiple Assessments for Instructional Planning

To create instructional profiles for your children, look for patterns in the results from the following assessment.

Running Records

Use the instructional reading level determined by the Running Record calculations for regrouping decisions.

Using Assessment Results

TESTED SKILLS	If ...	Then ...
COMPREHENSION	Children answer 0–3 items correctly ...	... reteach tested skills using the *Tier 2 Comprehension Intervention Online PDFs*
HIGH-FREQUENCY WORDS	Children answer 0–1 items correctly ...	... reteach tested skills using Section 3 of the *Tier 2 Fluency Intervention Online PDFs*
PHONEMIC AWARENESS	Children answer 0–3 items correctly ...	... reteach tested skills using the *Tier 2 Phonemic Awareness Intervention Online PDFs*
PHONICS	Children answer 0–3 items correctly ...	... reteach tested skills using the *Tier 2 Phonics/Word Study Intervention Online PDFs* and Sections 2 and 4 of the *Tier 2 Fluency Intervention Online PDFs*
CATEGORY WORDS	Children answer 0–1 items correctly ...	... reteach tested skills using the *Tier 2 Vocabulary Intervention Online PDFs*

Response to Intervention

Use the appropriate sections of the *Placement and Diagnostic Assessment* and children's assessment results to designate children requiring:

 **Tier 2 Intervention Online PDFs**

3 **WonderWorks Intervention Program**

→ Phonological and Phonemic Awareness

→ Phonics

→ Vocabulary

→ Comprehension

→ Fluency

Program Information

For Additional Resources

Unit Bibliography

Word Lists

Literature and Informational Text Charts

Web Sites

Resources

www.connected.mcgraw-hill.com

 SCOPE & SEQUENCE

	K	1	2	3	4	5	6
READING PROCESS							
Concepts About Print/Print Awareness							
Recognize own name							
Understand directionality (top to bottom; tracking print from left to right; return sweep, page by page)	✔						
Locate printed word on page	✔						
Develop print awareness (concept of letter, word, sentence)	✔						
Identify separate sounds in a spoken sentence	✔						
Understand that written words are represented in written language by a specific sequence of letters	✔						
Distinguish between letters, words, and sentences	✔						
Identify and distinguish paragraphs							
Match print to speech (one-to-one correspondence)	✔						
Name uppercase and lowercase letters	✔						
Understand book handling (holding a book right-side-up, turning its pages)	✔						
Identify parts of a book (front cover, back cover, title page, table of contents); recognize that parts of a book contain information	✔						
Phonological Awareness							
Recognize and understand alliteration							
Segment sentences into correct number of words							
Identify, blend, segment syllables in words		✔					
Recognize and generate rhyming words	✔	✔					
Identify, blend, segment onset and rime	✔	✔					
Phonemic Awareness							
Count phonemes	✔	✔					
Isolate initial, medial, and final sounds	✔	✔					
Blend spoken phonemes to form words	✔	✔					
Segment spoken words into phonemes	✔	✔					
Distinguish between long- and short-vowel sounds	✔	✔					
Manipulate phonemes (addition, deletion, substitution)	✔	✔					
Phonics and Decoding /Word Recognition							
Understand the alphabetic principle	✔	✔					
Sound/letter correspondence	✔	✔	✔	✔			
Blend sounds into words, including VC, CVC, CVCe, CVVC words	✔	✔	✔	✔			
Blend common word families	✔	✔	✔	✔			

KEY	✔ = Assessed Skill
	Tinted panels show skills, strategies, and other teaching opportunities.

	K	1	2	3	4	5	6
Initial consonant blends		✔	✔	✔			
Final consonant blends		✔	✔	✔			
Initial and medial short vowels	✔	✔	✔	✔	✔	✔	✔
Decode one-syllable words in isolation and in context	✔	✔	✔	✔			
Decode multisyllabic words in isolation and in context using common syllabication patterns		✔	✔	✔	✔	✔	✔
Distinguish between similarly spelled words	✔	✔	✔	✔	✔	✔	✔
Monitor accuracy of decoding							
Identify and read common high-frequency words, irregularly spelled words	✔	✔	✔	✔			
Identify and read compound words, contractions		✔	✔	✔	✔	✔	✔
Use knowledge of spelling patterns to identify syllables		✔	✔	✔	✔	✔	✔
Regular and irregular plurals	✔	✔	✔	✔	✔	✔	✔
Long vowels (silent *e*, vowel teams)	✔	✔	✔	✔	✔	✔	✔
Vowel digraphs (variant vowels)		✔	✔	✔	✔	✔	✔
r-Controlled vowels		✔	✔	✔	✔	✔	✔
Hard/soft consonants		✔	✔	✔	✔	✔	✔
Initial consonant digraphs		✔	✔	✔	✔	✔	
Medial and final consonant digraphs		✔	✔	✔	✔	✔	
Vowel diphthongs		✔	✔	✔	✔	✔	✔
Identify and distinguish letter-sounds (initial, medial, final)	✔	✔	✔				
Silent letters		✔	✔	✔	✔	✔	✔
Schwa words				✔	✔	✔	✔
Inflectional endings		✔	✔	✔	✔	✔	✔
Triple-consonant clusters		✔	✔	✔	✔	✔	
Unfamiliar and complex word families				✔	✔	✔	✔
Structural Analysis/Word Analysis							
Common spelling patterns (word families)		✔	✔	✔	✔	✔	✔
Common syllable patterns		✔	✔	✔	✔	✔	✔
Inflectional endings		✔	✔	✔	✔	✔	✔
Contractions		✔	✔	✔	✔	✔	✔
Compound words		✔	✔	✔	✔	✔	✔
Prefixes and suffixes		✔	✔	✔	✔	✔	✔
Root or base words			✔	✔	✔	✔	✔
Comparatives and superlatives			✔	✔	✔	✔	✔
Greek and Latin roots			✔	✔	✔	✔	✔
Fluency							
Apply letter/sound knowledge to decode phonetically regular words accurately	✔	✔	✔	✔	✔	✔	✔
Recognize high-frequency and familiar words	✔	✔	✔	✔	✔	✔	✔
Read regularly on independent and instructional levels							
Read orally with fluency from familiar texts (choral, echo, partner, Reader's Theater)							
Use appropriate rate, expression, intonation, and phrasing		✔	✔	✔	✔	✔	✔
Read with automaticity (accurately and effortlessly)		✔	✔	✔	✔	✔	✔
Use punctuation cues in reading		✔	✔	✔	✔	✔	✔

	K	1	2	3	4	5	6
Adjust reading rate to purpose, text difficulty, form, and style							
Repeated readings							
Timed readings		✔	✔	✔	✔	✔	✔
Read with purpose and understanding		✔	✔	✔	✔	✔	✔
Read orally with accuracy		✔	✔	✔	✔	✔	✔
Use context to confirm or self-correct word recognition		✔	✔	✔	✔	✔	✔

READING LITERATURE

Comprehension Strategies and Skills

	K	1	2	3	4	5	6
Read literature from a broad range of genres, cultures, and periods		✔	✔	✔	✔	✔	✔
Access complex text		✔	✔	✔	✔	✔	✔
Build background							
Preview and predict							
Establish and adjust purpose for reading							
Evaluate citing evidence from the text							
Ask and answer questions	✔	✔	✔	✔	✔	✔	✔
Inferences and conclusions, citing evidence from the text	✔	✔	✔	✔	✔	✔	✔
Monitor/adjust comprehension including reread, reading rate, paraphrase							
Recount/Retell	✔	✔					
Summarize			✔	✔	✔	✔	✔
Story structure (beginning, middle, end)	✔	✔	✔	✔	✔	✔	✔
Visualize							
Make connections between and across texts		✔	✔	✔	✔	✔	✔
Point of view		✔	✔	✔	✔	✔	✔
Author's purpose							
Cause and effect	✔	✔	✔	✔	✔	✔	✔
Compare and contrast (including character, setting, plot, topics)	✔	✔	✔	✔	✔	✔	✔
Classify and categorize		✔	✔				
Literature vs informational text	✔	✔	✔				
Illustrations, using	✔	✔	✔	✔			
Theme, central message, moral, lesson		✔	✔	✔	✔	✔	✔
Predictions, making/confirming	✔	✔	✔				
Problem and solution (problem/resolution)		✔	✔	✔	✔	✔	✔
Sequence of events	✔	✔	✔	✔	✔	✔	✔

Literary Elements

	K	1	2	3	4	5	6
Character	✔	✔	✔	✔	✔	✔	✔
Plot development/Events	✔	✔	✔	✔	✔	✔	✔
Setting	✔	✔	✔	✔	✔	✔	✔
Stanza				✔	✔	✔	✔
Alliteration						✔	✔
Assonance						✔	✔
Dialogue							
Foreshadowing						✔	✔

KEY	✔ = Assessed Skill Tinted panels show skills, strategies, and other teaching opportunities.

	K	1	2	3	4	5	6
Flashback						✔	✔
Descriptive and figurative language		✔	✔	✔	✔	✔	✔
Imagery					✔	✔	✔
Meter					✔	✔	✔
Onomatopoeia							
Repetition		✔	✔	✔	✔	✔	✔
Rhyme/rhyme schemes		✔	✔	✔	✔	✔	✔
Rhythm		✔	✔				
Sensory language							
Symbolism							

Write About Reading/Literary Response Discussions

	K	1	2	3	4	5	6
Reflect and respond to text citing text evidence		✔	✔	✔	✔	✔	✔
Connect and compare text characters, events, ideas to self, to other texts, to world							
Connect literary texts to other curriculum areas							
Identify cultural and historical elements of text							
Evaluate author's techniques, craft							
Analytical writing							
Interpret text ideas through writing, discussion, media, research							
Book report or review							
Locate, use, explain information from text features		✔	✔	✔	✔	✔	✔
Organize information to show understanding of main idea through charts, mapping							
Cite text evidence	✔	✔	✔	✔	✔	✔	✔
Author's purpose/ Illustrator's purpose							

READING INFORMATIONAL TEXT

Comprehension Strategies and Skills

	K	1	2	3	4	5	6
Read informational text from a broad range of topics and cultures	✔	✔	✔	✔	✔	✔	✔
Access complex text		✔	✔	✔	✔	✔	✔
Build background							
Preview and predict	✔	✔	✔				
Establish and adjust purpose for reading							
Evaluate citing evidence from the text							
Ask and answer questions	✔	✔	✔	✔	✔	✔	✔
Inferences and conclusions, citing evidence from the text	✔	✔	✔	✔	✔	✔	✔
Monitor and adjust comprehension including reread, adjust reading rate, paraphrase							
Recount/Retell	✔	✔					
Summarize				✔	✔	✔	✔
Text structure	✔	✔	✔	✔	✔	✔	✔
Identify text features		✔	✔	✔	✔	✔	✔
Make connections between and across texts	✔	✔	✔	✔	✔	✔	✔
Author's point of view					✔	✔	✔	✔
Author's purpose		✔	✔				

	K	1	2	3	4	5	6
Cause and effect	✔	✔	✔	✔	✔	✔	✔
Compare and contrast	✔	✔	✔	✔	✔	✔	✔
Classify and categorize		✔	✔				
Illustrations and photographs, using	✔	✔	✔	✔			
Instructions/directions (written and oral)		✔	✔	✔	✔	✔	✔
Main idea and key details	✔	✔	✔	✔	✔	✔	✔
Persuasion, reasons and evidence to support points/persuasive techniques						✔	✔
Predictions, making/confirming	✔	✔					
Problem and solution		✔	✔	✔	✔	✔	✔
Sequence, chronological order of events, time order, steps in a process	✔	✔	✔	✔	✔	✔	✔

Writing About Reading/Expository Critique Discussions

	K	1	2	3	4	5	6
Reflect and respond to text citing text evidence		✔	✔	✔	✔	✔	✔
Connect and compare text characters, events, ideas to self, to other texts, to world							
Connect texts to other curriculum areas							
Identify cultural and historical elements of text							
Evaluate author's techniques, craft							
Analytical writing							
Read to understand and perform tasks and activities							
Interpret text ideas through writing, discussion, media, research							
Locate, use, explain information from text features		✔	✔	✔	✔	✔	✔
Organize information to show understanding of main idea through charts, mapping							
Cite text evidence		✔	✔	✔	✔	✔	✔
Author's purpose/Illustrator's purpose							

Text Features

	K	1	2	3	4	5	6
Recognize and identify text and organizational features of nonfiction texts		✔	✔	✔	✔	✔	✔
Captions and labels, headings, subheadings, endnotes, key words, bold print	✔	✔	✔	✔	✔	✔	✔
Graphics, including photographs, illustrations, maps, charts, diagrams, graphs, time lines	✔	✔	✔	✔	✔	✔	✔

Self-Selected Reading/Independent Reading

	K	1	2	3	4	5	6
Use personal criteria to choose own reading including favorite authors, genres, recommendations from others; set up a reading log							
Read a range of literature and informational text for tasks as well as for enjoyment; participate in literature circles							
Produce evidence of reading by retelling, summarizing, or paraphrasing							

Media Literacy

	K	1	2	3	4	5	6
Summarize the message or content from media message, citing text evidence							
Use graphics, illustrations to analyze and interpret information	✔	✔	✔	✔	✔	✔	✔
Identify structural features of popular media and use the features to obtain information, including digital sources				✔	✔	✔	✔
Identify reasons and evidence in visuals and media message							
Analyze media source: recognize effects of media in one's mood and emotion							

KEY	✔ = Assessed Skill Tinted panels show skills, strategies, and other teaching opportunities.

	K	1	2	3	4	5	6
Make informed judgments about print and digital media							
Critique persuasive techniques							

WRITING

Writing Process

	K	1	2	3	4	5	6
Plan/prewrite							
Draft							
Revise							
Edit/proofread							
Publish and present including using technology							
Teacher and peer feedback							

Writing Traits

	K	1	2	3	4	5	6
Conventions		✔	✔	✔	✔	✔	✔
Ideas		✔	✔	✔	✔	✔	✔
Organization		✔	✔	✔	✔	✔	✔
Sentence fluency		✔	✔	✔	✔	✔	✔
Voice		✔	✔	✔	✔	✔	✔
Word choice		✔	✔	✔	✔	✔	✔

Writer's Craft

	K	1	2	3	4	5	6
Good topic, focus on and develop topic, topic sentence			✔	✔	✔	✔	✔
Paragraph(s); sentence structure			✔	✔	✔	✔	✔
Main idea and supporting key details			✔	✔	✔	✔	✔
Unimportant details							
Relevant supporting evidence			✔	✔	✔	✔	✔
Strong opening, strong conclusion			✔	✔	✔	✔	✔
Beginning, middle, end; sequence		✔	✔	✔	✔	✔	✔
Precise words, strong words, vary words			✔	✔	✔	✔	✔
Figurative and sensory language, descriptive details							
Informal/formal language							
Mood/style/tone							
Dialogue				✔	✔	✔	✔
Transition words, transitions to multiple paragraphs				✔	✔	✔	✔
Select focus and organization			✔	✔	✔	✔	✔
Points and counterpoints/Opposing claims and counterarguments							
Use reference materials (online and print dictionary, thesaurus, encyclopedia)							

Writing Applications

	K	1	2	3	4	5	6
Writing about text	✔	✔	✔	✔	✔	✔	✔
Personal and fictional narrative (also biographical and autobiographical)	✔	✔	✔	✔	✔	✔	✔
Variety of expressive forms including poetry	✔	✔	✔	✔	✔	✔	✔
Informative/explanatory texts	✔	✔	✔	✔	✔	✔	✔
Description	✔	✔	✔	✔			
Procedural texts		✔	✔	✔	✔	✔	✔
Opinion pieces or arguments	✔	✔	✔	✔	✔	✔	✔

	K	1	2	3	4	5	6
Communications including technical documents		✔	✔	✔	✔	✔	✔
Research report	✔	✔	✔	✔	✔	✔	✔
Responses to literature/reflection				✔	✔	✔	✔
Analytical writing							
Letters		✔	✔	✔	✔	✔	✔
Write daily and over short and extended time frames; set up writer's notebooks							
Penmanship/Handwriting							
Write legibly in manuscript using correct formation, directionality, and spacing							
Write legibly in cursive using correct formation, directionality, and spacing							

SPEAKING AND LISTENING

Speaking

	K	1	2	3	4	5	6
Use repetition, rhyme, and rhythm in oral texts							
Participate in classroom activities and discussions							
Collaborative conversation with peers and adults in small and large groups using formal English when appropriate							
Differentiate between formal and informal English							
Follow agreed upon rules for discussion							
Build on others' talk in conversation, adding new ideas							
Come to discussion prepared							
Describe familiar people, places, and things and add drawings as desired							
Paraphrase portions of text read alone or information presented							
Apply comprehension strategies and skills in speaking activities							
Use literal and nonliteral meanings							
Ask and answer questions about text read aloud and about media							
Stay on topic when speaking							
Use language appropriate to situation, purpose, and audience							
Use nonverbal communications such as eye contact, gestures, and props							
Use verbal communication in effective ways and improve expression in conventional language							
Retell a story, presentation, or spoken message by summarizing							
Oral presentations: focus, organizational structure, audience, purpose							
Give and follow directions							
Consider audience when speaking or preparing a presentation							
Recite poems, rhymes, songs							
Use complete, coherent sentences							
Organize presentations							
Deliver presentations (narrative, summaries, research, persuasive); add visuals							
Speak audibly (accuracy, expression, volume, pitch, rate, phrasing, modulation, enunciation)							
Create audio recordings of poems, stories, presentations							

Listening

	K	1	2	3	4	5	6
Identify musical elements in language							
Determine the purpose for listening							

KEY	✔ = Assessed Skill Tinted panels show skills, strategies, and other teaching opportunities.

	K	1	2	3	4	5	6
Understand, follow, restate, and give oral directions							
Develop oral language and concepts							
Listen openly, responsively, attentively, and critically							
Listen to identify the points a speaker makes							
Listen responsively to oral presentations (determine main idea and key details)							
Ask and answer relevant questions (for clarification to follow-up on ideas)							
Identify reasons and evidence presented by speaker							
Recall and interpret speakers' verbal/nonverbal messages, purposes, perspectives							

LANGUAGE

Vocabulary Acquisition and Use

	K	1	2	3	4	5	6
Develop oral vocabulary and choose words for effect							
Use academic language		✔	✔	✔	✔	✔	✔
Identify persons, places, things, actions		✔	✔	✔			
Classify, sort, and categorize words	✔	✔	✔	✔	✔	✔	✔
Determine or clarify the meaning of unknown words; use word walls		✔	✔	✔	✔	✔	✔
Synonyms, antonyms, and opposites		✔	✔	✔	✔	✔	✔
Use context clues such as word, sentence, paragraph, definition, example, restatement, description, comparison, cause and effect		✔	✔	✔	✔	✔	✔
Use word identification strategies		✔	✔	✔	✔	✔	✔
Unfamiliar words		✔	✔	✔	✔	✔	✔
Multiple-meaning words		✔	✔	✔	✔	✔	✔
Use print and online dictionary to locate meanings, pronunciation, derivatives, parts of speech		✔	✔	✔	✔	✔	✔
Compound words		✔	✔	✔	✔	✔	✔
Words ending in -er and -est		✔	✔	✔	✔		
Root words (base words)		✔	✔	✔	✔	✔	✔
Prefixes and suffixes		✔	✔	✔	✔	✔	✔
Greek and Latin affixes and roots			✔	✔	✔	✔	✔
Denotation and connotation					✔	✔	✔
Word families		✔	✔	✔	✔	✔	✔
Inflectional endings		✔	✔	✔	✔	✔	✔
Use a print and online thesaurus			✔	✔	✔	✔	✔
Use print and online reference sources for word meaning (dictionary, glossaries)		✔	✔	✔	✔	✔	✔
Homographs				✔	✔	✔	✔
Homophones			✔	✔	✔	✔	✔
Contractions	✔	✔	✔				
Figurative language such as metaphors, similes, personification				✔	✔	✔	✔
Idioms, adages, proverbs, literal and nonliteral language			✔	✔	✔	✔	✔
Analogies							
Listen to, read, discuss familiar and unfamiliar challenging text							
Identify real-life connections between words and their use							
Use acquired words and phrases to convey precise ideas							
Use vocabulary to express spatial and temporal relationships							

	K	1	2	3	4	5	6
Identify shades of meaning in related words	✔	✔	✔	✔	✔	✔	✔
Word origins				✔	✔	✔	✔
Morphology				✔	✔	✔	✔
Knowledge of Language							
Choose words, phrases, and sentences for effect							
Choose punctuation effectively							
Formal and informal language for style and tone including dialects							
Conventions of Standard English/Grammar, Mechanics, and Usage							
Sentence concepts: statements, questions, exclamations, commands		✔	✔	✔	✔	✔	✔
Complete and incomplete sentences; sentence fragments; word order		✔	✔	✔	✔	✔	✔
Compound sentences, complex sentences				✔	✔	✔	✔
Combining sentences		✔	✔	✔	✔	✔	✔
Nouns including common, proper, singular, plural, irregular plurals, possessives, abstract, concrete, collective		✔	✔	✔	✔	✔	✔
Verbs including action, helping, linking, irregular		✔	✔	✔	✔	✔	✔
Verb tenses including past, present, future, perfect, and progressive		✔	✔	✔	✔	✔	✔
Pronouns including possessive, subject and object, pronoun-verb agreement, indefinite, intensive, reciprocal; correct unclear pronouns		✔	✔	✔	✔	✔	✔
Adjectives including articles, demonstrative, proper adjectives that compare		✔	✔	✔	✔	✔	✔
Adverbs including telling how, when, where, comparative, superlative, irregular		✔	✔	✔	✔	✔	✔
Subject, predicate; subject-verb agreement		✔	✔	✔	✔	✔	✔
Contractions		✔	✔	✔	✔	✔	✔
Conjunctions				✔	✔	✔	✔
Commas			✔	✔	✔	✔	✔
Colons, semicolons, dashes, hyphens						✔	✔
Question words							
Quotation marks			✔	✔	✔	✔	✔
Prepositions and prepositional phrases, appositives		✔	✔	✔	✔	✔	✔
Independent and dependent clauses						✔	✔
Italics/underlining for emphasis and titles							
Negatives, correcting double negatives					✔	✔	✔
Abbreviations			✔	✔	✔	✔	✔
Use correct capitalization in sentences, proper nouns, titles, abbreviations		✔	✔	✔	✔	✔	✔
Use correct punctuation		✔	✔	✔	✔	✔	✔
Antecedents				✔	✔	✔	✔
Homophones and words often confused			✔	✔	✔	✔	✔
Apostrophes				✔	✔	✔	✔
Spelling							
Write irregular, high-frequency words	✔	✔	✔				
ABC order	✔	✔					
Write letters	✔	✔					
Words with short vowels	✔	✔	✔	✔	✔	✔	✔
Words with long vowels	✔	✔	✔	✔	✔	✔	✔

KEY	✔ = Assessed Skill Tinted panels show skills, strategies, and other teaching opportunities.

	K	1	2	3	4	5	6
Words with digraphs, blends, consonant clusters, double consonants		✔	✔	✔	✔	✔	✔
Words with vowel digraphs and ambiguous vowels		✔	✔	✔	✔	✔	✔
Words with diphthongs		✔	✔	✔	✔	✔	✔
Words with r-controlled vowels		✔	✔	✔	✔	✔	✔
Use conventional spelling		✔	✔	✔	✔	✔	✔
Schwa words				✔	✔	✔	✔
Words with silent letters			✔	✔	✔	✔	✔
Words with hard and soft letters			✔	✔	✔	✔	✔
Inflectional endings including plural, past tense, drop final e and double consonant when adding -ed and -ing, changing y to i		✔	✔	✔	✔	✔	✔
Compound words		✔	✔	✔	✔	✔	✔
Homonyms/homophones			✔	✔	✔	✔	✔
Prefixes and suffixes		✔	✔	✔	✔	✔	✔
Root and base words (also spell derivatives)				✔	✔	✔	✔
Syllables: patterns, rules, accented, stressed, closed, open				✔	✔	✔	✔
Words with Greek and Latin roots						✔	✔
Words from mythology						✔	✔
Words with spelling patterns, word families		✔	✔	✔	✔	✔	✔

RESEARCH AND INQUIRY

Study Skills

	K	1	2	3	4	5	6
Directions: read, write, give, follow (includes technical directions)			✔	✔	✔	✔	✔
Evaluate directions for sequence and completeness				✔	✔	✔	✔
Use library/media center							
Use parts of a book to locate information							
Interpret information from graphic aids		✔	✔	✔	✔	✔	✔
Use graphic organizers to organize information and comprehend text		✔	✔	✔	✔	✔	✔
Use functional, everyday documents				✔	✔	✔	✔
Apply study strategies: skimming and scanning, note-taking, outlining							

Research Process

	K	1	2	3	4	5	6
Generate and revise topics and questions for research				✔	✔	✔	✔
Narrow focus of research, set research goals				✔	✔	✔	✔
Find and locate information using print and digital resources		✔	✔	✔	✔	✔	✔
Record information systematically (note-taking, outlining, using technology)				✔	✔	✔	✔
Develop a systematic research plan				✔	✔	✔	✔
Evaluate reliability, credibility, usefulness of sources and information						✔	✔
Use primary sources to obtain information					✔	✔	✔
Organize, synthesize, evaluate, and draw conclusions from information							
Cite and list sources of information (record basic bibliographic data)					✔	✔	✔
Demonstrate basic keyboarding skills							
Participate in and present shared research							

Technology

	K	1	2	3	4	5	6
Use computer, Internet, and other technology resources to access information							
Use text and organizational features of electronic resources such as search engines, keywords, e-mail, hyperlinks, URLs, Web pages, databases, graphics							
Use digital tools to present and publish in a variety of media formats							

INDEX

A

B

G

M

N

O

alliteration, **7**:T44

repetition, **7**:T177, **9**:T177

rhyme/rhyme scheme, **6**:T44, **7**:T177, **9**:T177

rhythm, **7**:T177, **9**:T177

writing, **5**:T18, T32, T40, T50, T58

See also **Genre; Songs, rhymes, chants.**

Pre-Decodable Reader, **1**:S14, S24, S38, S48, S62, S72

Predict, **1**:S14, S24, S38, S48, S62, S72, T30, T48, T60, T68, T78, T112, T130, T194, T242, **2**:T60, T68, T78, T112, T142, T150, T156, T160, T224, T232, T238, T242, **3**:T30, T48, T60, T112, T130, T142, T150, T156, T160, T194, T212, T224, T232, T238, T242, **4**:T30, T60, T68, T74, T78, T112, T142, T150, T156, T160, T194, T224, T232, T238, T242, **5**:T60, T68, T74, T78, T112, T142, T150, T156, T160, T194, T224, T232, T238, T242, **6**:T30, T78, T112, T142, T150, T156, T160, T194, T224, T232, T238, T242, **7**:T30, T74, T78, T112, T142, T150, T156, T160, T194, T224, T232, T238, T242, **8**:T60, T68, T112, T142, T150, T156, T160, T194, T224, T232, T238, T242, **9**:T30, T60, T68, T74, T78, T112, T142, T150, T156, T194, T224, T238, T242, **10**:T32, T62, T70, T76, T114, T144, T152, T158, T162, T196, T226, T234, T240, T244

See also **Comprehension strategies: predictions, make, confirm, revise; Setting purposes for reading.**

Prefixes. *See* **Vocabulary strategies.**

Presentation, oral. *See* **Oral presentations.**

Previewing literature. *See* **Predict; Setting purposes for reading.**

Print awareness

book handling, opening, parts, **1**:S14, S24, S31, S38, S55, S62, S72, T12, T30, T48, T60, T94, T112, T130, T142, T176, T194, **2**:T12, T30, T48, T94, T112, T130, T176, T194, T212, **3**:T12, T30, T48, T60, T112, T130, T194, T212, **4**:T30, T48, T112, T130, T194, T212, **5**:T212, **9**:T194

book parts, **1**:T176, **2**:T212, T224, **3**:T48, **4**:T130, **5**:T12, T94

print type, **1**:T106

sentences, **6**:T12, T24, T30, T48, T68, T107, T130, T142, T150, T176, T194, T212, T224, **7**:T30, T48, T60, T130

uppercase and lowercase letters, **4**:T189, T194, T212, T232, **5**:T12, **6**:T224, **8**:T30

word boundaries, **2**:T176, T232, **5**:T94, **7**:T194, T212, **9**:T188, T194, T224, T232, **10**:T114, T178, T196, T214, T226

See also **Concepts of/about print.**

Procedural text. *See* **Genre: reading informational text.**

Punctuation. *See* **Grammar: punctuation of sentences.**

Q

Questions, asking. *See* **Comprehension strategies: ask and answer questions.**

R

Read alouds. *See* **Big Book, read the literature; Big Book, reread the literature; Interactive Read Aloud; Shared read.**

Reading across texts, **1**:S27, S51, S75, T44–T45, T126–T127, T208–T209, **2**:T44–T45, T126–T127, **3**:T44–T45, T126–T127, T208–T209, **4**:T44–T45, T126–T127, T208–T209, **5**:T44–T45, T126–T127, T208–T209, **6**:T44–T45, T126–T127, T208–T209, **7**:T44–T45, T126–T127, T208–T209, **8**:T44–T45, T126–T127, T208–T209, **9**:T44–T45, T126–T127, T208–T209, **10**:T46–T47, T128–T129, T210–T211

See also **Text connections: text to text.**

Reading independently, **1**:T67, T73, T77, T149, T155, T159, T231, T237, T241, **2**:T67, T73, T77, T149, T155, T159, T231, T237, T241, **3**:T67, T73, T77, T149, T155, T159, T231, T237, T241, **4**:T67, T73, T77, T149, T155, T159, T231, T237, T241, **5**:T67, T73, T77, T149, T155, T159, T231, T237, T241, **6**:T67, T73, T77, T149, T155, T159, T231, T237, T241, **7**:T67, T73, T77, T149, T155, T159, T231, T237, T241, **8**:T67, T73, T77, T149, T155, T159, T231, T237, T241, **9**:T67, T73, T77, T149, T155, T159, T231, T237, T241, **10**:T69, T75, T79, T151, T157, T161, T233, T239, T243

Reading purposefully, **1**:T67, T73, T77, T149, T155, T159, T231, T237, T241, **2**:T67, T73, T77, T149, T155, T159, T231, T237, T241, **3**:T67, T73, T77, T149, T155, T159, T231, T237, T241, **4**:T67, T73, T77, T149, T155, T159, T231, T237, T241, **5**:T67, T73, T77, T149, T155, T159, T231, T237, T241, **6**:T67, T73, T77, T149, T155, T159, T231, T237, T241, **7**:T67, T73, T77, T149, T155, T159, T231, T237, T241, **8**:T67, T73, T77, T149, T155, T159, T231, T237, T241, **9**:T67, T73, T77, T149, T155, T159, T231, T237, T241, **10**:T69, T75, T79, T151, T157, T161, T233, T239, T243

Rereading, **1**:S14, S17, S24, S38, S41, S48, S62, S65, S72, T31, T42, T49, T113, T124, T131, T195, T206, T213, **2**:T31, T49, T113, T131, T195, T213, **3**:T31, T49, T113, T131, T195, T213, **4**:T31, T48, T113, T130, T195, T212, **5**:T31, T42, T48, T113, T130, T195, T212, **6**:T31, T48, T113, T130, T195, T212, **7**:T31, T48, T113, T130, T195, T212, **8**:T31, T48, T113, T124, T131, T195, T212, **9**:T31, T48, T113, T130, T195, T206, T212, **10**:T33, T44, T50, T115, T126, T132, T197, T208, T214

See also **Big Book, reread the literature; Comprehension strategies: reread.**

Research and inquiry, **1**:T52–T55, T134–T137, T216–T219, **2**:T52–T55, T134–T137, T216–T219, **3**:T52–T55, T134–T137, T216–T219, **4**:T52–T55, T134–T137, T216–T219, **5**:T52–T55, T134–T137, T216–T219, **6**:T52–T55, T134–T137, T216–T219, **7**:T52–T55, T134–T137, T216–T219, **8**:T52–T55, T134–T137, T216–T219, **9**:T52–T55, T134–T137, T216–T219, **10**:T54–T55, T136–T139, T218–T221

Research process, **1**:T52–T53, T134–T135, T216–T217, **2**:T52–T53, T134–T135, T216–T217, **3**:T52–T53, T134–T135, T216–T217, **4**:T52–T53, T134–T135, T216–T217, **5**:T52–T53, T134–T135, T216–T217, **6**:T52–T53, T134–T135, T216–T217, T248–T249, **7**:T52–T55, T134–T135, T216–T217, T249, **8**:T52–T53, T134–T135, T216–T217, T249, **9**:T52–T53, T134–T135, T216–T217, **10**:T54–T55, T136–T137, T218–T219

Respond to reading

informational text, **1**:S31, S55, S60, T45, T127, T160–T161, T177, T225, T233, T239, T243, **2**:T13, T45, T61,

Key **X** = Unit X

T

U

Uppercase/lowercase letters

  letter recognition, **1**:S8, S13, S18, S23, S28, S32, S37, S42, S47, S52, S56, S61, S66, S71, S76

  penmanship, **1**:T16, T98, T180, **2**:T16, T98, **3**:T16, T98, T180, **4**:T16, T98, **5**:T16, T98, **6**:T16, T98, **7**:T16, T98, **8**:T16, T98, **9**:T16

V

Visualize. *See* **Comprehension strategies.**

Visual Vocabulary Cards, **1**:T11, T20, T34, T80, T81, T93, T102, T116, T162, T184, T198, T244, **2**:T20, T34, T47, T80, T93, T102, T116, T129, T163, T175, T198, **3**:T11, T34, T124, T162, T184, T198, **4**:T11, T20, T34, T80, T93, T102, T116, T175, T184, T198, **5**:T11, T20, T34, T80, T93, T102, T116, T175, T184, T198, **6**:T11, T20, T34, T75, T93, T102, T116, T124, T162, T175, T184, T198, **7**:T11, T20, T34, T93, T102, T116, T124, T162, T175, T184, T198, T206, **8**:T20, T34, T47, T80, T102, T116, T124, T129, T163, T175, T184, T198, **9**:T20, T34, T80, T81, T93, T102, T116, T162, T175, T198, T244, **10**:T11, T20, T36, T49, T82, T95, T104, T164, T177, T186, T200, T246

Vocabulary acquisition

  category words

    action words, **3**:T21, T43, T81

    animal homes, **7**:T185, T207, T245

    animal parts, **7**:T21, T43, T81

    baby animals, **10**:T187, T209, T247

    colors, **2**:T21, T43, T81

    days of the week, **1**:S59, S69

    family words, **1**:T103, T125, T163

    farm animals, **9**:T103, T125, T163

    feeling words, **1**:T21, T43, T81

    food words, **4**:T103, T125, T163, **5**:T185, T207, T245, **9**:T185, T207, T245

    household furniture, **9**:T21, T43, T81

    job words, **4**:T21, T43, T81

    movement words, **2**:T185, T207, T245

    names, **1**:S11, S21

    numbers, **1**:S35, S45

    opposites, **8**:T185, T207, T245, **10**:T105, T127, T165

    ordinal numbers, **8**:T103, T125, T163

    pets, **7**:T103, T125, T163

    position words, **4**:T185, T207, T245

    question words, **6**:T185, T207, T245, **10**:T21, T45, T83

    seasons, **6**:T21, T43, T81

    sensory words, **1**:T185, T207, T245

    sequence words, **3**:T185, T207, T245

    shape words, **2**:T103, T125, T163

    size words, **5**:T21, T43, T81

    sound words, **3**:T103, T125, T163

    tree parts, **5**:T103, T125, T163

    vehicles, **8**:T21, T43, T81

    weather words, **6**:T103, T125, T163

  cognates, **1**:T81, T163, T245, **2**:T81, T163, T245, **3**:T81, T163, T245, **4**:T81, T163, T245, **5**:T81, T163, T245, **6**:T81, T163, T245, **7**:T81, T163, T245, **8**:T81, T163, T245, **9**:T81, T163, T245, **10**:T83, T165, T247

  computer-related, **6**:T248, **7**:T248, **8**:T248, **9**:T248, **10**:T248

  domain-specific, **1**:T103, T125, T163, **4**:T21, T43, T81, T103, T125, T163, **5**:T103, T125, T163, T185, T207, T245, **6**:T21, T43, T81, T103, T125, T163, **7**:T21, T43, T81, T103, T125, T163, T185, T207, T245, **8**:T21, T43, T81, **9**:T21, T43, T81, T103, T125, T163, T185, T207, T245, **10**:T187, T209, T247

function words and phrases. *See* **English Language Learners: high-frequency words, vocabulary.**

  general academic, **1**:S14, S62, S69, T38, T52, T134, T176, T216, **2**:T52, T122, T126, T132, T134, T140

  oral vocabulary, **1**:S16, S20, S26, S40, S44, S50, S64, S68, S74, T10–T11, T20, T34, T42, T67, T77, T80, T92–T93, T102, T116, T124, T149, T159, T162, T174–T175, T184, T198, T206, T231, T241, T244, **2**:T10–T11, T20, T34, T42, T67, T77, T80, T92–T93, T116, T124, T149, T159, T162, T174–T175, T184, T198, T206, T231, T241, T244, **3**:T10–T11, T20, T34, T42, T67, T77, T80, T92–T93, T102, T116, T124, T149, T159, T162, T174–T175, T184, T198, T206, T231, T241, T244, **4**:T10–T11, T20, T34, T42, T77, T80, T92–T93, T102, T116, T124, T149, T159, T162, T174–T175, T184, T198, T206, T231, T241, T244, **5**:T10–T11, T20, T34, T42, T77, T80, T92–T93, T102, T116, T124, T149, T159, T162, T174–T175, T184, T198, T206, T231, T241, T244, **6**:T10–T11, T20, T34, T42, T67, T77, T80, T92–T93, T102, T116, T124, T149, T159, T162, T174–T175, T184, T198, T206, T231, T241, T244, **7**:T10–T11, T20, T34, T42–T43, T67, T77, T80, T92–T93, T102, T116, T124, T149, T159, T162, T174–T175, T184, T198, T206, T231, T241, T244, **8**:T10–T11, T20–T21, T34, T42, T67, T77, T80, T92–T93, T102, T116, T124, T149, T159, T162, T174–T175, T184, T198, T206, T231, T241, T244, **9**:T10–T11, T20, T34, T42, T67, T77, T80, T92–T93, T102, T116, T124, T149, T159, T162, T174–T175, T184, T198, T206, T231, T241, T244, **10**:T10–T11, T20, T36, T44, T69, T79, T82, T94–T95, T104, T118, T126, T151, T161, T164, T176–T177, T186, T200, T208, T233, T243, T246

  selection words, **2**:T12, T94, **4**:T12, T176, **7**:T12, **9**:T176, **10**:T178

  story words, **1**:T12, T94, T176, **2**:T176, **3**:T12, T94, T176, **4**:T94, **5**:T12, T94, T176, **6**:T12, T94, T176, **7**:T94, T176, **8**:T12, T94, T176, **9**:T12, **10**:T12, T96

  word walls, **1**:S33. *See also* **High-frequency words.**

  word webs, **1**:S16, S20, S26, S40, S44, S64, S68, T182, **2**:T182, **6**:T100, **7**:T18, **8**:T18, **10**:T136

  See also **Academic language; High-frequency words; Oral language.**

Vocabulary strategies

  ask and answer questions, **10**:T97

  compound words, **7**:T21, T43

  context clues, sentence clues, **5**:T207, **6**:T21, T43, **8**:T43, **9**:T185, T207, **10**:T21, T45

  figurative language, **6**:T103, T125, **7**:T185, T207

  inflectional endings, **5**:T103, T125

  plurals, **5**:T21, T43

  shades of meaning, **6**:T103, T125, **7**:T185, T207

Key **X** = Unit X

Common Core State Standards Correlations

English Language Arts

College and Career Readiness Anchor Standards for READING

The K–5 standards on the following pages define what students should understand and be able to do by the end of each grade. They correspond to the College and Career Readiness (CCR) anchor standards below by number. The CCR and grade-specific standards are necessary complements—the former providing broad standards, the latter providing additional specificity—that together define the skills and understandings that all students must demonstrate.

Key Ideas and Details

1. Read closely to determine what the text says explicitly and to make logical inferences from it; cite specific textual evidence when writing or speaking to support conclusions drawn from the text.

2. Determine central ideas or themes of a text and analyze their development; summarize the key supporting details and ideas.

3. Analyze how and why individuals, events, and ideas develop and interact over the course of a text.

Craft and Structure

4. Interpret words and phrases as they are used in a text, including determining technical, connotative, and figurative meanings, and analyze how specific word choices shape meaning or tone.

5. Analyze the structure of texts, including how specific sentences, paragraphs, and larger portions of the text (e.g., a section, chapter, scene, or stanza) relate to each other and the whole.

6. Assess how point of view or purpose shapes the content and style of a text.

Integration of Knowledge and Ideas

7. Integrate and evaluate content presented in diverse media and formats, including visually and quantitatively, as well as in words.

8. Delineate and evaluate the argument and specific claims in a text, including the validity of the reasoning as well as the relevance and sufficiency of the evidence.

9. Analyze how two or more texts address similar themes or topics in order to build knowledge or to compare the approaches the authors take.

Range of Reading and Level of Text Complexity

10. Read and comprehend complex literary and informational texts independently and proficiently.

CCSS Common Core State Standards
English Language Arts
Grade K

Each standard is coded in the following manner:

Strand	Grade Level	Standard
RL	K	1

Reading Standards for Literature

Key Ideas and Details		McGraw-Hill Reading Wonders
RL.K.1	With prompting and support, ask and answer questions about key details in a text.	**READING WRITING WORKSHOP BIG BOOK:** Unit 1, Week 3: 44-49 **LEVELED READERS:** Unit 1, Week 2: *Hop!* (A), *We Hop!* (O), *We Can Move!* (B) **Unit 2, Week 3:** *We Like Bugs!* (A), *The Bugs Run* (O), *I See a Bug!* (B) **Unit 3, Week 1:** *We Run* (A), *Go, Nat!* (O) **Unit 3, Week 2:** *A Noisy Night* (B) **Unit 4, Week 2:** *My Neighbors* (A), *Neighborhood Party* (O), *Parade Day* (B) **Unit 5, Week 1:** *My Garden* (A), *My Garden Grows* (O) **Unit 6, Week 2:** *The Rain* (A), *Weather Is Fun* (O), *Kate and Tuck* (B) **Unit 7, Week 3:** *We Want Water* (A), *A New Home* (O), *Bird's New Home* (B) **Unit 8, Week 3:** *Going Up* (A), *In the Clouds* (O), *How Sun and Moon Found Home* (B) **Unit 9, Week 1:** *Let Me Help You* (A), *How Can Jane Help?* (O), *I Used to Help Too* (B) **Unit 10, Week 1:** *Animal Band* (A), *We Want Honey* (O), *A Good Idea* (B) **YOUR TURN PRACTICE BOOK:** 29, 37, 45, 234 **READING WORKSTATION ACTIVITY CARDS:** 1, 2 **TEACHER'S EDITION:** Unit 1: T23, T106, T189 Unit 2: T177, T186-191 Unit 3: T25, T104-109 Unit 4: T35, T104-108, T142-143, T150-151, T186-191, T224-225, T232-233, T238-239 Unit 5: T61, T69, T238-239 Unit 6: T23-26, T61, T69, T75, T105-108, T143, T151, T186-191 Unit 7: T45, T107 Unit 8: T61, T69, T75, T105-108, T186-191 Unit 9: T22-26, T61, T69, T75, T104-109 Unit 10: T106-110, T145, T153, T159 **LITERATURE BIG BOOKS:** Unit 1, Week 1: *What About Bear?* Unit 2 Week 3: *I Love Bugs!* Unit 3, Week 1: *How Do Dinosaurs Go to School?* Unit 4, Week 2: *What Can You Do With a Paleta?* Unit 6, Week 1: *Mama, Is It Summer Yet?* Unit 6, Week 2: *Rain* Unit 7, Week 2: *The Birthday Pet* Unit 7, Week 3: *Bear Snores On* Unit 8, Week 1: *When Daddy's Truck Picks Me Up* Unit 9, Week 2: *Hen Hears Gossip* Unit 10, Week 2: *All Kinds of Families* **INTERACTIVE READ-ALOUD CARDS:** SS: "The Ugly Duckling", "Tikki Tikki Tembo" Unit 1, Week 1: "The Lion and the Mouse" Unit 1, Week 2: "The Tortoise and the Hare" Unit 2, Week 1: "Timimoto" Unit 4, Week 1: "Little Juan and the Cooking Pot" Unit 4, Week 3: "A Bundle of Sticks"
RL.K.2	With prompting and support, retell familiar stories, including key details.	**LEVELED READERS:** Unit 1, Week 2: *Hop!* (A), *We Hop!* (O, ELL), *We Can Move!* (B) **Unit 2, Week 3:** *I See a Bug!* (B) **Unit 3, Week 1:** *We Run* (A), *Go, Nat!* (O, ELL), *The Birdhouse* (B) **Unit 3, Week 2:** *City Sounds* (A), *Farm Sounds* (O, ELL), *A Noisy Night* (B) **Unit 4, Week 3:** *We Clean!* (A), *Can You Fix It?* (O, ELL), *Helping Mom* (B) **Unit 5, Week 1:** *The Mystery Seeds* (B) **Unit 6, Week 1:** *It Is Hot!* (A), *Little Bear* (O, ELL), *Ant and Grasshopper* (B) **Unit 6, Week 2:** *The Rain* (A), *Weather Is Fun* (O, ELL), *Kate and Tuck* (B) **Unit 8, Week 1:** *I Go Places* (A), *Run, Quinn!* (O, ELL), *Going to Gran's House* (B) **Unit 10, Week 2:** *My Box* (A), *Let's Make a Band* (O, ELL), *Going Camping* (B) **READING WORKSTATION ACTIVITY CARDS:** 5 **YOUR TURN PRACTICE BOOK:** 157, 167 **TEACHER'S EDITION:** Unit 1: T27, T109, T191 Unit 2: T75, T109, T143, T151, T157, T161, T186-191 Unit 3: T27, T109, T191 Unit 4: T109, T143, T151, T157, T225, T233, T239 Unit 5: T61, T69, T75, T79, T109, T143, T151, T157, T191, T225, T233, T239 Unit 6: T27, T61, T109, T191, T225 Unit 7: T109, T143, T144, T151, T157, T158, T191, T225, T233, T239 Unit 8: T61, T69, T75, T143, T151, T157, T191, T225, T233, T239 Unit 9: T27, T61, T69, T75, T79, T109, T143, T151, T159, T225, T233, T239 Unit 10: T29, T63, T71, T77, T81, T111, T145, T153, T157, T191, T227, T235, T241 **LITERATURE BIG BOOKS:** Unit 1, Week 1: *What About Bear?* Unit 1, Week 2: *Pouch!* Unit 3, Week 1: *How Do Dinosaurs Go to School?* Unit 3, Week 2: *Clang! Clang! Beep! Beep! Listen to the City* Unit 6, Week 1: *Mama, Is It Summer Yet?* Unit 7, Week 2: *The Birthday Pet*

Reading Standards for Literature

Key Ideas and Details		*McGraw-Hill Reading Wonders*
RL.K.3	With prompting and support, identify characters, settings, and major events in a story.	**LEVELED READERS: Unit 1, Week 2:** *Hop!* (A), *We Hop!* (O), *We Can Move!* (B) **Unit 2, Week 3:** *The Bugs Run* (O) **Unit 3, Week 2:** *A Noisy Night* (B) **Unit 3, Week 3:** *We Can Go* (A), *Going by Cab* (O), *Cal's Busy Week* (B) **Unit 4, Week 2:** *My Neighbors* (A), *Neighborhood Party* (O) **Unit 5, Week 1:** *My Garden* (A), *My Garden Grows* (O), *The Mystery Seeds* (B) **Unit 7, Week 2:** *My Cats* (A), *Their Pets* (O), *Will's Pet* (B) **Unit 8, Week 1:** *I Go Places* (A), *Run, Quinn!* (O), *Going to Gran's House* (B) **Unit 9, Week 2:** *Mike Helps Out* (A), *Clive and His Friend* (O), *Farmer White's Best Friend* **YOUR TURN PRACTICE BOOK:** 129, 217, 234 **READING WORKSTATION ACTIVITY CARDS:** 3, 4, 6, 7, 10, 11 **TEACHER'S EDITION: Unit 1:** T75, T108 **Unit 3:** T156-157, T186-191, T224-225 **Unit 4:** T104-109, T142-143, T150-151 **Unit 5:** T22-27, T60-61, T68-69, T74-75 **Unit 7:** T104-109, T142-143, T150-151, T156-157, T186-191, T224-225, T232-233, T238-239 **Unit 8:** T22-27, T60-61, T68-69, T75, T186-191 **Unit 9:** T22-29, T60-61, T68-69, T74-75, T104-109, T117, T142-143, T150-151, T156-157 **Unit 10:** T22-29, T62-63, T70-71, T76-77 **LITERATURE BIG BOOKS: Unit 3, Week 3:** *Please Take Me for a Walk* **Unit 4, Week 2:** *What Can You Do with a Paleta?* **Unit 7, Week 3:** *Bear Snores On* **Unit 8, Week 3:** *Bringing Down the Moon* **Unit 9, Week 1:** *Peter's Chair* **Unit 9, Week 2:** *Hen Hears Gossip* **Unit 10, Week 1:** *What's the Big Idea, Molly?* **INTERACTIVE READ-ALOUD CARDS: SS:** "The Ugly Duckling", "Tikki Tikki Tembo" **Unit 1, Week 1:** "The Lion and the Mouse" **Unit 1, Week 2:** "The Tortoise and the Hare" **Unit 3, Week 1:** "The Boy Who Cried Wolf" **Unit 4, Week 1:** "Little Juan and the Cooking Pot" **Unit 7, Week 3:** "Anansi: An African Tale" **Unit 9, Week 2:** "The Little Red Hen"
Craft and Structure		*McGraw-Hill Reading Wonders*
RL.K.4	Ask and answer questions about unknown words in a text.	**READING/WRITING WORKSHOP BIG BOOK: Unit 1, Week 2:** 32-37 **Unit 2, Week 1:** 8-13 **LEVELED READERS: Unit 4, Week 3:** *We Clean!* (A), *Can You Fix It?* (O, ELL), *Helping Mom* (B) **TEACHER'S EDITION: Unit 1:** T74 **Unit 4:** T127, T225, T238 **Unit 6:** T23, T189 **Unit 7:** T45 **Unit 9:** T45 **Unit 10:** T47
RL.K.5	Recognize common types of texts (e.g., storybooks, poems).	**LEVELED READERS: Unit 6, Week 1:** *Ant and Grasshopper* (B) **TEACHER'S EDITION: Unit 1:** T25, T208, T218 **Unit 4:** T126-127 **Unit 5:** T44-45, T54-55 **Unit 6:** T44, T74-75, T186 **Unit 7:** T44-45 **Unit 9:** T44-45, T126 **Unit 10:** T46 **LITERATURE BIG BOOK: Unit 1, Week 3:** *I Smell Springtime* **Unit 5, Week 1:** *Tommy* **Unit 6, Week 1:** *Covers* **Unit 7, Week 1:** *Kitty Caught a Caterpillar* **INTERACTIVE READ-ALOUD CARDS: SS:** "The Ugly Duckling", "Tikki Tikki Tembo" **Unit 1, Week 1:** "The Lion and the Mouse" **Unit 1, Week 2:** "The Tortoise and the Hare" **Unit 2, Week 1:** "Timimoto" **Unit 3, Week 1:** "The Boy Who Cried Wolf" **Unit 4, Week 3:** "A Bundle of Sticks" **Unit 5, Week 2:** "The Pine Tree" **Unit 6, Week 2:** "The Frog and the Locust" **Unit 6, Week 3:** "Rainbow Crow" **Unit 7, Week 3:** "Anansi: An African Tale" **Unit 8, Week 1:** "The King of the Winds" **Unit 9, Week 2:** "The Little Red Hen" **Unit 9, Week 3:** "Spider Woman Teaches the Navajo" **Unit 10, Week 1:** "The Elves and the Shoemakers"
RL.K.6	With prompting and support, name the author and illustrator of a story and define the role of each in telling the story.	**LEVELED READERS: Unit 2, Week 3:** *I See a Bug!* (B) **Unit 4, Week 2:** *Parade Day* (B), *Helping Mom* (B) **Unit 10, Week 1:** *A Good Idea* (B) **TEACHER'S EDITION: Unit 1:** T68, T94, T142 **Unit 2:** T176, T238-239 **Unit 3:** T12, T94, T176 **Unit 4:** T94, T156, T238 **Unit 5:** T12 **Unit 6:** T12, T94, T176 **Unit 7:** T94, T176 **Unit 8:** T12, T176 **Unit 9:** T12, T94-95 **Unit 10:** T12, T76, T96 **LITERATURE BIG BOOKS: Unit 1, Week 1:** *What About Bear?* **Unit 1, Week 2:** *Pouch!* **Unit 2, Week 3:** *I Love Bugs!* **Unit 3, Week 1:** *How Do Dinosaurs Go to School?* **Unit 5, Week 1:** *My Garden* **Unit 6, Week 2:** *Rain* **Unit 7, Week 2:** *The Birthday Pet* **Unit 8, Week 1:** *When Daddy's Truck Picks Me Up* **Unit 9, Week 2:** *Hen Hears Gossip* **Unit 10, Week 1:** *What's the Big Idea, Molly?* **READING WORKSTATION ACTIVITY CARDS:** 6

Reading Standards for Literature

Integration of Knowledge and Ideas		*McGraw-Hill Reading Wonders*
RL.K.7	With prompting and support, describe the relationship between illustrations and the story in which they appear (e.g., what moment in a story an illustration depicts).	**LEVELED READERS: Unit 5, Week 1:** *My Garden Grows* (O, ELL) **Unit 5, Week 3:** *Farm Fresh Finn* (B) **Unit 6, Week 1:** *It Is Hot!* **Unit 7, Week 3:** *Bird's New Home* (B) **READING WORKSTATION ACTIVITY CARDS:** 1, 4, 11 **TEACHER'S EDITION: Unit 1:** T25, T60-61, T108 **Unit 3:** T24, T60-T61, T68-T69 **Unit 5:** T22-27, T68-69, T238-239 **Unit 6:** T25, T60-61, T105, T188 **Unit 7:** T238-239 **Unit 8:** T25 **Unit 10:** T46-47 **LITERATURE BIG BOOKS: Unit 1, Week 1:** *What About Bear?* **Unit 2, Week 3:** *I Love Bugs!* **Unit 3, Week 1:** *How Do Dinosaurs Go to School?* **Unit 3, Week 2:** *Clang! Clang! Beep! Beep! Listen to the City* **Unit 5, Week 1:** *My Garden* **Unit 6, Week 3:** *Waiting Out the Storm* **Unit 8, Week 1:** *When Daddy's Truck Picks Me Up* **Unit 9, Week 1:** *The Clean Up!* **Unit 10, Week 1:** *The Variety Show* **Unit 10, Week 2:** *All Kinds of Families!* **INTERACTIVE READ-ALOUD CARDS: Unit 5, Week 2:** "The Pine Tree" **Unit 6, Week 2:** "The Frog and the Locust" **Unit 6, Week 3:** "Rainbow Crow"
RL.K.8	(Not applicable to literature.)	
RL.K.9	With prompting and support, compare and contrast the adventures and experiences of characters in familiar stories.	**LEVELED READERS: Unit 3, Week 1:** *Go, Nat!* (O, ELL) **READING WORKSTATION ACTIVITY CARD:** 15 **TEACHER'S EDITION: Unit 1:** S27, S51, S75, T35, T117, T136 **Unit 2:** T218-219 **Unit 3:** T35, T136, T218-219 **Unit 4:** T136-137 **Unit 6:** T54, T117, T136, T199, T218 **Unit 7:** T136-137, T199, T218 **Unit 8:** T35, T54, T218 **Unit 9:** T54, T117, T136 **Unit 10:** T37, T56, T138 **LITERATURE BIG BOOKS: Unit 1, Week 1:** *What About Bear?* **Unit 1, Week 2:** *Pouch!, Baby Animals on the Move* **INTERACTIVE READ-ALOUD CARDS: Unit 1, Week 1:** "The Lion and the Mouse" **Unit 1, Week 2:** "The Tortoise and the Hare" **Unit 2, Week 1:** "Timimoto" **Unit 7, Week 3:** "Anansi: An African Tale" **Unit 8, Week 1:** "The King of the Winds" **Unit 10, Week 1:** "The Elves and the Shoemakers"

Range of Reading and Level of Text Complexity		*McGraw-Hill Reading Wonders*
RL.K.10	Actively engage in group reading activities with purpose and understanding.	**READING/WRITING WORKSHOP BIG BOOKS: SS:** 36-41 **Unit 1:** 34-39, 46-51 **Unit 2:** 10-15, 28-33, 34-39 **Unit 3:** 10-15, 28-33, 46-51 **Unit 4:** 24-31, 38-45 **Unit 5:** 10-17, 38-45 **Unit 6:** 24-31, 38-45 **Unit 7:** 24-31, 38-45 **Unit 8:** 10-17, 24-31 **Unit 9:** 10-17, 24-31 **Unit 10:** 10-17, 24-31 **LEVELED READERS: Unit 5, Week 1:** *My Garden Grows* (ELL) **Unit 7, Week 2:** *Their Pets* (ELL) **Unit 7, Week 3:** *A New Home* (ELL) **TEACHER'S EDITION: Unit 1:** S12, S14, S17, S22, S24, S31, S36, S38, S41, S46, S48, S55, S62, S65, S70, S72, T22-27, T126-127 **Unit 2:** T30-31, T112-113, T130-131 **Unit 3:** T34-35, T94-95, T212-213 **Unit 4:** T112-113, T126-127, T130-131, T194-195, T199 **Unit 5:** T12-13, T48-49, T78-79, T117, T194-195 **Unit 6:** T12-13, T22-26, T94-95, T104-108, T117, T130-131, T176-177, T186-190, T194-195, T199 **Unit 7:** T112-113, T130-131, T160-161, T176-177, T194-195, T199, T212-213, T242-243 **Unit 8:** T12-13, T30-31, T34-35, T48-49, T112-113, T176-177, T212-213 **Unit 9:** T12-13, T30-31, T48-49, T94-95, T112-113, T117, T199, T212-213 **Unit 10:** T12-13, T32-33, T50-51, T96-97, T132-133 **INTERACTIVE READ-ALOUD CARDS: SS:** "The Ugly Duckling", "Tikki Tikki Tembo" **Unit 1, Week 1:** "The Lion and the Mouse" **Unit 1, Week 2:** "The Tortoise and the Hare" **Unit 3, Week 2:** "The Turtle and the Flute" **Unit 4, Week 1:** "Little Juan and the Cooking Pot" **Unit 4, Week 3:** "A Bundle of Sticks" **Unit 5, Week 2:** "The Pine Tree" **Unit 6, Week 2:** "The Frog and the Locust" **Unit 6, Week 3:** "Rainbow Crow" **Unit 7, Week 3:** "Anansi: An African Tale" **Unit 8, Week 1:** "The King of the Winds" **Unit 9, Week 2:** "The Little Red Hen" **Unit 9, Week 3:** "Spider Woman Teaches the Navajo" **Unit 10, Week 1:** "The Elves and the Shoemakers"

Reading Standards for Informational Text

Key Ideas and Details		McGraw-Hill Reading Wonders
RI.K.1	With prompting and support, ask and answer questions about key details in a text.	**READING/WRITING WORKSHOP BIG BOOKS:** Unit 2: 14-19 **LEVELED READERS:** Unit 1, Week 3: *The Beach* (A), *At School* (O), *See It Grow!* (B) Unit 2, Week 1: *We Need Tools* (A), *A Trip* (O), *What Can You See?* (B) Unit 2, Week 2: *Shapes!* (A), *Play with Shapes!* (O), *Use a Shape!* (B) Unit 4, Week 1: *You Cook* (A), *On the Job* (O), *The Neighborhood* (B) Unit 8, Week 2: *See This!* (A), *Places to See* (O), *My Trip to Yellowstone* (B) Unit 9, Week 3: *Look Where It Is From* (A), *What's for Breakfast?* (O), *Nature at the Craft Fair* (B) Unit 10, Week 3: *Help Clean Up* (A), *Let's Save Earth* (O), *Babysitters for Seals* (B) **YOUR TURN PRACTICE BOOK:** 53, 147 **READING WORKSTATION ACTIVITY CARDS:** 1 **TEACHER'S EDITION:** Unit 1: T126-127, T186-191, T225, Unit 2: T22-27, T44-45, T107 Unit 4: T22-27, T44-45, T61, T69, T75, T186-191, T208-209 Unit 5: T104-109, T151, T157, T186-191, T209 Unit 6: T23-26, T105-108, T187-188 Unit 7: T23, T25 Unit 8: T104-109, T126-127, T142-143, T151, T157, T209 Unit 9: T35, T127, T186-191 Unit 10: T188-193, T227, T241 **LITERATURE BIG BOOKS:** Unit 1, Week 2: *Baby Animals on the Move* Unit 1, Week 3: *Senses at the Seashore* Unit 2, Week 1: *The Handiest Things in the World, Discover with Tools* Unit 4, Week 1: *Whose Shoes? "A Shoe for Every Job"* Unit 4, Week 3: *Roadwork* Unit 5, Week 2: *A Grand Old Tree* Unit 5, Week 3: *An Orange in January* Unit 7, Week 1: *ZooBorns!* Unit 9, Week 3: *Bread Comes to Life* Unit 10, Week 3: *Panda Kindergarten* **INTERACTIVE READ-ALOUD CARDS:** SS: "Kindergarteners Can!" Unit 1, Week 3: "A Feast of the Senses" Unit 2, Week 3: "From Caterpillar to Butterfly" Unit 4, Week 2: "Cultural Festivals" Unit 9, Week 1: "Helping Out at Home" Unit 10, Week 2: "The Perfect Color"
RI.K.2	With prompting and support, identify the main topic and retell key details of a text.	**LEVELED READERS:** Unit 1, Week 3: *The Beach* (A), *At School* (O, ELL), *See It Grow!* (B) Unit 2, Week 1: *We Need Tools* (A), *A Trip* (O, ELL), *What Can You See?* (B) Unit 5, Week 2: *The Tree* (A), *Many Trees* (O, ELL), *Our Apple Tree* (B) Unit 5, Week 3: *The Farmers' Market* (A), *Let's Make a Salad!* (O, ELL) Unit 9, Week 3: *Look Where It Is From* (A) **READING WORKSTATION ACTIVITY CARDS:** 5 **TEACHER'S EDITION:** Unit 4: T191 Unit 5: T104-109, T126-127, T142-143, T150-151, T156-157, T186-T190, T208-209, T224-225 Unit 8: T104-109, T127, T160-161, T248-249 Unit 9: T127, T186-191, T224-225, T232-233, T248-249 Unit 10: T188-193, T211, T226-227, T240-241, T250-251 **LITERATURE BIG BOOKS:** Unit 1, Week 3: *Senses on the Seashore* Unit 5, Week 2: *A Grand Old Tree*, "From a Seed to a Tree" Unit 5, Week 3: *An Orange in January* Unit 8, Week 2: *Ana Goes to Washington, D.C.* Unit 9, Week 3: *Bread Comes to Life* Unit 10, Week 3: *Panda Kindergarten* **INTERACTIVE READ-ALOUD CARDS:** Unit 1, Week 3: "A Feast of the Senses" Unit 2, Week 3: "From Caterpillar to Butterfly" Unit 4, Week 2: "Cultural Festivals" Unit 9, Week 1: "Helping Out at Home" Unit 10, Week 2: "The Perfect Color"
RI.K.3	With prompting and support, describe the connection between two individuals, events, ideas, or pieces of information in a text.	**LEVELED READERS:** Unit 7: *Two Cubs* (A), *Animal Bodies* (O, ELL), *Two Kinds of Bears* (B); Unit 9: *Look Where It is From* (A), *What's for Breakfast?* (O, ELL) **READING WORKSTATION ACTIVITY CARDS:** 8, 9 **TEACHER'S EDITION:** Unit 6: T24, T25, T106 Unit 7: T22-26, T60-61, T68-69, T74-75, T208-209 Unit 8: T44-45, T95 **LITERATURE BIG BOOKS:** Unit 2, Week 2: *Shapes All Around* Unit 7, Week 1: *ZooBorns!* Unit 7, Week 3: "Animal Homes" Unit 8, Week 1: *Getting from Here to There* Unit 8, Week 2: *Ana Goes to Washington, D.C.* Unit 9, Week 3: *Bread Comes to Life* **INTERACTIVE READ-ALOUD CARDS:** Unit 2, Week 3: "From Caterpillar to Butterfly" Unit 6, Week 1: "A Tour of the Seasons" Unit 8, Week 2: "The Best of the West" Unit 9, Week 1: "Helping Out at Home" Unit 10, Week 3: "Protect the Environment"
Craft and Structure		**McGraw-Hill Reading Wonders**
RI.K.4	With prompting and support, ask and answer questions about unknown words in a text.	**LEVELED READERS:** Unit 1, Week 3: *At School* (O, ELL), *See It Grow!* (B) Unit 2, Week 1: *A Trip* (O, ELL) Unit 4, Week 1: *You Cook* (A), *On the Job* (O, ELL) Unit 5, Week 2: *The Tree* (A) Unit 5, Week 3: *The Farmers' Market* (A) Unit 7, Week 1: *Animal Bodies* (O, ELL) Unit 9, Week 3: *Nature at the Craft Fair* (B) Unit 10, Week 3: *Let's Save Earth* (O, ELL), *Babysitters for Seals* (B) **TEACHER'S EDITION:** Unit 4: T127 Unit 5: T107 Unit 7: T209 Unit 8: T127, T209 Unit 10: T234
RI.K.5	Identify the front cover, back cover, and title page of a book.	**READING/WRITING WORKSHOP:** Unit 1: 8-13, 26-31, 44-49 Unit 2: 8-13, 26-31, 44-49 Unit 3: 8-13, 26-31, 44-49 Unit 4: 8-15, 22-29, 36-43 **LEVELED READERS:** Unit 10, Week 3: *Help Clean Up* (A) **TEACHER'S EDITION:** Unit 1: T30-31, T176 Unit 4: T12 Unit 5: T94, T176, T232 Unit 7: T12, T60, T68, T74, T94 Unit 8: T87, T94 Unit 9: T176 Unit 10: T178, T226 **LITERATURE BIG BOOKS:** Unit 1, Week 3: *Senses at the Seashore* Unit 2, Week 1: *The Handiest Things in the World* Unit 4, Week 1: *Whose Shoes? A Shoe for Every Job*

Reading Standards for Informational Text

Craft and Structure		McGraw-Hill Reading Wonders
RI.K.6	Name the author and illustrator of a text and define the role of each in presenting the ideas or information in a text.	**LEVELED READERS:** Unit 5, Week 3: *Let's Make a Salad!* (O, ELL), **Unit 7, Week 1:** *Two Cubs* (A), *Animal Bodies* (O, ELL), *Two Kinds of Bears* (B) **READING WORKSTATION ACTIVITY CARDS:** 12 **TEACHER'S EDITION:** Unit 1: T176 Unit 2: T12 Unit 4: T12 Unit 5: T94, T176, T232 Unit 6: T12, T94, T176 Unit 7: T12, T60, T68, T74, T94 Unit 8: T94 Unit 9: T176 Unit 10: T178 **LITERATURE BIG BOOKS:** Unit 1, Week 3: *Senses at the Seashore* Unit 2, Week 1: *The Handiest Things in the World* Unit 2, Week 2: *Shapes All Around* Unit 8, Week 2: *Ana Goes to Washington, D.C.* Unit 9, Week 3: *Bread Comes to Life*

Integration of Knowledge and Ideas		McGraw-Hill Reading Wonders
RI.K.7	With prompting and support, describe the relationship between illustrations and the text in which they appear (e.g., what person, place, thing, or idea in the text an illustration depicts).	**READING/WRITING WORKSHOP BIG BOOK:** Unit 2, Week 1: 14-19 **LEVELED READERS:** Unit 1, Week 3: *The Beach* (A) Unit 2, Week 1: *We Need Tools* (A) Unit 2, Week 2: *Shapes!* (A), *Play with Shapes!* (O, ELL), *Use a Shape!* (B) Unit 9, Week 3: *What's for Breakfast?* (O, ELL) **READING WORKSTATION ACTIVITY CARDS:** 1 **TEACHER'S EDITION:** Unit 1: T126-T127, T186-191, T224-225 Unit 2: T24, T60-61, T124-T127, 143 Unit 3: T45, 127, T208-209 Unit 4: T22-27 Unit 6: T126-127, T209 Unit 9: T208-209, T232-233 Unit 10: T190, T244-245 **LITERATURE BIG BOOKS:** Unit 1, Week 3: *Senses at the Seashore*, pp. 4-34 Unit 2, Week 1: *The Handiest Things in the World* Unit 2, Week 2: *Shapes All Around* Unit 3, Week 2: *Sounds Are Everywhere* Unit 3, Week 3: *A Neighborhood* Unit 4, Week 1: *Whose Shoes? A Shoe for Every Job* Unit 6, Week 2: *Cloud Watch* Unit 9, Week 3: *Nature's Artists* **INTERACTIVE READ-ALOUD CARDS:** Unit 3, Week 3: "Field Trips" Unit 6, Week 1: "A Tour of the Seasons" Unit 9, Week 1: "Helping Out at Home"
RI.K.8	With prompting and support, identify the reasons an author gives to support points in a text.	**READING WORKSTATION ACTIVITY CARDS:** 12 **TEACHER'S EDITION:** Unit 2: T26, T108 Unit 4: T26, T190 Unit 5: T108, T190 Unit 8: T108 Unit 9: T190 Unit 10: T210-211 **LITERATURE BIG BOOKS:** Unit 1, Week 3: *Senses at the Seashore* Unit 2, Week 1: *The Handiest Things in the World* Unit 2, Week 2: *Shapes All Around* Unit 4, Week 1: *Whose Shoes? A Shoe for Every Job* Unit 4, Week 3: *Roadwork* Unit 5, Week 2: *A Grand Old Tree* Unit 5, Week 3: *An Orange in January* Unit 8, Week 2: *Ana Goes to Washington, D.C.* Unit 9, Week 3: *Bread Comes to Life* Unit 10, Week 3: *Save Big Blue!*
RI.K.9	With prompting and support, identify basic similarities in and differences between two texts on the same topic (e.g., in illustrations, descriptions, or procedures).	**READING/WRITING WORKSHOP BIG BOOK:** Unit 1, Week 3: *A Feast of the Senses* **READING WORKSTATION ACTIVITY CARDS:** 16 **TEACHERS EDITION:** Unit 1: T199 Unit 2: T54-55, T117, T126-127 Unit 4: T116-117, T218-219 Unit 5: T136-137, T198-199, T208-209, T218-219 Unit 7: T35, T54, T117 Unit 8: T136 Unit 9: T218 Unit 10: T128-129, T201, T220 **LITERATURE BIG BOOKS:** Unit 1, Week 3: *Senses at the Seashore* Unit 2, Week 1: *The Handiest Things in the World* Unit 2, Week 2: *Shapes All Around*, "Find the Shapes" Unit 5, Week 3: *An Orange in January*, "Farmers' Market" Unit 10, Week 2: *Good For You* **INTERACTIVE READ-ALOUD CARDS:** Unit 1, Week 3: "A Feast of the Senses" Unit 2, Week 2: "Kites in Flight" Unit 5, Week 3: "Farms Around the World" Unit 7, Week 1: "Baby Farm Animals" Unit 7, Week 2: "The Family Pet" Unit 10, Week 3: "Protect the Environment!"

Range of Reading and Level of Text Complexity		McGraw-Hill Reading Wonders
RI.K.10	Actively engage in group reading activities with purpose and understanding.	**READING/WRITING WORKSHOP BIG BOOKS:** Start Smart: 18-23, 53-58 Unit 1: 10-15, 28-33, 52-57 Unit 2: 16-21, 52-57 Unit 3: 34-39, 52-57 Unit 4: 10-17 Unit 5: 24-31 Unit 6: 10-17 Unit 7: 10-17 Unit 8: 38-45 Unit 9: 38-45 Unit 10: 38-45 **LEVELED READERS:** Unit 5, Week 2: *Many Trees* (ELL) **TEACHER'S EDITION:** Unit 1: S60, T112-113, T126-127, T199 Unit 2: T22-27, T44-45, T74-75, T186-191 Unit 3: T126-127, T198-199, T212-213 Unit 4: T12-13, T30-31, T116-117, T176-177 Unit 5: T34-35, T92-95, T160-161, T174-177, T198-199 Unit 6: T35, T126-127, T208-209 Unit 7: T12-13, T22-27, T30-31, T34-35, T48-49, T116-117 Unit 8: T94-95, T116-117 Unit 9: T34-35, T176-177, T194-195, T208-209 Unit 10: T118-119, T178-179, T201 **INTERACTIVE READ-ALOUD CARDS:** SS: "Kindergarteners Can!" Unit 1, Week 3: "A Feast of the Senses" Unit 2, Week 3: "From Caterpillar to Butterfly" Unit 3, Week 3: "Field Trips" Unit 4, Week 2: "Cultural Festivals" Unit 5, Week 1: "Growing Plants" Unit 5, Week 3: "Farms Around the World" Unit 6, Week 1: "A Tour of the Seasons" Unit 7, Week 1: "Baby Farm Animals" Unit 7, Week 2: "The Family Pet" Unit 8, Week 2: "The Best of the West" Unit 8, Week 3: "A View from the Moon" Unit 9, Week 1: "Helping Out at Home" Unit 10, Week 2: "The Perfect Color" Unit 10, Week 3: "Protect the Environment"

Reading Standards for Foundational Skills

These standards are directed toward fostering students' understanding and working knowledge of concepts of print, the alphabetic principle, and other basic conventions of the English writing system. These foundational skills are not an end in and of themselves; rather, they are necessary and important components of an effective, comprehensive reading program designed to develop proficient readers with the capacity to comprehend texts across a range of types and disciplines. Instruction should be differentiated: good readers will need much less practice with these concepts than struggling readers will. The point is to teach students what they need to learn and not what they already know—to discern when particular children or activities warrant more or less attention.

Note: In Kidergarten, children are expected to demonstrate increasing awareness and competence in the areas that follow.

Print Concepts		McGraw-Hill Reading Wonders
RF.K.1	Demonstrate understanding of the organization and basic features of print.	**TEACHER'S EDITION:** Unit 1: S10, S18, S23, S28, S29, S32, S37, S39, S42, S43, S47, S52, S53, S56, S61, S62, S63, S66, S71, S77, T12, T15, T16, T60, T97, T98, T180, T189, T192 **Unit 2:** T12, T15, T30, T97, T112, T179, T180, T212, T224 **Unit 3:** T15, T26, T94, T97, T106, T112, T130, T142, T176, T179, T211, T232 **Unit 4:** T12, T15, T23, T30, T47, T48, T60, T68, T94, T97, T105, T108, T112, T129, T130, T142, T150, T179, T187, T194, T211, T212, T224 **Unit 5:** T12, T15, T30, T47, T48, T60, T68, T94, T97, T112, T129, T130, T142, T150, T176, T179, T211, T212, T224, T232 **Unit 6:** T12, T15, T29, T37, T47, T97, T129, T179, T211 **Unit 7:** T15, T16, T47, T94, T97, T98, T129, T150, T176, T179, T180, T211, T212, T232 **Unit 8:** T12, T15, T47, T48, T68, T94, T97, T129, T142, T179 **Unit 9:** T12, T15, T25, T47, T60, T94, T97, T129, T142, T176, T179, T211 **Unit 10:** T12, T15, T49, T62, T96, T97, T13, T144, T178, T179, T213
RF.K.1a	Follow words from left to right, top to bottom, and page by page.	**READING/WRITING WORKSHOP:** Start Smart: 4-5, 22-23, 40-41 **LITERATURE BIG BOOK:** Start Smart, Week 3: *ABC Big Book* Unit 4, Week 2: *What Can You Do With a Paleta?* **TEACHER'S EDITION:** Unit 1: S10, S62, T12, T60, T189 **Unit 2:** T30, T112, T224 **Unit 3:** T26, T94, T176 **Unit 4:** T12, T23, T30, T48, T60, T68, T94, T105, T108, T112, T130, T142, T150, T187, T194, T212, T224 **Unit 5:** T68, T94, T112, T130, T142, T150, T176, T212, T224, T232 **Unit 6:** T12 **Unit 7:** T94, T150 **Unit 8:** T12, T68, T94, T142 **Unit 9:** T12, T25, T60, T94, T142 **Unit 10:** T12, T62, T96, T144, T178
RF.K.1b	Recognize that spoken words are represented in written language by specific sequences of letters.	**TEACHER'S EDITION:** Unit 1: S39, S63 **Unit 2:** T212 **Unit 3:** T47-129, T211 **Unit 4:** T47, T129, T211 **Unit 5:** T47, T129, T211 **Unit 6:** T29, T37, T47, T129, T211 **Unit 7:** T47, T129, T176, T211, T212 **Unit 8:** T47, T48, T129, T211 **Unit 9:** T47, T129, T176, T211 **Unit 10:** T49, T131, T213
RF.K.1c	Understand that words are separated by spaces in print.	**TEACHER'S EDITION:** Unit 1: S29, S39, S43, S53, S63, S77 **Unit 2:** T12, T180 **Unit 3:** T94, T106, T112, T130, T142, T232 **Unit 5:** T12, T30, T48, T60, T94 **Unit 7:** T232
RF.K.1d	Recognize and name all upper- and lowercase letters of the alphabet.	**YOUR TURN PRACTICE BOOK:** 3, 7, 8, 11, 15, 16, 20, 24, 34, 42, 50, 58, 66, 84, 92, 100, 108, 116, 134, 142, 143-144, 162, 172, 192, 202, 212, 222, 232 **TEACHER'S EDITION:** Unit 1: S23, S18, S23, S28, S32, S37, S42, S47, S52, S56, S61, S66, S71, T15, T16, T97, T98, T180, T192 **Unit 2:** T15, T97, T179 **Unit 3:** T15, T97, T179 **Unit 4:** T15, T97, T179 **Unit 5:** T15, T97, T179 **Unit 6:** T15, T97, T179 **Unit 7:** T15, T16, T97, T98, T179, T180 **Unit 8:** T15, T97, T179 **Unit 9:** T15, T97, T179 **Unit 10:** T15, T97, T179
Phonological Awareness		McGraw-Hill Reading Wonders
RF.K.2	Demonstrate understanding of spoken words, syllables, and sounds (phonemes).	**TEACHER'S EDITION:** Unit 1: S13, S18, S23, S42, S47, S52, S56, S61, S66, S71, T14, T36, T102, T118, T124, T184, T206 **Unit 2:** T14, T20, T42, T70, T96, T102, T124, T144, T178, T184, T206, T210, T226 **Unit 3:** T20, T36, T42, T62, T96, T102, T118, T124, T144, T184, T206, T226 **Unit 4:** T20, T28, T42, T56, T62, T70, T102, T118, T128, T138, T145, T152, T184, T192, T200, T206, T210, T220, T226 **Unit 5:** T14, T20, T28, T36, T42, T62, T63, T72, T102, T110, T118, T124, T138, T144, T145, T152, T184, T192, T206, T210, T226, T227, T234 **Unit 6:** T20, T28, T36, T42, T46, T56, T62, T63, T70, T102, T124, T138, T144, T152, T154, T184, T192, T206, T210, T220, T227, T234 **Unit 7:** T20, T28, T36, T42, T46, T62, T102, T110, T118, T124, T128, T138, T144, T145, T178, T184, T206, T210, T220, T226, T234 **Unit 8:** T20, T28, T42, T46, T56, T62, T63, T102, T110, T118, T124, T128, T138, T144, T145, T152, T184, T200, T206, T226, T227, T234 **Unit 9:** T14, T20, T42, T62, T102, T124, T144, T184, T206, T210, T220, T226, T227, T234 **Unit 10:** T20, T44, T48, T58, T64, T72, T104, T126, T130, T140, T146, T147, T154, T212, T222, T229, T236
RF.K.2a	Recognize and produce rhyming words.	**LITERATURE BIG BOOKS:** Start Smart, Weeks 1-3: *Big Book of Rhymes* **TEACHER'S EDITION:** Unit 1: S23, S42, S47, S52, T102, T124 **Unit 2:** T210 **Unit 3:** T20, T42, T62 **Unit 4:** T184, T206, T226 **Unit 5:** T184, T206, T226 **Unit 6:** T102, T124, T144 **Unit 7:** T102, T124, T144 **Unit 8:** T102, T124, T144 **Unit 9:** T102, T124, T144
RF.K.2b	Count, pronounce, blend, and segment syllables in spoken words.	**LITERATURE BIG BOOK:** Smart Start, Week 3: *Big Book of Rhymes* **TEACHER'S EDITION:** Unit 1: S56, S61, S66, S71 **Unit 2:** T184, T206, T226 **Unit 3:** T184, T206, T226 **Unit 5:** T20, T42, T62 **Unit 9:** T20, T42, T62, T184, T206, T226 **Unit 10:** T20, T44, T64

Reading Standards for Foundational Skills

Phonological Awareness		McGraw-Hill Reading Wonders
RF.K.2c	Blend and segment onsets and rimes of single-syllable spoken words.	**YOUR TURN PRACTICE BOOK:** 88, 96, 104, 112, 124, 130, 138, 148, 158, 168, 182, 183, 188, 198, 208, 228, 242, 243, 248, 256, 264, 272, 280, 293 **TEACHER'S EDITION:** Unit 1: T184, T206 Unit 2: T102, T124, T144 Unit 3: T102, T124, T144 Unit 4: T20, T42, T62 Unit 5: T102, T124, T144 Unit 6: T20, T42, T62 Unit 7: T20, T42, T62, T184, T206, T226 Unit 8: T20, T42, T62, T184, T206, T226 Unit 10: T104, T126, T146
RF.K.2d	Isolate and pronounce the initial, medial vowel, and final sounds (phonemes) in in three-phoneme (consonant-vowel-consonant, or CVC) words. (This does not include CVCs ending with /l/, /r/, or /x/.)	**YOUR TURN PRACTICE BOOK:** 80, 193 **TEACHER'S EDITION:** Unit 1: T14, T36, T118 Unit 2: T14, T70, T96, T178 Unit 3: T36, T96, T118 Unit 4: T28, T70, T110, T118, T128, T138, T145, T152, T192, T200, T210, T220 Unit 5: T14, T28, T36, T63, T72, T110, T118, T138, T145, T152, T192 Unit 6: T28, T36, T46, T56, T62, T63, T70, T138, T152, T154, T184, T192, T206 Unit 7: T28, T36, T110, T118, T178 Unit 8: T28, T46, T56, T63, T110, T118, T145, T152
RF.K.2e	Add or substitute individual sounds (phonemes) in simple, one-syllable words to make new words.	**TEACHER'S EDITION:** Unit 5: T210, T220, T227, T234 Unit 6: T210, T220, T227, T234 Unit 7: T128, T138, T145, T152, T210, T220, T227, T234 Unit 8: T128, T138, T145, T152, T200, T227, T234 Unit 9: T210, T220, T227, T234 Unit 10: T48, T58, T72, T130, T140, T147, T154, T212, T222, T229, T236

Phonics and Word Recognition		McGraw-Hill Reading Wonders
RF.K.3	Know and apply grade-level phonics and word analysis skills in decoding words.	**TEACHER'S EDITION:** Unit 1: S19, S43, S67, T28, T29, T97, T105, T121, T179, T181, T210, T211, T220, T245 Unit 2: T15, T39, T46, T97, T128-129, T179, T203, T221 Unit 3: T15, T38, T39, T46, T56, T97, T110, T111, T128, T179, T181, T210 Unit 4: T15, T17, T28-29, T30-31, T37, T39, T46, T47, T48-49, T57, T66, T73, T76, T81, T97, T99, T110, T111, T112-113, T121, T128, T129, T130-131, T139, T148, T155, T158, T163, T179, T181, T193, T194-195, T203, T210, T211, T212-213, T221, T230, T237, T240, T245 Unit 5: T14, T17, T28, T29, T30-31, T36, T39, T47, T48-49, T56, T57, T66, T73, T76, T81, T99, T110-111, T112-113, T118, T119, T121, T128, T129, T130-131, T138, T139, T146, T148, T153, T155, T158, T163, T181, T192, T193, T194-195, T200, T203, T210, T211, T212-213, T220, T221, T228, T230, T237, T240, T245 Unit 6: T15, T17, T29, T30-31, T39, T46, T47, T48-49, T57, T66, T73, T81, T97, T99, T111, T112-113, T121, T128, T129, T130-131, T139, T148, T155, T158, T163, T178, T179, T181, T193, T194-195, T201, T203, T210, T212-213, T221, T230, T237, T240, T245 Unit 7: T15, T17, T28-29, T30-31, T37, T46, T47, T48-49, T56, T57, T64, T65, T66, T73, T76, T81, T96, T97, T99, T110, T112-113, T119, T121, T128, T129, T130-131, T139, T146, T148, T155, T158, T163, T178, T179, T181, T192, T193, T194-195, T201, T203, T210, T211, T212-213, T220, T221, T230, T237, T240, T245 Unit 8: T15, T17, T29, T30-31, T39, T46, T47, T48-49, T57, T66, T73, T76, T81, T97, T99, T111, T112-113, T121, T128, T129, T130-131, T139, T148, T155, T158, T163, T179, T181, T193, T194-195, T201, T203, T210, T211, T212-213, T220, T221, T230, T237, T240, T245 Unit 9: T15, T17, T29, T30-31, T37, T39, T46, T47, T48-49, T56, T57, T64, T65, T66, T71, 72, T73, T76, T81, T97, T99, T110-111, T112-113, T119, T120, T121, T128, T129, T130-131, T138, T139, T146, T147, T148, T153, T154, T155, T158, T163, T179, T181, T192-193, T194-195, T201, T202, T203, T210, T211, T212-213, T220, T221, T228, T229, T230, T235, T236, T237, T240, T245 Unit 10: T15, T17, T30-31, T32-33, T39, T40, T41, T48, T49, T50-51, T58, T59, T66, T67, T68, T74, T75, T83, T97, T99, T101, T110, T112-113, T114-115, T121, T123, T130, T131, T140, T141, T148, T149, T150, T156, T157, T160, T165, T179, T181, T182, T183, T191, T194-195, T196-197, T203, T204, T205, T212-213, T222, T223, T230, T231, T232, T238, T239, T242, T247
RF.K.3a	Demonstrate basic knowledge of one-to-one letter-sound correspondences by producing the primary or many of the most frequent sounds for each consonant.	**PHONICS/WORD STUDY WORKSTATION ACTIVITY CARDS:** 1, 2, 3, 4, 5, 6, 7, 8, 9, 10, 11, 12, 13, 14, 15, 16, 17, 18, 19, 20, 21, 22, 23, 24 **TEACHER'S EDITION:** Unit 1: T28, T179, T210, T220 Unit 2: T15, T97, T179 Unit 3: T97, T110, T179 Unit 4: T97, T110, T179 Unit 5: T14, T28, T36, T56, T118, T138, T192, T200, T220, T228 Unit 6: T15, T97, T179 Unit 7: T56, T96, T97, T110, T146, T178, T179, T192, T220 Unit 8: T15, T97, T179 Unit 10: T97, T110, T179

Reading Standards for Foundational Skills

Phonics and Word Recognition		McGraw-Hill Reading Wonders
RF.K.3b	Associate the long and short sounds with the common spellings (graphemes) for the five major vowels.	**YOUR TURN PRACTICE BOOK:** 36, 62, 101-102, 135-136, 138, 246, 248, 254, 256, 262, 264, 270, 278 **PHONICS/WORD STUDY WORKSTATION ACTIVITY CARDS:** 2, 7, 10, 14, 19, 25, 26, 27, 28, 29, 30 **TEACHER'S EDITION: Unit 1:** T97, T105 **Unit 2:** T46, T128–T129, T221 **Unit 3:** T15, T38, T56 **Unit 4:** T15, T28-29, T37 **Unit 5:** T110-111, T119, T146, T153 **Unit 6:** T193, T201, T211 **Unit 7:** T15, T28-29, T37, T46, T64, T65, T119, T201 **Unit 8:** T201, T220 **Unit 9:** T15, T29, T37, T56, T64, T65, T71, 72, T76, T97, T110-111, T119, T120, T138, T146, T147, T153, T154, T179, T192-193, T201, T202, T220, T228, T229, T235, T236 **Unit 10:** T15, T30-31, T39, T40, T58, T66, T67, T74, T99, T112-113, T121, T140, T148, T149, T156, T181, T182, T191, T194-195, T203, T204, T222, T230, T231, T238

Phonological Awareness		McGraw-Hill Reading Wonders
RF.K.3c	Read common high-frequency words by sight (e.g., *the, of, to, you, she, my, is, are, do, does*).	**READING/WRITING WORKSHOP: Start Smart:** 9, 16-22, 27 **Unit 1:** 7-13, 14-19, 25-31 **Unit 2:** 7-13, 14-19, 25-31 **Unit 3:** 7-13, 25-31, 32-37 **Unit 4:** 7-15, 21-29, 35-43 **Unit 5:** 7-15, 21-29, 35-43 **Unit 6:** 7-15, 21-29, 35-43 **Unit 7:** 7-15, 21-29, 35-43 **Unit 8:** 7-15, 21-29, 35-43 **Unit 9:** 7-15, 21-29, 35-43 **Unit 10:** 7-15, 21-29, 35-43 **YOUR TURN PRACTICE BOOK:** 4, 9-10, 12, 17-18, 21, 25-26], 31-32, 39-40, 47-48, 55-56, 63-64, 71-72, 89-90, 97-98, 105-106, 113-114,121-122, 131-132, 139-140, 149-150, 159-160, 169-170, 179-180, 189-190, 199-200, 209-210, 219-220, 229-230, 239-240, 249-250, 257-258, 265-266, 273-274, 281-282, 291-292 **TEACHER'S EDITION: Unit 1:** S19, S43, S67, T29, T121, T181, T211, T245 **Unit 2:** T39, T129, T203 **Unit 3:** T39, T111, T181 **Unit 4:** T17, T29, T30-31, T39, T47, T48-49, T57, T66, T73, T76, T81, T99, T111, T112-113, T121, T129, T130-131, T139, T148, T155, T158, T163, T181, T193, T194-195, T203, T211, T212-213, T221, T230, T237, T240, T245 **Unit 5:** T17, T29, T30-31, T39, T47, T48-49, T57, T66, T73, T76, T81, T99, T111, T112-113, T121, T129, T130-131, T139, T148, T155, T158, T163, T181, T193, T194-195, T203, T211, T212-213, T221, T230, T237, T240, T245 **Unit 6:** T17, T29, T30-31, T39, T47, T48-49, T57, T66, T73, T81, T99, T111, T112-113, T121, T129, T130-131, T139, T148, T155, T158, T163, T181, T193, T194-195, T203, T211, T212-213, T221, T230, T237, T240, T245 **Unit 7:** T17, T29, T30-31, T39, T47, T48-49, T57, T66, T73, T76, T81, T99, T111, T112-113, T121, T129, T130-131, T139, T148, T155, T158, T163, T181, T193, T194-195, T203, T211, T212-213, T221, T230, T237, T240, T245 **Unit 8:** T17, T29, T30-31, T39, T47, T48-49, T57, T66, T73, T76, T81, T99, T111, T112-113, T121, T129, T130-131, T139, T148, T155, T158, T163, T181, T193, T194-195, T203, T211, T212-213, T221, T230, T237, T240, T245 **Unit 9:** T17, T29, T30-31, T39, T47, T48-49, T57, T66, T73, T76, T81, T99, T111, T112-113, T121, T129, T130-131, T139, T148, T155, T158, T163, T181, T193, T194-195, T203, T211, T212-213, T221, T230, T237, T240, T245 **Unit 10:** T17, T31, T32-33, T41, T49, T50-51, T59, T68, T75, T78, T83, T101, T113, T114-115, T123, T131, T141, T150, T157, T160, T165, T183, T195, T196-197, T205, T212-213, T223, T232, T239, T242, T247
RF.K.3d	Distinguish between similarly spelled words by identifying the sounds of the letters that differ.	**TEACHER'S EDITION: Unit 2:** T46, T128 **Unit 3:** T46, T128, T210 **Unit 4:** T46, T128, T210 **Unit 5:** T128, T210 **Unit 6:** T46, T128, T210 **Unit 7:** T46, T128, T210 **Unit 8:** T46, T128, T210 **Unit 9:** T46, T128, T210 **Unit 10:** T48, T130, T212

Reading Standards for Foundational Skills

Fluency		McGraw-Hill Reading Wonders
RF.K.4	Read emergent-reader texts with purpose and understanding.	**READING/WRITING WORKSHOP:** Unit 1: 32-37, 44-49, 50-55 Unit 2: 32-37, 44-49, 50-55 Unit 3: 8-13, 32-37, 50-55 Unit 4: 8-15, 22-29, 36-43 Unit 5: 8-15, 22-29, 36-43 Unit 6: 8-15, 22-29, 36-43 Unit 7: 8-15, 22-29, 36-43 Unit 8: 8-15, 22-29, 36-43 Unit 9: 8-15, 22-29, 36-43 Unit 10: 8-15, 22-29, 36-43
		LEVELED READERS: Unit 1, Week 1: *Soup!* (A), *Mouse and Monkey* (O, ELL), *Come and Play!* (B) Unit 1 Week 2: *Hop!* (A), *We Hop!* (O, ELL) *We Can Move!* (B) Unit 1, Week 3: *The Beach* (A), *At School* (O, ELL), *See It Grow!* (B) Unit 2, Week 1: *We Need Tools* (A), *A Trip* (O, ELL), *What Can You See?* (B) Unit 2, Week 2: *Shapes!* (A), *Play with Shapes!* (O, ELL), *Use a Shape!* (B) Unit 2, Week 3: *We Like Bugs!* (A), *The Bugs Run* (O, ELL), *I See a Bug!* (B) Unit 3, Week 1: *We Run* (A), *Go, Nat!* (O, ELL), *The Birdhouse* (B) Unit 3, Week 2: *City Sounds* (A), *Farm Sounds* (O, ELL), *A Noisy Night* (B) Unit 3, Week 3: *We Can Go* (A), *Going by Cab* (O, ELL), *Cal's Busy Week* (B) Unit 4, Week 1: *You Cook* (A), *On the Job* (O, ELL), *The Neighborhood* (B) Unit 4, Week 2: *My Neighbors* (A), *Neighborhood Party* (O, ELL), *Parade Day* (B) Unit 4, Week 3: *We Clean!* (A) *Can You Fix It?* (O, ELL), *Helping Mom* (B) Unit 5, Week 1: *My Garden* (A), *My Garden Grows* (O, ELL), *The Mystery Seeds* (B) Unit 5, Week 2: *The Tree* (A), *Many Trees* (O, ELL), *Our Apple Tree* (B) Unit 5, Week 3: *The Farmer* (A), *Let's Make a Salad!* (O, ELL), *Farm Fresh Finn* (B) Unit 6, Week 1: *It Is Hot!* (A), *Little Bear* (O, ELL), *Ant and Grasshopper* (B) Unit 6, Week 2: *The Rain* (A), *Weather Is Fun* (O, ELL), *Kate and Tuck* (B) Unit 6 Week 3: *Bad Weather* (A), *Getting Ready* (O, ELL), *The Storm* (B) Unit 7, Week 1: *Two Cubs* (A), *Animal Bodies* (O, ELL), *Two Kinds of Bears* (B) Unit 7, Week 2: *My Cats* (A), *Their Pets* (O, ELL), *Will's Pet* (B) Unit 7, Week 3: *We Want Water* (A) *A New Home* (O, ELL), *Bird's New Home* (B) Unit 8, Week 1: *I Go Places* (A), *Run, Quinn!* (O, ELL), *Going to Gran's House* (B) Unit 8, Week 2: *See This!* (A), *Places to See* (O, ELL), *My Trip to Yellowstone* (B) Unit 8, Week 3: *Going Up* (A), *In the Clouds* (O, ELL), *How Sun and Moon Found Home* (B) Unit 9, Week 1: *Let Me Help You* (A), *How Can Jane Help?* (O, ELL), *I Used to Help, Too* (B) Unit 9, Week 2: *Mike Helps Out* (A), *Clive and His Friend* (O, ELL), *Farmer White's Best Friend* (B) Unit 9, Week 3: *Look Where It Is From* (A), *What's for Breakfast?* (O, ELL), *Nature at the Craft Fair* (B) Unit 10, Week 1: *Animal Band* (A), *We Want Honey* (O, ELL), *A Good Idea* (B) Unit 10, Week 2: *My Box* (A), *Let's Make a Band* (O, ELL), *Going Camping* (B) Unit 10, Week 3: *Help Clean Up* (A), *Let's Save Earth* (O, ELL), *Babysitters for Seals* (B)
		TEACHER'S EDITION: Unit 1: S14, S48, T48-49, T112-113, T150-151, T232-233 Unit 2: T48-49, T130-131, T224-225 Unit 3: T60-61, T130-131, T212-213 Unit 4: T30-31, T48-49, T60-61, T65, T68-69, T72, T74-75, T78-79, T112-113, T130-131, T142-143, T147, T150-151, T156-157, T160-161, T194-195, T212-213, T224-225, T229, T232-233, T236, T238-239, T242-243 Unit 5: T30-31, T48-49, T60-61, T65, T68-69, T72, T74-75, T78-79, T112-113, T130-131, T142-143, T147, T150-151, T156-157, T160-161, T194-195, T212-213, T224-225, T229, T232-233, T236, T238-239, T242-243 Unit 6: T30-31, T48-49, T60-61, T65, T68-69, T72, T74-75, T78-79, T112-113, T130-131, T142-143, T147, T150-151, T194-195, T212-213, T224-225, T229, T232-233, T236 Unit 7: T30-31, T48-49, T60-61, T65, T68-69, T72, T74-75, T78-79, T112-113, T130-131, T142-143, T147, T150-151, T156-157, T160-161, T194-195, T212-213, T224-225, T229, T232-233, T236, T238-239, T242-243 Unit 8: T30-31, T48-49, T60-61, T65, T68-69, T72, T74-75, T78-79, T112-113, T10-131, T142-143, T147, T150-151, T156-157, T160-161, T194-195, T212-213, T224-225, T229, T232-233, T236, T238-239, T242-243 Unit 9: T30-31, T48-49, T60-61, T65, T68-69, T72, T74-75, T78-79, T112-113, T130-131, T142-143, T147, T150-151, T156-157, T160-161, T194-195, T212-213, T224-225, T229, T232-233, T236, T238-239, T242-243 Unit 10: T32-33, T50-51, T62-63, T67, T70-71, T74, T76-77, T80-81, T114-115, T132-133, T144-145, T149, T152-153, T156, T158-159, T162-163, T196-197, T214-215, T226-227, T231, T234-235, T238, T240-241, T244-245

College and Career Readiness Anchor Standards for WRITING

The K–5 standards on the following pages define what students should understand and be able to do by the end of each grade. They correspond to the College and Career Readiness (CCR) anchor standards below by number. The CCR and grade-specific standards are necessary complements—the former providing broad standards, the latter providing additional specificity—that together define the skills and understandings that all students must demonstrate.

Text Types and Purposes

1. Write arguments to support claims in an analysis of substantive topics or texts, using valid reasoning and relevant and sufficient evidence.

2. Write informative/explanatory texts to examine and convey complex ideas and information clearly and accurately through the effective selection, organization, and analysis of content.

3. Write narratives to develop real or imagined experiences or events using effective technique, well-chosen details, and well-structured event sequences.

Production and Distribution of Writing

4. Produce clear and coherent writing in which the development, organization, and style are appropriate to task, purpose, and audience.

5. Develop and strengthen writing as needed by planning, revising, editing, rewriting, or trying a new approach.

6. Use technology, including the Internet, to produce and publish writing and to interact and collaborate with others.

Research to Build and Present Knowledge

7. Conduct short as well as more sustained research projects based on focused questions, demonstrating understanding of the subject under investigation.

8. Gather relevant information from multiple print and digital sources, assess the credibility and accuracy of each source, and integrate the information while avoiding plagiarism.

9. Draw evidence from literary or informational texts to support analysis, reflection, and research.

Range of Writing

10. Write routinely over extended time frames (time for research, reflection, and revision) and shorter time frames (a single sitting or a day or two) for a range of tasks, purposes, and audiences.

Common Core State Standards
English Language Arts
Grade K

Writing Standards

Text Types and Purposes		McGraw-Hill Reading Wonders
W.K.1	Use a combination of drawing, dictating, and writing to compose opinion pieces in which they tell a reader the topic or the name of the book they are writing about and state an opinion or preference about the topic or book (e.g., My favorite book is…).	**READING/WRITING WORKSHOP:** Unit 1: 38-39 **Unit 3:** 58 **Unit 5:** 32-33 **Unit 6:** 18-19 **Unit 9:** 18-19 **Unit 10:** 46-47 **TEACHER'S EDITION:** Unit 1: T87, T100, T114, T122 **Unit 3:** T196, T204, T214 **Unit 5:** T100, T114, T122-123, T132, T144 **Unit 6:** T32, T40, T41 **Unit 9:** T5, T18, T32, T40-41, T50 **Unit 10:** T17, T184, T198, T206, T216 **WRITING WORKSTATION ACTIVITY CARDS:** 5, 20
W.K.2	Use a combination of drawing, dictating, and writing to compose informative/explanatory texts in which they name what they are writing about and supply some information about the topic.	**READING/WRITING WORKSHOP:** Unit 2: 20-21 **Unit 4:** 44 **Unit 5:** 44-45 **Unit 6:** 44 **Unit 7:** 16-17, 44 **Unit 8:** 30-31 **Unit 9:** 44 **TEACHER'S EDITION:** Unit 1: S15, S33, S53, S67, S77, T182, T196, T204 **Unit 2:** T100, T122, T164 **Unit 3:** T18, T32, T40 **Unit 4:** T18, T32, T40, T114, T122, T196, T204 **Unit 5:** T182, T196, T204 **Unit 6:** T52-53, T135 **Unit 7:** T18, T32, T40, T100, T114, T122 **Unit 8:** T53, T100, T114, T122, T135 **Unit 9:** T182, T196, T204, T214 **Unit 10:** T18, T34, T42-43, T52 **WRITING WORKSTATION ACTIVITY CARDS:** 18, 23
W.K.3	Use a combination of drawing, dictating and writing to narrate a single event or several loosely linked events, tell about the events in the order in which they occurred, and provide a reaction to what happened.	**READING/WRITING WORKSHOP:** Unit 3: 38-39, 56 **Unit 5:** 44 **Unit 6:** 30 **Unit 8:** 16, 46-47 **Unit 9:** 30 **Unit 10:** 16 **TEACHER'S EDITION:** Unit 2: T196, T204, T246 **Unit 3:** T114, T122, T164 **Unit 5:** T32, T40, T82, T164, T246 **Unit 6:** T114, T123, T164, T246 **Unit 8:** T32, T40, T82, T196, T204 **Unit 9:** T82, T100, T114, T122-123, T132 **Unit 10:** T18, T34, T42, T43, T52, T84, T116, T166, T248 **WRITING WORKSTATION ACTIVITY CARDS:** 1, 4, 5, 7, 15

Writing Standards

Production and Distribution of Writing		McGraw-Hill Reading Wonders
W.K.4	(Begins in grade 3.)	
W.K.5	With guidance and support from adults, respond to questions and suggestions from peers and add details to strengthen writing as needed.	**TEACHER'S EDITION: Unit 1:** T32, T40 (Go Digital: Writing), T50, T58 (Go Digital: Writing), T122 (Go Digital: Writing), T132, T140 (Go Digital: Writing), T204 (Go Digital: Writing), T214, T222 (Go Digital: Writing) **Unit 2:** T40 (Go Digital: Writing), T50, T58 (Go Digital: Writing), T122 (Go Digital: Writing), T132, T140 (Go Digital: Writing), T204 (Go Digital: Writing), T214, T222 (Go Digital: Writing) **Unit 3:** T40 (Go Digital: Writing), T50, T58 (Go Digital: Writing), T122 (Go Digital: Writing), T132, T140 (Go Digital: Writing), T204 (Go Digital: Writing), T222 (Go Digital: Writing) **Unit 4:** T40 (Go Digital: Writing), T50, T58 (Go Digital: Writing), T122 (Go Digital: Writing), T132, T140 (Go Digital: Writing), T204 (Go Digital: Writing), T214, T222 (Go Digital: Writing) **Unit 5:** T40 (Go Digital: Writing), T50, T58 (Go Digital: Writing), T122 (Go Digital: Writing), T132, T140 (Go Digital: Writing), T204 (Go Digital: Writing), T214, T222 (Go Digital: Writing) **Unit 6:** T40 (Go Digital: Writing), T50, T58 (Go Digital: Writing), T122 (Go Digital: Writing), T132, T140 (Go Digital: Writing), T204 (Go Digital: Writing), T214, T222 (Go Digital: Writing) **Unit 7:** T40 (Go Digital: Writing), T58 (Go Digital: Writing), T122 (Go Digital: Writing), T140 (Go Digital: Writing), T164, T204 (Go Digital: Writing), T222 (Go Digital: Writing) T246 **Unit 8:** T40 (Go Digital: Writing), T50, T58 (Go Digital: Writing), T122 (Go Digital: Writing), T132, T140 (Go Digital: Writing), T164, T204 (Go Digital: Writing), T214, T222 (Go Digital: Writing), T246 **Unit 9:** T40 (Go Digital: Writing), T50, T58 (Go Digital: Writing), T122 (Go Digital: Writing), T132, T140 (Go Digital: Writing), T204 (Go Digital: Writing), T214, T222 (Go Digital: Writing) **Unit 10:** T42 (Go Digital: Writing), T52, T60 (Go Digital: Writing), T124 (Go Digital: Writing), T134, T142 (Go Digital: Writing), T166, T206 (Go Digital: Writing), T224 (Go Digital: Writing), T248 **WRITING WORKSTATION ACTIVITY CARDS:** 10, 11, 12, 13, 14, 16
W.K.6	With guidance and support from adults, explore a variety of digital tools to produce and publish writing, including in collaboration with peers.	**TEACHER'S EDITION: Unit 1:** T134 **Unit 2:** T216 **Unit 6:** T248-249 **Unit 7:** T52, T134, T216, T248-249 **Unit 8:** T52, T134, T216, T248-249 **Unit 9:** T216, T248-249 **Unit 10:** T218, T250-251 **ConnectED Digital Resources:** My Binder (My Work)

Research to Build and Present Knowledge		McGraw-Hill Reading Wonders
W.K.7	Participate in shared research and writing projects (e.g., explore a number of books by a favorite author and express opinions about them).	**TEACHER'S EDITION: Unit 1:** T52, T134, T216 **Unit 2:** T52, T134, T216 **Unit 3:** T52, T134, T216 **Unit 4:** T52, T134, T216 **Unit 5:** T52, T100, T114, T122-123 **Unit 6:** T52, T134, T216 **Unit 7:** T52, T134, T216, T248-249 **Unit 8:** T52, T134, T216 **Unit 9:** T52, T134, T216 **Unit 10:** T54, T136, T218 **WRITING WORKSTATION ACTIVITY CARDS:** 20, 23 **ConnectED Digital Resources:** Collaborate (Projects)
W.K.8	With guidance and support from adults, recall information from experiences or gather information from provided sources to answer a question.	**READING/WRITING WORKSHOP: Unit 7:** 44 **TEACHER'S EDITION: Unit 1:** T32, T40, T100 **Unit 2:** T52, T134, T216 **Unit 3:** T100, T214 **Unit 4:** T18, T52, T100, T134, T182, T216 **Unit 5:** T18, T52, T134, T216 **Unit 6:** T52, T100, T134, T216 **Unit 7:** T50, T52, T132, T134, T196, T204, T214, T216 **Unit 8:** T52, T134, T216 **Unit 9:** T52, T134, T216 **Unit 10:** T54, T102, T136, T218
W.K.9	(Begins in grade 4.)	

Range of Writing		McGraw-Hill Reading Wonders
W.K.10	(Begins in grade 3.)	

College and Career Readiness Anchor Standards for **SPEAKING** AND **LISTENING**

The K–5 standards on the following pages define what students should understand and be able to do by the end of each grade. They correspond to the College and Career Readiness (CCR) anchor standards below by number. The CCR and grade-specific standards are necessary complements—the former providing broad standards, the latter providing additional specificity—that together define the skills and understandings that all students must demonstrate.

Comprehension and Collaboration
1. Prepare for and participate effectively in a range of conversations and collaborations with diverse partners, building on others' ideas and expressing their own clearly and persuasively.
2. Integrate and evaluate information presented in diverse media and formats, including visually, quantitatively, and orally.
3. Evaluate a speaker's point of view, reasoning, and use of evidence and rhetoric.

Presentation of Knowledge and Ideas
4. Present information, findings, and supporting evidence such that listeners can follow the line of reasoning and the organization, development, and style are appropriate to task, purpose, and audience.
5. Make strategic use of digital media and visual displays of data to express information and enhance understanding of presentations.
6. Adapt speech to a variety of contexts and communicative tasks, demonstrating command of formal English when indicated or appropriate.

CCSS Common Core State Standards
English Language Arts
Grade K

Speaking and Listening Standards

Comprehension and Collaboration		McGraw-Hill Reading Wonders
SL.K.1	Participate in collaborative conversations with diverse partners about kindergarten topics and texts with peers and adults in small and larger groups.	**TEACHER'S EDITION:** Unit 1: S10-11, S44, S58, T11, T54-55, T117, T134, T136-137, T216 **Unit 2:** T34, T51, T52, T134, T222 **Unit 3:** T20, T33, T45, T175, T216 **Unit 4:** T11, T20, T52, T54, T58, T93, T134, T136, T140, T175, T216, T218 **Unit 5:** T11, T20, T52, T93, T120, T136, T174, T175, T216, T222 **Unit 6:** T11, T52, T54, T93, T136, T140, T216, T218 **Unit 7:** T10-11, T52, T54, T55, T93, T134, T136, T137, T175, T218, T219 **Unit 8:** T11, T54, T58, T80, T92, T93, T134, T136, T140, T175, T218, T222 **Unit 9:** T10-11, T52, T54, T93, T136, T140, T175, T218, T222 **Unit 10:** T11, T20, T56, T60, T95, T104, T136, T138, T142, T177, T186, T220, T224
SL.K.1a	Follow agreed-upon rules for discussions (e.g., listening to others and taking turns speaking about the topics and texts under discussion).	**READING/WRITING WORKSHOP:** Unit 1: 6-7, 24-25 **Unit 2:** 24-25 **Unit 3:** 6-7, 24-25, 42-43 **Unit 4:** 6-7, 20-21, 34-35 **Unit 5:** 6-7, 20-21, 34-35 **Unit 6:** 6-7, 20-21, 36-43 **Unit 7:** 6-7, 20-21, 34-35 **Unit 8:** 6-7, 20-21 **Unit 9:** 6-7, 8-15, 20-21, 34-35 **Unit 10:** 6-7, 20-21 **YOUR TURN PRACTICE BOOK:** 31-32, 45, 68, 70-71, 81-82, 93 **READING WORKSTATION ACTIVITY CARDS:** 1, 6, 18, 19 **WRITING WORKSTATION ACTIVITY CARDS:** 1, 11, 13, 21+D89 **TEACHER'S EDITION:** Unit 1: T11, T134, T216 **Unit 2:** T52, T134, T222 **Unit 3:** T175, T216 **Unit 4:** T11, T52, T58, T93, T134, T140, T216 **Unit 5:** T11, T52, T93, T175, T216 **Unit 6:** T11, T52, T93, T140, T216 **Unit 7:** T11, T52, T55, T93, T134, T137, T219 **Unit 8:** T11, T58, T93, T134, T140, T222 **Unit 9:** T11, T52, T93, T140, T175, T222 **Unit 10:** T11, T60, T95, T142, T224
SL.K.1b	Continue a conversation through multiple exchanges.	**READING/WRITING WORKSHOP:** Unit 1: SS4-SS5, SS22-SS23, SS40-SS41, 6-7, 24-25, 42-43 **Unit 2:** 6-7, 8, 14-19, 24, 25, 42-43, 46, 47, 48, 51, 54, 55, 58 **Unit 3:** 6-7, 14-19, 24-35, 42-43 **Unit 4:** 6-7, 20-21, 34-35 **Unit 5:** 6-7, 20-21, 34-35 **Unit 6:** 8-15 **Unit 7:** 6-7, 8-15, 20-21, 22-29, 34-35, 36-43 **Unit 8:** 6-7, 8-15, 20-21, 22-29, 34-35, 36-43 **Unit 9:** 6-7, 8-15, 20-21, 22-29, 34-35 **Unit 10:** 6-7, 8-15, 20-21, 22-29, 34-35, 36-43 **YOUR TURN PRACTICE BOOK:** 29, 45, 53, 61, 68 **READING WORKSTATION ACTIVITY CARDS:** 1, 6, 17, 18 **WRITING WORKSTATION ACTIVITY CARDS:** 1, 9, 11 **PHONICS/WORD STUDY WORKSTATION ACTIVITY CARDS:** W11, W12, R2, R3 **SCIENCE/SOCIAL STUDIES WORKSTATION ACTIVITY CARDS:** W4, W26, R10 **LITERATURE BIG BOOKS:** Smart Start: *Animals in the Park* **Unit 2, Week 1:** *The Handiest Things in the World* **Unit 2, Week 2:** *Shapes All Around* **Unit 3, Week 2:** *Clang! Clang! Beep! Beep! Listen to the City* **Unit 4, Week 1:** *Whose Shoes? A Shoe for Every Job* **Unit 4, Week 2:** *What Can You Do with a Paleta?* **Unit 4, Week 3:** *Roadwork* **Unit 5, Week 3:** *An Orange in January* **Unit 6, Week 1:** *Mama, Is It Summer Yet?* **Unit 6, Week 2:** *Rain* **Unit 7, Week 1:** *ZooBorns!* **Unit 7, Week 2:** *The Birthday Pet* **Unit 8, Week 1:** *When Daddy's Truck Picks Me Up* **Unit 8, Week 2:** *Ana Goes to Washington, D.C.* **Unit 9, Week 3:** *Bread Comes to Life* **Unit 10, Week 3:** *Panda Kindergarten* **TEACHER'S EDITION:** Unit 1: S10-S11, S21, S26-S27, S34-S35, S44-S45, S54, S58-S59, S64, S68-S69, S74-S75, T11, T34, T35, T52, T53, T54-55, T81, T84, T93, T101, T117, T123, T133, T134, T135, T136-137, T162, T175, T183, T197, T199, T215, T216, T217, T218 **Unit 2:** T11, T19, T33, T41, T51, T52, T64, T93, T134, T136, T137, T175, T204, T215, T216, T217, T218 **Unit 3:** T11, T19, T54-55, T58, T93, T117, T134, T135, T136-137, T175, T216, T217, T218 **Unit 4:** T11, T54, T93, T134, T136, T175, T216, T218 **Unit 5:** T11, T52, T54, T93, T136, T175, T216, T218 **Unit 6:** T11, T52, T54, T136, T218 **Unit 7:** T10-11, T52, T54, T93, T134, T136, T175, T218 **Unit 8:** T11, T54, T58, T80, T92, T93, T136, T140, T175, T218, T222 **Unit 9:** T10-11, T54, T93, T136, T140, T175, T218 **Unit 10:** T11, T56, T95, T136, T138, T177, T220 **INTERACTIVE READ-ALOUD CARDS:** Smart Start, Week 1: "The Ugly Duckling" **Smart Start, Week 2:** "Tikki Tikki Tembo" **Smart Start, Week 3:** "Kindergarteners Can!" **Unit 1, Week 1:** "The Lion and the Mouse" **Unit 1, Week 2:** "The Tortoise and the Hare" **Unit 1, Week 3:** "A Feast of the Senses" **Unit 2, Week 1:** "Timimoto" **Unit 2, Week 2:** "Kites in Flight" **Unit 2, Week 3:** "From Caterpillar to Butterfly" **Unit 3, Week 1:** "The Boy Who Cried Wolf" **Unit 3, Week 2:** "The Turtle and the Flute" **Unit 3, Week 3:** "Field Trips" **Unit 4, Week 1:** "Little Juan and the Cooking Pot" **Unit 4, Week 2:** "Cultural Festivals" **Unit 4, Week 3:** "The Bundle of Sticks" **Unit 5, Week 1:** "Growing Plants" **Unit 5, Week 2:** "The Pine Tree" **Unit 5, Week 3:** "Farmers Around the World" **Unit 6, Week 1:** "A Tour of the Seasons" **Unit 6, Week 1:** "The Frog and the Locust" **Unit 6, Week 3:** "Rainbow Crow" **Unit 7, Week 1:** "Baby Farm Animals" **Unit 7, Week 2:** "The Family Pet" **Unit 7, Week 3:** "Anansi, An African Tale" **Unit 8, Week 1:** "The King of the Winds" **Unit 8, Week 2:** "The Best of the West" **Unit 8, Week 3:** "A View From the Moon" **Unit 9, Week 1:** "Helping Out at Home" **Unit 9, Week 2:** "The Little Red Hen" **Unit 9, Week 3:** "Spider Woman Teaches the Navajo" **Unit 10, Week 1:** "The Elves and the Shoemakers" **Unit 10, Week 1:** "Good for You!" **Unit 10, Week 1:** "Help Save Big Blue!"

Speaking and Listening Standards

Comprehension and Collaboration		*McGraw-Hill Reading Wonders*
SL.K.2	Confirm understanding of a text read aloud or information presented orally or through other media by asking and answering questions about key details and requesting clarification if something is not understood.	**READING/WRITING WORKSHOP:** Unit 1: 6-7, 26-31, 33, 35, 37, 42-43, 45, 47, 49, 51, 53, 55 **Unit 2:** 6-7, 8, 9, 10, 13, 14-19, 24-25, 27, 28, 30, 33, 34, 35, 46, 47, 48, 51, 54, 55, 58 **Unit 3:** 6-7, 9, 12, 13, 16, 17, 19, 33, 34, 37, 42-43, 46, 47, 49, 51, 53, 55 **Unit 4:** 6-7, 9-15, 20-21, 23-25, 28-29, 34-43 **Unit 5:** 8-15, 23-28 **Unit 6:** 8-15, 22-29 **Unit 7:** 8-15, 18-19, 20-21, 22-29, 34-35, 36-43 **Unit 8:** 6-7, 8-15, 20-21, 22-29, 34-35, 36-43 **Unit 9:** 6-7, 8-15, 20-21, 22-29, 34-35, 36-43 **Unit 10:** 6-7, 8-15, 20-21, 22-29, 34-35, 36-43

LEVELED READERS: Unit 1, Week 3: *The Beach* (A), *See It Grow!* (O, ELL), *At School* (B) **Unit 2, Week 1:** *We Need Tools* (A), *A Trip* (O, ELL), *What Can You See?* (B) **Unit 3, Week 1:** *We Run* (A), *Go, Nat!* (O, ELL), *The Birdhouse* (B) **Unit 4, Week 2:** *My Neighbors* (A), *Neighborhood Party* (O, ELL), *Parade Day* (B) **Unit 5, Week 1:** *My Garden* (A), *My Garden Grows* (O, ELL), *The Mystery Seeds* (B) **Unit 5, Week 3:** *The Farmer* (A), *Let's Make a Salad!* (O, ELL), *Farm Fresh Finn* (B) **Unit 6, Week 1:** *It Is Hot!* (A), *Little Bear* (O, ELL), *Ant and Grasshopper* (B) **Unit 7, Week 2:** *My Cats* (A), *Their Pets* (O, ELL), *Will's Pet* (B) **Unit 7, Week 3:** *We Want Water* (A), *A New Home* (O, ELL), *Bird's New Home* (B) **Unit 8, Week 2:** *See This!* (A), *Places to See* (O, ELL), *My Trip to Yellowstone* (B) **Unit 8, Week 3:** *Going Up* (A), *In the Clouds* (O, ELL) *How Sun and Moon Found Home* (B) **Unit 9, Week 2:** *Mike Helps Out* (A), *Clive and His Friend* (O, ELL), *Farmer White's Best Friend* (B) **Unit 9, Week 3:** *Look Where It Is From* (A), *What's for Breakfast?* (O, ELL), *Nature at the Craft Fair* (B) **Unit 10, Week 2:** *My Box* (A), *Let's Make a Band* (O, ELL), *Going Camping* (B) **Unit 10, Week 3:** *Help Clean Up* (A), *Let's Save Earth* (O, ELL) *Babysitters for Seals* (B)

YOUR TURN PRACTICE BOOK: 29-30, 35-38, 45-46, 53, 59-61, 68, 79-80, 85-86, 93-94, 99, 101-103, 107, 109-111, 115, 118, 123, 127-128, 129, 137, 141, 143-144, 147, 153-154, 164-165, 174, 187, 207, 217, 221, 227, 231, 234

READING WORKSTATION ACTIVITY CARDS: 7, 8, 16, 20

WRITING WORKSTATION ACTIVITY CARDS: 4, 6, 9

TEACHER'S EDITION: Unit 1: T11, T22-26, T186-191 **Unit 2:** T35, T186-191, T244 **Unit 3:** T104-108, T137, T175 **Unit 4:** T11, T55, T92, T137, T175, T219, T244 **Unit 5:** T11, T52, T93, T175, T186 **Unit 6:** T11, T20, T26, T93, T175 **Unit 7:** T11, T52, T55, T93, T137, T175, T219, T242 **Unit 8:** T11, T55, T78, T92-93 **Unit 9:** T11, T52, T55, T80, T93, T137, T162, T175, T219, T242 **Unit 10:** T11, T57, T80, T95, T139, T221, T244

LITERATURE BIG BOOKS: Unit 1, Week 1: *What About Bear?* **Unit 1, Week 2:** *Pouch!* **Unit 1, Week 3:** *Senses at the Seashore* **Unit 2, Week 1:** *The Handiest Things in the World* **Unit 2, Week 2:** *Shapes All Around* **Unit 3, Week 1:** *How Do Dinosaurs Go to School?* **Unit 3, Week 2:** *Clang! Clang! Beep! Beep! Listen to the City* **Unit 3, Week 3:** *Please Take Me for a Walk* **Unit 4, Week 1:** *Whose Shoes? A Shoe for Every Job* **Unit 4, Week 2:** *What Can You Do with a Paleta?* **Unit 4, Week 3:** *Roadwork* **Unit 5, Week 1:** *My Garden* **Unit 5, Week 2:** *A Grand Old Tree* **Unit 6, Week 3:** *Waiting Out the Storm* **Unit 7, Week 3:** *Bear Snores On* **Unit 8, Week 3:** *Bringing Down the Moon* **Unit 9, Week 1:** *Peter's Chair* **Unit 9, Week 2:** *Hen Hears Gossip* **Unit 10, Week 1:** *What's the Big Idea, Molly?* **Unit 10, Week 2:** *All Kinds of Families*

INTERACTIVE READ-ALOUD CARDS: Smart Start, Week 1: "The Ugly Duckling" **Smart Start, Week 2:** "Tikki Tikki Tembo" **Smart Start, Week 3:** "Kindergarteners Can!" **Unit 1, Week 1:** "The Lion and the Mouse" **Unit 1, Week 2:** "The Tortoise and the Hare" **Unit 1, Week 3:** "A Feast of the Senses" **Unit 2, Week 1:** "Timimoto" **Unit 2, Week 2:** "Kites in Flight" **Unit 2, Week 3:** "From Caterpillar to Butterfly" **Unit 4, Week 1:** "Little Juan and the Cooking Pot" **Unit 4, Week 2:** "Cultural Festivals" **Unit 4, Week 3:** "The Bundle of Sticks" **Unit 5, Week 1:** "Growing Plants" **Unit 5, Week 2:** "The Pine Tree" **Unit 6, Week 1:** "A Tour of the Seasons" **Unit 6, Week 2:** "The Frog and the Locust" **Unit 6, Week 3:** "Rainbow Crow" **Unit 8, Week 1:** "The King of the Winds" **Unit 8, Week 2:** "The Best of the West" **Unit 8, Week 3:** "A View From the Moon" **Unit 9, Week 1:** "Helping Out at Home" **Unit 9, Week 2:** "The Little Red Hen" **Unit 9, Week 3:** "Spider Woman Teaches the Navajo" **Unit 10, Week 1:** "Help Save Big Blue!"

Speaking and Listening Standards

Comprehension and Collaboration		McGraw-Hill Reading Wonders
SL.K.3	Ask and answer questions in order to seek help, get information, or clarify something that is not understood.	**READING/WRITING WORKSHOP: Unit 1:** 6-7, 26-31, 33, 36, 37, 42-43, 45, 47, 49, 51, 53, 55 **Unit 2:** 6, 7, 14-19 **Unit 3:** 8-13, 14-19, 42-43 **Unit 4:** 6-7, 9, 11, 14, 20-29, 34-43 **Unit 5:** 6-7, 9, 11, 14, 20-29, 34-43 **Unit 6:** 6-7, 9, 11, 14, 20-29, 34-43 **Unit 7:** 6-7, 20-21 **Unit 8:** 6-7, 20-21 **Unit 9:** 6-7, 20-21 **Unit 10:** 6-7 **LEVELED READERS: Unit 2, Week 1:** *We Need Tools* (A), *What Can You See?* (O, ELL), *A Trip* (B) **Unit 4, Week 1:** *You Cook* (A), *On the Job* (O, ELL), *The Neighborhood* (B) **Unit 4, Week 3:** *We Clean!* (A), *Can You Fix It?* (O, ELL), *Helping Mom* (B) **Unit 5, Week 1:** *My Garden* (A), *My Garden Grows* (O, ELL), *The Mystery Seeds* (B) **Unit 5, Week 3:** *The Farmer* (A), *Let's Make a Salad!* (O, ELL), *Farm Fresh Finn* (B) **Unit 6, Week 1:** *It Is Hot!* (A), *Little Bear* (O, ELL), *Ant and Grasshopper* (B) **Unit 6, Week 3:** *Bad Weather* (A), *Getting Ready* (O, ELL), *The Storm* (B) **Unit 7, Week 1:** *Two Cubs* (A), *Animal Bodies* (O, ELL), *Two Kinds of Bears* (B) **Unit 8, Week 2:** *See This!* (A), *Places to See* (O, ELL), *My Trip to Yellowstone* (B) **Unit 9, Week 1:** *Let Me Help You* (A) *How Can Jane Help?* (O, ELL), *I Used to Help Too* (B) **Unit 10, Week 1:** *Animal Band* (A), *We Want Honey* (O, ELL), *A Good Idea* (B) **Unit 10, Week 3:** *Help Clean Up* (A), *Let's Save Earth* (O, ELL) *Babysitters for Seals* (B) **READING WORKSTATION ACTIVITY CARDS:** 7, 16, 20 **WRITING WORKSTATION ACTIVITY CARDS:** 4, 6, 9 **TEACHER'S EDITION: Unit 1:** T13, T216, T233 **Unit 2:** T95, T131, T137 **Unit 3:** T31, T49 **Unit 4:** T11, T55, T93, T137, T216, T219 **Unit 5:** T11, T52, T134, T216 **Unit 6:** T11, T93 **Unit 7:** T52, T93, T134, T182, T196, T205 **Unit 8:** T11, T93, T175 **Unit 9:** T13, T22, T52, T55 **Unit 10:** T11, T95, T97 **LITERATURE BIG BOOKS: Unit 1, Week 1:** *What About Bear?* **Unit 1, Week 2:** *Pouch!* **Unit 1, Week 3:** *Senses at the Seashore* **Unit 2, Week 1:** *The Handiest Things in the World* **Unit 2, Week 2:** *Shapes All Around* **Unit 3, Week 1:** *How Do Dinosaurs Go to School?* **Unit 3, Week 2:** *Clang! Clang! Beep! Beep! Listen to the City* **Unit 3, Week 3:** *Please Take Me for a Walk* **Unit 4, Week 1:** *Whose Shoes? A Shoe for Every Job* **Unit 4, Week 2:** *What Can You Do with a Paleta?* **Unit 4, Week 3:** *Roadwork* **Unit 9, Week 1:** *Peter's Chair* **Unit 9, Week 2:** *Hen Hears Gossip* **Unit 10, Week 2:** *All Kinds of Families!* **Unit 10, Week 3:** *Panda Kindergarten* **INTERACTIVE READ-ALOUD CARDS: Unit 1, Week 1:** "The Lion and the Mouse" **Unit 1, Week 2:** "The Tortoise and the Hare" **Unit 1, Week 3:** "A Feast of the Senses" **Unit 2, Week 1:** "Timimoto" **Unit 2, Week 2:** "Kites in Flight" **Unit 2, Week 3:** "From Caterpillar to Butterfly" **Unit 3, Week 1:** "The Boy Who Cried Wolf" **Unit 3, Week 2:** "The Turtle and the Flute" **Unit 4, Week 1:** "Little Juan and the Cooking Pot" **Unit 4, Week 2:** "Cultural Festivals" **Unit 9, Week 2:** "The Little Red Hen"
Presentation of Knowledge and Ideas		**McGraw-Hill Reading Wonders**
SL.K.4	Describe familiar people, places, things, and events and, with prompting and support, provide additional detail.	**READING/WRITING WORKSHOP BIG BOOK: Unit 1:** 6-7, 42-43 **Unit 2:** 6-7, 24-25, 42-43 **Unit 3:** 6-7, 24-25, 42-43 **Unit 4:** 6-7, 20-21, 34-35 **Unit 5:** 6-7, 20-21, 34-35 **Unit 6:** 6-7, 20-21, 34-35 **Unit 7:** 6-7, 20-21, 34-35 **Unit 8:** 6-7, 20-21, 34-35 **Unit 9:** 6-7, 20-21, 34-35 **Unit 10:** 6-7, 20-21, 34-35 **YOUR TURN PRACTICE BOOK:** 27-28, 35-38, 51-52, 61, 67, 68, 83, 85-86, 93-94, 103, 107, 109-110, 115, 117, 118, 141, 157, 167, 174, 193, 221, 231 **READING WORKSTATION ACTIVITY CARDS:** 10, 12, 14, 16 **WRITING WORKSTATION ACTIVITY CARDS:** 1, 2, 8, 16, 19, 22 **TEACHER'S EDITION: Unit 1:** S58, S74-75, T19, T33, T134, T183, T197, T205 **Unit 2:** T175, T182 **Unit 3:** T11, T93, T175, T177 **Unit 4:** T10-11, T18-19, T92, T114-115, T132-133, T135, T175, T182-183, T197, T214-215 **Unit 5:** T54, T136, T175, T218 **Unit 6:** T11, T13, T52, T54, T136, T175, T218 **Unit 7:** T54, T136, T163, T175, T218 **Unit 8:** T54, T175, T216 **Unit 9:** T11, T93, T136, T175, T183 **Unit 10:** T102, T116, T136, T177 **LITERATURE BIG BOOKS: Smart Start:** *Animals in the Park* **Unit 1, Week 1:** *What About Bear?* **Unit 1, Week 2:** *Pouch!* **Unit 1, Week 3:** *Senses at the Seashore* **Unit 2, Week 3:** *I Love Bugs!* **Unit 4, Week 1:** *Whose Shoes? A Shoe for Every Job* **Unit 4, Week 2:** *What Can You Do with a Paleta?* **Unit 4, Week 3:** *Roadwork* **Unit 5, Week 1:** *My Garden* **Unit 5, Week 2:** *A Grand Old Tree* **Unit 5, Week 3:** *An Orange in January* **Unit 6, Week 1:** *Mama, Is It Summer Yet?* **Unit 6, Week 2:** *Rain* **Unit 7, Week 1:** *ZooBorns!* **Unit 7, Week 2:** *The Family Pet* **Unit 7, Week 3:** *Bear Snores On* **Unit 8, Week 1:** *When Daddy's Truck Picks Me Up* **Unit 8, Week 2:** *Ana Goes to Washington, D.C.* **Unit 9, Week 1:** *Peter's Chair* **Unit 9, Week 2:** *Hen Hears Gossip* **Unit 9, Week 3:** *Bread Comes to Life* **Unit 10, Week 1:** *What's the Big Idea, Molly?* **Unit 10, Week 2:** *All Kinds of Families!* **INTERACTIVE READ-ALOUD CARDS: Smart Start, Week 2:** "Tikki Tikki Tembo" **Smart Start, Week 3:** "Kindergarteners Can!" **Unit 1, Week 1:** "The Lion and the Mouse" **Unit 1, Week 2:** "The Tortoise and the Hare" **Unit 1, Week 3:** "A Feast of the Senses" **Unit 2, Week 1:** "Timimoto" **Unit 2, Week 2:** "Kites in Flight" **Unit 2, Week 3:** "From Caterpillar to Butterfly" **Unit 3, Week 1:** "The Boy Who Cried Wolf" **Unit 3, Week 2:** "The Turtle and the Flute" **Unit 4, Week 3:** "The Bundle of Sticks" **Unit 5, Week 3:** "Farms Around the World" **Unit 6, Week 3:** "Rainbow Crow" **Unit 7, Week 3:** "Anansi: An African Tale" **Unit 8, Week 3:** "A View From the Moon" **Unit 9, Week 3:** "Spider Woman Teaches the Navajo" **Unit 10, Week 1:** "The Elves and the Shoemakers" **Unit 10, Week 1:** "Good for You!"

Speaking and Listening Standards

Presentation of Knowledge and Ideas		McGraw-Hill Reading Wonders
SL.K.5	Add drawings or other visual displays to descriptions as desired to provide additional detail.	**YOUR TURN PRACTICE BOOK:** 27-28, 30-32, 35-38, 43-46, 51-53, 59-60, 61, 62, 67-70, 77-80, 83, 85-86, 88, 93-94, 99, 101-102, 103-104, 107, 109-112, 115, 117-118, 123, 127-128, 129, 130, 133, 135-136, 137, 138, 141, 143-144, 147, 148, 151, 153-154, 157, 158, 164-165, 167, 168, 174, 187, 193, 207, 217, 221, 227, 231, 234 **READINGWORK STATION ACTIVITY CARDS:** 1, 6, 12, 15, 16, 20 **WRITING WORKSTATION ACTIVITY CARDS:** 1, 2, 4, 9, 17, 20, 23 **TEACHER'S EDITION: Unit 1:** T32, T41, T123, T214 **Unit 2:** T40-41, T123, T132 **Unit 3:** T41, T134, T217 **Unit 4:** T32, T41, T52, T123, T134, T205 **Unit 5:** T53, T134, T217 **Unit 6:** T53, T122-123, T135, T140, T163, T197, T205, T222 **Unit 7:** T33, T41, T114, T123 **Unit 8:** T53, T132, T134, T216 **Unit 9:** T41, T53, T123, T205, T214, T241 **Unit 10:** T43, T137, T216
SL.K.6	Speak audibly and express thoughts, feelings, and ideas clearly.	**READING/WRITING WORKSHOP: Unit 1:** 6-7, 8-13, 14-19, 24-25, 26-31, 42-43 **Unit 2:** 6-7, 8, 9, 10, 13, 14-19, 24-25, 33, 34, 35, 42-43, 46, 47, 48, 51, 54, 55, 58 **Unit 3:** 6-7, 13, 26, 27, 30, 31, 42-43, 44-49 **Unit 4:** 6-8, 22-29, 34-35 **Unit 5:** 6-7 **Unit 6:** 6-7 8-15, 22-29 **Unit 7:** 6-7 **Unit 8:** 20-21, 34-35 **LEVELED READERS: Unit 1, Week 2:** *Hop!* (A), *We Hop!* (O, ELL), *We Can Move!* (B) **Unit 2, Week 3:** *We Like Bugs!* (A), *The Bugs Run* (O, ELL), *I See a Bug* (B) **Unit 3, Week 1:** *We Run* (A), *Go, Nat!* (O, ELL), *The Birdhouse* (B) **Unit 5, Week 3:** *The Farmer* (A), *Let's Make a Salad!* (O, ELL), *Farm Fresh Finn* (B) **Unit 6, Week 1:** *It Is Hot!* (A), *Little Bear* (O, ELL), *Ant and Grasshopper* (B) **Unit 6, Week 2:** *The Rain* (A), *Weather Is Fun* (O, ELL), *Kate and Tuck* (B) **YOUR TURN PRACTICE BOOK:** 29, 37, 39-40, 43-44, 45, 47-48, 53, 61, 68, 71-72, 81-82, 83, 89-90, 97-98, 103, 105-106, 107, 113-114, 115, 121-122, 129, 131-132, 137, 141, 147, 149-150, 151, 187, 221, 227, 231 **READING WORKSTATION ACTIVITY CARDS:** 1, 3, 12, 17 **WRITING WORKSTATION ACTIVITY CARDS:** 1, 2, 6, 20, 25 **TEACHER'S EDITION: Unit 1:** T134, T175, T222 **Unit 2:** T58, T175, T222 **Unit 3:** T58, T140, T222 **Unit 4:** T58, T140, T175, T222 **Unit 5:** T11, T58, T140, T222 **Unit 6:** T11, T58, T140, T175, T222 **Unit 7:** T52, T58, T140, T175, T222 **Unit 8:** T11, T58, T93, T40, T175, T222 **Unit 9:** T11, T52, T58, T140, T222, T245 **Unit 10:** T11, T95, T142, T177, T224 **LITERATURE BIG BOOKS: Unit 1, Week 1:** *What About Bear?* **Unit 1, Week 2:** *Pouch!* **Unit 1, Week 3:** *Senses at the Seashore* **Unit 2, Week 1:** *The Handiest Things in the World* **Unit 2, Week 2:** *Shapes All Around* **Unit 2, Week 3:** *I Love Bugs!* **Unit 3, Week 2:** *A Grand Old Tree* **Unit 3, Week 3:** *An Orange in January* **Unit 5, Week 1:** *My Garden* **Unit 6, Week 1:** *Mama, Is It Summer Yet?* **Unit 8, Week 2:** *Ana Goes to Washington, D.C.* **INTERACTIVE READ-ALOUD CARDS: Unit 1, Week 1:** "The Lion and the Mouse" **Unit 1, Week 2:** "The Tortoise and the Hare" **Unit 1, Week 3:** "A Feast of the Senses" **Unit 2, Week 1:** "Timimoto" **Unit 2, Week 2:** "Kites in Flight" **Unit 2, Week 3:** "From Caterpillar to Butterfly" **Unit 3, Week 1:** "The Boy Who Cried Wolf" **Unit 3, Week 2:** "The Turtle and the Flute" **Unit 3, Week 3:** "Field Trips" **Unit 4, Week 1:** "Little Juan and the Cooking Pot" **Unit 4, Week 2:** "Cultural Festivals" **Unit 4, Week 3:** "The Bundle of Sticks" **Unit 5, Week 1:** "Growing Plants" **Unit 7, Week 2:** "The Family Pet"

College and Career Readiness Anchor Standards for LANGUAGE

The K–5 standards on the following pages define what students should understand and be able to do by the end of each grade. They correspond to the College and Career Readiness (CCR) anchor standards below by number. The CCR and grade-specific standards are necessary complements—the former providing broad standards, the latter providing additional specificity—that together define the skills and understandings that all students must demonstrate.

Conventions of Standard English
1. Demonstrate command of the conventions of standard English grammar and usage when writing or speaking.
2. Demonstrate command of the conventions of standard English capitalization, punctuation, and spelling when writing.

Knowledge of Language
3. Apply knowledge of language to understand how language functions in different contexts, to make effective choices for meaning or style, and to comprehend more fully when reading or listening.

Vocabulary Acquisition and Use
4. Determine or clarify the meaning of unknown and multiple-meaning words and phrases by using context clues, analyzing meaningful word parts, and consulting general and specialized reference materials, as appropriate.
5. Demonstrate understanding of figurative language, word relationships, and nuances in word meanings.
6. Acquire and use accurately a range of general academic and domain-specific words and phrases sufficient for reading, writing, speaking, and listening at the college and career readiness level; demonstrate independence in gathering vocabulary knowledge when encountering an unknown term important to comprehension or expression.

CCSS Common Core State Standards
English Language Arts
Grade K

Language Standards

Conventions of Standard English		McGraw-Hill Reading Wonders
L.K.1	Demonstrate command of the conventions of standard English grammar and usage when writing or speaking.	**TEACHER'S EDITION: Unit 1:** T16, T19, T32-33, T41, T36, T98, T101, T114-115, T122-123, T125, T133, T141, T165, T180, T183, T197, T205, T214-215, T223, T247 **Unit 2:** T16, T18-19, T32-33, T40-41, T50-51, T59, T83, T98, T101, T115, T123, T133, T141, T165, T180, T183, T185, T197, T205, T215, T223 **Unit 3:** T16, T98, T180, T183, T197, T215 **Unit 4:** T16, T18-19, T32-33, T40-41, T47, T51, T59, T98, T101, T114-115, T122-123, T129, T133, T139, T141, T180, T182-183, T196-197, T204-205, T211, T215, T221, T223 **Unit 5:** T16, T21, T43, T83, T98, T103, T180, T196, T247 **Unit 6:** T16, T19, T33, T41, T44, T47, T51, T53, T59, T83, T98, T101, T114, T115, T123, T129, T133, T141, T180, T183, T185, T197, T205, T207, T211, T215, T223, T247 **Unit 7:** T16, T19, T33, T41, T47, T51, T83, T98, T114-115, T123, T129, T133, T139, T141, T165, T180, T182, T183, T196, T197, T204-205, T211, T215, T223, T247 **Unit 8:** T16, T19, T21, T33, T41, T47, T50-51, T83, T98, T101, T115, T123, T129, T133, T141, T180, T182-183, T196-197, T205, T211, T215, T223 **Unit 9:** T16, T19, T21, T32-33, T41, T47, T51, T59, T83, T98, T101, T103, T114-115, T123, T133, T141, T165, T129, T180, T183, T185, T197, T205, T211, T215, T223, T247 **Unit 10:** T16, T21, T34, T42, T49, T85, T100, T131, T182, T187, T198, T213, T249
L.K.1a	Print many upper- and lowercase letters.	**TEACHER'S EDITION: Unit 1:** T16, T98, T180 **Unit 2:** T16, T98, T180 **Unit 3:** T16, T98, T180 **Unit 4:** T16, T47, T98, T129, T139, T180, T211, T221 **Unit 5:** T16, T98, T180 **Unit 6:** T16, T47, T98, T129, T180, T211 **Unit 7:** T16, T47, T98, T129, T139, T180, T211 **Unit 8:** T16, T47, T98, T129, T180, T211 **Unit 9:** T16, T47, T98, T129, T180, T211 **Unit 10:** T16, T49, T100, T131, T182, T213 **YOUR TURN PRACTICE BOOK:** 34, 42, 50, 58, 66, 76, 84, 92, 100, 108, 116, 126, 134, 142, 152, 162, 172, 184, 192, 202, 212, 222, 232, 244, 252, 260, 268, 276, 284
L.K.1b	Use frequently occurring nouns and verbs.	**TEACHER'S EDITION: Unit 1:** T19, T32-33, T41, T36, T101, T114-115, T122-123, T125, T133, T141, T165, T183, T197, T205, T214-215, T223, T247 **Unit 2:** T18-19, T32-33, T40-41, T50-51, T59, T83, T101, T115, T123, T133, T141, T165, T183, T185, T197, T205, T215, T223 **Unit 5:** T103 **Unit 6:** T19, T33, T44, T51, T53, T83, T114, T223, T247 **Unit 7:** T19, T33, T41, T51, T83, T114-115, T123, T133, T141, T165, T183, T197, T205, T215, T223, T247 **Unit 8:** T10, T18, T114, T115 **Unit 9:** T21, T103, T185 **Unit 10:** T187 **YOUR TURN PRACTICE BOOK:** 23, 41, 65, 73, 83, 107, 115, 141, 151, 161, 191, 201, 211, 221, 241, 251, 259, 267, 295
L.K.1c	Form regular plural nouns orally by adding /s/ or /es/ (e.g., *dog, dogs; wish, wishes*).	**TEACHER'S EDITION: Unit 5:** T21, T43 **Unit 6:** T33, T41, T51, T59, T101, T115, T123, T133, T141, T183, T197, T205, T215
L.K.1d	Understand and use question words (interrogatives) (e.g., *who, what, where, when, why, how*).	**TEACHER'S EDITION: Unit 3:** T183, T197, T215 **Unit 6:** T185, T207 **Unit 7:** T182, T196, T204-205 **Unit 9:** T103, T125 **Unit 10:** T21
L.K.1e	Use the most frequently occurring prepositions (e.g., *to, from, in, out, on, off, for, of, by, with*).	**TEACHER'S EDITION: Unit 3:** T29, T47 **Unit 5:** T193, T211 **Unit 7:** T29, T47 **Unit 8:** T19, T33, T41, T50-51, T83, T101, T115, T123, T133, T141, T183, T197, T205, T223
L.K.1f	Produce and expand complete sentences in shared language activities.	**TEACHER'S EDITION: Unit 4:** T18-19, T32-33, T40-41, T51, T59, T101, T114-115, T122-123, T133, T141, T182-183, T196-197, T204-205, T215, T223 **Unit 5:** T83, T196, T247 **Unit 8:** T182-183, T196-197, T215, T223; **Unit 9:** T19, T32-33, T41, T51, T59, T83, T101, T114-115, T123, T133, T141, T165, T183, T197, T205, T215, T223, T247 **Unit 10:** T34, T42, T85, T198, T249

Language Standards

Conventions of Standard English		McGraw-Hill Reading Wonders
L.K.2	Demonstrate command of the conventions of standard English capitalization, punctuation, and spelling when writing.	**TEACHER'S EDITION: Unit 1:** T16, T72, T129, T211, T221 **Unit 2:** T47, T57, T129, T139, T211, T221 **Unit 3:** T19, T47, T50-51, T53, T57, T59, T83, T101, T115, T120, T123, T132-133, T139, T141, T183, T196-197, T205, T211, T214-215, T221, T223, T247 **Unit 4:** T16, T47, T57, T98, T129, T139, T211, T221 **Unit 5:** T16, T47, T57, T98, T101, T115, T123, T139, T180, T211, T221 **Unit 6:** T12, T16, T47, T57, T98, T129, T139, T176, T211, T221 **Unit 7:** T16, T47, T57, T98, T129, T139, T180, T211, T214, T221 **Unit 8:** T16, T32, T47, T98, T101, T114, T129, T132, T164, T211, T221 **Unit 9:** T47, T129, T211 **Unit 10:** T49, T53, T103, T116, T131, T213, T216
L.K.2a	Capitalize the first word in a sentence and the pronoun *I*.	**TEACHER'S EDITION: Unit 3:** T19, T50-51, T53, T59, T83, T115, T123, T132-133, T197, T223 **Unit 5:** T101, T115, T123 **Unit 8:** T32, T101, T114, T132 **Unit 10:** T53, T103, T116, T216
L.K.2b	Recognize and name end punctuation.	**TEACHER'S EDITION: Unit 3:** T101, T115, T123, T132-133, T141, T183, T196-197, T205, T214-215, T223, T247 **Unit 6:** T12, T176 **Unit 7:** T214 **Unit 8:** T32, T101, T114, T132, T164
L.K.2c	Write a letter or letters for most consonant and short-vowel sounds (phonemes).	**TEACHER'S EDITION: Unit 1:** T16, T72, T129, T211 **Unit 2:** T47, T129, T211 **Unit 3:** T47, T120, T211 **Unit 4:** T16, T47, T98, T129, T139, T211, T221 **Unit 5:** T16, T47, T98, T180, T211 **Unit 6:** T16, T47, T98, T129, T211 **Unit 7:** T16, T47, T57, T98, T129, T139, T180, T211 **Unit 8:** T16, T47, T98, T129, T211 **Unit 9:** T47, T129, T211 **Unit 10:** T49, T131, T213 **YOUR TURN PRACTICE BOOK:** 34, 42, 50, 58, 51-52, 62, 66, 76, 84, 85, 86, 88, 92, 100, 104, 108, 116, 126, 130, 134, 138, 142, 148, 158, 162, 164-165, 168, 172, 192, 202, 212, 222, 232 **PHONICS AND WORD STUDY WORKSTATION ACTIVITY CARDS:** 1, 2, 3, 4, 5, 6, 7, 8, 9, 10, 11, 12, 13, 14, 15, 16, 17, 18, 19, 20, 21, 22, 23, 24
L.K.2d	Spell simple words phonetically, drawing on knowledge of sound-letter relationships.	**TEACHER'S EDITION: Unit 1:** T221 **Unit 2:** T57, T139, T221 **Unit 3:** T57, T139, T221 **Unit 4:** T47, T57, T129, T139, T211, T221 **Unit 5:** T57, T139, T221 **Unit 6:** T57, T139, T221 **Unit 7:** T47, T57, T129, T139, T211, T221 **Unit 8:** T47, T129, T139, T211, T221 **YOUR TURN PRACTICE BOOK:** 30, 38, 46, 54, 62, 74, 75, 80, 88, 96, 104, 112, 124, 125, 130, 138, 148, 158, 168, 182, 183, 188, 198, 208, 228, 242, 243, 256, 264, 272, 280, 293, 294

Knowledge of Language		McGraw-Hill Reading Wonders
L.K.3	(Begins in grade 2.)	

Vocabulary Acquisition and Use		McGraw-Hill Reading Wonders
L.K.4	Determine or clarify the meaning of unknown and multiple-meaning words and phrases based on *kindergarten reading and content*.	**TEACHER'S EDITION: Unit 4:** T127 **Unit 5:** T45, T46, T108, T187 **Unit 6:** T21, T23, T33, T41 **Unit 7:** T24, T45, T189, T209 **Unit 9:** T21, T24, T25, T43, T185, T189, T207 **Unit 10:** T25, T187, T209
L.K.4a	Identify new meanings for familiar words and apply them accurately (e.g., knowing *duck* is a bird and learning the verb to *duck*).	**TEACHER'S EDITION: Unit 5:** T108, T185, T187 T207 **Unit 6:** T21, T189 **Unit 7:** T24, T45, T189 **Unit 8:** T21 **Unit 9:** T25, T45, T185, T207 **Unit 10:** T25, T47
L.K.4b	Use the most frequently occurring inflections and affixes (e.g., *-ed, -s, re-, un-, pre-, -ful, -less*) as a clue to the meaning of an unknown word.	**TEACHER'S EDITION: Unit 5:** T45, T46, T187 **Unit 6:** T23, T33, T41 **Unit 9:** T21, T24, T43, T189 **Unit 10:** T187, T209

Language Standards

Vocabulary Acquisition and Use		*McGraw-Hill Reading Wonders*
L.K.5	With guidance and support from adults, explore word relationships and nuances in word meanings.	**TEACHER'S EDITION: Unit 1:** T10-11, T34, T43 **Unit 2:** T10, T43, T103, T116, T125, T135, T175, T185, T207, T245 **Unit 3:** T10, T116, T175 **Unit 4:** T10-11, T12-13, T21, T34, T43, T44-45, T54, T67, T80, T81, T83, T92-93, T94-95, T103, T116, T125, T126-127, T133, T136, T141, T149, T165, T174-175, T176-177, T183, T185, T188, T198, T207, T208-209, T218, T231, T245, T247 **Unit 5:** T10-11, T12-13, T21, T34, T43, T54, T67, T80, T81, T92-93, T94-95, T116, T149, T174-175, T185, T195, T207, T218, T245 **Unit 6:** T10-11, T20, T34, T35, T42, T43, T44, T67, T81, T92-93, T103, T108, T116, T125, T126-127, T136, T149, T163, T174-175, T176-177, T185, T198, T208-209, T218, T231, T245 **Unit 7:** T10-11, T12-13, T21, T25, T34, T43, T54, T67, T81, T92-93, T94-95, T103, T116, T126-127, T136, T149, T163, T174-175, T185, T190, T207, T208-209, T218, T231, T245 **Unit 8:** T10-11, T12-13, T21, T23, T34, T43, T44-45, T54, T67, T81, T92-93, T94-95, T103, T116, T125, T126-127, T136, T149, T163, T174-175, T185, T198, T207, T208-209, T218, T231, T245 **Unit 9:** T10-11, T12-13, T34, T44-45, T54, T67, T81, T92-93, T103, T116, T126-127, T136, T149, T163, T174-175, T176-177, T185, T198, T207, T208-209, T218, T231, T245 **Unit 10:** T10-11, T25, T36, T46-47, T56, T69, T83, T94-95, T96-97, T105, T106-111, T118, T127, T128-129, T136-137, T138, T151, T165, T176-177, T178-179, T187, T189, T190, T200, T209, T210-211, T220, T233, T247
L.K.5a	Sort common objects into categories (e.g., shapes, foods) to gain a sense of the concepts the categories represent.	**TEACHER'S EDITION: Unit 2:** T43, T103, T125, T135 **Unit 4:** T103, T183 **Unit 5:** T21, T185, T207 **Unit 6:** T43 **Unit 8:** T43 **Unit 10:** T127, T129, T136-137
L.K.5b	Demonstrate understanding of frequently occurring verbs and adjectives by relating them to their opposites (antonyms).	**YOUR TURN PRACTICE BOOK:** 241, 283 **TEACHER'S EDITION: Unit 6:** T44 **Unit 7:** T25 **Unit 8:** T23, T185, T207 **Unit 9:** T189 **Unit 10:** T25, T105, T127, T189, T190
L.K.5c	Identify real-life connections between words and their use (e.g., note places at school that are colorful).	**READING/WRITING WORKSHOP: Unit 1:** Smart Start: 4-5, 22-23, 40-41; 6-7, 24-25, 42-43 **Unit 2:** 6-7, 24-25, 42-43 **Unit 3:** 6-7, 24-25, 42-43 **Unit 4:** 6-7, 20-21, 34-35 **Unit 5:** 6-7, 20-21, 34-35 **Unit 6:** 6-7, 20-21, 34-35 **Unit 7:** 6-7, 20-21, 34-35 **Unit 8:** 6-7, 20-21, 34-35 **Unit 9:** 6-7, 20-21, 34-35 **Unit 10:** 6-7, 20-21, 34-35 **YOUR TURN PRACTICE BOOK:** 23, 33, 41, 49, 57, 65, 73, 83, 107, 115, 133, 141, 151, 161, 171, 191, 201, 211, 221, 241, 251, 259, 267, 275, 283, 295 **TEACHER'S EDITION: Unit 1:** T10-11, T34, T43 **Unit 2:** T10, T116, T175 **Unit 3:** T10, T116, T175 **Unit 4:** T10-11, T12-13, T21, T34, T43, T44-45, T54, T67, T80, T81, T83, T92-93, T94-95, T103, T116, T125, T126-127, T133, T136, T141, T149, T165, T174-175, T176-177, T183, T185, T198, T207, T208-209, T218, T231, T245, T247 **Unit 5:** T10-11, T12-13, T21, T34, T43, T54, T67, T80, T81, T92-93, T94-95, T116, T149, T174-175, T185, T198, T218, T245 **Unit 6:** T10-11, T20, T34, T35, T42, T67, T81, T92-93, T103, T116, T125, T126-127, T136, T149, T163, T174-175, T176-177, T185, T198, T208-209, T218, T231, T245 **Unit 7:** T10-11, T12-13, T21, T25, T34, T43, T54, T67, T81, T92-93, T94-95, T103, T116, T126-127, T136, T149, T163, T174-175, T185, T207, T208-209, T218, T231, T245 **Unit 8:** T10-11, T34, T81, T92-93, T102, T116, T124, T136, T149, T163, T174-175, T185, T198, T207, T208-209, T218, T231, T245 **Unit 9:** T10-11, T12-13, T20, T34, T42-43, T54, T67, T92-93, T103, T116-117, T124-125, T136, T149, T174-175, T176-177, T185, T198, T206-207, T218, T231 **Unit 10:** T10-11, T25, T36, T46-47, T56, T69, T83, T94-95, T96-97, T106-111, T118, T128-129, T138, T151, T165, T176-177, T178-179, T187, T190, T200, T209, T210-211, T220, T233, T247 **INTERACTIVE READ-ALOUD CARDS: SS:** "The Ugly Duckling", "Kindergarteners Can!", "Tikki Tikki Tembo" **Unit 1, Week 1:** "The Lion and the Mouse" **Unit 1, Week 2:** "The Tortoise and the Hare" **Unit 2, Week 3:** "From Caterpillar to Butterfly" **Unit 3, Week 2:** "The Turtle and the Flute" **Unit 4, Week 1:** "Little Juan and the Cooking Pot" **Unit 4, Week 2:** "Cultural Festivals" **Unit 4, Week 3:** "A Bundle of Sticks" **Unit 6, Week 3:** "Rainbow Crow" **Unit 7, Week 3:** "Anansi: An African Tale" **Unit 9, Week 2:** "The Little Red Hen" **Unit 9, Week 3:** "Spider Woman Teaches the Navajo" **Unit 10, Week 1:** "The Elves and the Shoemakers" **ConnectED Digital Resources:** Visual Glossary

Language Standards

Vocabulary Acquisition and Use		McGraw-Hill Reading Wonders
L.K.5d	Distinguish shades of meaning among verbs describing the same general action (e.g., *walk, march, strut, prance*) by acting out the meanings.	**TEACHER'S EDITION:** Unit 2: T185, T207, T245 Unit 4: T188 Unit 6: T35, T108 Unit 7: T185, T190, T207
L.K.6	Use words and phrases acquired through conversations, reading and being read to, and responding to texts.	**READING/WRITING WORKSHOP:** Smart Start: 4-5, 22-23, 40-41 Unit 1: 6-7, 24-25, 42-43 Unit 2: 6-7, 24-25, 42-43 Unit 3: 6-7, 24-25, 42-43 Unit 4: 6-7, 20-21, 34-35 Unit 5: 6-7, 20-21, 34-35 Unit 6: 6-7, 20-21, 34-35 Unit 7: 6-7, 20-21, 34-35 Unit 8: 6-7, 20-21, 34-35 Unit 9: 6-7, 20-21, 34-35 Unit 10: 6-7, 20-21, 34-35 **TEACHER'S EDITION:** Unit 1: S26, S34, S44 Unit 2: T20-21, T93, T198 Unit 3: T20, T93, T198 Unit 4: T10-11, T12-13, T20-21, T22-27, T34, T42-43, T44-45, T54-55, T67, T80, T81, T92-93, T94-95, T176-177, T184-185, T186-191, T198, T205, T206-207, T208-209, T215, T218-219, T223, T218-219, T231, T244, T245 Unit 5: T10-11, T12-13, T20-21, T22-27, T34, T42-43, T44-45, T54-55 , T117, T162-163, T174-175, T176-177, T184-185, T186-191, T198, T199, T206-207, T208-209, T218-219, T231, T244-245 Unit 6: T10-11, T20-21, T34-35, T42-43, T44-45, T54-55, T67, T80, T81, T92-93, T94-95, T102-103, T104-109, T116, T124-125, T126-127, T136-137, T149, T231, T244 Unit 7: T10-11, T12-13, T20-21, T22-27, T34-35, T42-43, T44-45, T54-55, T67, T80, T81, T92-93, T94-95, T102-103, T104-109, T116, T124-125, T126-127, T136-137, T149, T231, T244, T245 Unit 8: T10-11, T12-13, T20-21, T22-27, T34-35, T42-43, T44-45, T54-55, T67, T80, T81, T92-93, T94-95, T102-103, T104-109, T116, T124-125, T126-127, T136-137, T149, T231, T244, T245 Unit 9: T10-11, T12-13, T20-21, T22-27, T34-35, T42-43, T44-45, T54-55, T162, T163, T174-175, T176-177, T184-185, T186-191, T198, T199, T206-207, T208-209, T218-219, T231, T244, T245 Unit 10: T10-11, T12-13, T20-21, T22-29, T36, T44-45, T46-47, T56-57, T69, T82, T83, T94-95, T96-97, T104-105, T106-111, T118, T126-127, T128-129, T138-139, T151, T179, T233, T246, T247 **LITERATURE BIG BOOKS:** Unit 1, Week 2: *Pouch!* Unit 2, Week 2: *Shapes All Around* Unit 2, Week 3: *I Love Bugs!* Unit 3, Week 1: *How Do Dinosaurs Go to School?* Unit 4, Week 1: *Whose Shoes? A Shoe for Every Job* Unit 4, Week 2: *What Can You Do with a Paleta?* Unit 5, Week 2: *A Grand Old Tree* Unit 5, Week 3: *An Orange in January* Unit 6, Week 1: *Mama, Is It Summer Yet?* Unit 7, Week 1: *ZooBorns!* Unit 7, Week 2: *The Birthday Pet* Unit 8, Week 2: *Ana Goes to Washington, D.C.* Unit 8, Week 3: *Bringing Down the Moon* Unit 9, Week 3: *Bread Comes to Life* Unit 10, Week 1: *What's the Big Idea, Molly?* Unit 10, Week 2: *All Kinds of Families!* **INTERACTIVE READ-ALOUD CARDS:** SS: "The Ugly Duckling", "Kindergarteners Can!", "Tikki Tikki Tembo" Unit 1, Week 1: "The Lion and the Mouse" Unit 1, Week 2: "The Tortoise and the Hare" Unit 2, Week 3: "From Caterpillar to Butterfly" Unit 3, Week 2: "The Turtle and the Flute" Unit 4, Week 1: "Little Juan and the Cooking Pot" Unit 4, Week 2: "Cultural Festivals" Unit 4, Week 3: "A Bundle of Sticks" Unit 6, Week 3: "Rainbow Crow" Unit 7, Week 3: "Anansi: An African Tale" Unit 9, Week 2: "The Little Red Hen" Unit 9, Week 3: "Spider Woman Teaches the Navajo" Unit 10, Week 1: "The Elves and the Shoemakers"

Master the Common Core State Standards!

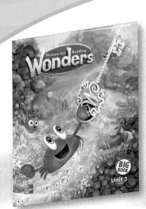

- eBooks
- Interactive Texts
- Level Reader Search
- Listening Library
- Interactive Activities

Leveled Readers

DIFFERENTIATE

Leveled Readers
Small Group Instruction
with Differentiated Texts

- Online Research
- Interactive Group Projects

Collection of Texts

INTEGRATE

Research and Inquiry
Research Projects

Text Connections
Reading Across Texts

Talk About Reading
Analytical Discussion

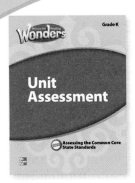

- Online Assessment
- Test Generator
- Reports

Unit
Assessment

Benchmark
Assessment

ASSESS

Unit Assessment

Benchmark Assessment

PROGRAM COMPONENTS

Big Book and Little Book of Reading/ Writing Workshop

Literature Big Books

Interactive Read-Aloud Cards

Teacher Editions

Teaching Posters

   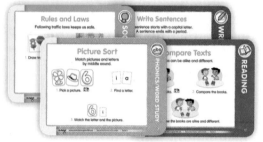

Puppet

Leveled Readers

Your Turn Practice Book

Visual Vocabulary Cards

Leveled Workstation Activity Cards

 **Assessing the Common Core State Standards**

Retelling Cards

Photo Cards

High-Frequency Word Cards

the

Sound- Spelling Cards

Response Board

Unit Assessment

Benchmark Assessment

 Go Digital

For the Teacher

For the Students

 Plan
Customizable Lesson Plans

 Assess
Online Assessments Reports and Scoring

 Professional Development
Lesson and CCSS Videos

 My To Do List
Assignments Assessment

 Words to Know
Build Vocabulary

 Teach
Classroom Presentation Tools Instructional Lessons

 Collaborate
Online Class Conversations Interactive Group Projects

Additional Online Resources
ELL Activities
Tier 2 Intervention
Interactive Games and Activities
Word-Building Cards
Sound-Spelling Songs
Sound Pronunciation Audio

 Read
eBooks
Interactive Texts

 Play
Interactive Games

 Manage and Assign
Student Grouping and Assignments

 School to Home
Digital Open House Activities and Messages

 Write
Interactive Writing

 School to Home
Activities for Home Messages from the Teacher Class Wall of Student Work

www.connected.mcgraw-hill.com